Writing Research Papers

A COMPLETE GUIDE

Tenth Edition

James D. Lester
Austin Peay State University

James Lester, Jr.
Clayton College and State University

Longman

New York San Francisco Boston
London Toronto Sydney Tokyo Singapore Madrid
Mexico City Munich Paris Cape Town Hong Kong Montreal

Editor-in-Chief: Joseph Terry
Acquisitions Editor: Susan Kunchandy
Development Manager: Janet Lanphier
Development Editor: Carol Hollar-Zwick
Marketing Manager: Christopher Bennem
Supplements Editor: Donna Campion
Senior Production Manager: Valerie Zaborski
Project Coordination, Text Design, and Electronic Page Makeup: Electronic Publishing
Services Inc., NYC
Cover Designer/Manager: Nancy Danahy
Cover Illustration: ©Garry Nichols (s)/SIS
Photo Researcher: Julie Tesser
Manufacturing Manager: Lucy Hebard
Printer and Binder: Banta Book Group
Cover Printer: Phoenix Color Corps.

For permission to use copyrighted material, grateful acknowledgment is made to the copyright holders on pp. C-1–C-3, which are hereby made part of this copyright page.

Library of Congress Cataloging-in-Publication Data

Lester, James D.,
  Writing research papers: a complete guide / James D. Lester, James Lester, Jr.–10th ed.
    p. cm
  Includes bibliographical references and index.
  ISBN 0-321-08207-9 – ISBN 0-321-08208-7 (spiral)
    1. Report writing. 2. Research. I. Lester, James D., II. Title.

  LB2369 .L4 2001
   808'.202 – dc21   2001029723

Please visit our website at http://www.ablongman.com

ISBN 0-321-08207-9 (paperbound version)
ISBN 0-321-08208-7 (tabbed version)

1 2 3 4 5 6 7 8 9 10—BAE—04 03 02 01

Contents

Preface to the Instructor

For thirty-four years *Writing Research Papers: A Complete Guide* has served over three million students and thousands of instructors. The journey has been a marvelous adventure. With this edition, James D. Lester, Jr., joins the project as co-author. Jim brings his experience as a classroom teacher at Mt. Zion High School in Jonesboro, Georgia, and as instructor of composition at Clayton College and State University in Morrow, Georgia. Together, we bring you a tenth edition for the new millennium.

As in previous editions, the text features advice on the judicious handling of research materials, but it now offers high-tech features, such as extensive coverage of electronic research and methods for publishing on the Web. It remains rooted in the fundamentals of thorough library research but encourages Internet searching as well as the value of field research. It endorses the written word while recognizing the value of graphics, audio, video, and slide presentations.

We have given *Writing Research Papers: A Complete Guide* a complete overhaul, and here are features you will find.

- New chapters that address crucial issues, including one on electronic publishing
- New organization to focus the student on each essential task
- New high-tech features and help with Internet research
- A fresh new design that facilitates navigation within the text and to the Web
- Confirmation of the standards set by the MLA, APA, CBE, and CMS
- New sample papers that show real students expressing their findings
- Free research booklets on argument, literature, and writing across the curriculum
- A complete and well-designed ancillary package

New Chapters

Three new chapters strengthen the text in key areas:

New opening chapter. "Writing from Research" introduces students to the research project as a whole, suggests various approaches to the research task, and explains the value of a prearranged schedule.

New chapter on academic ethics. "Practicing Academic Integrity" addresses such issues as credibility, property rights, plagiarism, collaborative work, and publishing on the Web.

New chapter on electronic publishing. "Preparing Electronic Research Projects" introduces students to various kinds of electronic publishing, from word processing to slide presentations to web pages and websites.

New Organization

To focus the content of each chapter, several chapters have been divided and rearranged. For example, the former Chapter 2 on gathering data has been divided into three chapters:

"Gathering Data in the Library" (Chapter 3)

"Searching the World Wide Web" (Chapter 4)

"Collecting Data outside the Library" (Chapter 5)

The former Chapter 6 on writing the paper has been divided into three chapters:

"Drafting the Paper in an Academic Style" (Chapter 10)

"Writing the Introduction, Body, and Conclusion" (Chapter 12)

"Revising, Proofreading, and Formatting the Rough Draft" (Chapter 13)

Also, the long chapter on form and style for other disciplines has been divided into two chapters to concentrate respectively on:

"CMS Style: Using Footnotes or Endnotes" (Chapter 16)

"CBE Style for the Natural and Applied Sciences" (Chapter 17)

New High-Tech Features and Help with Internet Research

Internet research, popular with students but still relatively uncharted, now receives substantial coverage in a single chapter. In addition, other sections of the text have been overhauled to provide up-to-date coverage. For example:

- Coverage of web search engines now includes metasearch engines and specialized search engines, as well as standard and educational search engines.
- Potential research tools, such as listserv, Usenet, and chat groups are covered in depth.
- New coverage of Internet bibliographies instructs students in using the Internet to assemble a list of potential sources.
- A new section on conducting archival research helps students locate rare and historic material.
- A checklist, "Evaluating Internet Sources," helps students gauge the quality of Internet articles.

- Appendix B, "Finding Sources for a Specific Discipline," features those in print form in the library, electronic sources on the library's network (such as the *MLA International Bibliography*), and those accessible on the Internet from a home computer.

Fresh, Navigable Design

For the first time, *Writing Research Papers: A Complete Guide* is printed with four-color text and artwork to make the information easier to find and more pleasing to read. It brings strong, visual elements to the instruction. New "Where to Look" boxes, signaled with an eyeglass icon, make the many cross-references in this comprehensive textbook easier to spot. A globe icon directs students to a website that supports and expands on the text.

The spiral-bound version of *Writing Research Papers* has cardboard tabs to divide the text and make information easier to find. Printed on one side of each tab are suggested websites for additional and appropriate information. The other side of the tab features a table of contents to that section of the book.

Confirmation of Academic Styles

This new tenth edition remains up-to-date with fidelity to the standards of the fifth edition of the *MLA Handbook for Writers of Research Papers* (1999). APA style is kept current by references to updates at ⟨http://www.apa.org/journals/webref.html⟩. APA has published a new fifth edition of the *Publication Manual of the American Psychological Association,* 2001. Fidelity to *The CBE Manual* and *The Chicago Manual of Style* are maintained

New Student Papers

Student writing examples, all new in this tenth edition of *Writing Research Papers: A Complete Guide*, show how real students tackled a wide range of topics. Of these, five are polished and fully documented manuscripts which demonstrate the different academic styles.

"The Poetry of Langston Hughes" (MLA)

"Functional Foods as Preventive Medicine" (MLA)

"Treating Children with Attention-Deficit-Hyperactivity-Disorder" (APA)

"Organ Donation" (CMS)

"Managing Diabetes" (CBE)

Additional samples include abstracts in MLA and APA style, a literature review, and an annotated bibliography. Other sample papers are available in the *Instructor's Manual, Model Research Papers from Across the Curriculum,* and three booklets to research in literature, argument, and writing across the curriculum, as described next.

Free Booklets on Argument, Literature, and Writing across the Curriculum

Upon adoption of *Writing Research Papers: A Complete Guide,* instructors may request one of three booklets to be shrink wrapped with student copies.

Argument and Research introduces students to the complexities of developing a persuasive essay. The revised booklet explains methods for discovering a valid argument, investigating the evidence, and making claims. It discusses systems of reasoning, such as the rhetorical triangle and the Toulmin system. A sample paper is included.

Literature and Research introduces students to the nuances of literary research, showing how to identify a problem, investigate secondary literature, and interpret and analyze the work using various methods of inquiry. A sample paper is included.

Writing across the Curriculum and Research introduces students to the conventions and requirements of research in different disciplines. This guide explains methods for identifying and investigating a problem and methods of inquiry. It explains what constitutes acceptable evidence and how to report it in science and technology, in the social sciences, and in the humanities. The formats of APA, CBE, and CMS are explained and illustrated with seven student papers.

Gift copies of these informative booklets are available to instructors from Longman representatives.

The Ancillary Package

In addition to the booklets described above, the publication package includes these additional features:

Two versions of *Writing Research Papers: A Complete Guide.* Instructors may choose the traditional paper-bound version or the spiral-bound version with handy tab dividers. Both versions feature four-color art and a new, more accessible design.

Integrated website. The companion website (www.ablongman.com/lester) will provide activities specific to each chapter's content, such as using keywords to find and narrow a topic, using listserv archives as potential research areas, and evaluating different kinds of web materials. A web icon within the text signals to students (and instructors) that a web activity is available.

CD-ROM. Packaged with the text will be a CD-ROM that features a searchable online version of *Writing Research Papers* with additional instructional tools and practice exercises.

Model Research Papers from across the Disciplines, Fifth Edition. Written by Diane Gould (Shoreline Community College), this booklet examines student papers on topics from a variety of disciplines. Introductions and annotations examine each paper's features in detail. Available to instructors upon request.

Instructor's Manual. This handy guide contains chapter-by-chapter classroom exercises, research assignments, quizzes, and duplication masters. Available to instructors upon request, and also available on the website.

Acknowledgments

The preface would not be complete without the recognition of many key people who served in the development of *Writing Research Papers: A Complete Guide,* Tenth Edition.

For helping with the appendix of reference sources, we thank Anne Berwind, head of Information Services at Austin Peay State University. For helping to develop Chapter 18 on electronic publishing, we thank Miles Kimball of Murray State University. For her work on the website to accompany the book, we thank Kimberly Dozier. As you will see in the text and the ancillary material, we owe thanks to several students: Adele Gelvin, Northeastern Junior College; Sarah E. Bemis, Edgewood College; Katie Hebert, University of Wisconsin–Stevens Point; Ashley Barnette, Clayton College and State University; and from Austin Peay State University Shannon Williams, Gena Messersmith, and Michael Hook.

For submitting student papers, we thank four instructors: Pam Berns, Northeastern Junior College; Ann Cameron, Indiana University–Kokomo; Winifred Morgan, Edgewood College; and James Stokes, University of Wisconsin–Stevens Point.

For editorial assistance that kept us focused, we thank the Longman group of Carol Hollar-Zwick, Lynn Huddon, Valerie Zaborski, and Susan Kunchandy. Finally, we want to recognize a great group of reviewers who offered penetrating and perceptive suggestions for this new edition: Louise Ackley, Boise State University; Kevin Ball, Youngstown State University; Bob Baron, Mesa Community College; Pam Berns, Northeastern Junior College; Jacob S. Blumner, University of Michigan–Flint; Doyle W. Burke, Mesa Community College; Ann Cameron, Indiana University–Kokomo; Rita Carey, Clark College; Paul Cerda, Shoreline Community College; Rae Colley, State University of West Georgia; Charles L. Darr, University of Pittsburgh–Johnstown; Michael Doyle, Casper College; Sarah L. Dye, Elgin Community College; Heidi Estrem, Eastern Michigan University; Shearle Furnish, West Texas A&M University; Kevin J. Gardner, Baylor University; Susanmarie Harrington, Indiana University, Purdue University–Indianapolis; Jaime H. Herrera, Mesa Community College; Pamela Howell, Midland College; Dollie Hudspeth, St. Philip's College; Daniel Kies, College of DuPage; Katharine W. Mangelsdorf, University of Texas–El Paso; Cindy Moore, Indiana University, Purdue University–Fort Wayne; Winifred Morgan, Edgewood College; Ralph D. Powell Jr., Indiana University Northwest; Peggy L. Richards, University of Akron; Barbara M. Smith, Western Wyoming Community College; James Stokes, University of Wisconsin–Stevens Point; Marlene L. Szymona, Philadelphia University;

Richard C. Taylor, East Carolina University; Deborah Coxwell Teague, Florida State University; Vicki L. Trussel, Blue River Community College; and Stephanie Zirkel, Penn Valley Community College.

James D. Lester
Clarksville, Tennessee

James D. Lester, Jr.
Morrow, Georgia

Preface to the Student

Within the academic community you will be asked to write "researched" essays that require you to go beyond what you know and think to incorporate ideas by others. To work on such assignments, you will need to access the Internet, to check out books from the library, and perhaps to interview several people. As you consult such sources, you will absorb the words and opinions of the experts and bring them to bear on your topic. You become a facilitator, one who pulls together and makes sense of divergent views.

A research assignment may take various forms, such as these:

"Write a paper that explores the former Berlin Wall as a symbol for the rise and fall of communism in the Soviet Union."

"What are you curious about? Find a problem, question, or issue that piques your interest and that requires research."

"Defend the contributions to American society of a famous but controversial person, such as Martin Luther King or Alexander Hamilton."

These three examples merely touch the surface of possible assignments, but they demonstrate an important point: a research assignment may be open-ended or highly specific. Whatever kind of assignment you receive, you will need to follow a logical procedure for developing the paper. That's what *Writing Research Papers: A Complete Guide* is all about. We have designed it to carry you step-by-step to a finished research project.

Frequently-Asked Questions and Where to Find Answers

- Why do research at all?
Chapter 1 explains why we conduct research and report what we find.

- Need a research topic?
Chapter 2 helps you find a topic that will interest you and your readers.

- Need to find information?
Chapters 3–5 show you how to find information in the library, on the Internet, and in the real world through interviews, observation, questionnaires, and the like.

- Need to get organized?
Chapter 6 helps you organize your notes and ideas for a focused paper.

- Need to know which sources are reliable and worth citing?
Chapter 7 helps you judge the sources you find so you will know which to read and cite and which to dismiss.

- What about plagiarism and publishing on my website?
Chapter 8 addresses matters of academic integrity and honesty in reporting.

- Need guidelines for taking notes?
Chapter 9 shows how to write effective notes that will transfer easily into your text.

- What about writing the paper and blending the sources into my paragraph?
Chapters 10–13 help give your writing an academic style, one that blends sources effectively into your prose and encourages strength and purpose in your introduction, body, and conclusion.

- What happens when the instructor says "Use APA style" or "Reference your sources with footnotes"?
Chapters 14–17 provide detailed instruction and examples of four academic styles—MLA (English), APA (social sciences), CMS (humanities), and CBE (sciences).

- How do I publish my research paper on the Web?
Chapter 18 helps you present your paper electronically, including releasing it on the World Wide Web.

The new learning aids in this edition, shown on the opposite page, have been designed with you in mind. These features will help you better learn and understand the research process and provide you with additional resources for areas in which you may need further help.

Writing Research Papers: A Complete Guide, now in its tenth edition, has served almost three million students by maintaining up to date views on student research. Early editions encouraged students to write with the computer, later editions advocated research on the Internet, and this edition motivates students like you to publish the paper in an electronic form, not merely on paper. We welcome any thoughts and suggestions you may have on this text as you work through it. We wish you well.

J. D. L.
JamesDLester@aol.com

J. D. L., Jr.
JLester@mzhs.ccps.ga.net

Hint and **Note** boxes throughout the text offer additional information on key topics.

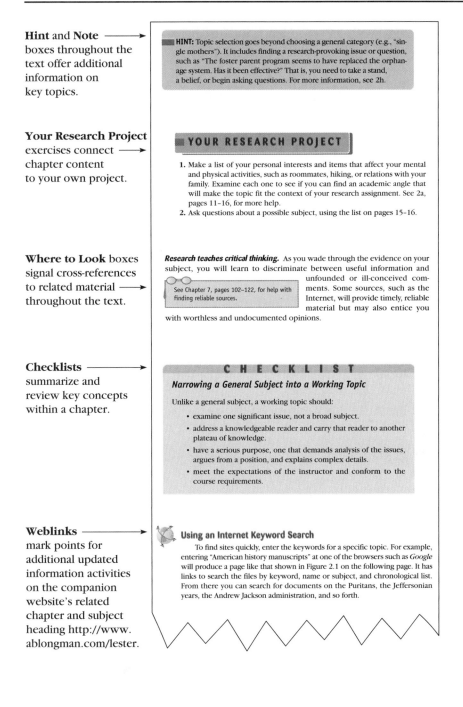

HINT: Topic selection goes beyond choosing a general category (e.g., "single mothers"). It includes finding a research-provoking issue or question, such as "The foster parent program seems to have replaced the orphanage system. Has it been effective?" That is, you need to take a stand, a belief, or begin asking questions. For more information, see 2h.

Your Research Project exercises connect chapter content to your own project.

YOUR RESEARCH PROJECT

1. Make a list of your personal interests and items that affect your mental and physical activities, such as roommates, hiking, or relations with your family. Examine each one to see if you can find an academic angle that will make the topic fit the context of your research assignment. See 2a, pages 11–16, for more help.
2. Ask questions about a possible subject, using the list on pages 15–16.

Where to Look boxes signal cross-references to related material throughout the text.

Research teaches critical thinking. As you wade through the evidence on your subject, you will learn to discriminate between useful information and unfounded or ill-conceived comments. Some sources, such as the Internet, will provide timely, reliable material but may also entice you with worthless and undocumented opinions.

See Chapter 7, pages 102–122, for help with finding reliable sources.

Checklists summarize and review key concepts within a chapter.

C H E C K L I S T

Narrowing a General Subject into a Working Topic

Unlike a general subject, a working topic should:

- examine one significant issue, not a broad subject.
- address a knowledgeable reader and carry that reader to another plateau of knowledge.
- have a serious purpose, one that demands analysis of the issues, argues from a position, and explains complex details.
- meet the expectations of the instructor and conform to the course requirements.

Weblinks mark points for additional updated information activities on the companion website's related chapter and subject heading http://www.ablongman.com/lester.

Using an Internet Keyword Search

To find sites quickly, enter the keywords for a specific topic. For example, entering "American history manuscripts" at one of the browsers such as *Google* will produce a page like that shown in Figure 2.1 on the following page. It has links to search the files by keyword, name or subject, and chronological list. From there you can search for documents on the Puritans, the Jeffersonian years, the Andrew Jackson administration, and so forth.

1

Writing from Research

We conduct informal research all the time. We examine various models and their options before buying a car, and we check out another person informally before proposing or accepting a first date. We sometimes search the classified ads to find a summer job, or we roam the mall to find a new tennis racket, the right pair of sports shoes, or the latest CD. Research, then, is not foreign to us. However, in the classroom, we begin thinking about a serious and systematic activity, one that involves the library, the Internet, or field research.

A research paper, like a personal essay, requires you to choose a topic that you care about and to invest many hours in thinking about it. However, unlike a personal essay, you develop your ideas by gathering information and reading sources. As you pull your project together, you continue to express personal ideas, but now they are supported by and based on the collective evidence and the opinions of experts on the topic.

Some instructors prefer the description "research*ed* writing," for this type of writing grows from investigation, and the research is used in different ways, in different amounts, and for different purposes. Each classroom and each instructor will make different demands on your talents. The guidelines here are general; your instructors will provide the specifics.

This text therefore introduces research as an engaging, sometimes exciting pursuit on several fronts—your personal knowledge, ideas gleaned from sources, and research in the field.

1a Why Do Research?

Instructors ask you to write a research paper for several reasons:

Research teaches methods of discovery. A research project asks you to discover both what you already know about a complex topic and what others can teach you. The discovery process will usually include reading, and it often requires or motivates you to venture into the field for interviews, observation, and experimentation. You may not arrive at any final answers or solutions, but you will come to understand the different views on a subject. In your final paper, you will synthesize your ideas and discoveries with the knowledge and opinions of others.

Research teaches investigative skills. A research project requires you to investigate a subject, grasp the essentials of it, and disclose your findings. The exercise teaches important methods for gaining knowledge on a complex topic. Your success will depend on your negotiating the various sources of information, from reference books in the library to computer databases and from special archival collections to the most recent articles in the printed periodicals. The Internet, with its vast amounts of information, will challenge you to find "reliable" sources. If you conduct research by observation, interviews, surveys, and laboratory experiments, you will discover additional methods of investigation.

For tips on finding material on the Internet and beyond, examine Chapter 4, pages 54–77.

Research teaches critical thinking. As you wade through the evidence on your subject, you will learn to discriminate between useful information and unfounded or ill-conceived comments. Some sources, such as the Internet, will provide timely, reliable material but may also entice you with worthless and undocumented opinions.

See Chapter 7, pages 102–22, for help with finding reliable sources.

Research teaches logic. Like a judge in the courtroom, the research paper asks for your perceptive judgment about the issues surrounding a specific topic. Your decisions about the issues, in effect, will be based upon the wisdom gained from research about the topic. Your paper and your readers will rely upon your logical response to your reading, observation, interviews, and testing.

Research teaches the basic ingredients of argument. In most cases, a research paper requires you to make a claim and support it with reasons and evidence. For example, if you argue that "urban sprawl has invited wild animals into our backyards," you will learn to anticipate challenges to your theory and to defend your assertion with evidence.

For help with making a claim and establishing a thesis, see 1c, pages 3–8.

1b   Learning Format Variations

Scholarly writing in each scholarly discipline follows certain conventions; that is, special forms are required for citing the sources and for designing the pages. These rules make uniform the numerous articles written internationally by millions of different scholars. The society of language and literature scholars, the Modern Language Association, has a set of guidelines generally known as the MLA style. Similarly, the American Psychological Association has its own APA style. Other groups of scholars prefer to use a footnote system, while others use a numbering system. These variations are not meant to confuse; they have evolved within disciplines as the preferred style. What is important for you, right now, is to determine which format to use. Many composition instructors will ask you to use MLA style, as explained primarily in Chapters 11–14, but they are just as likely to ask for APA style (Chapter 15) if your topic concerns one of the social sciences. In a like manner, your art appreciation instructor might expect the Chicago Manual's footnote style but could just as easily request the APA style. Ask early and organize accordingly.

MLA Style, pages 224–76
APA Style, pages 277–309
Chicago Footnote Style, pages 310–35
CBE Number Style, pages 336–51

1c Understanding a Research Assignment

Beyond picking a good topic, you will need a reason for writing the paper. Literature instructors might expect you to make judgments about the structure of a story or poem. Education instructors might ask you to examine the merits of a testing program. History instructors might want you to explore an event, perhaps the causes and consequences of Desert Storm, the war on Iraq.

Your inquiry is often a response to a question, such as "Should school children receive medication for hyperactive behavior?" One student, Gena Messersmith, gathered evidence to answer affirmatively in her paper (see pages 300–09). Another student considered this one: "Has medical science advanced tissue and organ transplantation faster than the public has kept pace with donations?" (See pages 323–35 for Adele Gelvin's paper.) Different kinds of topics and questions can motivate you to explore your own thoughts and discover what others are saying.

Understanding the Terminology

Assignments in literature, history, and the fine arts will often require you to *interpret, evaluate,* and perform *causal analysis.* Assignments in education, psychology, political science, and other social science disciplines will usually require *analysis, definition, comparison,* or a search for *precedents* leading to a *proposal.* In the sciences your experiments and testing will usually require a discussion of the *implications* of your findings.

Evaluation

To evaluate, you first need to establish clear criteria of judgment and then explain how the subject meets these criteria. For example, student evaluations of faculty members are based on a set of expressed criteria—an interest in student progress, a thorough knowledge of the subject, and so forth. Similarly, you may be asked to judge the merits of a poem, art show, or new computer software. Your first step should be to create your criteria. What makes a good movie? How important is form to a poem? Is space a special factor in architecture? You can't expect the sources to provide the final answers; you need to experience the work and make your final judgments on it.

Let's see how it develops with one student who was asked to examine the Title IX statute. Being female, she quickly asserted its value for providing funds and integrity to women's athletic programs. But upon entering the intellectual conversation as found in the literature on the topic, she developed several ideas on an argument that Title IX does not damage men's programs.

The same evaluative process would apply to other subjects. For example, Katie Hebert (see pages 210–23) conducted her inquiry on how nutritional foods might prevent disease. Her work produced not only a few answers but charts showing the relative values of such foods. In many ways, every research paper is an evaluation.

Interpretation

To interpret, you must usually answer, "What does it mean?" You may be asked to explain the symbolism in a piece of literature, examine a point of law, or make sense of test results. Questions often point toward interpretation:

What does this passage mean?
What does this data tell us?
Can you explain your reading of the problem to others?

For example, your instructor might ask you to interpret the Supreme Court's ruling in *Roe v. Wade,* interpret test results on pond water at site A and site B, or interpret a scene from Shakespeare's *A Midsummer Night's Dream.*

Definition

Sometimes you will need to provide an extended definition to show that your subject fits into a selected and well-defined category. Note these examples:

1. Slapping a child on the face is child abuse.
   You will need to define child abuse and then show that an act of slapping fits the definition.
2. Title IX is a law, not an option, for athletic programs.
   You will need to define the law in detail.
3. Plagiarism should be considered a criminal misdemeanor.
   You will need to define a criminal misdemeanor and prove that plagiarism fits the definition
4. Cheerleaders are athletes who deserve scholarships.
   You will need to define "athletes who deserve scholarships" and find a way to place cheerleaders within that category.

These examples demonstrate how vague and illusive our language can be. We know what an athlete is in general, but the argument needs a careful analysis of the term "scholarship athlete." The writer will need to work carefully to reach agreement with the reader about the terminology. What's more, the writer will need to define in some detail the term "cheerleader."

A good definition usually includes three elements: the subject (cheerleaders), the class to which the subject belongs (athlete), and the difference from others in this class (gymnast). The assumption is that a gymnast is a scholarship athlete. If the writer can associate the cheerleader with the gymnast, then the argument might have merit.

Definition will almost always become a part of your work when some of the terminology is subjective. If you argue, for example, that medical experiments on animals are cruel and inhumane, you may need to define what you mean by "cruel" and explain why human standards should be applied to animals that are not human. Thus, definition might serve as your major thesis.

Definition is also necessary with technical and scientific terminology, as shown by Gena Messersmith (see pages 300–09). She understood Attention Deficit Hyperactivity Disorder (ADHD) because her daughter was diagnosed with ADHD. Yet Messersmith also needed a careful, detailed definition of the medical disorder, not merely a discourse on the behavioral problems of her daughter. By her inquiry, she reached her conclusion that medication, not behavior modification, would best serve children who have ADHD.

Thus, most writers build their paper on an issue that gives them a reason for inquiry and investigation of their own attitudes and beliefs as well as ideas from written sources, interviews, observation, and other research methods.

Proposal

This type of argument says to the reader, "We should do something." It often has practical applications, as shown by these examples:

1. We should change the annual yearbook into a semiannual magazine because student interest, participation, and response to a yearbook are extremely poor.
2. We should cancel all drug testing of athletes because it presumes guilt and demeans the innocent.
3. A chipping mill should not be allowed in this area because its insatiable demand for timber will strip our local forests.

As shown by these examples, the proposal argument calls for action—a change in policy, a change in the law, and sometimes an alteration of accepted procedures. Again, the writer must advance the thesis and support it with reasons and evidence.

In addition, a proposal demands special considerations. First, writers should convince readers that a problem exists and is serious enough to merit action. In the example above about chipping mills, the writer will need to establish that, indeed, chipping mills have been proposed and perhaps even approved for the area. Then the writer will need to argue that they endanger the environment: they grind vast amounts of timber of any size and shave timber into chips that are reprocessed in various ways. As a result, lumberjacks cut even the immature trees, stripping forests into barren wastelands. The unstated assumption is that clear-cutting damages the land.

Second, the writer must explain the consequences to convince the reader that the proposal has validity. The paper must defend the principle that clear-cutting damages the land, and should show, if possible, how chipping mills in other parts of the country have damaged the environment.

Third, the writer will need to address any opposing positions, competing proposals, and alternative solutions. For example, chipping mills produce chip board for decking the floors of houses, thus saving trees that might be required for making expensive plywood boards. Without chipping mills, we might run short on paper and homebuilding products. The writer will need to note opposing views and consider them in the paper.

Adele Gelvin's inquiry into organ and tissue donation includes a proposal (see pages 323–35). It explains the problem—that donors are needed—and the consequences—people are dying as they wait for certain organs. Along the way, Gelvin dismisses the many myths about tissue and organ donation and proposes that her readers sign a donor card.

Causal Argument

Unlike proposals, which predict consequences, causal arguments show that a condition exists because of specific circumstances. That is, something has caused or created this situation, and we need to know why. For example, a student's investigation uncovered why schools in one state benefit greatly from a lottery but not in another.

Let's look at a student who asked the question: Why do numerous students, like me, who otherwise score well on the ACT test, score poorly in the math section of the test and, consequently, enroll in developmental courses that offer no college credit? This question merited his investigation, so he gathered evidence from his personal experience as well as from data drawn from interviews, surveys, critical reading, and accumulated test results. Ultimately, he explored and wrote on a combination of things—poor study skills by students, bias in the testing program, and inadequate instruction in grade school and high school. He discovered something about himself and many things about the testing program.

Sarah Bemis, a student writer, used a similar kind of causal argument in her essay on diabetes management (see pages 344–51). Bemis traces the causes for the disease and then examines the methods for controlling it: medication, diet, and exercise.

Comparison and Analogy

An argument often compares and likens a subject to something else. You might be asked to compare a pair of poems or compare stock markets—Nasdaq with Dow Jones. Comparison is seldom the focus of an entire paper, but it can be useful in a paragraph that compares, let's say, the banking policy of Andrew Jackson with that of his congressional opponents.

On the other hand, an analogy is a figurative comparison that allows the writer to draw several parallels of similarity. For example, the human circulatory system is like a transportation system with a hub, a highway system, and a fleet of trucks to carry the cargo.

Shannon Williams, a student writer, considered using comparison in a couple of ways for her paper on the poet Langston Hughes (pages 204-09). She saw Hughes as a key figure in the Harlem Renaissance just as Shakespeare served the Elizabethan Renaissance and as Ralph Waldo Emerson inspired the American Renaissance. She also considered the willingness of Hughes to use the vernacular language, which compares favorably with the music writers of today, such as rap artists.

Precedence

Precedence refers to conventions or customs, usually established in the past. In judicial decisions, it is a standard set by previous cases, a *legal precedent.* Therefore, a thesis statement built on precedence requires a past event that establishes a rule of law or a point of procedure. As an example, let's return to the argument against the chipping mill. If the researcher can prove that another mill in another part of the country ruined the environment, then the researcher has a precedent for how damaging such an operation can be.

The sample papers printed within this book also demonstrate the use of precedence. Shannon Williams (204-09) argues that Langston Hughes set a precedent for the use of African American vernacular in poetry. Katie Hebert (210-23) suggests that the precedent for healing foods was set long ago in tribal medicine, and Sarah Bemis (344-51) indicates that the precedent of diet and exercise to maintain diabetic balance might be just as important, if not more so, than some medications.

Implications

If you conduct any kind of test or observation, you will probably make field notes in a research journal and tabulate your results at regular intervals. At some point, however, you will be expected to explain your findings, arrive at conclusions, and discuss the implications of your scientific inquiry. Lab reports are elementary forms of this task. What did you discover and what does it mean?

For example, one student explored the scientific world of drug testing before companies place their products on the market. His discussions had chilling implications for consumers. Another student examined the role of mice as reservoir carriers of Lyme disease. This work required reading as well as field research and testing to arrive at final judgments. In literature, a student examined the recurring images of birds in the poetry of Thomas Hardy to discuss the implications of the birds in Hardy's basic themes.

In review, fit one of more of these arguments to the context of your project:

Evaluation
Interpretation
Definition
Proposal
Causal Argument

Comparison and Analogy
Precedence
Implications

1d   Establishing a Schedule

The steps for producing a research paper have remained fundamental for many years. You will do well to follow them, even to the point of setting deadlines on the calendar for each step. In the spaces below, write dates to remind yourself when deadlines should be met.

_____ *Topic approved by the instructor.* The topic must have a built-in question or argument so that you can interpret an issue and cite the opinions found in the source materials.

_____ *Reading and creating a working bibliography.* Preliminary reading establishes the basis for your research, helping you to discover the quantity and quality of available sources. If you can't find much, your topic is too narrow. If you find far too many sources, your topic is too broad and needs narrowing. Chapter 3 will explain the process of finding reliable, expert sources.

_____ *Organizing.* Instructors will require different types of plans. For some, your research journal will indicate the direction of your work. Others will ask for a formal outline. In either case, see Chapter 6.

_____ *Creating notes.* Begin entering notes in your computer or on note cards. Write plenty of notes and collect a supply of photocopied pages, which you should carefully label. Some notes will be summaries, others will need carefully drawn quotations from the sources, and some will be paraphrases written in your own voice. Chapter 9 explains these various techniques.

_____ *Drafting the paper.* During your writing, let your instructor scan the draft to give you feedback and guidance. He or she might see further complications for your exploration and also steer you clear of any simplistic conclusions. Drafting is also a stage for peer review, in which one or more classmates look at your work. The instructor may also have classroom workshops that will offer in-class review of your work in progress. Chapters 10, 11, and 12 explain matters of drafting the paper.

_____ *Formatting the paper.* Proper manuscript design places your paper within the required design for your discipline, such as the number system for a scientific project or the APA style for an education paper. Chapters 14–17 provide the guidelines for the various disciplines. See also Appendix A.

_____ *Writing a list of sources.* You will need to list in the proper format the various sources used in your study. Chapters 14–17 provide documentation guidelines.

_____ *Revision and proofreading.* Be conscientious about examining your manuscript and making all necessary corrections. With the aid of computers, you can check spelling and some aspects of style. Chapter 13 provides tips on revision and editing.

_____ *Submitting the manuscript.* Like all writers, you will need at some point to "publish" the paper and release it to the audience, which might be your instructor, your classmates, or perhaps a larger group. Plan well in advance to meet this final deadline. You may publish the paper in a variety of ways—on paper, on a disk, on a CD-ROM, on your own website.

For details about preparing the research paper in an electronic format, see Chapter 18, pages 352–62.

2

Finding a Topic

An informed choice of a subject is crucial for fulfilling the research assignment. You might be tempted to write from a personal interest, such as "Fishing at Lake Cumberland"; however, the content and the context of your course and the assignment itself should drive you toward a serious, scholarly perspective: "The Effects of Toxic Chemicals on the Fish of Lake Cumberland." This topic would probably send you into the field for hands-on investigation, just what causal analysis might require.

You will need a special edge or angle. The topic "Symbolism in Hawthorne's Fiction" has no originality, but "Hester Prynne in the 21st Century" has a touch of originality. Similarly, "The Sufferings of Native Americans" could be improved to "Urban Sprawl in Morton County: The Bulldozing of Indian Burial Grounds." Shannon Williams on page 204 considered the title "Langston Hughes: Father to the Rap Artists," to relate the historical poet to the contemporary scene. Yet keep in mind that your special position need not appear in the title. Gena Messersmith's essay on pages 300–09 was driven by her own experiences with her hyperactive child.

In another example, you might be tempted by the topic "Computer Games," but the research assignment requires an evaluation of issues, not a description. It also requires detailed definition. A better topic might be "Learned Dexterity with Video and Computer Games," which requires the definition of learned dexterity and how some video games promote it. Even in a first-year composition class, your instructor may expect discipline-specific topics, such as:

EDUCATION:	The Visually Impaired: Options for Classroom Participation
POLITICAL SCIENCE:	Conservative Republicans and the Religious Right
LITERATURE:	Kate Chopin's *The Awakening* and the Women's Movement
HEALTH:	The Effects of Smoking during Pregnancy
SOCIOLOGY:	Parents Who Lie to Their Children

These topics produce inquiry-based learning or problem-based learning. That is, your inquiry into the issues or your effort to solve the problem will

C H E C K L I S T

Narrowing a General Subject into a Working Topic

Unlike a general subject, a working topic should:

- examine one significant issue, not a broad subject.
- address a knowledgeable reader and carry that reader to another plateau of knowledge.
- have a serious purpose, one that demands analysis of the issues, argues from a position, and explains complex details.
- meet the expectations of the instructor and conform to the course requirements.

empower the learning process. When your topic addresses such issues, you have a reason to:

- Examine specific sources in the library, on the Internet, and in the field.
- Share your investigation of the issues with the reader.
- Write a meaningful conclusion.

This chapter will help you mold a general subject into a workable topic. It explains how to relate your personal ideas to a scholarly problem (see 2a), how to use interviews and chat groups (2b), how to search computer sources for issues worthy of investigation (see 2c), how to examine the library's sources (see 2d, 2e, 2f, 2g), and how to write a proposal with an effective thesis (2h and 2i).

2a | Relating Your Personal Ideas to a Scholarly Problem

Try to make a connection between your interests and the inherent issues of the subject. For instance, a student whose mother became seriously addicted to the Internet developed a paper from the personal experiences of her dysfunctional family. She worked within the sociology discipline and consulted journals of that field. Another student who worked at Walmart, developed a research project on discount pricing and its effect on small-town shop owners. She worked within the discipline of marketing and business management, reading appropriate literature in those areas. Sarah Bemis, whose paper appears on pages 344–51, researched a variety of sources for information on diabetes, a topic that concerned her because diabetes had afflicted both her grandmother and her mother. Begin with two activities:

1. Relate your experiences to scholarly problems and academic disciplines.
2. Speculate about the subject by listing issues, asking questions, engaging in free writing, and using other idea-generating techniques.

Connecting Personal Experience to Scholarly Topics

You can't write a personal essay and call it a research paper, yet you can choose topics close to your life. Examine your responses to television shows, magazine articles, friends and associates, the workplace, and your leisure-time activities. Then use one of the techniques described below:

1. Combine personal interests with an aspect of academic studies:

PERSONAL INTEREST:	Skiing
ACADEMIC SUBJECT:	Sports medicine
POSSIBLE TOPICS:	"Protecting the Knees," "Therapy for Strained Muscles," or "Skin Treatments"

2. Consider social issues that affect you and your family:

PERSONAL INTEREST:	The education of my child
SOCIAL ISSUE:	The behavior of my child in school
POSSIBLE TOPICS:	"Children Who Are Hyperactive" "Should School Children Take Medicine to Calm Their Hyperactivity"

3. Consider scientific subjects if appropriate:

PERSONAL INTEREST:	The ponds and well water on the family farm
SCIENTIFIC SUBJECT:	Chemical toxins in the water
POSSIBLE TOPIC:	"The Poisoning of Underground Water Tables"

4. Let your cultural background prompt you toward detailed research into your roots, your culture, and the mythology and history of your ethnic background:

ETHNIC BACKGROUND:	Native American
PERSONAL INTEREST:	History of the Apache tribes
POSSIBLE TOPIC:	"The Indian Wars from the Native American's Point of View"

ETHNIC BACKGROUND:	Hispanic
PERSONAL INTEREST:	Struggles of the Mexican child in an American classroom
POSSIBLE TOPIC:	"Bicultural Experiences of Hispanic Students: The Failures and Triumphs"

HINT: Every discipline, whether sociology, geology, or literature, will limit a discussion to analytical categories that require detailed study, such as the *demographics* of a target audience (marketing), the *function* of loops and arrays (computer science), or *observation* of human subjects (psychology). Part of your task is learning the terminology and using it appropriately.

Speculating about Your Subject to Discover Ideas and to Focus on the Issues

At some point you may need to sit back, relax, and use your imagination to contemplate the issues and generate ideas worthy of investigation. Ideas can be generated in the following ways:

Keeping a Research Journal

Unlike a diary of personal thoughts about your daily activities or a journal of creative ideas, such as poems, stories, or scenarios, the research journal is a place to record ideas in one source book or computer file. It can feature a list of issues, sets of questions, miscellaneous notes, and bits of free writing, as shown in the example below. A notebook with pockets provides space for photocopied materials and other loose papers. If you keep the journal on a computer file, you can download materials from the Internet and use a scanner for other items.

Free Writing

To free write, merely focus on a topic and write whatever comes to mind. Do not worry about grammar, style, or penmanship, but keep writing nonstop for a page or so to develop valuable phrases, comparisons, personal anecdotes, and specific thoughts that help focus issues of concern. Below, Katie Hebert explores certain aspects of her topic (see pages 210-23 for the final version):

> Although I do not advocate canceling all future doctor appointments, it seems clear to me that functional foods have exhibited strength in the fight for cancer prevention and the control of coronary heart disease. These are two causes of a tremendous number of deaths in America each year. So Americans are taking a new serious look at foods high in the antioxidants found in Vitamin C, E, and beta-carotene, as well as fatty acids, soluble fiber, and green and black teas. Disease prevention makes better sense to me than late-in-life attempts to heal a disease.

This free writing has set the path for this writer's investigation into the role of diet in controlling illness. She has found her position—that prevention through diet has merit.

Listing Key Words

Note fundamental terms and concepts that might focus the direction of your research. One student, while considering a topic on Langston Hughes, listed several terms and phrases associated with the poet:

Harlem Renaissance	vernacular language	jazz verse
race relations	racial oppression	racial pride
jazz music	poetic symbolism	racial strength

These key words set the stage for writing the rough outline, as explained on the following page.

Arranging Key Words into a Rough Outline

As you develop ideas and begin listing key terms and subtopics, you should recognize the hierarchy of major and minor issues.

> Langston Hughes
>> Harlem Renaissance
>>> The rise of African American poetry and music
>> Language
>>> The use of the vernacular
>> Personal integrity
>>> African American pride
>> Symbolism
>>> Symbols of strength and dignity
>> Jazz
>>> The new rhythms of Harlem

This initial ranking of ideas would grow in length and mature in depth during Shannon Williams's research process (see pages 204–09 for her paper).

Clustering

Another method for discovering the hierarchy of your primary topics and subtopics is to cluster ideas around a central subject. The cluster of related topics can generate a multitude of interconnected ideas.

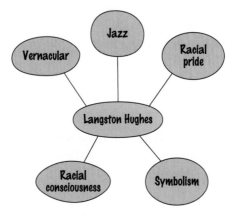

Narrowing by Comparison

Comparison limits a discussion to specific differences. Any two works, any two persons, any two groups may serve as the basis for a comparative study. Historians compare Robert E. Lee and Ulysses S. Grant. Political scientists compare conservatives and liberals. Literary scholars compare the merits of free verse with patterned verse. However, the study should focus on issues, as shown below in a preliminary outline in which Katie Hebert (see pages 210–23) compares the various properties of foods to determine those best suited for maintaining good health. She also compares the economic and health benefits:

Economic benefits	Health benefits
lower cost of food	lower cholesterol
rising cost of medicine	less heart disease
	may prevent cancer

The plan limits the discussion to potential benefits of food, which include both economic and health benefits.

Asking Questions

Stretch your imagination with questions.

1. General questions examine terminology, issues, causes, etc. For example, having read Henry Thoreau's essay "Civil Disobedience," one writer asked:

> What is "civil disobedience"?
> Is dissent legal? Is it moral? Is it patriotic?
> Is dissent a liberal activity? Conservative?
> Should the government encourage or stifle dissent?
> Is passive resistance effective?

Answering the questions can lead the writer to a central issue or argument, such as "Civil Disobedience: Shaping Our Nation."

2. Rhetorical questions use the modes of writing as a basis. One student framed these questions:

COMPARISON:	How does a state lottery compare with horse racing?
DEFINITION:	What is a lottery in legal terms? In religious terms?
CAUSE/EFFECT:	What are the consequences of a state lottery on funding for education, highways, prisons, and social programs?
PROCESS:	How are winnings distributed?
CLASSIFICATION:	What types of lotteries exist and which are available in this state?
EVALUATION:	What is the value of a lottery to the average citizen? What are the disadvantages?

3. Academic disciplines across the curriculum provide questions, as framed by one student on the topic of sports gambling.

ECONOMICS:	Does sports gambling benefit a college's athletic budget? Does it benefit the national economy?
PSYCHOLOGY:	What is the effect of gambling on the mental attitude of the college athlete who knows huge sums hang in the balance on his/her performance?

> **HISTORY:**   Does gambling on sporting events have an identifiable tradition?
>
> **SOCIOLOGY:**   What compulsion in human nature prompts people to gamble on athletic prowess?

4. Journalism questions explore the basic elements of a subject: Who? What? Where? When? Why? and How? For example:

WHO?   Athletes

WHAT?   Illegal drugs

WHEN?   During off-season training and also on game day

WHERE?   Training rooms and elsewhere

WHY?   To enhance performance

HOW?   By pills and injections

The journalist's questions direct you toward the issues, such as "win at all costs" or "damaging the body for immediate gratification."

5. Kenneth Burke's *pentad* questions five aspects of a topic: act, agent, scene, agency, purpose.

WHAT HAPPENED (THE ACT)?	crucifixion scene in *The Old Man and the Sea*
WHO DID IT (AGENT)?	Santiago, the old fisherman
WHERE AND WHEN (SCENE)?	at the novel's end
HOW DID IT OCCUR (AGENCY)?	Santiago carries the mast of his boat up the Cuban hillside
WHAT IS A POSSIBLE MOTIVE FOR THIS EVENT (PURPOSE)?	Hemingway wanted to make a martyr of the old man

Example from a journal entry:

> The crucifixion scene in Hemingway's *The Old Man and Sea* shows Santiago hoisting the mast of his boat on his shoulder and struggling up the Cuban hillside. Hemingway suggests Christian connotations with this scene, so I wonder if, perhaps, he has used other Christian images in the novel.

This researcher can now search the novel with a purpose—to find other Christian images, rank and classify them, and determine if, indeed, the study has merit.

2b   Talking with Others to Refine the Topic

Personal Interviews

Like some researchers, you may need to consult with your instructor or sit on a park bench with a friend. Explore a subject for key ideas while having coffee or a soda with a colleague, relative, or work associate. Ask people in your community for ideas and for their reactions to your general subject.

For example, one writer had considered "organ donation" as her possible topic. While chatting with a few friends, one said, "I heard about this guy who went to a party and woke up the next morning in a bathtub full of ice. His kidneys were stolen for sale on the black market." The writer, Adele Gelvin, seized upon the absurdity of this urban legend and decided to explore the myths surrounding the topic of organ donation.

> Adele Gelvin's paper on organ and tissue donation can be found on pages 323–335.

Casual conversations which contribute to your understanding of the subject need not be documented. However, the conscientious writer will credit a formal interview or an in-depth discussion with an expert. Also, when participating in a collaborative research project, you will surely want each member of the team to receive credit for the work accomplished.

Internet Discussion Groups

What are other people saying about your subject? You might use the computer to share ideas and messages with other scholars interested in your subject. Somebody may answer a question or point to an interesting aspect which has not occurred to you. With discussion groups you have a choice:

> See 4h, pages 71–72, for a more complete discussion of listserv and chat groups.

- E-mail news groups in which you post a message to a listserv site and then wait for the reply.
- MUD and MOO discussion groups on the Internet. These are multi-user domains explained in greater detail in section 4h, page 71.
- Real-time chatting with participants online at the same time, even with audio and video in some cases.

For example, your instructor may set up an informal classroom discussion list and expect you to participate online with her and your fellow students. You and your classmates will correspond by e-mail messages. In other cases, the instructor might suggest that you investigate a specific site, such as alt.religion for a religious subject or alt.current-events.usa for a paper on gun control laws. Alt.religion, for example, offers these news groups among a list of about 50:

    alt.religion.wicca.moderated
    alt.religion.scientology
    alt.religion.jehovahs-witn
    alt.religion.christian.roman-catholic
    alt.religion.mormom
    alt.religion.christian

C H E C K L I S T

Exploring Ideas with Others

- Consult with your instructor.
- Discuss your topic with three or four classmates.
- Listen to the concerns of others.
- Conduct a formal interview (see pages 78–79).
- Join a computer discussion group.
- Take careful notes.
- Adjust your research accordingly.

By joining, you become a part of the open forum on fairly specific topics, which can help you narrow your work to one issue. Note: Some members do not like the intrusion of uninformed newcomers, so you should probably "lurk" at first, read any FAQs (frequently asked questions), and get a feel for the group before posting your queries.

> For additional information on discussion groups see section 4h, pages 71–72.

You can find discussion groups by going to **www.tile.net**, which catalogs thousands of lists by name, description, and domain and which also provides instructions on how to subscribe and unsubscribe. Real-time chatting is becoming more and more popular as machines increase in speed and capacity. Some programs, such as CUSeeMe, support video and audio exchanges (try it at **www.cuseemeworld.com**). Thus, Internet Relay Chat (IRC) enables you to conduct online interviews as well as discuss your topic and your findings.

2c   Using the World Wide Web to Refine Your Topic

An article or two on the World Wide Web can give you tips about how others approach the subject, which might enable you to focus on a specific issue. The online articles might also provide links to additional articles.

> See also Chapter 4, pages 54–77 for detailed information about Internet searches.

Using an Internet Subject Directory

Many search engines have a directory of subjects on the home page. This list will enable you to move quickly from a general subject to a specific topic. This type of search will be hierarchical; that is, each mouse click narrows the topic. For example, one student studying Thomas Jefferson consulted *AltaVista's* subject categories and clicked on **Reference**, where she found

Archives, then **Early American Archives**, and eventually *Early American Review*, a journal that featured an article on "Jefferson and His Daughters." Although it appears time consuming, the search occurs quickly. Within minutes you will be examining the words of others speaking on your subject.

> **HINT:** The Internet has made it difficult to apply traditional evaluations to an article: is it accurate, authoritative, objective, current, and thorough in coverage? Some Internet sites are advocates for special interests, some sites market products or sprinkle the site with banners to commercial sites, some sites are personal home pages, and many sites offer objective news and scholarly information. The answers:
>
> 1. Go to the reliable databases available through your library, such as *InfoTrac, PsycINFO, UMI ProQuest, Electric Library,* or *EBSCOhost.* You can reach these from remote locations at home or the dorm room by connecting to your library. They are monitored sites that give information filtered by editorial boards and peer review. Many articles on the Internet appeared first in print. Yet all articles must be examined with a critical eye.
> 2. Go to the website accompanying this book for additional tips on methods for evaluating Internet sources, with examples, at **www.ablongman.com/lester**.

Using an Internet Keyword Search

To find sites quickly, enter the keywords for a specific topic. For example, entering "American history manuscripts" at one of the browsers such as *Google* will produce a page like that shown in Figure 2.1 on the following page. It has links to search the files by keyword, name or subject, and chronological list. From there you can search for documents on the Puritans, the Jeffersonian years, the Andrew Jackson administration, and so forth.

Internet search engines will force you to narrow your general subject. For example, one student entered "Internet+addiction," which brought up thou-

See Chapter 4, pages 63–65, for detailed help with keyword searches on the Internet.

sands of sources. By tightening the request to the phrase "Internet addiction," enclosed within quotation marks, she cut the list considerably and discovered other keywords: cyber-wellness, weboholics, and netaddiction. She realized that she had a workable topic.

2d   Using the Library's Electronic Databases to Narrow the Subject

Most college libraries now have electronic databases, such as *InfoTrac, Silverplatter,* or *UMI ProQuest.* Unlike a general search engine with multiple spiders going in search of *every* mention of your keywords, these database

FIGURE 2.1. A Library of Congress site "Words and Deeds in American History," found by using a keyword search for American history manuscripts.
Reproduced with the permission of the Library of Congress.

files are reliable because they refer you to thousands of magazine and journal articles that have been either peer reviewed by experts or filtered through magazine and newspaper editorial processes. In many cases you can read an abstract of the article and often read or print the full text of an article. Libraries will vary in their electronic databases, so be sure to consult with the reference librarians. Follow these steps:

1. Select a database. Some databases, such as *UMI ProQuest,* are general; others focus on one discipline (for example, *PsycINFO* indexes psychological sources and *ERIC* indexes educational sources). *InfoTrac* is a general database with several divisions on health, contemporary authors, and general academic topics. These databases will move you quickly to a list of articles on your topic.

2. Enter a key phrase that describes your topic, enclosed within quotation marks. Avoid using just one general word. For example, the word *food* on the *EBSCOhost* database produced 10,000 possible sites. The two-word phrase "healing foods" produced a manageable twenty-two sites. Here are six of the twenty-two entries:

> **1.** *Healing foods could keep you healthy, wealthy and wise.* By: Schrader, Michael; Nation's Restaurant News, 06/19/2000. Vol. 34 Issue 25, p34, 1/3p *Full Text*

2. *Eat These Healing Foods*. Runner's World, Nov99, Vol. 34 Issue 11, p29, 2/5p *Full Text*

3. *Healing Foods*. Psychology Today, Jul/Aug99, Vol. 32 Issue 4, p24, 1/4p *Full Text*

4. *Big E*. By: Ball, Aimee Lee; Harper's Bazaar, Aug99 Issue 3453, 4p *Full Text*

5. *Healing Foods*. By: Martin, Jeanne Marie; Total Health, Feb94, Vol. 16 Issue 1, 3p *Full Text*

6. *Healing Foods*. By: Kane, Ed; Cats Magazine, Jul98, Vol. 54 Issue 7, 5p, 1 chart *Full Text*

3. Examine the list for relevant articles and browse the descriptions, the abstracts, and in some cases the full text.

A researcher would need to look at the list of entries above and consider possibilities, dismissing 1, 2, and 3 because they are too short, $\frac{1}{3}$ page being the longest. Number 4 has four pages in *Harper's Bazaar,* a woman's magazine; checking it reveals that the Big E is *estrogen,* which plays important roles in a woman's body—the researcher should read it for relevance since the full text is available. Number 5 has three pages from *Total Health,* a relevant magazine—again, the researcher should read it since the full text is available. Number 6 can be dismissed because it's devoted to cats, not humans.

> For more information on evaluating a set of listed sources, see pages 102–22 and also this book's website at www.ablongman.com/lester.

Thus, the researcher has two of six articles that might shed light on the topic. That's probably about the average for the library databases. The ratio will worsen when the researcher goes to a general search engine like *AltaVista* or *Google,* where maybe two of twenty titles will suggest relevance.

2e Using a Library's Electronic Book Catalog

College libraries now have computerized indexes to their holdings. Called by different names at each library (e.g., *Acorn, Felix, Access*), a computerized index lists all books housed in the library, plus film strips, video tapes, and similar items. It will not index the titles of articles in magazines and journals, but it will tell you which periodicals are housed in the library and whether they are housed in printed form or on microforms. Like the electronic databases, described in 2d, it will help you find a workable topic by guiding you quickly from general subjects to subtopics and finally to specific books. It will confirm that your subject has been treated with in-depth studies. Instructors will want to see a few books in your bibliography, so follow these steps:

1. Enter a topic that will generate a reasonably sized list. Katie Hebert, for example, first entered "food" and found 326 entries. She shifted to "nutrition" for 266 records. "Nutritional food" produced just one entry,

Your Search: **Subject Keyword = "diet therapy"**
Displaying Record: **2 of 34**

Title:	Krause's food, nutrition, & diet therapy / - edited by L. Kathleen Mahan, Sylvia Escott-Stump.
Edition:	10th ed.
Publisher:	Philadelphia : W.B. Saunders, c2000.
Description:	xxxiv, 1194 p. : ill. (some col.) ; 29 cm.
Subject:	Diet therapy Nutrition Food
Other Authors:	Mahan, L. Kathleen. Escott-Stump, Sylvia.
Alternate Titles:	Food, nutrition, & diet therapy Krause's food, nutrition and diet therapy Food, nutrition, and diet therapy
Contents:	Digestion, absorption, transport, and excretion of nutrients – Energy – Macronutrients: carbohydrates, proteins, and lipids – Vitamins – Minerals – Water, electrolytes, and acid-base balance – Nutrition during pregnancy and lactation – Nutrition in infancy – Nutrition for the low-birth-weight infant – Nutrition in childhood – Nutrition in adolescence – Nutrition in adult years – Nutrition in aging – Nutrition in the community – Guidelines for dietary planning – Dietary and clinical assessment – Laboratory data in nutrition assessment –Interactions between drugs and nutrients.
ISBN:	0721679048
Publication date:	c2000.

Detailed Holding Information			
Collection	**Call #**	**Copy**	**Note**
General Book Collection, Level 3	RM216.M285 2000		

Detailed Circulation Information		
Status	**Holdings**	**Hold Status**
Available		Not on hold

FIGURE 2.2. Description of a book in an electronic book catalog.
Reproduced with the permission of Woodward Library, Austin Peay State University.

a book from 1979. During the search, however, she studied the entries for keywords, such as "food allergy" and "food habits." One entry, "diet therapy," caught her eye and yielded a reasonable list of thirty-four books, including two titles published in 2000 and six in 1999.

2. Examine the various entries in detail, starting with the most recent. Notice Figure 2.2, which reproduces the detailed description of the book. Under the description of the contents, the researcher can quickly determine if this book will serve well.

3. Print the entry and use it for your trip into the stacks to find the book and to examine it for possible checkout. TIP: While in the stacks, examine nearby books, for they will likely treat the same subject.

HINT: The electronic catalog may provide a gateway or link to other libraries or to networked information, even to the Internet (see page 73 for more about hypertext links). The gateway enables you to examine the holdings in a nearby library or in distant libraries which offer interlibrary loans.

2f Using Compact Diskettes

Browsing in an encyclopedia on a CD will give you a good feel for the depth and strength of the subject and a list of likely topics. For general information, consult an encyclopedia on an individual disk, such as *Grolier's Encyclopedia, Encarta,* or *Electronic Classical Library.* For specific information, you might try the discipline-related CDs, such as the *Oxford English Dictionary, IBM Dictionary of Computing, McGraw-Hill Encyclopedia of World Economies, The History of American Literature, America's Civil War: A Nation Divided, Leading Black Americans,* and others. Your library may not house the individual CD relevant to your search, so look for additional disks at department offices and at the offices of individual professors.

Figure 2.3 on the following page shows one page from the Encarta Encyclopedia 2000 with a notation to key words that might produce a research paper topic. This material can be found at http://encarta.msn.com/index/conciseindex/13/0133e000htm?z=1&pg=2&br=1

2g Using Printed Materials to Evaluate Your Potential Topic

With your working topic in hand, do some exploratory reading in reference books, biographies, or periodicals. This early reading will enhance your understanding of the topic, give you hints about refining it, and confirm that sufficient literature exists.

Scanning Periodicals and Books

As with Internet sources, look to see how your subject is discussed in the literature. Carefully read the *titles* of books and articles, noting any key terms:

"The Lessons of the French Revolution"
"Napoleon's Ambition and the Quest for Domination"
"Perspectives: Napoleon's Relations with the Catholic Church"

These titles provide several key words and possible topics for a research paper: *Napoleon's ambition, Napoleon and the church, the French Revolution.*

Hughes, Langston (1902-1967), American writer, known for the use of jazz and black folk rhythms in his poetry. James Mercer Langston Hughes was born in Joplin, Missouri, and educated at Lincoln University in Pennsylvania. He published his first poem, "The Negro Speaks of Rivers," in *Crisis* magazine in 1921 and studied at Columbia University from 1921-1922. He then lived for a time in Paris. After his return to the United States, he worked as a busboy in Washington, D.C. There, in 1925, his literary skills were discovered after he left three of his poems beside the plate of American poet Vachel Lindsay, who recognized Hughes's abilities and subsequently helped publicize Hughes's work.

Perhaps I can use this as my topic

Hughes wrote in many genres, but he is best known for his poetry, in which he disregarded classical forms in favor of musical rhythms and the oral and improvisatory traditions of black culture. In the 1920s, when he lived in New York city, he was a prominent figure during the Harlem Renaissance and was referred to as the Poet Laureate of Harlem. His innovations in form and voice influenced many black writers. Hughes also wrote the drama *Mulatto* (1935), which was performed on Broadway 373 times. Beginning in the 1930s, Hughes was active in social and political causes, using his poetry as a vehicle for social protest. He traveled to the Union of Soviet Socialist Republics (USSR), Haiti, and Japan, and he served as the Madrid correspondent for a Baltimore, Maryland newspaper during the Spanish Civil War (1936–1939).

In the 1940s, first for the *Chicago Defender* and later for the *New York Post*, Hughes wrote a newspaper column in the voice of the character Simple (also called Jesse B. Semple), who expressed the thoughts of young black Americans. Simple's plain speech, humor, and use of dialect belied his wisdom and common sense. The character became famous and later figured in many of Hughes short stories.

Hughes wrote more than 50 books. His works include the poetry volumes *Weary Blues* (1926), *The Dream Keeper* (1932), *Shakespeare in Harlem* (1942), and *Fields of Wonder* (1947) and the short story collections *The Ways of White Folks* (1934), *Simple Speaks His Mind* (1950), *Simple Takes a Wife* (1953), and *Best of Simple* (1961). Hughes also wrote the novels *Not Without Laughter* (1930) and *Tambourines to Glory* (1958), the autobiographical books *The Big Sea* (1940) and *I Wonder as I Wander* (1957), and the children's books *Black Misery* (1969) and *The Sweet and Sour Animal Book* (written 1936, published 1994). *The Collected Poems of Langston Hughes* was published in 1994.

FIGURE 2.3. "Langston Hughes" from Microsoft Encarta Encyclopedia 2000. With highlighting and marginal note by the student.

Reproduced by permission of the Microsoft Corporation (copyright).

Inspect a book's *table of contents* to find topics of interest. A typical history book might display these headings in the table of contents:

The French Revolution
The Era of Napoleon
Reaction to Napoleon and More Revolutions
The Second Empire of France

If any of these headings look interesting, go to the book's *index* for additional headings, such as this sample:

Napoleon
    becomes Emperor, 174–176
    becomes First Consul, 173
    becomes Life Consul, 174
    and the Catholic Church, 176–178
    character of, 168–176
    and codes of law, 178–179
    defeats Austrians, 170
    extends empire in Europe, 180–189
    encounters opposition, 190–191
    defeated by enemies, 192–197
    sent to Elba, 197
    seizes power for "One Hundred Days," 198
    sent to St. Helena, 199

If you see something that looks interesting, read the designated pages to consider the topic further. For example, you might read about Napoleon's return from Elba for a few additional days of glory before the darkness of confinement at St. Helena.

Searching the Headings in the Printed Indexes

If you do not have access to an electronic database, the printed indexes categorize and subdivide topics by alphabetical order. These are works such as the *Readers' Guide to Periodical Literature, Bibliographic Index,* or *Humanities Index.* Searching under a key word or phrase will usually locate a list of critical articles on the subject, and studying the titles might suggest a narrowed topic. For example, looking under the heading *Single Mothers* might produce several possible topics, such as "welfare moms," "single motherhood," or "racial differentials in child support."

HINT: Topic selection goes beyond choosing a general category (e.g., "single mothers"). It includes finding a research-provoking issue or question, such as "The foster parent program seems to have replaced the orphanage system. Has it been effective?" That is, you need to take a stand, adopt a belief, or begin asking questions. For more information, see 2h.

2h   Drafting a Research Proposal

A research proposal comes in two forms: (1) a short paragraph to iden-tify the project for yourself and your instructor or (2) a formal, multipage report that provides background information, your rationale for conducting the study, a review of the literature, your methods, and the conclusions you hope to prove.

The Short Proposal

A short proposal identifies five essential ingredients of your work:

- The specific topic.
- The purpose of the paper (explain, analyze, argue).
- The intended audience (general or specialized).
- Your voice as the writer (informer or advocate).
- The preliminary thesis sentence or opening hypothesis.

For example, here is the proposal of Gena Messersmith (see her paper on pages 300–09):

> This report will deal with the issues facing parents who have children who are diagnosed with Attention Deficit Hyperactivity Disorder (ADHD). I'm one of those parents, so this study touches my life. In it, I will try to determine if medication is the best treatment for this disorder. Respected authorities in the field state over and over again that medication is the only known solution to the treatment of this disorder. Even with experts backing medication, there is still resistance to medicating children. To support my claim, I have planned for interviews with people who either have ADHD or have children with ADHD.

This writer has identified the basic nature of her project and can now go in search of evidence that will defend the argument.

The Long Proposal

Some instructors may assign the long proposal, which may include some or all of the following elements:

1. *Cover page* with title of the project, your name, and the person or agency to whom you are submitting the proposal:

The Dangers of Internet Addiction

Submitted to

The University Committee on Computers

By Tiffany Bledsoe

2. An *abstract* that summarizes your project in fifty to one hundred words (see p. 211 for an example).

3. A *purpose statement* with your *rationale* for the project. In essence this is your thesis sentence, your identification of the audience that your work will address, and the role you will play as investigator and advocate (see the short proposal above for an example and the discussion below, "Explaining Your Purpose in the Research Proposal").

4. A *statement of qualification* that explains your experience and perhaps the special qualities you bring to the project; Gena Messersmith, for example, says in her short proposal above, "I'm one of those parents, so this study touches my life." Another student made this qualification:

> I bring first-hand experience to this study. I used to drink the
> water from our farm's well, but now the water is contaminated. My
> parents and I do not dare drink it. This project will examine the
> damage to the environment by chemicals seeping into the ground
> from several different sources. It will serve as a warning to all
> landowners that industrial pollution seeps many miles from the
> source.

If you have no experience with the subject, you can omit the statement of qualification.

5. A *review of the literature,* which will survey the articles and books that you have examined in your preliminary work (see pages 120–22 for an explanation with an example).

6. A description of your *research methods*, which is the design of the *materials* you will need, your *timetable*, and, where applicable, your *budget*. These elements are often a part of a scientific study, so see Chapters 15 and 17 for work in the social, physical, and biological sciences.

Explaining Your Purpose in the Research Proposal

Research papers accomplish different tasks:

- They explain and define the topic.
- They analyze the specific issues.
- They persuade the reader with the weight of the evidence.

Use *explanation* to review and itemize factual data. One writer explained how diabetes can be managed (see Sarah Bemis's essay on pages 344–51). Another writer explained how organ donation has lagged far behind the demand for tissue and organs (see Adele Gelvin's essay on pages 323–35).

Use *analysis* to classify various parts of the subject and to investigate each one in depth. One writer examined various foods that might be instrumental in preventing certain diseases. The analysis required her to classify and itemize the foods and give a breakdown of their various benefits.

Use *persuasion* to question the general attitudes about a problem and then to affirm new theories, advance a solution, recommend a course of

C H E C K L I S T

Addressing the Reader

- *Identify your audience.* Have you visualized your audience, its expertise, and its expectations? Your perception of the reader will affect your voice, style, and your choice of words.

- *Identify your discipline.* Readers in each discipline will bring differing expectations to your paper with regard to content, language, design, and documentation format.

- *Meet the needs of your readers.* Are you saying something worthwhile? Something new? Do not bore them with known facts from an encyclopedia. (This latter danger is the reason many instructors discourage your use of an encyclopedia as a source.

- *Engage and even challenge your readers.* Find an interesting or different point of view. For example, a report on farm life can become a challenging examination of chemical contamination because of industrial sprawl into rural areas, and an interpretation of a novel can become an examination of the prison system rather than a routine discourse on theme or characterization.

action, or—in the least—invite the reader into an intellectual dialogue. Katie Hebert urges the reader to eat wisely (210-23), Gena Messersmith encourages the use of medication for children diagnosed with ADHD (300-09), and Adele Gelvin encourages us to sign our donor cards (323-35).

Identifying Your Audience in the Research Proposal

Academic readers will have certain expectations, based upon the focus of your work, so adjust your topic and critical approach to the people who will read your paper. Readers of a paper on social issues (i.e., working mothers, latchkey children, overcrowded prisons) will expect analysis that points toward a *social theory* or answer. Readers of an academic interpretation of a novel will expect to read *literary theories* on the novel's symbolism, narrative structure, or characterization. Readers of a business report on outdoor advertising will expect *statistical evidence* that will defend a general proposition, especially as it reflects the demographics of the targeted consumers and the cost of reaching them.

Identifying Your Role as a Researcher in the Proposal

Your voice should reflect the investigative nature of your work, so try to display your knowledge. In short, make it *your* discourse, not a collection of quotations from experts in the books and journals. Your role as a researcher is to investigate, explain, argue the issues at hand, and defend your ideas with proper citations. Refer often to your authorities and quote them, but not lavishly; that is, quote a key, pivotal sentence, not an entire paragraph. Provide charts or graphs that you have created or copied from the sources. Just be certain that you provide in-text citations to the sources to reflect your academic honesty.

2i Expressing Your Thesis

A thesis sentence expands your topic into a scholarly proposal, one that you will try to prove and defend in your paper. It does not state the obvious, such as: "Langston Hughes was a great poet from Harlem." That sentence will not provoke an academic discussion because your readers know that any published poet has talent. The writer must narrow and isolate one issue by finding a critical focus, such as this one that a student considered for her essay:

> Langston Hughes used a controversial vernacular language that paved the way for later artists, even today's rap musicians.

This sentence advances an idea that the writer can develop fully and defend with evidence. The writer has made a connection between the subject, *Langston Hughes,* and the focusing agent, *vernacular language.* Look at two other writers' thesis statements:

THESIS: Certain nutritional foods can prevent disease.

THESIS: More people must become organ donors despite their initial resistance.

In the first, the writer begins a causal analysis on the effects of selected foods. In the second, the writer advances a proposal on a medical issue as well as a moral one. Accordingly, each writer's critical approach to a subject affects the thesis.

Depending on the critical approach, one topic might produce several issues from which the writer might pick:

BIOLOGICAL APPROACH: Nutritional foods may be a promising addition to the diet of those who wish to avoid certain diseases.

ECONOMIC APPROACH: Nutritional foods can become an economic weapon in the battle against rising health care costs.

HISTORIC APPROACH: Other civilizations, including primitive tribes, have known about food's healing properties for centuries. Why did we let modern chemistry blind us to its benefits?

Each statement above will provoke a response from the reader, who will demand a carefully structured defense in the body of the paper.

Your thesis is not your conclusion or your answer to a problem. Rather, the thesis anticipates your conclusion by setting in motion the examination of facts and pointing the reader toward the special idea of your paper, which you will save for the conclusion. Note below how three writers developed different thesis sentences even though they had the same topic, "Santiago in Hemingway's *The Old Man and the Sea*." (Hemingway's novel narrates the toils of an old Cuban fisherman named Santiago, who desperately needs the money to be gained by returning with a good catch of fish. On this day he catches a marlin. After a long struggle, Santiago ties the huge marlin to the side of his small boat. However, during the return in the darkness, sharks attack the marlin so that he arrives home with only a skeleton of the fish. He removes the boat's mast and carries it, like a cross, up the hill to his home.)

THESIS: Poverty forced Santiago to venture too far and struggle beyond reason in his attempt to land the marlin.

This writer will examine the economic conditions of Santiago's trade.

THESIS: The giant marlin is a symbol for all of life's obstacles and hurdles, and Santiago is a symbol for all suffering humans.

This writer will examine the religious and social symbolism of the novel.

THESIS: Hemingway's portrayal of Santiago demonstrates the author's deep respect for Cuba and its stoic heroes.

This writer takes a social approach in order to examine the Cuban culture and its influence on Hemingway.

Make the preliminary thesis sentence a part of your research proposal:

> This paper will interpret a novel, *The Old Man and the Sea*, by Ernest Hemingway. My purpose is to explain to fellow literature students the novel's setting and the social conditions of the old Cuban. I suspect that poverty forced Santiago to venture too far and struggle beyond reason in his attempt to land the marlin. —Ramon Lopez

This writer and his instructor now have an understanding of the paper's purpose, its audience, the role of the student as a literary interpreter, and the paper's narrow focus on Santiago's economic status.

Using an Enthymeme

Some of your instructors might want the research paper to develop an argument as expressed in an enthymeme, which is a claim supported with a *because* clause. Examples:

ENTHYMEME: Hyperactive children need medication because ADHD is a medical disorder, not a behavioral problem.

The claim that children need medication is supported by the stated reason that the condition is a medical problem, not one of behavior. This writer will need to address any unstated assumptions, for example, that medication alone will solve the problem.

ENTHYMEME: Health-conscious Americans should eat functional foods because they protect against cancer and heart problems.

The claim that food can protect one's health is supported by the stated reason that some foods protect human organs against disease. Again, this writer will need to address any unstated assumptions, for example, that diet alone can produce good health.

◼ YOUR RESEARCH PROJECT

1. Make a list of your personal interests and items that affect your mental and physical activities, such as roommates, hiking, or relations with your family. Examine each one to see if you can find an academic angle that will make the topic fit the context of your research assignment. See 2a, pages 11–16, for more help.
2. Ask questions about a possible subject, using the list on pages 15–16.
3. Look around your campus or community for subjects. Talk with your classmates and even your instructor about campus issues. Focus on your hometown community in search of a problem, such as the demise of the main street merchants. Investigate any environmental concerns in your area, from urban sprawl to beach erosion to waste disposal. Think seriously about a piece of literature you have read, perhaps Fitzgerald's *The Great Gatsby*. If you are a parent, consider issues related to children, such as finding adequate child care. Once you have a subject of interest, apply the narrowing techniques described on pages 13–16, such as clustering, free writing, or listing key words.
4. To determine if sufficient sources will be available and to narrow the subject even further, visit the Internet, investigate *InfoTrac* or one of the other databases, such as the *Electronic Book Catalog* at your library. Keep printouts of any interesting articles or book titles.
5. Write a brief research proposal for submission to your instructor (see pages 26–31).

3

Gathering Data in the Library

With a refined topic in hand, you can begin research in three different places—the library, the Internet, and the field. The next three chapters will explore these options.

3a Launching the Search

Your research strategy in the library should include four steps, with adjustments for your individual needs.

1. Conduct a preliminary search for relevant sources. Scan the reference section of your library for its electronic sources as well as the abundance of printed indexes, abstracts, bibliographies, and reference books. Search the library's electronic book catalog and dip into the electronic networks, such as *InfoTrac's* Academic Index. This preliminary work will serve several purposes:

- It shows the availability of source materials with diverse opinions.
- It provides a beginning set of reference citations, abstracts, and full-text articles.
- It defines and restricts your subject.
- It gives you an overview of the subject by showing how others have researched it.

Your preliminary search should include a survey of the library if orientation classes have not given you an overview.

2. Refine the topic and evaluate the sources. On this first trip to the library or on later visits, narrow your topic to something that you believe will be manageable. As soon as you refine the topic, you can spend valuable time reading abstracts, articles, and pertinent sections of books. Most instructors will expect you to cite from the library's scholarly sources, so a mix of journal articles and books should accompany your Internet articles and field research.

3. Take shortcuts. First, consult Appendix B of this book, "Finding Sources for a Selected Discipline" (pages A-31–A-45), which gives you several appropriate electronic and printed sources. It sends you to key sources in psychology, art, literature, and many other disciplines. For example, if your work is on an education topic, it sends you to *ERIC* (online), *Current Index to Journals in Education,* and *Edweb* (online). If your work is on a computer science topic, it sends you to *INSPEC* (online) or to *Computer Literature Index.* In addition, you will need to access a variety of computer searches in the library, such as the electronic book catalog (see page 35) and the electronic services like *InfoTrac* and *Silverplatter* (see pages 40–43). Without leaving the computer work station in the reference room of the library, you can develop a working bibliography, read a few abstracts and full-text articles, and in general make substantive advances before you ever enter the library stacks.

Note: Most of the reference works described in this chapter are now available on the various databases available on the library's electronic network. You will need to log in with your ID before accessing the references, and then examine them on campus or off.

4. Read and take notes: Examine books, articles, essays, reviews, computer printouts, and government documents. Whenever possible, write complete notes as you read so that you can transcribe them or paste them into your text. Don't delay the writing task until you face a huge, imposing pile of data.

> **HINT:** Just as we are learning proper behavior on Internet sites, a similar behavior is rudimentary in the library, such as talking softly out of respect for others and no food or drinks in the library. Do not reshelve books and periodicals; leave them at the reshelving bins so that librarians can return them to the correct place. Rewind microfilm and leave it in the reshelving bin. Avoid breaking down the spine of books in attempts to copy the pages. At the computer station, analyze sources and then print; do not randomly print everything. (See pages 65–66 for methods of analyzing a source.)

3b Developing a Working Bibliography

A working bibliography provides the list of the sources that you plan to read before drafting your paper. Producing a set of bibliography entries has three purposes:

1. It locates articles and books for note-taking purposes.
2. It provides information for the in-text citations, as in this example in MLA style:

> The healing properties of certain foods have been noted by Milner (682-88) and Hasler (6-10).

3. It provides information for the final reference page (see Chapters 14–17). Therefore, you should preserve all computer printouts and handwritten notes.

Consult the index for the form to use for other sources (e.g., anthology, lecture, map). Then, turn to the appropriate pages in Chapters 14–17 for examples.

Whether you keyboard your sources or make handwritten cards for easy shuffling, each working bibliography entry should contain the following information, with variations, of course, for books, periodicals, and government documents:

Author's name
Title of the work
Publication information
Library call number
(Optional) A personal note about the contents of the source
The URL for Internet sources

Bibliography Entry for a Book (MLA style)

RM216.G946 2000

Grodner, Michele, Sara Long Anderson, and Sandra DeYoung.
Foundations and Clinical Applications of Nutrition: A
Nursing Approach. St. Louis: Mosby, 2000.

Books, Level 3

Bibliography Entry for a Journal Article (MLA style)

Smith, Bruce R. "Premodern Sexualities." PMLA 155 (2000):
318-29.

Bibliography Entry for a Magazine Article (MLA style)

McCord, Holly, and Gloria McVeigh. "Super Stroke Stoppers."
Prevention July 2000: 62.

Bibliography Entry for an Internet Article (MLA style)

Garbarino, James. "Some Kids Are Orchids." Time.Com Magazine
(20 Dec. 1999). 12 Feb. 2000 http://www.pathfinder.com/
time/magazine/articles/0,3266,35858.00.html.

3c Finding Books on Your Topic

The library is no longer a repository of only printed materials. It has gone high tech like the business world. Thus, much of your research will be conducted on the library's electronic network with call numbers to its own books and with links to sources around the world.

Using Your Library's Electronic Book Catalog

Your library's computerized catalog to its holdings probably has a special name, such as LIBNET, FELIX, ACORN, or UTSEARCH. In theory, it will include every book in the library filed by subject, author, and title. Begin your research at the catalog by using a *keyword search* to a subject, such as "nutrition." You will get a list of books on the monitor, and you can click the mouse on each one to gather more information. See Figure 3.1.

The next procedure is to get the full details with call number on a print-out, as shown in Figure 2.2 in Chapter 2, page 22. Important elements of the printout are highlighted. Use the printout to find the book in the stacks.

You can also find bibliographies here. At the electronic book catalog, type the word "bibliographies" plus your topic. For instance, one student entered *bibliographies + women's studies.* The catalog provided a large list of sites, each appearing as a hypertext link to full data on the source. Here's an example of four items from a list of thirty or more.

> *Bibliographies on Native American Women's Theatre (2000)*
> *Bibliography: Gender and Technology (1994)*
> *Bibliography of Ecofeminist Resources (2000)*
> *Biblography on Women and the Internet (1997)*

HINT: Many college libraries as well as public libraries are part of a network of libraries. This network expands the holdings of every library because one library will loan books to another. Therefore, if a book you need is unavailable in your library, ask a librarian about an interlibrary loan. Understand, however, that you may have to wait several days for its delivery. Periodical articles usually come more quickly by fax.

Show Detail	Title	Foundations and clinical applications of nutrition
	Author	Grodner, Michele
	Date	2000
Show Detail	Title	Krauses's food, nutrition, & diet therapy
	Date	2000
Show Detail	Title	Diet and nutrition sourcebook
	Date	1999
Show Detail	Title	Encyclopedia of human nutrition
	Date	1999

FIGURE 3.1. Keyword Results

Using the Online and Printed Bibliographies

Generally speaking, the electronic databases give access to sources written only in the last few years. Thus, you may want to supplement your computer printouts by searching various printed reference guides, bibliographies, and indexes. If your topic fits a clearly defined discipline, skip to Appendix B, pages A-31–A-45, which will list some of the best indexes and research guides for your field. If you are still trying to formulate a clear focus, begin with general guides, as discussed next.

Starting the Search with General Bibliographies

When ordering its research databases, the library subscribes to electronic online versions or print versions. You will need to determine which ones are available.

Three general works provide page numbers to many different books and journals that contain bibliographies on numerous subjects.

> *Bibliographic Index: A Cumulative Bibliography of Bibliographies.* New York: Wilson, 1938–date. Available both in print and online with your library's network.

> Hillard, James, et al. *Where to Find What: A Handbook to Reference Service.* 4th ed. Metuchen, NJ: Scarecrow, 1999.

> Balay, Robert, et al. *Guide to Reference Books.* 11th ed. Chicago: ALA, 1996.

You can also access such guides and bibliographies by a keyword search at the computer station. The keyword "bibliography" will provide a list of reference books like these, which can be accessed quickly by the hypertext link:

Z5071.A1 B4
Agriculture; a bibliography of bibliographies.   Copies: 1
Besterman, Theodore, 1904–1976.   Pub: 1971

PR56.B34 1995
A research guide for undergraduate students;   Copies: 1
English and American literature / Nancy L. Baker   Pub: 1995

Z3501.A1 B52 1994
Bibliographies for African studies, 1987–1993 /   Copies: 1
edited by Yvette Scheven and Nancy Huling.   Pub: 1994

Figure 3.2 shows how *Bibliographic Index* will send you to bibliographic lists that are hidden inside books, sources that you might not find otherwise. In this case, the bibliography will be found on pages 105–12 of Sarnoff's book.

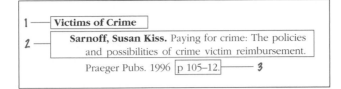

FIGURE 3.2.
Example from *Bibliographic Index,* 2000, showing (1) subject heading, (2) entry of a book that contains a bibliography, (3) specific pages on which the bibliography is located.

If it fits your research, you would probably want to write a bibliography entry for this source to examine the bibliography for additional articles on this topic.

Saranoff, Susan Kiss. <u>Paying for Crime: The Policies and</u>
<u>Possibilities of Crime Victim Reimbursement</u>. New York:
Praeger, 1996.
Bibl on 105-12

Using the Trade Bibliographies

Trade bibliographies, intended primarily for use by booksellers and librarians, can help you in three ways:

1. Discover sources not listed in other bibliographies or in the card catalog.
2. Locate facts of publication, such as place and date.
3. Determine if a book is in print.

Search this work for your topic:

Subject Guide to Books in Print (New York: Bowker, 1957–date).

Note: Online it may appear as **Books in Print**.

Use this work for its subject classifications, any one of which will provide a ready-made bibliography to books on your subject. Figure 3.3 shows a sample from the 2000 issue found with the keyword "diet."

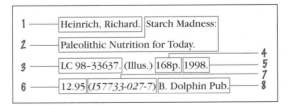

FIGURE 3.3.
From *Subject Guide to Books in Print,* 2000, showing (1) author, (2) title, (3) Library of Congress number, (4) number of pages, (5) date of publication, (6) price, (7) International Standard Book Number (used when ordering), (8) publisher.

You may also find valuable sources in the following trade bibliographies that may be available online or in printed versions.

Books in Print lists by author and title all books currently in print.

Publishers' Weekly offers the most current publication data on new books and new editions.

Paperbound Books in Print locates all paperback books on one topic; these are usually books available at local bookstores.

Cumulative Book Index provides complete publication data on one book but will also locate *all* material in English on a particular subject.

Library of Congress Catalog: Books, Subject provides a ready-made bibliography to books on hundreds of subjects.

Ulrich's International Periodicals Directory helps you locate current periodicals, both domestic and foreign, and to order photocopies of articles.

Using Appendix B

Appendix B of this book, alphabetized by discipline, furnishes a guide to the library's key references, some online, some in print, and others on the World Wide Web. Here are examples of four items from Appendix B under "Language and Literature." (*Note:* The phrase "online and print" means the work may be online in the library's electronic network or it is available in a printed version.)

Essay and General Literature. New York: Wilson, 1900–present. The best source for finding individual essays that might be buried within a book's contents. Online and print.

MLA International Bibliography of Books and Articles on the Modern Languages and Literatures. New York: MLA, 1921–present. The best overall index to major literary figures, literary issues, and language topics. Online and print.

Project Gutenberg http://promo.net/pg This site provides literary texts in the public domain that can be downloaded via FTP. There are three divisions: light literature such as fables, heavy literature such as *The Scarlet Letter*, and reference works.

Voice of the Shuttle http://humanitas.ucsb.edu For the language or literary scholar, this site gives a massive collection of bibliographies, textual criticism, news groups, and links to classical studies, history, philosophy, and other related disciplines.

Searching for Encyclopedia Bibliographies

Search for specialized encyclopedias in your field at the electronic book catalog or on the Internet. Entering "encyclopedia of psychology" might give you a list that looks like this:

BF31.E52 2000
  Encyclopedia of psychology

BF31.E52 2001
    The Corsini encyclopedia of psychology and behavioral science
BF 31.B25 1999
    Baker encyclopedia of psychology and counseling

Clicking on the link will give you more information on each encyclopedia. After you find and read an article on your specific topic, examine any bibliography at the end of the article. It might point you to additional sources, like the one shown in Figure 3.4.

Examining the Bibliography at the End of a Book

When you get into the stacks or read a book online, look for bibliographies at the end of books. An example of one is shown in Figure 3.5.

Searching for Bibliographies at the End of Journal Articles

Look for bibliographies in scholarly journals at the end of articles. For example, students of history depend upon the bibliographies within various issues of *English Historical Review,* and students of literature find bibliographies in *Studies in Short Fiction.* In addition, the journals themselves provide subject indexes to their own contents. For example, if your subject is "Adoption," you will discover that a majority of your sources are located in a few key

---

FURTHER REFERENCES

Clarke, E., & Dewhurst, K. *An illustrated history of brain function.*
Clarke, E., & O'Malley, C. D. *The human brain and spinal cord.*
Ferrier, D. *The functions of the brain.*
Finger, S., & Stein, D. G. *Brain damage and recovery: Research and clinical perspectives.*
McHenry, L. C., Jr. *Garrison's history of neurology.*

FIGURE 3.4. Sample bibliography from the end of an article in *Encyclopedia of Psychology 2nd ed., vol. 1, p. 287, edited by Raymond J. Corsini. Reprinted by permission of John Wiley & Sons, Inc.*

SECONDARY SOURCES

Abbott, Edith. "The Civil War and the Crime Wave of 1865–70." *Social Service Review,* 1977.
Amis, Mosews N. *Historical Raleigh,* 1913.
Andrews, Marietta M. *Scraps of Paper.* 1929.
Badeau, Adam. *Military History of U. S. Grant.* 1885
Bailey, Mrs. Hugh. "Mobile's Tragedy: The Great Magazine Explosion of 1865." *Alabama Review,* 1968.
Bakeless, John. "The Mystery of Appomattox." *Civil War Times Illustrated,* 1970.

FIGURE 3.5. A portion of a bibliography list at the end of N. A. Trudeau's book, *Out of the Storm*

journals. In that instance, going straight to the annual index of one of these journals will be a shortcut.

3d   Finding Articles in Magazines and Journals

An index furnishes the exact page numbers to specific sections of books and to individual articles in magazines, journals, and newspapers. The library's online index not only directs you to articles in magazines, but it also gives you an abstract of the article, and often provides the full text.

Searching the Electronic Indexes to Periodicals

On the library network you will have access to electronic databases like *InfoTrac, Silverplatter, ProQuest, Academic Universe, EbscoHost,* and others. One of these will usually guide you to several sources, provide an abstract, and then provide a full-text version of the article or send you into the stacks armed with a printed bibliography entry, like the one shown in Figure 3.6 in response to the keywords "child care education."

If you click to retrieve more data, you can read the abstract and even the full article. See Figure 3.7.

Finding Indexes Devoted to Your Discipline

The databases mentioned above and Internet seach engines will help you find discipline-specific indexes. For example, entering the keywords "music indexes" will produce entries such as these with hyperlinks to full information:

ML 118.M825
> Orchestral music in print

RILM (online)
> International Repertory of Music Literature

ML 118.M825
> Organ music in print

You can also find discipline-specific indexes in Appendix B, which shows, among other references, these indexes for music:

> *Bibliographic Guide to Music.* Boston: Hall, 1976–present. Annu-
> ally. Provides an excellent subject index to almost every
> topic in the field of music. Will give you the bibliographic
> data to several articles on most topics in the field.

☐ **Create** public schools **at work: how to give working parents more time with their kids.**
(Outlook 1998)(Cover Story) Barbra Murray.
   U.S. News & World Report Dec 29, 1997 v123 n25 p88(2)
View text and retrieval choices

FIGURE 3.6. *InfoTrac* printout

Music Article Guide. Philadelphia: Information Services, 1966–present. Indexes music education and instrumentation in such journals as *Brass and Wind News, Keyboard, Flute Journal,* and *Piano Quarterly.*

Music Index. Warren, MI: Information Coordinators, 1949–date. Indexes music journals such as *American Music Teacher, Choral Journal, Journal of Band Research, Journal of Music Therapy.*

The New Grove Dictionary of Music and Musicians. Ed. S. Sadie. 20 vols. New York: Macmillan, 1986. This mammoth work will provide you with information on almost every topic related to music. A good place to find technical definitions.

Expanded Academic ASAP

◀ **Article 14 of 41** ▶

☐ *U.S. News & World Report,* Dec 29, 1997 v123 n25 p88(2)
Mark

Create public schools at work: how to give working parents more time with their kids. (Outlook 1998)(Cover Story)
Barbra Murray.

Abstract: A few progressive corporations have established on-site schools for their employee's children. These schools, known as satellite learning centers, are usually funded by the company, but run by the public school system. The schools allow employees to have more interaction with their children.

Full Text: COPYRIGHT 1997 U.S. News and World Report Inc.

Like millions of American fathers, Mark Politte drops off his child--4-year-old Anna--at school every morning. But unlike most other dads, he also picks his child up after school each day. He has lunch with her occasionally, too. He never misses a parent-teacher conference. He knows most of the other kids in Anna's class by their first names, and he knows most of their parents pretty well. He will even show up in her class at a moment's notice when summoned by the teacher to lend support on a disciplinary matter or to comfort Anna over a skinned knee. And no, he is not a stay-at-home father. He is the director of room operations at the Radisson Twin Towers Hotel in Orlando, Fla., a demanding 50-hour-a-week job. …

FIGURE 3.7. InfoTrac printout with abstract and a small portion of the full text

Using the H. W. Wilson Indexes

For many years the H. W. Wilson Company in Minneapolis has provided excellent indexes to periodical literature. The indexing firm has kept current by providing its indexes online as well as in printed versions. They index topics that send you to articles in a wide variety of periodicals in many disciplines.

Readers' Guide to Periodical Literature

The *Readers' Guide to Periodical Literature* (online or in print) indexes important reading for the early stages of research in magazines such as:

Aging	*Foreign Affairs*	*Psychology Today*
American Scholar	*Foreign Policy*	*Scientific Review*
Astronomy	*Health*	*Science Digest*
Bioscience	*Negro History*	*Science*
Business Week	*Oceans*	*SciQuest*
Earth Science	*Physics Today*	*Technology Review*

An entry from the *Readers' Guide to Periodical Literature* is shown in Figure 3.8. Make a bibliography entry to a source if it looks promising.

Port, O. "Now, Electronic 'Eyes' for the Blind." <u>Business Week</u> 31
    Jan. 2000: 56 + .

Social Sciences Index

The *Social Sciences Index* (online or in print) indexes journal articles for 263 periodicals in these fields:

anthropology	geography	political science
economics	law and criminology	psychology
environmental science	medical science	sociology

FIGURE 3.8.
Sample entry from Readers' Guide to Periodical Literature showing (1) subject, (2) title of article, (3) author, (4) illustrations, (5) periodical title and publication data.

Humanities Index

The *Humanities Index* (online or in print) catalogs 260 publications in several fields:

archaeology	folklore	philosophy
classical studies	history	religion
language and	literary criticism	theology
literature	political criticism	
area studies	performing arts	

Other Indexes

Other indexes of importance include:

Applied Science and Technology Index for articles in chemistry, engineering, computer science, electronics, geology, mathematics, photography, physics, and other related fields.

Biological and Agricultural Index for articles in biology, zoology, botany, agriculture, and related fields.

Education Index for articles in education, physical education, and related fields.

Business Periodicals Index for articles in business, marketing, accounting, advertising, and related fields.

Recently Published Articles for articles in history and related fields.

In addition to these major indexes, you should examine the indexes for your discipline as listed in Appendix B of this book.

Searching for an Index to Abstracts

An abstract is a brief description of an article, usually written by the author. An index to abstracts can accelerate your work by allowing you to read the abstract before you assume the task of locating and reading the entire work. You may find them at the electronic book catalog by entering the keyword *abstracts,* which will produce a list with great variety. It will look something like this:

Show detail	Abstracts of current studies
Show detail	Dissertation abstracts international
Show detail	Social work abstracts
Show detail	Women studies abstracts

A more specific keyword search will include your discipline, such as "psychology abstracts." This will produce a reference, most likely, to *PsycINFO,* the searchable database produced by the American Psychological Association. It will give you the type of entry shown in Figure 3.9.

You may also wish to examine the abstracts to the dissertations of graduate students in *Dissertation Abstracts International,* which you can access online at the electronic book catalog under *ProQuest Digital Dissertation,* or

```
        Record 1 of 34 in PsycINFO 1999-2001/01
1 ———   AN: 2000-15373-006
2 ———   DT: Journal-Article
3 ———   TI: Evaluating an electronic monitoring system for people
        who wander.
4 ———   AU: Altus,-Deborah-E; Mathews,-R.-Mark; Xaverius,-Pamela-K;
        Engelman,-Kimberely-K; Nolan,-Beth-A-D
5 ———   SO: American-Journal-of-Alzheimer's Disease. 2000 Mar-Apr;
        Vol 15(2): 121-125
6 ———   PB: US: Prime National Publishing Corp.
7 ———   IS: 0182-5207
8 ———   PY: 2000
        AB: Wandering away from home, or elopement, is a behavior that
        places persons with dementia at risk of serious injury and may
        lead family caregivers to place their loved ones in institutions or
        to severely restrict their independence. This study evaluated the
        Mobile Locator, an electronic device designed to help caregivers
        quickly locate a person who has eloped. This 6 month pilot study
9 ———   included case studies of 7 users and an opinion survey of family
        caregivers, professional caregivers, and search and rescue
        workers. The survey results showed that respondents were
        positively impressed by the device, only identifying cost as a
        potential drawback.  Case studies revealed that the equipment
        was easy to use, effective, and helpful to caregivers' peace of
        mind. These results suggest that the Mobile Locator is a valuable
        tool deserving of further study. (PsycINFO Database Record ©
        2000 APA, all rights reserved)
```

FIGURE 3.9. Sample entry from PsycINFO
(1) AN = accession number; (2) DT = document type; (3) TI = title of the article; (4) AU = author;
(5) SO = source; (6) PB = publisher; (7) IS = ISSN number; (8) PY = publication year;
(9) AB = abstract of the article.

you can find a printed version in the reference room. In the printed version, you will need to look for issue No. 12, Part II, of each volume, for it contains the cumulative subject and author indexes for Issues 1–12 of the volume's two sections—*A: Humanities and Social Sciences* and *B: Sciences and Engineering.* For an example from the index of *Dissertation Abstracts International* of June 1999, see Figure 3.10. The abstract of Kristen Johansen's dissertation is shown in Figure 3.11.

You may cite an abstract in your paper, but let your readers know that you have cited an abstract, not an actual dissertation. If you need the full dissertation and have time, order a copy of the complete work from Bell & Howell Information and Learning Company. Copies of dissertations may be obtained by addressing your request to Bell & Howell Information and Learning Company (formerly UMI) 300 north Zeeb Road, Ann Arbor, MI 48106-1346 USA. Telephone: (734) 761-7400; E-mail: info@bellhowell.infolearning.com; Web page: http://www.bellhowell.infolearning.com.

Novels

1 —— Constructions of power in Thomas Hardy's major novels.
  2 —— *Johansen, Kristen.*, *p.4436A* —— 3
  Modern novels: The disruption of form, the incorporation of
    space. *De Weille, Karin Gerry, p.4424A*
  The limits of doubt: A critique of representational scepticism
    in the late novels of Henry James. *Kohan, Keven*
    Michael, p.4427A

▨**FIGURE 3.10.**
From the index to vol. 59, *Dissertation Abstracts International,* 1999, showing (1) title of dissertation, (2) author, (3) page number where abstract can be found.
The excerpt contained here is published with permission of Bell & Howell Information and Learning Company. Further reproduction is prohibited without permisission.

---

1 —— **Constructions of power in Thomas Hardy's major novels.**
2 —— Johansen, Kristen., *Ph.D. Bowling Green State University, 1998.*
3 —— 171pp. Advisor: Khani Begum —— 4
5 —— **Order Number DA9913585**

6 —
Thomas Hardy's fiction works to unravel and expose the many facets surrounding the productions of power. In short, who has power, why, and how can it be resisted? The answers to these questions are as varied as his five major novels; common to all the constructions of power, however, is that power is composed and maintained at multiple levels, in multiple points and in multiple intersections. Specifically, power in Hardy's novels tends to function in the realms of gender and class, and the ways these two categories are inscribed in sexuality and on the body. And because encompassing power constructions such as knowledge, discourse, gender, sexuality, and class are constituted by the reiteration of small acts, gestures, and speech acts, power functions differently in different contexts. Hardy's work, when illuminated by theorists such as Michel Foucault and Judith Butler, details how these factors work together and against one another to aid or oppose the individual, generally, and the independent woman, more specifically. Ultimately, Hardy's fiction serves as an alternative layer of historical sedimentation, an example of how gender regimes are maintained or changed in a particular historical moment.

▨**FIGURE 3.11.**
From *Dissertation Abstracts International,* 1999, showing (1) title of dissertation, (2) author, degree earned, school, and date, (3) total number of pages of the dissertation, (4) faculty chairman of the dissertation committee, (5) order number if you desire to order a copy of the complete work, (6) the abstract.
The excerpt contained here is published with permission of Bell & Howell Information and Learning Company. Further reproduction is prohibited without permisission.

3e Searching for a Biography

Biographies appear in books and articles, so you will need to use a variety of sources. The electronic card catalog will usually provide multiple sources if you enter the keywords "biography + index."

Show detail	Black biography, 1790–1950
Show detail	Index to literary biography
Show detail	Index to artistic biography
Show detail	Biography index

Several electronic indexes, like *InfoTrac* or *ProQuest,* will provide you with abstracts and even full-text articles:

Biography Reference Bank
Current Biography: 1940-Present
Current Biography Illustrated
Marquis Who's Who Online
Wilson Biographies Plus Illustrated

Several printed indexes, which may soon be online, also have value for finding biographies.

Biography Index

The *Biography Index* in its printed form has long been a starting point for studies of famous persons. It will lead you to biographical information for people of all lands. See Figure 3.12 for the type of information provided.

Current Biography Yearbook

Current Biography Yearbook provides a biographical sketch of important people. Most articles are three to four pages in length and, of importance, they include references to other sources at the end. It is current, thorough, and has international scope.

	2	*3*
1 — **Clinton, Hillary Rodham,** 1947-, **lawyer and wife of Bill Clinton**		
4 — Baldwin, Louis. Turning points; pivotal moments in the careers of		
5 — 83 famous figures. McFarland & Co. 1999 p50-2 — 8 7		
Brank, J. 9 things you didn't know about Hillary. Il pors — 9 6		
10 — *Glamour* v97 no9 p210 S 1999		
Junod, T. You'll never look at Hillary Clinton the same way again.		
Il pors *Esquire* v132 no4 p114-19+ O 1999		

FIGURE 3.12.

From *Biography Index*, 2000, showing (1) subject, (2) dates of subject's birth and death, (3) subject's profession, (4) author of the biography, (5) title of the biography, (6) publisher, (7) publication date, (8) specific pages, (9) contains portraits, (10) publication data for a periodical.

Contemporary Authors

Contemporary Authors provides a biographical guide to current writers in fiction, nonfiction, poetry, journalism, drama, motion pictures, television, and a few other fields. It provides an overview of most contemporary writers, giving a list of writings, biographical facts (including a current address and agent), a sidelights, and in many cases an interview by the editors of *CA* with the author. Most entries include a bibliography of additional sources on the writer. It has good coverage of major writers and stays current with second and third articles.

Dictionary of Literary Biography

The *Dictionary of Literary Biography* provides a profile of thousands of writers in more than one hundred volumes under such titles as these:

American Humorists, 1800-1950
Victorian Novelists after 1885
American Newspaper Journalists, 1926-1950

3f Searching for Articles in the Newspaper Indexes

For many years, searching for newspaper articles was difficult if not impossible. There were no indexes capable of doing the task. Now the electronic networks enable you to find newspaper articles from across the nation. Your library may have a newspaper search engine on its network, or you may need to go to the World Wide Web and access

Newspapers.com

It will take you quickly to one of over 800 newspapers, from the *Aspen Times* to the *Carbondale Valley Journal.* In most cases, an online newspaper will have its own internal search engine that enables you to examine articles from its archives. Figure 3.13 on the following page shows the opening page of the online site for the *Herald Citizen* of Cookeville, Tennessee.

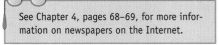

See Chapter 4, pages 68–69, for more information on newspapers on the Internet.

Notice especially the hyperlink at the lower left, "Search our Archives," a feature that enables you to search the back issues for topics of interest.

In addition, several helpful print indexes are being placed online:

Bell and Howell's Index to the Christian Science Monitor
The New York Times Index
Official Index to *The London Times*
Wall Street Journal Index

3g Searching the Indexes to Pamphlet Files

Librarians routinely clip items of interest from newspapers, bulletins, pamphlets, and miscellaneous materials and file them alphabetically by subject in

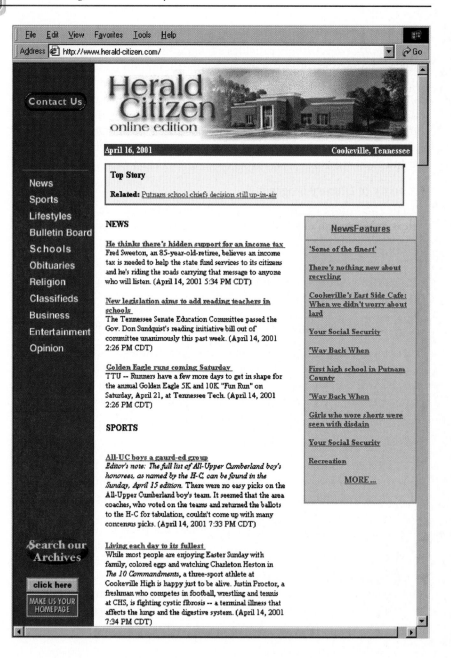

FIGURE 3.13. Opening page of the online edition of the *Herald Citizen,* a Cookeville, Tennessee, newspaper

loose-leaf folders. Make the pamphlet file a regular stop during preliminary investigation. Sometimes called the *vertical file,* it will have clippings on many topics, such as:

Asbestos in the Home
Carpal Tunnel Syndrome
Everything Doesn't Cause Cancer
Medicare and Coordinated Care Plans

Check at your library electronic card catalog to see if your librarians have created an online index to local pamphlets. The *Vertical File Index,* the principal index to published pamphlets, gives a description of each entry, the price, and the information for ordering the pamphlet.

Also important to you are published pamphlets that feature articles on a common topic. The *Social Issues Resources Series (SIRS),* online or in print, collects articles on special topics and reprints them as one unit on a special subject, such as abortion, AIDS, prayer in schools, pollution. With *SIRS* you will have ten or twelve articles readily available in one booklet.

The *CQ Researcher,* online and in print, will have one pamphlet, like *SIRS,* devoted to one topic, such as "Energy and the Environment." It will examine central issues on the topic, give background information, show a chronology of important events or processes, express an outlook, and provide an annotated bibliography. In one place you have material worthy of quotation and paraphrase as well as a list of additional sources. Figure 3.14 shows one of numerous sources on this topic as listed in the *CQ Researcher's* bibliography.

> **HINT:** For the correct citation forms to articles found in *SIRS* or *CQ Researcher,* see page 245.

3h Searching for Government Documents

All branches of the government publish massive amounts of material. Many documents have great value for researchers, so investigate the following if your topic is one that government agencies might have investigated.

Gelbspan, Ross. *The Heat Is On: The High Stakes Battle over Earth's Threatened Climate,* Addison-Wesley Publishing Co., 1997.

As scientific data increasingly support the theory that global warming is already well under way, environmental advocates, countries that are at risk of flooding from rising sea levels, and global insurance companies are joining hands in a campaign to support international efforts to slow climatic change.

FIGURE 3.14. An annotated bibliography from the *CQ Researcher* (2000)

```
        Record 5 of 366 in GPO on SilverPlatter 1976-2000/10
1 ──── AN: 99053103
2 ──── SUA: Y 4.AG 4:S.HRG.106-444
3 ──── CA: United States. Congress. Senate. Special Committee on Aging.
4 ──── TI: Nursing home residents: short-changed by staff shortages : forum
        before the Special Committee on Aging, United States Senate, One
        Hundred Sixth Congress, first session, Washington, DC,
        November 3,1999.
5 ──── SO: Washington: U.S. G.P.O.: For sale by the U.S. G.P.O., Supt. of
        Docs. Congressional Sales Office, 1999 [i.e. 2000].
6 ──── SE: United States. Congress. Senate. S. hrg.; 106-444.
7 ──── IT: 1009-B-01 1009-C-01 (MF)
```

FIGURE 3.15. From GPO on Silverplatter
(1) AN = accession number, (2) SUA = document number; (3) CA = corporate author;
(4) TI = title; (5) SO = source; (6) SE = series; (7) IT = GPO item number.

GPO on Silverplatter on your library's network
or
GPOAccess on the Internet

Either of these sites will take you to files of the Government Printing Office. The database list includes *Congressional Bills, Congressional Record, Economic Indicators, Public Laws,* the *U.S. Constitution*, and much more. A keyword search will provide an entry similar to that shown in Figure 3.15.

Most federal publications are published by the Government Printing Office (GPO) in Washington, D.C., regardless of the branch of government that issues them. Thus, a working bibliography entry to a Senate hearing, for example, should look like this:

S.HRG.106–444
United States. Congress. Senate. Special Committee on Aging.
    "Nursing Home Residents: Short-Changed by Staff
    Shortages." Washington: GPO, 1999.

Other works provide valuable information on matters of the government:

The *Monthly Catalog of the United States Government Publications* is the printed version of GPO.

Public Affairs Information Service Bulletin (PAIS), online and in print, indexes articles and documents published by miscellaneous organizations. It's a good place to start because of its excellent index.

The *Congressional Record,* online and in print, is a daily publication that provides Senate and House bills, documents, and committee reports.

Public Papers of the Presidents of the United States, online and in print, is the publication of the Executive Branch, including not only papers of the president but also papers of all members of the president's cabinet and various agencies.

The U.S. Code, online and in print. The Supreme Court regularly publishes decisions, codes, and other rulings, as do appellate and district courts. State courts also publish rulings and court results on a regular basis.

See pages 252–54 for correct methods of writing bibliography citations for government documents.

3i Searching for Essays within Books

Some essays get lost within collections and anthologies. You can find such essays, listed by subject, on this database at your library:

Essay and General Literature Index on *Silverplatter*

The print version is:

Essay and General Literature Index, 1900–1933. New York: H. W. Wilson, 1934. Supplements, 1934–date.

This reference work helps you find essays hidden within anthologies. It indexes material of both a biographical and a critical nature. The essay listed in the example below might easily have been overlooked by any researcher.

King, Martin Luther, 1929–1968
  Raboteau, A. J. Martin Luther King and the tradition of black religious protest. (*In* Religion and the life of the nation; ed. by R. A. Sherrill, pp. 46–65).

Your electronic book catalog will give you the call number to Sherrill's book.

C H E C K L I S T

The Library Search

When you start your research on a topic, you will need to switch back and forth from the computer terminals to the stacks and also to the printed bibliographies and indexes, according to the resources in your library. Start, perhaps, with the sources on this list.

- To find books:
  electronic book catalog with keyword
  online with keywords "bibliographies" + "your discipline"

continued

C H E C K L I S T

The Library Search, continued

- To find periodical articles:
  an electronic database with a keyword
  online with keywords "indexes" + "your discipline"
  the Wilson indexes

- To find an abstract:
  online with keywords "abstracts" + "your discipline"

- To find biographies in books and periodicals:
  online with keywords "biography" + "indexes"
  Biography Index, online or in print

- To find newspaper articles:
  Internet at **http://www.newspapers.com**
  electronic database under keyword "newspapers"

- To find pamphlet files:
  Online with the library's network to *SIRS* and *CQ Researcher*
  Ask your librarian for local files

- To find government documents:
  Online with the library network to **GPO on Silverplatter**
  Internet access to **GPOAccess**

- To find essays within books:
  Essay and General Literature Index, online or in print

- To find microforms:
  Online with the library network to **ERIC**

3j | Using the Microforms

The online sources are gradually replacing the microforms, but your library may have magazines and newspapers converted to a small sheet of film called a microfiche (flat sheet of film) or microfilm (a roll). Your library will specify in the cardex files (the list of periodicals) how journals and magazines are housed—bound printed volumes or microforms. Use a microfilm reader, usually located near the microfilm files, to browse the articles. Should you need a printed copy of a microfilmed article, the library has coin-operated machines or the clerks will copy it for you.

Your library may also house guides to special microform holdings, which carry such titles as *American Culture 1493-1806: A Guide to the Microfilm Collection* or perhaps *American Periodicals 1800-1850: A Guide to the*

Microfilm Collection. Every library has its own peculiar holdings of microfilm and microfiche materials; the librarian can help you.

YOUR RESEARCH PROJECT

1. If you have not done so with an orientation group, take the time to stroll through your library. Identify its various sections and the types of information available there. Especially learn about the reference room, the stacks, and the printed periodical articles. Pick up a bound volume of a journal, open it, and notice how it contains twelve issues (or six) of one year's publications.

2. At the library, sit down at one of the computer terminals and investigate its various options. Make up a topic for the moment and go searching for books or articles at the terminal. Try to find an abstract or a full-text article and then print it.

3. Go to the reference desk and ask the librarian for a specialized bibliography on your topic. Say something like this, substituting your topic: "Do you have a specialized bibliography on global warming?"

4. Locate the library's holdings of the *CQ Researcher* and *Social Issues Resources Series*. Page through the various booklets to note how they provide several penetrating articles on a common topic. If the works are online, use a keyword to see if your topic has been treated by a special issue.

5. To test the various resources of the library, go in search of information about the day you were born. Don't limit yourself to major events of the day; go also in search of local hometown news, and look at the advertisements to see what people were wearing and what things cost back then.

4

Searching the World Wide Web

Like the library, the **Internet** is now a major source of research information. It offers instant access to millions of computer files relating to almost any subject, including articles, illustrations, sound and video clips, and raw data. For easy access to this network, most researchers now use the **World Wide Web,** which is a set of files connected by hypertext links and accessed by means of a **browser,** such as *Netscape Navigator* and *Microsoft Explorer.* The Internet does not replace the library, just as it cannot replace field research, as discussed in Chapter 5. Plus, what it offers is the best and the worst of information, all easily accessed but not readably identified. Thus, one of your major tasks when citing from an Internet article is to judge its authority and veracity. Therefore, this chapter will help you with two tasks: (1) to become efficient searchers for academic information and (2) to become an accomplished evaluator of websites.

Despite the electronic wizardry of the age, a basic credo still remains for writers of research papers—give readers clear documentation to the sources used in the paper. Thus, as you gather data on the Internet, remember to keep accurate records. Search for facts about the author. Does the author have a home page? Is the author listed at Amazon.com? Is the author affiliated with an institution or organization? Sometimes you will need to truncate the URL to discover the sponsoring institution and the publication facts. Through it all, you will need to evaluate each source for its scholarly value (see page 65-66 for a checklist on this important matter).

4a   Reading an Internet Address

In the library you must employ the call number to find a book. On the Internet you will employ a Uniform Resource Locator (URL), like this one:

http://www.georgetown.edu/library_catalogues.html

The *protocol* (http://) transmits data.

The *server* (www [World Wide Web]) is the global Internet service that connects the multitude of computers and the Internet files.

The *domain* (georgetown.edu) names the organization feeding information into the server, with a *suffix* to label the type of organization: *.com* commercial, *.edu* educational, *.gov* government, *.mil* military, *.net* network organization, and *.org* organization. These soon may include new domains: *.aero* (air transprot industry), *.biz* (businesses), *.coop* (non-profits), *.info* (unricticed), *.name* (individual), *.museum* (parks, zoos, and museums), and *.pro* (accountants, lawyers, physicians).

The *directory/file* (library_catalogues) finds one of the server's directories and then a specific file.

The *hypertext markup language* (html) names the computer language used to write the file.

Often, knowing just the protocol and the server.domain will get you to a home site from which you can search deeper for files. The URL http://lcweb. loc.gov/homepage will take you to the Library of Congress (see Figure 4.1).

FIGURE 4.1. The home page for the Library of Congress

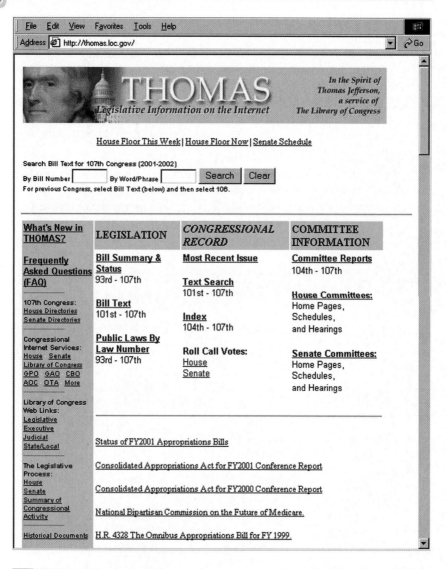

FIGURE 4.2. Home page to Thomas, the congressional site for the Library of Congress

At the home page you can select a specific directory, such as Thomas: Legislative Information (see Figure 4.2). In Thomas you have access to legislation of both the House and Senate, with links to many other sites and a search engine for finding specific information.

You can search the current Congress for the text of bills. At the Thomas search engine, enter a word or phrase, such as "student financial aid," and the site will take you to a list of resolutions, bills, and acts, like the three listed here:

1. To amend the Internal Revenue Code of 1986 to permit the disclosure of return information to verify the accuracy of information provided on applications for Federal student financial...(Introduced in the House) [*H.R.4661.IH*]

2. Resolved, That the resolution from the House of Representative (H. Con. Res. 68) entitled 'Concurrent resolution establishing the congressional budget for the United State Government...(Engrossed Senate Amendment) [*H.CON.RES.68.EAS*]

3. Access to Excellence in Education for the 21st Century Act (Introduced in the House)[*H.R.2719.IH*]

At this point, you can click on the link to H.R.2719.IH to read the bill. See Figure 4.3 on the following page for a portion of the legislation entitled "Findings."

In effect, you will have moved rather quickly from the home page of the Library of Congress to a specific piece of legislation that you might wish to use in your paper.

> **NOTE:** The technology of the Internet advances so rapidly that the instructions in this text for documenting online sources may be dated. However, the authors of this book are committed to keeping it current, so if a brochure named Citing Cyberspace was enclosed with this book, please consult it for up-to-date advice about citing from the Internet.

4b Using a Search Engine

Internet search engines locate specific Internet sites devoted to your topic. They offer both subject directories and keyword searches. Sets of computer instructions called HTTP (*hypertext transfer protocol*) connect the various sites to each other using *hypertext links,* which will carry you from one site to another. You will know that text is "hot" when it is underlined and colored in blue, green, red, or some color other than black; also, with most browsers the pointer changes form when it moves over "hot" text.

Many search engines exist. They differ in design and performance. You will need to find the ones you prefer.

Subject Directory Search Engines

These engines are human compiled and indexed to guide you to general areas that are then subdivided to specific categories. Your choices control the list.

About.com	http://home.about.com/index.htm
Go.network	http://www.go.com
Lycos	http://www.lycos.com
Yahoo!	http://www.yahoo.com

Figure 4.4 on page 59 shows the opening page from *Yahoo!* that features fourteen major categories as links to further information. Clicking on Health, for example, will take you to another site, as shown in Figure 4.5 on page 61.

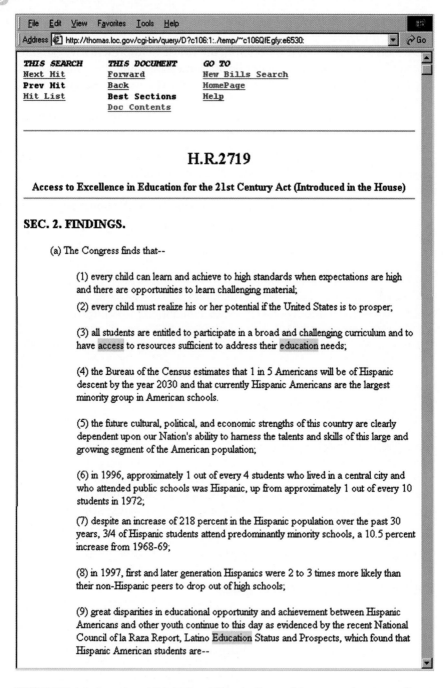

FIGURE 4.3. A portion of H.R.2719, a bill in the House of Representatives on excellence in education

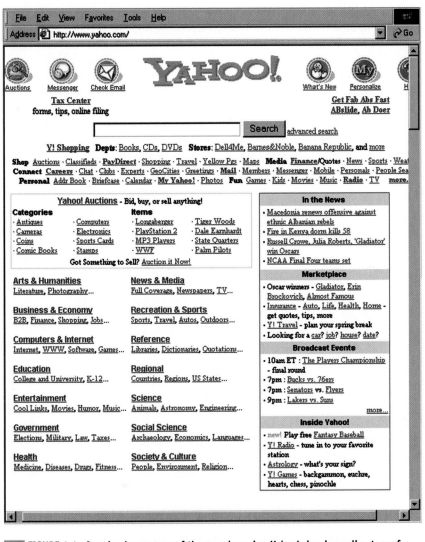

FIGURE 4.4. Opening home page of the search engine *Yahoo!* showing a directory of fourteen categories, each one serving as a link to Internet files.

Reproduced with permission of Yahoo! Inc. ©2000 by Yahoo! Inc. YAHOO! and the YAHOO! logo are trademarks of Yahoo! Inc.

Figure 4.5 shows a list that includes Teen Health where, by clicking on it, you would find twenty-three links to articles, such as these two:

AMA Adolescent Health On-Line from the American Medical Association.

Cool Nurse.com information for teens on sexuality, fitness and nutrition, substance abuse, mental health, and more.

Clicking on one of these will take you to the site and various articles on teen health. One sounds really "neat"—Cool Nurse, and the other sounds a bit stuffy. Which should you select? Begin with the AMA site because it is sponsored by a professional organization. Enter the "Cool Nurse" site with caution because it is a ".com" site, that is, a commercial site where you will encounter banners advertising all sorts of things. In addition, you cannot know if a reputable organization sponsors the site. In this case, a nurse named Amy operates the site. This one-person operation does not mean the information is not sound, but given a choice you should, as a young scholar, use the AMA site, where material has been judged by professionals for its accuracy.

Robot-Driven Search Engines

Another set of engines respond to a keyword by electronically scanning millions of web pages. Your keyword phrase and Boolean operators control the list.

AltaVista	**http://altavista.digital.com/**
Excite	**http://www.excite.com**
Google	**http://www.google.com/**
Hotbot	**http://www.hotbot.com**
Webcrawler	**http://www.webcrawler.com**

Metasearch Engines

A metasearch will examine your topic in several of the search engines listed above. Thus, you need not search each major engine separately. For example, when you enter a query at the **Mamma.com** website, the engine simultaneously queries about ten of the major search engines, such as *Yahoo!, Webcrawler, Magellan.* It then provides you with a short, relevant set of results. You will get fewer results than what might appear at one of the major search engines. For example, the request for "chocolate + children" produced 342,718 results on *AltaVista* but only fifty on *Mamma.com.* The claim is that a metasearch engine gives you the more relevant sites. This claim is based on the fact that the metasearch engine selects the first few listings from each of the other engines under the theory that each engine puts the most relevant sites at the top of its list. Here

are four metasearch engines:

Dogpile	**http://dogpile.com**
InferenceFind	**http://www.infind.com/**
Mamma.com	**http://mamma.com**
Metacrawler.com	**http://metacrawler.com**

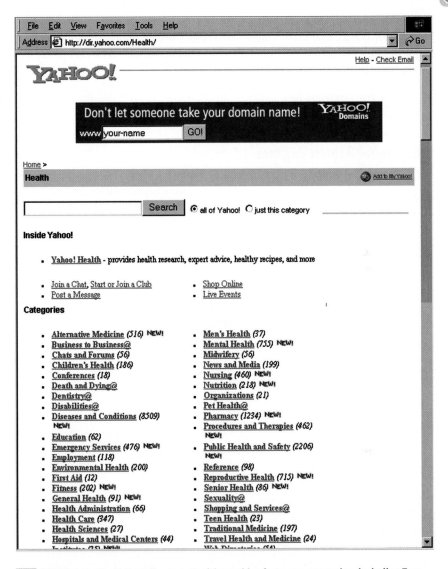

Specialized Search Engines

Other search engines specialize in one area, such as *WWWomen* (women's studies), *TribalVoice* (Native American Studies), and *Bizweb* (business studies). In addition, large Web sites, such as the Library of Congress or *New York Times Online,* have search engines just for themselves.

To discover any specialized search engine, go to one of the major sites, such as *AltaVista,* and ask, "Where can I find a search engine on journalism?" or "Where can I find a search engine on the environment?" The computer will name specialized search engines, such as these two:

www.journalism.net
www.gis.org (Geographical Information System)

Educational Search Engines

Educational search engines provide subject indexes to the various disciplines (Humanities or Sciences) and to subtopics under those headings (History, Literature, Biochemistry, etc.). One of these will get you started:

For additional sites and updates on search engines, consult the website to accompany this book at: **www.ablongman.com/ lester.**

Argus Clearinghouse	**http://www.clearinghouse.net**
English Server	**http://eserver.org.**
Internet Public Library	**http://ipl.sils.umich.edu/**
Knowledge Source (SIRS)	**http://www.sirs.com**
Library of Congress Subject Guide to Internet Resources	**http://lcweb.loc.gov/global/ www.subject. html**
Planet Earth	**http://www.nosc.mil/planet earth/info.html**
SavvySearch	**http://www.cs.colostate.edu/ ~dreiling/ smartform.html**
Searchedu	**http://www.searchedu.com**
Voice of the Shuttle	**http://humanitas.ucsb.edu/**

HINT: Most Web programs, such as *Netscape,* include a "bookmark" tool for configuring an icon that enables you to save addresses for quick access. When you find a search engine or a file that you need to access on a regular basis, create a bookmark to the site so that you can revisit it with just a click of the mouse. For example, in *Netscape* simply click on *Bookmarks*, then click on *Add Bookmark.* This will automatically add the URL to the list of bookmarks. In Microsoft Internet Explorer use the button bar marked *Favorites* to make your bookmarks. Note: if you are working at a university computer laboratory, do not add bookmarks to the hard drive. Instead, save the bookmarks to your disk by using *save as* in the *file* menu of *Netscape.*

4c Using a Subject Directory

A **subject directory** will take you through a sequence of Internet sub-jects. Subject-tree directories are hierarchical; that is, they move you methodically to narrower topics. You might start with *history,* move to *mil-itary history,* move to *Civil War History,* move to *Civil War Battles,* and arrive finally at *The Battle at Get-tysburg.* In effect, the subject directory will have carried you from the general to the specific.

> See Figures 4.4 and 4.5 for examples and an explanation of the role of a subject directory.

This tool is especially helpful when you have no preconceived notion about the topic you wish to write about.

4d Using a Keyword Search

Selecting a search engine is important, but so is your choice of keywords to launch the search. Use the words you would like to find in the title, description, or text of an Internet site.

The mechanism of the search engines usually places the most relevant sites first, so the first five to ten entries will be likely sources with your key-word in the title.

Tips for Searching

One Word

If you search for a common or general word, such as *gettysburg,* you will get a mammoth search of every document that contains this term. Lowercase words also will find capitalized words (e.g., "gettysburg" will find *gettysburg, Gettysburg, GETTYSBURG*).

Not all search engines use words and symbols interchangeably, so you may need to read the Help menu of each one for details.

Two or More Words Joined by and, not, or

If you provide two or more words with *and* or the "+" sign between each one, the search engine will find only sources that combine all words.

gettysburg *and* Lee
gettysburg + Lee

Attach a *not* or a minus (−) sign in front of words that *must not* be a part of the search:

gettysburg + Lee − Lincoln
gettysburg *and* Lee *not* Lincoln

This request will give you documents that mention Gettysburg and Robert E. Lee but will eliminate any documents that include Lincoln's name.

Lee *or* Lincoln + gettysburg

The *or* will broaden the search to include both men.

The Title

Use a *t:* to restrict the search to sites that contain the title, be it a book, article, poem, document, or speech:

t: "*gettysburg address*"

A Phrase

Use quotation marks around two or more words to make them one unit (although proper names do not need quotation marks).

"Robert E. Lee's military strategy" + Gettysburg

The phrase above produced the Internet article found in Figure 4.6, a site that also displays links to many other sources. Therefore, make your request in phrases whenever possible; that is, ask for "migraine headaches" (2,000 hits), not "migraine and headaches" (10,000 hits). *Netscape Navigator,* for example, gives you a search option for *phrase* as well as by *any* word or *all* words.

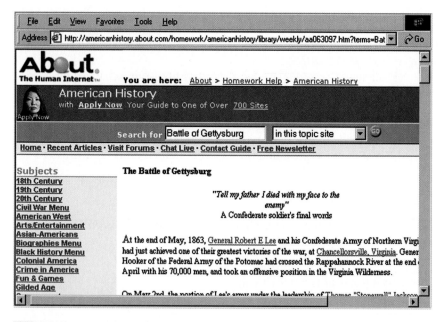

FIGURE 4.6. Article on the battle at Gettysburg found by the use of a search engine. Note links to other sites.

Truncation

By truncating the word or using its root, followed by an asterisk, you can retrieve variants of it. For example, if you wish to write a paper on women's issues, you can enter *femini** and find sites on feminine, feminist, femininity, and so forth.

C H E C K L I S T

Evaluating Internet Sources

The Internet supplies huge amounts of material, some of it excellent and some not so good. You must make judgments about the validity and veracity of these materials. In addition to your commonsense judgment, here are a few guidelines:

1. Prefer the "edu" and "org" sites. Usually, these will be domains developed by an educational institution, such as Ohio State University, or by a professional organization, such as the American Psychological Association. Of course, "edu" sites also include many student papers which can include unreliable information. New domains that may prove useful are *.pro, .museum,* and *.biz.*

2. The "gov" (government) and "mil" (military) sites usually have reliable materials. The "com" (commercial) sites become suspect for several reasons: (a) they are selling advertising space; (b) they often charge you for access to their files; (c) they can be ISP sites (Internet Service Provider) which people pay to use and to post their "material." Although some ISP sites might have good information, they are usually no more reliable than vanity presses or want ads.

3. Look for the *professional* affiliation of the writer, which you will find in the opening credits or an e-mail address. Go in search of the writer's home page. Type in the writer's name at a search engine to see how many results are listed. Also, type in the writer's name at Amazon.com for a list of his or her books. If you find no information on the writer, you will need to rely on a sponsored website. That is, if the site is not sponsored by an organization or institution, you should probably abandon the source and look elsewhere.

4. Look for a bibliography that accompanies the article, which will indicate the scholarly nature of this writer's work.

5. Usenet discussion groups offer valuable information at times, but some articles lack sound, fundamental reasoning or evidence to support the opinions.

6. Treat e-mail messages as "mail," not scholarly articles. A similar rule applies to "chat."

(continued)

C H E C K L I S T

Evaluating Internet Sources, continued

7. Does the site give you hypertext links to other professional sites or to commercial sites? Links to other educational sites serve as a modern bibliography to more reliable sources. Links to commercial sites are often attempts to sell you something.

8. Learn to distinguish from among the different types of websites, such as advocacy pages, personal home pages, informational pages, and business and marketing pages. One site provides evaluation techniques; see http://www2.widener.edu/Wolfgram-Memorial-Library/webeval.htm.

9. Your skills in critical thinking can usually determine the validity of a site. For more help in critical thinking, visit Robert Harris's site http://www.virtualsalt.com/evalu8it.htm.

4e Accessing Online Sources

Home Pages

You can locate home pages for individuals, institutions, and organizations by using a search engine, such as *Yahoo!* or *AltaVista* (see page 57). Type in James D. Lester + Homepage and you will get:

James D. Lester

Clicking on this colored link will take you to Lester's home page at "apsu.edu." You can also list an organization, such as the American Psychological Association, and you will get a link to the site:

http://www.apa.org/

Since the home page itself will have little research value, look for links, a directory, an index, or an internal search engine that will take you quickly to specific material.

Articles

A search engine will take you to many articles on the Web, some isolated without documentation and credentials and others that list the author as well as the association to which the author belongs. For example, a search for "child care centers" will usually produce local sites, such as "Apple Tree Family Child Care." Private sites like these will infuse your research with local knowledge. Adding another relevant term, such as "child care regulations" will take you to state and national sites, such as the National Resource Center for Health and Safety in Child Care.

HINT: Most serious writers will avoid articles that have no author listed and no affiliation with an organization or institution. A documented essay generally requires these items in the bibliography:

> Author
> Date
> Title
> Affiliation or organization
> Address (which will be the URL for websites)

Sometimes, one or two of these items might be missing; the organization might be the author or the date might be missing. However, a reference that contains only a title and the URL cannot be properly documented and should be avoided.

Journals

You can find online journals in one of three ways.

- First, access your favorite search engine and use a keyword search for *journals* plus the name of your subject. For example, one student accessed *Alta Vista* and used a keyword search for "journals + fitness." The search produced links to twenty online journals devoted to fitness, such as *Health Page, Excite Health,* and *Physical Education*. Another student's search for "women's studies + journals" produced a list of relevant journals, such as *Feminist Collections, Resources for Feminist Research,* and *Differences*. By accessing one of these links, you can examine abstracts and articles.
- Second, access a search engine's subject directory. In *Yahoo!,* for example, one student selected Social Science from the key directory, clicked on Sociology, clicked on Journals, and accessed links to several online journals, such as *Edge: The E-Journal of Intercultural Relations* and *Sociological Research Online*.
- Third, if you already know the name of a journal, go to your favorite search engine to make a keyword query, such as *Psycholoquy,* a social science journal.

Many of the online periodicals offer indexes or keyword searches to their articles. In addition, they often provide full-text articles from hard-to-find periodicals that may not be housed in your library.

Caution: some journals will require a fee or require you to join the association before they permit your access.

Magazines

Several directories exist for searching out magazine articles:

NewsDirectory.Com   **http://www.newsdirectory.com/new/**

Takes you to magazine home pages where you can begin your free search in that magazine's archives. Under "current events," for example, it will send you to *Atlantic Monthly* **theatlantic.com,** *Harper's* **Harpers.org,** or *Newsweek* **Newsweek.com.**

Electric Library   **http://wwws.elibrary.com/**

Has a good search engine; requires membership, which is free for one month. Remember to cancel your membership after research is finished or charges will accrue.

Pathfinder   **http://www.time.com/time/index.htm**

Gives free access to *Time Magazine*; has a good search engine to thousands of archival articles.

ZD Net   **http://www.zdnet.com/**

Provides excellent access to industry-oriented articles in banking, electronics, computers, management, and so on. Offers two weeks of free access before charges begin to accrue.

Another way to access online magazines is through a search engine's directory. For example, one student accessed *Alta Vista,* clicked on Health and Fitness in the directory on the home page, clicked on publications, then magazines. The result was a list of forty magazines devoted to various aspects of health and fitness, such as *Healthology* and *The Black Health Net.*

Newspapers and News Sources

Most major news organizations maintain Internet sites. Consult one of these:

Chronicle of Higher Education   **http://www.chronicle .com**
 Requires a paid subscription, but has great value for students in education.

CNN Interactive **http://www.cnn.com** Has a good search engine and takes you quickly without cost to transcripts of its broadcasts. A good source for research in current events.

C-SPAN Online **http://www.c-span.org** Emphasizes public affairs and offers both a directory and a search engine to transcripts. A valuable source for research in public affairs, government, political science.

Fox News **http://www.foxnews.com** Watch for the source; some articles come not from Fox News but Reuters and other news providers.

London Times **http://www.the-times.co.uk/news/ pages/Times/frontpage.html** Offers directories and indexes, but not a search engine, so improve your search for articles in the *Times* with **searchuk.com**.

National Public Radio Online **http://www.npr.org** Provides audio articles by RealPlayer or some other audio engine. Be prepared to take careful notes.

New York Times on the Web **http://www.nytimes.com** You can read recent articles for free. However, if you search the 365-day archive, be prepared with your credit card. Articles cost $2.50. After purchase, they appear on the monitor for printing or downloading.

USA Today DeskTopNews **http://www.usatoday.com** Has a fast search engine and will provide information about current events.

U.S. News Online **http://www.usnews.com** Has a fast search engine and provides free, in-depth articles on current political and social issues.

Wall Street Journal **http://www.wsj.com** Has excellent business and investment information, but it requires a subscription.

Washington Times **http://www.washingtontimes.com/** Has up-to-the-minute political news.

CQ Weekly **http://library.cq.com** This magazine, formerly *Congressional Quarterly Weekly,* keeps tabs on congressional activities in Washington.

To find other newspapers and online media, search for "newspapers" on *Yahoo!* or *AltaVista*. Your college library may also provide LEXIS-NEXIS, which will search news sources for you.

Books

One of the best sources of full-text, online books is the Online Books Page at the University of Pennsylvania:

http://digital.library.upenn.edu/books/

This site indexes books by author, title, and subject. It has a search engine that will take you quickly to the full text of Thomas Hardy's *A Pair of Blue Eyes* or to Linnea Hendrickson's *Children's Literature: A Guide to the Criticism*. This site is adding new textual material almost every day, so consult it first. Understand, however, that contemporary books, still under copyright protection, are not included. That is, you can freely download an Oscar Wilde novel but not one by John Updike.

4f Using Online Rather than Print Versions

Online versions of articles offer advantages:

- You can view them almost instantly on the monitor rather than searching, threading, and viewing microfilm or microfiche.
- You can use the online indexes or search engines to locate appropriate articles.
- You can save or print an abstract or article without the hassle of photocopying.
- You can download material to your disk and, where appropriate, insert it into your paper.
- You can copy or scan graphics and photographs into your text.

However, careful writers usually understand that the text may differ from the original printed version and may even be a digest. Therefore, cite the Internet source to avoid giving the appearance that you are citing from the printed version. There are often major differences between the same article in *USA Today* and in *USA Today DeskTopNews*. Remember, too, that abstracts may not accurately represent the full article. In fact, some abstracts are not written by the author at all but by an editorial staff. Therefore, resist the desire to quote from the abstract; write a paraphrase instead, or, better, find the full text and cite from it (see also pages 111–15). Finally, you may need to subscribe at a modest cost to some sites. A company has the right to make demands before giving us access.

4g Using Gopher, FTP, Telnet

Although Web sources now dominate the Internet, valuable material still exists on other protocols, such as gopher, FTP, and telnet. These sources look different because they have no hypertext format (they are not linked to other sources) and most do not have graphics and color.

Gopher is an Internet browser that burrows deeper and deeper into layers of information, unlike the Web, which allows you to move from site to site regardless of level of specificity. Fortunately, most gopher files have been redesigned as files for the World Wide Web.

File Transfer Protocol (FTP) is a step-by-step process by which you copy files—text, graphics, video, sound, and so forth—from the Internet into your computer. Thus, you can access files by using FTP to copy what you need. To access FTP files go to **http://computers.lycos.com/downloads/dindex. asp** or go to **http://www.dogpile.com** and click on **ftp** before launching the search. An FTP site will have an address like this: **ftp5/new/articles/misc/ health/diabetes**. At this site you are likely to find several hundred smaller numbered sites, such as **172620**. Some will be articles; others will be Usenet-type conversations.

Telnet is not a protocol for file transfer but a remote operations protocol. For example, it lets you access your school's computer from your home or a dorm room. You will need to have an account on the server and a username and password that permit you to logon and begin working. You may need help for accessing your specific system from a librarian, instructor, or an expert at the computer center.

4h Using Listserv, Usenet, and Chat Groups

Listserv E-mail News Groups

The word *Listserv* is used to describe discussion groups that correspond via e-mail about a specific educational or technical subject. For example, your literature professor might ask everybody in the class to join a Listserv group on Victorian literature. To participate, you must have an e-mail address and subscribe to the list.

To access Listserv on your own, consult one of these sites:

L-Soft http://www.lsoft.com/products/default.asp?item-
 listserv Browse any of about 42,000 public Listserv lists on
 the Internet.

Egroups http://groups.yahoo.com/local/news.html Join a
 Listserv group in such areas as Health & Fitness, Home,
 Recreation, Reference and Education, Science, Sports, and
 others.

Liszt http://www.liszt.com Search Liszt's main directory of
 more than 90,000 mailing lists. Also click on a topic, such as
 Computers (250 lists), Health (271 lists), Humanities (254
 lists), and many others.

Tile.net http://www.tile.net/ Provides access to lists, Usenet
 news groups, and FTP sites.

At some point you may wish to join a list, and each site will explain the procedure for subscribing and participating via e-mail in a discussion. Katie Hebert, whose paper appears on pages 210–23, researched the term "functional food" in Tile.net. She found a description for the list "Biochem for health," as shown in Figure 4.7.

Real-Time Chatting

Usenet and Chat groups use Internet sites rather than e-mail. To access Usenet, go to dogpile.com or metacrawler.com and click the Usenet button before launching the search. Typing "diabetes" takes one to a site such as alt.support.diabetes, which addresses such topics as "Is diabetes increasing?" or "Symptoms of diabetes." These discussions, in the main, are serious commentaries by persons with a personal stake in the subject. The site includes, usually, the real name of the person speaking, along with an e-mail address. Thus they have some validity and *might* be used in a research paper, but you have no way of authenticating the person's credentials. Thus, let the

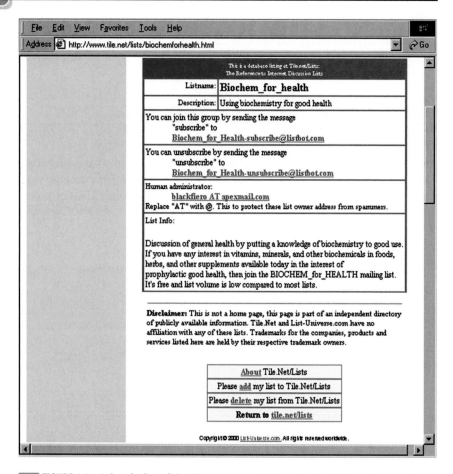

File   Edit   View   Favorites   Tools   Help

Address ⌕ http://www.tile.net/lists/biochemforhealth.html   ▼   ⟳ Go

> This is a database listing at Tile.net/Lists:
> The Reference to Internet Discussion Lists

Listname:	**Biochem_for_health**
Description:	Using biochemistry for good health

You can join this group by sending the message
   "subscribe" to
   Biochem_for_Health-subscribe@listbot.com

You can unsubscribe by sending the message
   "unsubscribe" to
   Biochem_for_Health-unsubscribe@listbot.com

Human administrator:
   blackfiero AT apexmail.com
Replace "AT" with @. This to protect these list owner address from spammers.

List Info:

Discussion of general health by putting a knowledge of biochemistry to good use.
If you have any interest in vitamins, minerals, and other biochemicals in foods,
herbs, and other supplements available today in the interest of
prophylactic good health, then join the BIOCHEM_for_HEALTH mailing list.
It's free and list volume is low compared to most lists.

Disclaimer: This is not a home page, this page is part of an independent directory
of publicly available information. Tile.Net and List-Universe.com have no
affiliation with any of these lists. Trademarks for the companies, products and
services listed here are held by their respective trademark owners.

About Tile.Net/Lists
Please add my list to Tile.Net/Lists
Please delete my list from Tile.Net/Lists
Return to tile.net/lists

FIGURE 4.7. A description of the Listserv group *Biochem for Health* found by accessing
Tile.net

reader know something about the source: "Lori Silfen in a recent Usenet conversation reminded her audience to refer to 'a person with diabetes,' not to a
'diabetic person.'"

   Yahoo!, *AltaVista,* and other search engines offer their own chat groups;
a click of the mouse gets you into the site. By using a fictional username, you
can avoid giving out your identity and your e-mail address. *Yahoo!* has a "Chat"
key that will take you to various discussion groups. Another way to find discussion groups is through a keyword search for "List of online chat groups"
at one of the search engines. If you want a commercial site that requires a
monthly fee, try **Usenet.com.**

CAUTION: Avoid citing in your research paper any type of information
from somebody using a fictional name. You might find some interesting things by participating in a chat group but not anything you can cite
in your paper as authoritative information.

A few additional aspects of Listserv and Usenet are FAQs, lurking, and moderated and unmoderated lists.

FAQs (frequently asked questions) provide answers to questions submitted by users.

Lurking is to watch messages on the list without participating.

A *moderated list* has an editor who screens messages that go out.

Unmoderated lists automatically distribute any message that comes through.

4i Examining Library Holdings Via Internet Access

Most major libraries offer access to their library catalog via the Web, which will allow you to search their collections for books, videos, dissertations, audio tapes, special collections, and other items. You may sometimes order books through interlibrary loan online. Additionally, some of the libraries now post full-text documents, downloadable bibliographies, databases, and links to other sites. If you need identification of all books on a topic, as copyrighted and housed in Washington, D.C., consult:

Library of Congress **http://www.loc.gov** This site allows you to search by word, phrase, name, title, series, and number. It provides special features, such as an American Memory Home Page, full-text legislative information, and exhibitions, such as the various drafts of Lincoln's Gettysburg Address.

For an Internet overview of online libraries, their holdings, and addresses, consult:

LIBCAT **http://www.metronet.lib.mn.us/lc/lc1.cfm** This site gives you easy access to almost 3000 online library catalogs.

LIBWEB **http://sunsite.berkeley.edu/libweb** This site takes you to home pages of academic, public, and state libraries. You will be prompted for a public-access login name, so follow the directions for entering and exiting the programs.

Another kind of online library is:

Carl UnCover **http://uncweb.carl.org** This site provides a keyword search of 17,000 journals by author, title, or subject. Copies of the articles will be faxed, usually within the hour, for a small fee.

4j Finding an Internet Bibliography

You can quickly build a bibliography on the Internet in two ways: by using an Internet search engine, or by using an online bookstore.

A Search Engine

At a search engine on the Internet, such as *Alta Vista,* enter a descriptive phrase, such as "Child Abuse Bibliographies." You will get a list of bibliographies, and you can click the mouse on one of them, such as:

Child Abuse
Child Abuse. Child Abuse Articles. Child Abuse Reports
http://www.childwelfare,com/kinds/pr01.htm

Clicking with the mouse on the hypertext address will carry you to a list:

Child Abuse Articles
Child Abuse Reports
Child Sexual Abuse
Substance Abuse

Clicking on the first item will produce a set of hypertext links to articles that you might find helpful, such as this one:

"Suffer the children: How government fails its most vulnerable citizens—abused and neglected kids" by David Stoesz and Howard Jacob Karger (*The Washington Monthly,* 1996).

Online Bookstore

Use the search engines of *Amazon.com* and *Barnes&Noble.com* to gain a list of books currently in print. In most cases, the books on the list will be available in your library. For example, one student searched *Barnes&Noble.com* for books on "Fad Dieting." She received the list shown in Figure 4.8, which gave her the beginnings of a bibliography.

In review, the Internet offers a vast set of sources for researchers.

- You can quickly find articles via a keyword search or by tracking along the subject directories of the browsers.
- You can access home pages and individual articles or go in search of magazines, journals, newspapers, and books.
- You can monitor and participate in Listserv groups by e-mail or join Usenet discussion groups on the Internet.

4k Conducting Archival Research

The Internet has made possible all kinds of research in library and museum archives. You may have an interest in this type of work. If so, consider several ways to approach the study.

Go to the Library

Go physically into a library and ask about the archival material housed there. Even small libraries often have very valuable collections, and the librarian can get you started.

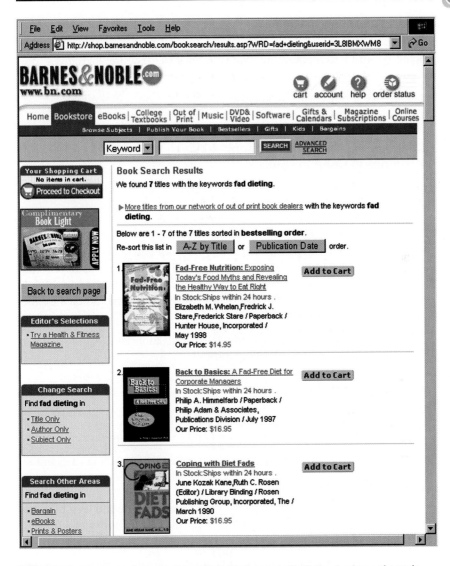

Use the Library's Electronic Catalog

Go into the library and search its electronic book catalog to see if it offers any special collections and archives. The Stanford University Library, for example, offers links to antiquarian books, manuscripts, and university archives. It also provides ways to find material by subject, title, and collection number. It carries the researcher to links such as: London (Jack) Papers, 1897–1916 (m0077) [html]. Clicking here takes the researcher to file descriptions and the files. These can be accessed by Internet if the researcher has the proper credentials for entering and using the Stanford collection.

Go to an Edited Search Engine

Go to an edited search engine, such as *Yahoo!,* for it may give you results quickly. For example, requesting "Native American literature + archives" produced such links as:

American native press archives
Native American History Archive
Native Americans and the Environment
Indigenous Peoples' Literature
Sayings of Chief Joseph

One or more of these collections might open the door to an interesting topic and enlightening research.

Go to a Metasearch Engine

Go to a metasearch engine such as *dogpile.com* and make a request, such as "native American literature + archives." It will list such sites as **Reference Works and Research Material for Native American Studies**, which is located at **www.stanford.edu**. There, the Native American Studies Collections offers several valuable lists:

Native American Studies Encyclopedias and Handbooks
Native American Studies Bibliographies
Native American Studies Periodical Indexes
Native American Biography Resources
Native American Studies Statistical Resources
Links to other Native American sites on the Internet
Links to Usenet discussion groups related to Native Americans

Thus, the researcher would have a wealth of archival information to examine.

Use Search Engine Directories

Use the directory and subdirectories of a search engine and let it take you deeper and deeper into the files. Remember, this tracing goes quickly. Here are examples of links at several engines:

Excite Guide: Lifestyle: Cultures and Groups: Native Americans: Literature
Lycos: Entertainment: Books: Literature: Native American Literature
AltaVista: Society: History: Indigenous People: Native Americans: Art
The latter site, for example, carried one researcher to the Red Earth Museum in Oklahoma City (see Figure 4.9).

Look for a Listserv or Usenet Group

Using a search engine, simply join your topic with the word *listserv*: "Native American literature + listserv." The search engine will produce such links as **Native-L: Native Literature listserv and archives**. By following the proper procedures, you can log on and begin corresponding. Participants might quickly point you in the direction of good topics and sources for developing the paper.

File Edit View Favorites Tools Help

Address http://www.redearth.org/museum.htm   Go

RED EARTH

Red Earth Museum - Preserving Native Cultures

Red Earth Museum, Central Oklahoma's only museum dedicated to encouraging the preservation of American Indian cultures, has since 1978 benefitted the education of thousands of Oklahoma schoolchildren and adults. Through unique educational programs and exhibitions focusing on the Native American way of life, Red Earth is often a visitors' first exposure to American cultures and history. The collections at Red Earth Museum play an

FIGURE 4.9. The home page to the Red Earth Museum where a student might find archival information on Native Americans

YOUR RESEARCH PROJECT

1. To look for an Internet discussion group on your topic, go to metacrawler.com and, before entering your subject, select the button for searching news groups rather than the Web. Explore the choices. You may also search the lists described in 4h, pages 71-73.
2. *Voice of the Shuttle* is a large and powerful search engine for educational information. Enter URL http://humanitas.ucsb.edu/ and search for your topic. If unsuccessful, try one of the other educational search engines listed on page 62.
3. When you have found an Internet article directly devoted to your subject, apply to it an evaluation as described on pages 65-66. Ask yourself, "Does this site have merit?" Apply that same test to other Internet articles as you find them.
4. Practice using the Bookmark feature of your browser. That is, rather than print an article from the Internet, bookmark it instead for future reference (see page 62).
5. As with library sources, begin making bibliography entries and writing notes of promising Internet sources. Build a computer file of promising sources with Bookmarks or Favorites. (See page 34 for an example of a bibliography entry to an Internet source).

5

Collecting Data Outside the Library

For many students and research teams, the library is only one place for locating information. Material exists in many other places. Be prepared, therefore, to conduct primary research in the laboratory and in the field whenever your topic demands it. Converse with other people in person, by letter, or e-mail; if time permits it, conduct in-depth interviews or use a questionnaire. Watch for television specials, visit courthouse archives, and perhaps do some observational research under the guidance of an instructor (see pages 83–85).

Set up your field research in an objective manner in order to control any subjective feelings. Student Gena Messersmith (see pages 300–09) had strong, personal feelings about her daughter's condition as she researched Attention Deficit Hyperactivity Disorder, so she had to force herself to look objectively at the evidence. Questionnaires and observations that are slanted to get a desired report should be avoided. Allow your instructor to review your methods and apparatus before launching the study. All writers get deeply involved in the subject, but they must couple that involvement with the skill of detachment. What are the facts? What conclusions do they support? Let conclusions arrive from the evidence, not your previously drawn ideas.

5a   Investigating Hometown Sources

Interviewing Knowledgeable People

Talk to persons who have experience with your subject. Personal interviews can elicit valuable in-depth information. They provide information that few others will have. Look to organizations for experienced persons (for example, if writing on a folklore topic, you might contact the county historian, a senior citizens' organization, or a local historical society). If necessary, post a notice soliciting help: "I am writing a study of local folklore. Wanted: people who have a knowledge of regional tales." Another way to accomplish this task is to request information on a listserv list, which will bring you commentary from a group of experts interested in a particular field (see pages 71–73 for more details). For accuracy, record the interview with a tape recorder (with permission of the person interviewed, of course). When finished, make a bibliography entry just as you would for a book:

Thornbright, Mattie Sue. Personal interview. 15 Jan. 2001.

In addition to the guidelines listed on page 80 and also pages 16–18, you need to remember several vital matters. First, be prepared. That means you know your interviewee's professional background and that you have a set of pertinent questions, with follow-ups. Second, keep your focus on the principal issue. Subjects may wish to wander toward tangential ideas, so always bring them back to the central subject with an appropriate question. Third, maintain an ethical demeanor that honors with accuracy the statements of the subject.

Writing Letters and Corresponding by E-mail

Correspondence provides a written record for research. As you would in an interview, ask pointed questions so that correspondents will respond directly to your central issues. Tell the person who you are, what you are attempting to do, and why you have chosen to write this particular person or set of persons. If germane, explain why you have chosen this topic and what qualifies you to write about it.

Gena Messersmith
12 Morningside Road
Clarksville, TN

Ms. Rachel G. Warren, Principal
Sango High School
Clarksville, TN

Dear Ms. Warren:

I am a college student conducting research into methods for handling hyperactive children in the public school setting. I am surveying each elementary school principal in the country. I have contacted the central office also, but I wished to have perspectives from those of you on the front lines. I have a child with ADHD, so I have a personal as well as a scholarly reason for this research. I could ask specific questions on policy, but I have gotten that from the central office. What I would like from you is a brief paragraph that describes your policy and procedure when one of your teachers reports a hyperactive child. In particular, do you endorse the use of medication for calming a child with ADHD? May I quote you in my report? I will honor your request to withhold your name.
I have enclosed a self-addressed, stamped envelope for your convenience. You may e-mail me at messersmith@apsu.edu.

Sincerely,

Gena Messersmith

Gena Messersmith

This letter makes a fairly specific request for a minimum amount of information. It does not require an expansive reply. Should Messersmith use a quotation from the reply, she should provide a bibliography entry on her works cited page.

> Warren, Rachel G. Principal of Sango High School, Clarksville, TN. E-mail to the author. 5 Apr. 2000.

Reading Personal Papers

Search for letters, diaries, manuscripts, family histories, and other personal materials that might contribute to your study. The city library may house private collections, and the city librarian can usually help you contact the county historian and other private citizens who have important documents. Obviously, handling private papers must be done with the utmost decorum and care. Again, make a bibliography entry for such materials:

> Joplin, Lester. "Notes on Robert Penn Warren." Unpublished paper. Nashville, 1997.

Attending Lectures and Public Addresses

Watch bulletin boards and the newspaper for a featured speaker who might visit your campus. When you attend, take careful notes and, if available, request a copy of the lecture or speech. Remember, too, that many lectures, reproduced on video, will be available in the library or in departmental files. Always make a bibliography entry for any words or ideas you use.

C H E C K L I S T

Interviews, Letters, Private Papers, Courthouse Documents

- Set your appointments in advance.
- Consult with experienced persons. If possible, talk to several people in order to weigh the different opinions. Telephone interviews are acceptable.
- Be courteous and on time for interviews.
- Be prepared in advance with a set of focused, pertinent questions for initiating and conducting the interview.
- Handle private and public papers with great care.
- For accuracy, record the interview with a tape recorder (with permission of the person interviewed, of course).
- Double-check direct quotations with the interviewee or the tape.
- Get permission before citing a person by name or quoting their exact words.
- Send helpful people a copy of your report along with a thank you note.

Petty-Rathbone, Virginia. "Edgar Allan Poe and the Image of
Ulalume." Lecture. Heard Library, Vanderbilt U., 2000.

Investigating Government Documents

Documents are available at three levels of government—county, state, and
federal. As a constituent, you are entitled to examine many kinds of records
on file at various agencies. If your topic demands it, you may contact the
mayor's office, attend and take notes at a city council assembly, or search out
printed documents.

Local Government

Visit the courthouse or county clerk's office where you can find facts on
each election, census, marriage, birth, and death. These archives will include
wills, tax rolls, military assignments, deeds to property, and much more.
Therefore, a trip to the local courthouse can be rewarding, helping you trace
the history of the land and its people.

State Government

Contact by phone a state office that relates to your research, such as
Consumer Affairs (general information), Public Service Commission (which
regulates public utilities such as the telephone company), or the Department of Human Services (which administers social and welfare services).
The agencies may vary by name in your state. Remember, too, that the state
will have an archival storehouse which will make its records available for
public review.

Federal Government

Your United States senator or representative can send you booklets
printed by the Government Printing Office. A list of these materials, many of
which are free, appears in a monthly catalog issued by the Superintendent of
Documents, *Monthly Catalog of United States Government Publications*,
Washington, DC 20402. Most college libraries will have this catalog in print
form or the electronic network. In addition, you can gain access to the
National Archives Building in Washington, D.C., or to one of the regional
branches in Atlanta, Boston, Chicago, Denver, Fort Worth, Kansas City, Los
Angeles, New York, Philadelphia, or Seattle. Their archives contain court
records and government documents which you can review in two books:
Guide to the National Archives of the United States and *Select List of Publications of the National Archives and Record Service.* You can borrow some
documents on microfilm if you consult *Catalog of National Archives Microfilm Publications.* One researcher, for example, found the table shown in Figure 5.1 while looking for information on shifts in population.

The researcher also made a bibliography entry to record the source of
this table.

Population change, 1980-1990

Cities with the most rapid population growth

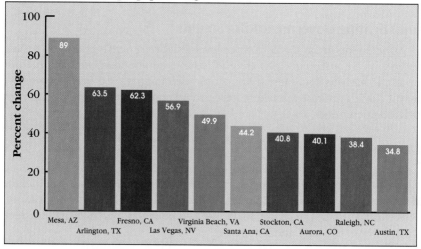

FIGURE 5.1. **Table on cities with the most rapid population growth**
From Courtenay M. Slater and George E. Hall, eds., 1993 County and City Extra. Reproduced by permission of Slater-Hall Information Products, from Bernan Press, Lanham, Md., 1993 (copyright).

REF/HA/202/A37

"Population Change, 1980–1990." <u>1993 County and City Extra:</u>
    <u>Annual Metro, City and County Data Book</u>. Ed. Courtney M.
    Slater and George E. Hall. Lanham, MD: Bernan Press, 1993.

5b Examining Audiovisual Materials, Television, and Radio

Important data can be found in audiovisual materials: films, filmstrips, music, phonograph recordings, slides, audio cassettes, and video cassettes. You will find these sources on and off campus. Consult such guides as *Educators Guide* (film, filmstrips, and tapes), *Media Review Digest* (nonprint materials), *Video Source Book* (video catalog), *The Film File*, or *International Index to Recorded Poetry*. Television, with its many channels, such as *The History Channel*, offers invaluable data. With a VCR you can record a program for detailed examination. Again, write bibliography entries for any materials that contribute to your paper.

"Nutrition and AIDS." Narr. Carolyn O'Neil. CNN. 12 Jan. 1997.

5c Conducting a Survey with a Questionnaire

Questionnaires can produce current, firsthand data that you can tabulate and analyze. Of course, to achieve meaningful results, you must survey a random sample, one that is representative of the whole population in terms of

C H E C K L I S T

Using Media Sources

- Watch closely the opening and closing credits to capture the necessary data for your bibliography entry. The format is explained on pages 275–76.
- Your citations may refer to a performer, director, or narrator, depending upon the focus of your study.
- As with the live interview, be scrupulously accurate in taking notes. It's best to write direct quotations because paraphrases of television commentary can unintentionally be distorted and colored by bias.
- Preplan the review of a media presentation, even to the point of preparing a set of criteria to help with your judgment or a list of questions in search of answers.

age, sex, race, education, income, residence, and other factors. Various degrees of bias can creep into the questionnaire unless you remain objective. Thus, use the formal survey only when you are experienced with tests and measurements as well as with statistical analysis or when you have an instructor who will help you with the instrument. Be advised that most schools have a Human Subjects Committee that sets guidelines, draws up consent forms, and requires anonymity of participants for information gathering that might be intrusive. An informal survey gathered in the hallways of campus buildings lacks credibility in the research paper. If you build a table or graph from the results, see pages A-13–A-16 for examples and instructions.

Label your survey in the bibliography entry:

Mason, Valerie, and Sarah Mossman. "Child Care Arrangements of
  Parents Who Attend College." Questionnaire. Knoxville: U of
  Tennessee, 2000.

5d Conducting Experiments, Tests, and Observation

Empirical research, usually performed in a laboratory, can determine why and how things exist, function, or interact with one another. Your paper will explain your methods and findings in pursuit of a hypothesis (your thesis). An experiment thereby becomes primary evidence for your paper.

Observation occurs generally outside the lab in the field, which might be a child-care center, a movie theater, a parking lot, or the counter of a McDonald's restaurant. The field is anywhere you can observe, count, and record behavior, patterns, and systems. You might test the water in a stream, study the growth of certain wildflowers, or observe the nesting patterns of deer. Retail merchandisers observe our buying habits, and basketball coaches

C H E C K L I S T

Conducting a Survey

- Keep the questionnaire short, clear, and focused on your topic.
- Write unbiased questions. Let your professor review the instrument before using it.
- Design it as a quick response to a scale (Choose A, B, or C), to a ranking (first choice, second choice, etc.), or to fill in the blanks.
- Arrange for an easy return of the questionnaire, even to the point of providing a self-addressed, stamped envelope.
- Retain e-mail responses until the project is complete.
- Provide a sample questionnaire and your tabulations in an appendix.
- Tabulate the results objectively. Even negative results that deny your hypothesis have value.

analyze the shot selections of team members. Gathering data is a way of life—by television networks, politicians, and thousands of marketing firms.

Most experiments and observations begin with a *hypothesis*, which is similar to a thesis sentence (see pages 29–31). The hypothesis is a statement assumed to be true for the purpose of investigation. *Hummingbirds live as extended families governed by a patriarch* is a hypothesis needing data to prove its validity. *The majority of people will not correct the poor grammar of a speaker* is a hypothesis that needs testing and observation to prove its validity.

However, you can begin observation without a hypothesis and let the results lead you to conclusions. The research project for this chapter asks you to conduct a double-entry observation for one week and to write a short reflection about what you learned by keeping the field notes. This could be your introduction into field research.

Generally, a report on an experiment or observation follows an expected format that provides four distinct parts: introduction, method, results, discussion. Understanding these elements will help you design your survey.

Introduction to explain the design of your experiment:

- Present the point of the study.
- State the hypothesis and how it relates to the problem.
- Provide the theoretical implications of the study.
- Explain the manner in which this study relates to previously published work.

Method to describe what you did and how you conducted the study:

- Describe the subjects who participated, whether human or animal.

C H E C K L I S T

Conducting an Experiment or Observation

- Express a clear hypothesis.
- Select the proper design for the study—lab experiment, observation, or the collection of raw data in the field.
- Include a review of the literature if appropriate.
- Keep careful records and accurate data.
- Don't let your expectations influence the results.
- Maintain respect for human and animal subjects. In that regard, you may find it necessary to get approval for your research from a governing board.

- Describe the apparatus to explain your equipment and how you used it.
- Summarize the procedure in the execution of each stage of your work.

Results to report your findings:

- Summarize the data that you collected.
- Provide the necessary statistical treatment of the findings with tables, graphs, and charts.
- Include findings that conflict with your hypothesis.

Discussion that explains the implications of your work:

- Evaluate the data and its relevance to the hypothesis.
- Interpret the findings as necessary.
- Discuss the implications of the findings.
- Qualify the results and limit them to your specific study.
- Make inferences from the results.

Your experiment and the writing of the report will require the attention of your instructor. Seek his or her advice often.

 Consult the Lester website (www.ablongman.com/lester) for additional information, examples, and links to sites that discuss in greater detail the matters of experiment and observation.

YOUR RESEARCH PROJECT

1. Select an event or object from nature to observe daily for one week. Record field notes in a double-entry format by using the left side of the page to record and the right side of the page to comment and reflect on

what you have observed. Afterwards, write a brief paragraph discussing your findings.

Record:	*Response:*
Day 1	
10 minute session at window, three hummingbirds fighting over the feeder.	Is the male chasing away the female or is the female the aggressor?
Day 2	
10 minute session at window, saw eight single hummingbirds and one guarding feeder 2 by chasing others away.	I did some research and the red-throated male is the one that's aggressive.

2. Look carefully at your subject to determine if research outside the library will be helpful for your project. If so, what kind of research: correspondence? local records? the news media? a questionnaire? an observation or experiment?
3. Work closely with your instructor to design an instrument that will affect your research and your findings. In fact, most instructors will want to examine any questionnaire that you will submit to others and will want to approve the design of your experiment or observation.
4. Follow university guidelines on testing with humans and animals.

6

Organizing Ideas and Setting Goals

Initially, research is haphazard and your work space will be cluttered with bits of information scattered through your notes and on sheets of photocopied material or printouts from the Internet. So after the initial search to confirm the availability of sources, you need to organize your ideas so that reading and note-taking will relate directly to your specific needs. Your needs become clear when you draw plans, such as a research proposal, a list of ideas, a set of questions, or a rough outline. In addition, the design of your study should match an appropriate organizational model, called a *paradigm.* You may also be required to create a final outline to keep your manuscript well ordered. The organizational ideas in this chapter may help you find your way through the maze.

Careful organization and the presentation of evidence will augment your voice and give it a touch of authority, which will invite readers to share your position. When you take a position, as with urging people to sign their donor card for organ and tissue donations, you will be appealing to the reader's ethical sense. Your voice and control of the material will need to convince the reader that you have in mind the best interests of all.

6a Charting a Direction and Setting Goals

Instead of plunging too quickly into note-taking, first decide *what* to look for and *why* you need it. One or more of these exercises will help your organization:

- Revisit your research proposal, if you developed one, for essential issues.
- List key words, ideas, and issues that you must explore in the paper.
- Rough out an initial outline.
- Ask a thorough set of questions.
- Use modes of development (i.e., definition or cause/effect) to identify key issues.
- Search issues across the curriculum (e.g., economics or psychology or biology).
- Let your thesis sentence point you toward the basic issues.

Each of these techniques is explored on the following pages.

Using Your Research Proposal to Direct Your Note-taking

Your research proposal, if you developed one, will introduce issues worthy of research. For example, the last sentence of this research proposal names four topics:

> I want to address young people who think they need a tan in order to be beautiful. Preliminary investigation indicates that ultraviolet radiation causes severe skin damage that is cumulative; that is, it builds adverse effects with each exposure. My role is to investigate the facts and explore options for those who desire a good tan. I need information on skin types, sun exposure, tanning beds, and types of skin damage.

This writer can go in search of evidence about skin types, sun exposure, tanning beds, and types of skin damage. The paper can thereby explore the consequences of sun bathing.

See Chapter 2, pages 26–29, for a detailed discussion of the research proposal.

Another writer sketched the following research proposal, which lists the types of evidence necessary to accomplish the project.

> This paper will study organ and tissue donation. It will expose the myths that prevail in the public's imagination and, hopefully, dispel them. It will explore the serious need and benefits derived from donated organs and tissue. It will also itemize the organs and their use to rehabilitate the diseased and wounded. It will evaluate but it will also be a proposal—sign the donor card!

Listing Key Words and Phrases to Set Directions for Note-Taking

Follow two fairly simple steps: (1) jot down ideas or words in a rough list, and (2) expand the list to show a hierarchy of major and minor ideas. Student Katie Hebert started by writing these key words on nutritional foods:

garlic	green and black tea	meats, fish, cheese
oatmeal, oatbran	low-fat milk	fruit juice
pasta	rice	whole-grain bread

Hebert could begin note-taking with this list and write one of the words at the top of each note.

> **HINT:** What you are looking for at this point are terms that will speed your search on the Internet and in the library's various indexes.

Writing a Rough Outline

As early as possible, organize your key terminology in a brief outline, arranging the words and phrases in an ordered sequence, as shown in this example.

To help cholesterol
>   oatmeal, oat bran, cereal, pasta, whole grain bread

To fight cancer
>   garlic, low-fat meats and fish, vegetables, fruit, fiber, tomato
>   products, carrots, broccoli

To reduce heart disease
>   low-fat foods, vegetables, fruit, fiber, soy products, tomato products,
>   green and black tea

To control osteoporosis
>   milk, juice, pasta, rice

This outline, although sketchy, provides the terminology needed for keyword searches on the Internet and for conducting interviews or questionnaires on food consumption (see 5a, pages 78–82 and 5c, pages 82–83).

Using Questions to Identify Issues

Questions can invite you to develop answers in your notes. (See also 2a, "Asking Questions," pages 15–16.)

What is a functional food?
How does it serve the body in fighting disease?
Can healthy eating really lower health care costs?
Can healthy eating really prolong one's life?
Can we identify the components of nutritional foods which make them
>   work so effectively?

What is an antioxidant? A carcinogen? A free radical? A triglyceride?

You should try to answer every question with at least one written note. One question might lead to others, and your answer to a question (Are nutritional foods something new?) might produce a topic sentence for a paragraph:

> Although medical professionals are just beginning to open their
> minds and eyes to the medicinal power of food, others have known
> about food's healthful properties for centuries.

Setting Goals by Using the Modes of Development

Try to anticipate the kinds of development you will need to build effective paragraphs and to explore your topic fully. Then base your notes on the modes of development: *definition, comparison and contrast, process, illustration, cause and effect, classification, analysis,* and *description.*

<u>Define</u> tissue donation

<u>Contrast</u> myths, religious views, and ethical considerations

<u>Illustrate</u> organ and tissue donation with several examples

Use <u>statistics</u> and <u>scientific data</u>

Search out <u>causes</u> for a person's reluctance to sign a donor card

Determine the <u>consequences</u> of donation with a focus on saving the lives of children

Read and use a <u>case study</u> on a child's death and organ donation by the parents of the child

Explore the step-by-step stages of the <u>process</u> of organ donation

<u>Classify</u> the types and <u>analyze</u> the problem

Give <u>narrative</u> examples of several people whose lives were saved

With this list in hand, a writer can search for material to develop as *contrast, process, definition*, and so forth.

> **HINT:** Try developing each important item on your list into a full paragraph. Write a definition paragraph. Write a paragraph to contrast abuse and discipline. Write another paragraph that gives four or five examples. By so doing, you will be well on your way to developing the paper.

One student recorded this note that defines the subject:

Organ and tissue donation is the gift of life. Each year many people confront health problems due to diseases or congenital birth defects. Organ transplants give these people the chance to live a somewhat normal life. Organs that can be successfully transplanted include the heart, lungs, liver, kidneys, and pancreas (Barnill 1). Tissues that can be transplanted successfully include bone, corneas, skin, heart valves, veins, cartilage, and other connective tissues (Taddonio 1).

Using Approaches Across the Curriculum to Chart Your Major Ideas

Each scholarly field gives a special insight into any given topic. Suppose, for example, that you wish to examine an event from American history, such as the Battle of Little Big Horn. Different academic disciplines will help you approach the topic in different ways.

POLITICAL SCIENCE:	Was Custer too hasty in his quest for political glory?
ECONOMICS:	Did the government want to open the western lands for development that would enrich the nation?
MILITARY SCIENCE:	Was Custer's military strategy flawed?
PSYCHOLOGY:	Did General Custer's ego precipitate the massacre?
GEOGRAPHY:	Why did Custer stage a battle at this site?

These approaches can also produce valuable paragraphs, if developed, such as this:

> The year 1876 stands as a monument to the western policies of Congress and the President, but Sitting Bull and Custer seized their share of glory. Custer's egotism and political ambitions overpowered his military savvy (Lemming 6). Also, Sitting Bull's military tactics (he told his braves to kill rather than show off their bravery) proved devastating for Custer and his troops who no longer had easy shots at "prancing, dancing Indians" (Potter 65).

Using Your Thesis to Chart the Direction of Your Research

Often, the thesis sentence will set the direction of the paper's development. **Argument** grows from some statements, as shown next.

THESIS: Misunderstandings about organ donation can distort reality and cause serious limits on the availability of a cornea, a liver, or a healthy heart for those persons in need.

Argument 1. Many myths mislead people into believing that donation is unethical.

Argument 2. Some fear that as a patient they might be put down early.

Argument 3. Religious views sometimes get in the way of donation.

The outline above, though brief, gives this writer three categories that require detailed research in support of the thesis.

Cause and effect issues will derive from some thesis sentences. Notice that the next writer's thesis on television's educational values points the way to four very different areas worthy of investigation.

THESIS: Television can have positive effects on a child's language development.

Consequence 1. Television introduces new words.

Consequence 2. Television reinforces word usage and proper syntax.

Consequence 3. Literary classics come alive verbally on television.

Consequence 4. Television provides the subtle rhythms and musical effects of accomplished speakers.

The outline above can help the writer produce four positive consequences of television viewing.

Chapter 2, pages 29–31, gives additional information on formulating an effective thesis sentence.

Evaluation will evolve from thesis sentences that judge a subject by a set of criteria, such as the analysis of a poem, movie, or museum display. Notice how the next student's thesis sentence invites evaluation of an architectural plan.

> ## C H E C K L I S T
>
> ### *Evaluating Your Overall Plan*
>
> **1.** What is my thesis? Will my notes and records defend and illustrate my proposition? Is the evidence convincing?
>
> **2.** Have I found the best plan for developing the thesis with elements of argument, evaluation, cause-effect, or comparison?
>
> **3.** Should I use a combination of elements (evaluation, comparison, causal analysis), and then set out the argument?

THESIS: The architectural drawing for the university's new student center is not friendly to the handicapped.

Evaluation 1.   The common areas seemed cramped, narrow, and with few open areas for students to cluster.

Evaluation 2.   Steps and stairs seem all too common in the design.

Evaluation 3.   Only one elevator appears in the plans when three would be fair and equitable.

Evaluation 4.   Only the first floor restrooms are handicapped accessible.

Evaluation 5.   The handicapped parking spaces are designated for an entrance with steps, not a ramp.

Comparison has importance for a thesis sentence that judges the value of two sides of an issue, as shown in one student's rough outline:

THESIS: Discipline often involves punishment, but child abuse adds another element: the gratification of the adult.

Comparison 1:   A spanking has the interest of the child at heart but a beating or a caning has no redeeming value.

Comparison 2:   Time outs remind the child that relationships are important and to be cherished but lock outs in a closet only promote hysteria and fear.

Comparison 3:   The parent's ego and selfish interests often take precedence over the welfare of the child or children.

6b Using Academic Models (Paradigms)

A paradigm is a universal outline, one that governs most papers of a given type. It is not content specific; rather, it provides a general model, a broad scaffold, and a basic academic pattern of reasoning for all papers with a certain purpose. In contrast, a traditional outline, with its specific detail on various levels of subdivision, is useful for only one paper. Start with a paradigm, an ideal pattern for many different papers, and finish with an outline, a content-oriented plan for one paper only.

A General All-Purpose Model

If you are uncertain about the design of your paper, start with this bare-bones model and expand it with your material. Readers, including your instructor, are accustomed to this sequence for research papers. It offers plenty of leeway.

Identify the subject
    Explain the problem
    Provide background information
    Frame a thesis statement
Analyze the subject
    Examine the first major issue
    Examine the second major issue
    Examine the third major issue
Discuss your findings
    Restate your thesis and point beyond it
    Interpret the findings
    Provide answers, solutions, a final opinion

To the introduction you can add a quotation, an anecdote, a definition, or comments from your source materials. Within the body you can compare, analyze, give evidence, trace historical events, and handle other matters. In the conclusion you can challenge an assumption, take exception to a prevailing point of view, and reaffirm your thesis. Flesh out each section, adding subheadings as necessary, and you will thereby create an outline.

Chapter 12 explores in detail the development of these three major sections of a research paper. For tips about the introduction, see pages 180–85; for the body, see pages 185–90; for the conclusion, see pages 190–93.

Paradigm for Advancing Your Ideas and Theories

See also Chapter 15, pages 277–78, for a discussion on writing theory in APA style.

If you want to advance a theory in your paper, use this next design, but adjust it to eliminate some items and add new elements as necessary.

Introduction
    Establish the problem or question
    Discuss its significance
    Provide the necessary background information
    Introduce experts who have addressed the problem
    Provide a thesis sentence that addresses the problem
    from a fresh perspective if at all possible
Body
    Evaluate the issues involved in the problem
    Develop a past-to-present examination
    Compare and analyze the details and minor issues

Cite experts who have addressed the same problem
Conclusion
Advance and defend your theory as it grows out of evidence in the body
Offer directives or a plan of action
Suggest additional work and research that is needed

Paradigm for the Analysis of Creative Works

If you plan to analyze musical, artistic, or literary works, such as an opera, a set of paintings, or a novel, adjust this next paradigm to your subject and purpose.

Introduction
Identify the work
Give a brief summary in one sentence
Provide background information that relates to the thesis
Offer biographical facts about the artist that relate to the specific issues
Quote and paraphrase authorities to establish the scholarly traditions
Write a thesis sentence that establishes your particular views of the literary work
Body
Provide evaluative analysis divided according to such elements as imagery, theme, character development, structure, symbolism, narration, language, and so forth
Conclusion
Keep a fundamental focus on the artist of the work, not just the elements of analysis as explained in the body
Offer a conclusion that explores the contributions of the artist in accord with your thesis sentence

Paradigm for Argument and Persuasion Papers

If you write persuasively or argue from a set position, your paper should conform in general to this next paradigm. Select the elements that fit your design.

Introduction
In one statement establish the problem or controversial issue that your paper will examine
Summarize the issues
Define key terminology
Make concessions on some points of the argument
Use quotations and paraphrases to clarify the controversial nature of the subject
Provide background information to relate the past to the present

Write a thesis to establish your position
Body
  Develop arguments to defend one side of the subject
  Analyze the issues, both pro and con
  Give evidence from the sources, including quotations as appropriate
Conclusion
  Expand your thesis into a conclusion that makes clear your position,
    which should be one that grows logically from your analysis and dis-
    cussion of the issues

Paradigm for Analysis of History

If you are writing a historical or political science paper that analyzes
events and their causes and consequences, your paper should conform in general to the following plan.

Introduction
  Identify the event
  Provide the background leading up to the event
  Offer quotations and paraphrases from experts
  Give the thesis sentence
Body
  Analyze the background leading up to the event
  Trace events from one historic episode to another
  Offer a chronological sequence that explains how one event relates
    directly to the next
  Cite authorities who have also investigated this event in history
Conclusion
  Reaffirm your thesis
  Discuss the consequences of this event, explaining how it altered the
    course of history

Paradigm for a Comparative Study

A comparative study requires that you examine two schools of thought,
two issues, two works, or the positions taken by two persons. The paper
examines the similarities and differences of the two subjects, generally using
one of three arrangements for the body of the paper.

Introduction
  Establish A
  Establish B
  Briefly compare the two
  Introduce the central issues
  Cite source materials on the subjects
  Present your thesis

Body (choose one)

Examine A	Compare A & B	Issue 1
Examine B	Contrast A & B	Discuss A & B
Compare and contrast A & B	Discuss the central issues	Issue 2
		Discuss A & B
		Issue 3
		Discuss A & B

Conclusion
    Discuss the significant issues
    Write a conclusion that ranks one over the other
      or
    Write a conclusion that rates the respective ideas of each side

For the paradigm of a scientific report, see Chapter 5, pages 83–85, which explains the arrangement of introduction, method, results, discussion. See also Chapters 15 and 16 for details about scholarly writing in the social sciences, natural sciences, and applied sciences.

Remember that the models provided above are general guidelines, not ironclad rules. Adjust each as necessary to meet your special needs.

6c Writing a Formal Outline

Not all papers require the formal outline, nor do all researchers need one. A short research paper can be created from key words, a list of issues, a rough outline, and a first draft. However, a formal outline sometimes becomes important, for it classifies the issues of your study into clear, logical categories with main headings and one or more level of subheadings. An outline will change miscellaneous notes, computer drafts, and photocopied materials into an ordered progression of ideas.

HINT: A formal outline is not rigid and inflexible; you may, and should, modify it while writing and revising. In every case, treat an outline or organizational chart as a tool. Like an architect's blueprint, it should contribute to, not inhibit, the construction of a finished product.

You may wish to experiment with the "outline" feature of your software, which will allow you to view the paper at various levels of detail and to highlight and "drop" the essay into a different organization.

Using Standard Outline Symbols

List your major categories and subtopics in this form:

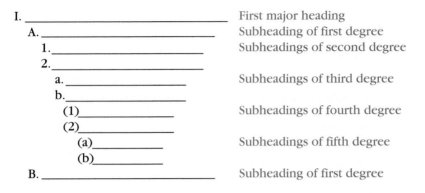

I. _____   First major heading
   A. _____   Subheading of first degree
     1._____   Subheadings of second degree
     2._____
       a._____   Subheadings of third degree
       b._____
         (1)_____   Subheadings of fourth degree
         (2)_____
           (a)_____   Subheadings of fifth degree
           (b)_____
   B. _____   Subheading of first degree

The degree to which you continue the subheads will depend, in part, upon the complexity of the subject. Subheads in a research paper seldom carry beyond subheadings of the third degree, the first series of small letters.

An alternative form, especially for papers in business and the sciences, is the *decimal outline*, which divides material by numerical divisions:

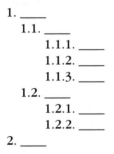

1. ____
   1.1. ____
      1.1.1. ____
      1.1.2. ____
      1.1.3. ____
   1.2. ____
      1.2.1. ____
      1.2.2. ____
2. ____

Writing a Formal Topic Outline

If your purpose is to arrange quickly the topics of your paper without detailing your data, build a topic outline of balanced phrases. The topic outline may use noun phrases:

III. The senses
   A. Receptors to detect light
     1. Rods of the retina
     2. Cones of the retina

It may also use gerund phrases:

III. Sensing the environment
   A. Detecting light
     1. Sensing dim light with retina rods
     2. Sensing bright light with retina cones

And it may also use infinitive phrases:

III. To use the senses
   A. To detect light
      1. To sense dim light
      2. To sense bright light

No matter which grammatical format you choose, you should follow it consistently throughout the outline. Student Sarah Bemis's topic outline follows.

I. Diabetes defined
   A. A disease without control
      1. A disorder of the metabolism
      2. The search for a cure
   B. Types of diabetes
      1. Type 1, juvenile diabetes
      2. Type 2, adult onset diabetes
II. Health complications
   A. The problem of hyperglycemia
      1. Signs and symptoms of the problem
      2. Lack of insulin
   B. The conflict of the kidneys and the liver
      1. Effects of ketoacidosis
      2. Effects of artereoclerosis
III. Proper care and control
   A. Blood sugar monitoring
      1. Daily monitoring at home
      2. Hemoglobin test at a laboratory
   B. Medication for diabetes
      1. Insulin injections
      2. Hypoglycemia agents
   C. Exercise programs
      1. Walking
      2. Swimming
      3. Aerobic workouts
   D. Diet and meal planning
      1. Exchange plan
      2. Carbohydrate counting
IV. Conclusion: Balance of all the factors

Writing a Formal Sentence Outline

The sentence outline requires full sentences for each heading and sub-heading. It has two advantages over the topic outline:

1. Many entries in a sentence outline can serve as topic sentences for paragraphs, thereby accelerating the writing process.
2. The subject/verb pattern establishes the logical direction of your thinking (for example, the phrase "Vocabulary development" becomes "Television viewing can improve a child's vocabulary").

Consequently, the sentence outline brings into the open any possible organizational problems rather than hiding them as a topic outline might do. The time devoted to writing a complete sentence outline, like writing complete, polished notes (see pages 133–44), will serve you well when you write the rough draft and revise it.

A portion of Adele Gelvin's outline follows.

Outline

THESIS: Organ and tissue donation and transplantation is an option every person has, but many people do not take advantage of it because of myths and other ethical issues; nevertheless, all people should choose to donate their organs and tissues after death to help save someone else's life.

   I. Organ and tissue donation is the gift of life.
      A. Organs that can be successfully transplanted include the heart, lungs, liver, kidneys, and pancreas.
      B. Tissues that can be transplanted successfully include bone, corneas, skin, heart valves, veins, cartilage, and other connective tissues.
      C. The process of becoming a donor is easy.
      D. Many people receive organ and tissue transplants each year, but still many people die because they did not receive the needed transplant.
  II. Many myths mislead people into believing donation is bad and unethical.
      A. The fire of these myths is "I heard about this guy who went to a party, and he woke up the next morning in a bathtub full of ice. His kidneys were stolen for sale on the black market."
      B. This is a prime example of how myths are started to scare people away from opportunities that could be advantageous to others.
      C. "If I'm in an accident and the hospital knows I want to be a donor, the doctors won't try to save my life!" is another well-circulated myth.

As shown on the previous page, the thesis sentence often appears as a separate item in the outline. It is the main idea of the entire paper, so try not to label it as Item I in the outline. Otherwise, you may search fruitlessly for parallel ideas to put in II, III, and IV. (See also page 180 on using the thesis in the opening.)

To see Gelvin's paper, turn to pages 323–35.

Using Your Notes, Photocopies, Internet Printouts, and the Research Journal to Enrich Your Organizational Plan

If you have kept a research journal, you have probably developed a number of paragraphs on the topic. Therefore, review the journal and assign each paragraph to a section of your outline. Do this by making a note, such as "put in the conclusion," or by assigning an outline number, "use in II.A.1." Do the same thing with your other materials. Then assign them to a spot in your outline, as shown in this brief example from an outline:

> A. Television viewing can improve the vocabulary of children.
> 1. Negative views
>   Cite Powell; cite Winkeljohann
> 2. Positive views
>   Cite Rice and Woodsall; cite Singer; cite Postman

Using a Basic, Dynamic Order to Chart the Course of Your Work

Finally, the finished paper should trace the issues, defend and support a thesis, and provide dynamic progression of issues and concepts that point forward to the conclusion. The paper should provide these elements:

> Identification of the problem or issue
> A review of the literature on the topic
> Your thesis or hypothesis
> Analysis of the issues
> Presentation of evidence
> Interpretation and discussion of the findings

In every case you must generate the dynamics of the paper by (1) building anticipation in the introduction, (2) investigating the issues in the body, and (3) providing a final judgment. In this way, you will satisfy the demands of the academic reader who will expect you to:

- examine a problem
- cite literature on it
- offer your ideas and interpretation of it

All three are necessary in almost every instance. Consequently, your early organization will determine, in part, the success of your research paper.

YOUR RESEARCH PROJECT

1. Scratch out an outline for your project. List your general thesis and below that establish several divisions that will require careful and full development. Test more than one plan. Do you need several criteria of judgment? Causal issues? Arguments? Type of evidence? Which seems to work best for you?
2. Select one of the paradigms, as found on pages 92–96, and develop it fully with the information in your scratch outline (see item 1 immediately above).
3. If you are familiar with the design of web pages, you realize that the hierarchical ideas have value because readers can click various hot keys that will carry them deeper into the various files. The hierarchy looks something like this:

See Chapter 18, pages 352–62, for more information on planning and constructing the various pages of a website.

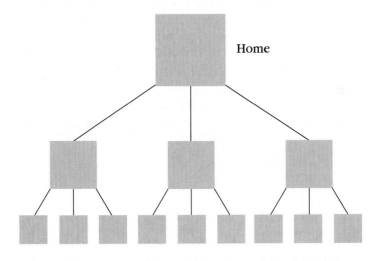

Home

Test your outline, as developed in items 1 and 2, by filling the blanks above with topics that merit a paragraph of development.

7

Finding and Reading the Best Sources

The research paper assignment is an exercise in inquiry as you try to discover what you know on a topic and what others can teach you. The process emphasizes your curiosity as you probe a complex subject. You may not arrive at any final answers or solutions, but you will enter the intellectual discussion. Your paper will invite others into your thinking and synthesize the words of others into your own. This chapter cuts to the heart of the matter: How do I find the best, most appropriate sources? Should I read all or just part of a source? How do I respond to it?

Be skeptical about accepting every printed word as being the truth. Constantly review and verify to your own satisfaction the words of your sources, especially in this age of electronic publication. It would be wise to consider every article on the Internet as suspect until you verify its scholarship (see pages 65–66 for guidelines on judging the value of Internet articles).

HINT: Some student researchers photocopy entire journal articles and carry an armload of books from the library. Such diligence is misplaced. The quality of your citations and the way you position them far outweigh the quantity of your source materials.

 ## 7a Finding the Best Source Materials

Do not hesitate to ask your instructor for help in finding sources. Instructors know the field, know the best writers, and can provide a brief list to get you started. Sometimes instructors will even pull books from their office shelves to give you a starting point.

Librarians know the resources of the library. Their job is to serve your needs. If you appeal for help, they will often walk into the stacks with you to find the appropriate reference books or relevant journal articles.

Try to use recent sources. A book may look valuable, but if its copyright date is 1955 the content has probably been replaced by recent research and current developments. Scientific and technical topics always require up-to-date research. Learn to depend on monthly and quarterly journals as well as books.

The best techniques for finding and evaluating your sources will be described in this chapter. First, however, examine the inverted pyramid below that shows you a progression from excellent sources to less reliable sources. The pyramid chart does not ask you to dismiss items at the bottom, but it endorses a sponsored website over an individual website and favors an encyclopedia over a chat group.

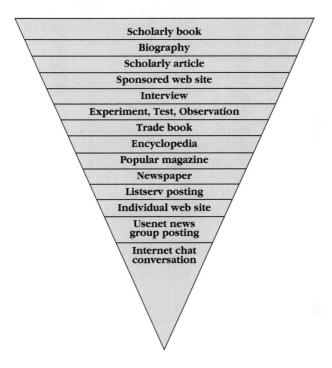

Scholarly book
Biography
Scholarly article
Sponsored web site
Interview
Experiment, Test, Observation
Trade book
Encyclopedia
Popular magazine
Newspaper
Listserv posting
Individual web site
Usenet news group posting
Internet chat conversation

Scholarly Book

Like journal articles, scholarly books are subjected to careful review before publication. They are published because they give the very best treatment on a subject. They are not published to make money; in fact, many scholarly books lose money for the publishers. Scholarly books, including textbooks, treat academic topics with in-depth discussions and careful documentation of the evidence. A college library is a repository for scholarly books—technical and scientific works, doctoral dissertations, publications of the university presses, and many textbooks.

Two works will help you evaluate a book:

Book Review Digest provides an evaluation of several thousand books each year. Arranged alphabetically, it features summaries and brief quotations from the reviews to uncover the critical reception of the work.

The Booklist, a monthly magazine that reviews new books for librarians, includes brief summaries and recommendations.

Other reviews are hidden here and there in magazines and journals. To find them, use one of the following indexes.

Book Review Index will send you to reviews in 225 magazines and journals.

Index to Book Reviews in the Humanities indexes reviews in humanities periodicals devoted to history, philosophy, literature, art, and similar fields. Items are listed by author, title, and then reviewer.

Index to Book Reviews in the Social Sciences indexes the reviews in social science periodicals devoted to education, psychology, political science, and similar fields. Items are listed by author, title, and then reviewer.

Current Book Review Citations gives an author-title index to book reviews in more than 1,000 periodicals.

A sample page of *Book Review Digest* shows you the type of information available in a review of books (see Figure 7.1). After bibliographic details, it summarizes the book and then provides the reviews, one from *Booklist* and another from *The Library Journal.* Both reviewers give a positive response to the book, so a researcher could feel good about using the book as a source.

Biography

The librarian can help you find an appropriate printed biography from among the thousands available. They are in works such as *Contemporary Authors, Dictionary of American Negro Biography,* and *Who's Who in Philosophy.*

You can also learn about a notable person on the Internet. Using a search engine, such as *AltaVista,* type in the name of an author, inventor, politician, or industrialist and see what develops. Famous people will usually have several sites devoted to them.

You may need a biography for several reasons:

1. To verify the standing and reputation of somebody that you want to paraphrase or quote in your paper.
2. To provide biographical details in your introduction. For example, the primary topic may be Carl Jung's psychological theories of the unconscious, but some information about Jung's career might be appropriate in the paper.
3. To discuss a creative writer's life in relation to his or her work. That is, Joyce Carol Oates's personal life may shed some light on her stories or novels.

See Appendix B, pages A-31–A-45, for a list of reference works for almost every field; these works will point you toward biographies of important people.

A *critical biography* is a book devoted to the life of one person, such as Richard Ellmann's *Oscar Wilde,* a study of the British poet and playwright, or Alf Mapp's

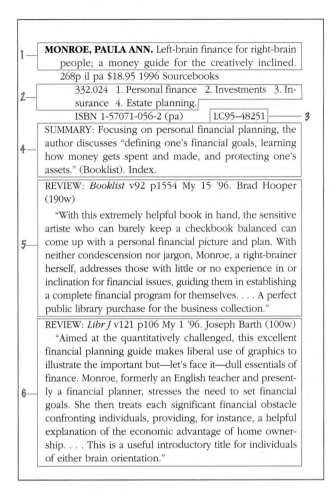

FIGURE 7.1. From *Book Review Digest,* 1997
(1) Author and title. (2) Dewey call number and subject entries for card catalog. (3) Library of Congress call number. (4) First entry is a description of the work. (5) *Booklist's* evaluation of the book. (6) *Library Journal's* evaluation of the book.

Thomas Jefferson: A Strange Case of Mistaken Identity, which interprets the life and times of the former president. To find a critical biography, use the electronic card catalog at the library or go online to Amazon.com or Barnes& Noble.com, which are bookstore sites that will show what biographies might be available.

Scholarly Article

A scholarly article can appear in a magazine, newspaper, or journal. In general, scholarly journals offer more reliable evidence than popular magazines, yet don't be deceived. Many magazines are noted for their quality—*Atlantic Monthly, Scientific Review, Psychology Today*, and many others. The major newspapers—*New York Times, Atlanta Constitution, Wall Street Journal,* and others—hire the best writers and columnists, so some scholarly articles will be found in both printed newspapers and newspapers online. With a journal article you may feel more confident in its authenticity because the authors of journal articles write for academic honor, they document all sources, and they publish through university presses and academic organizations that use a jury to judge an article before its publication. Thus, a journal article about child abuse found in *Child Development* or *Journal of Marriage and the Family* should be reliable, but an article about child abuse in a popular magazine may be less reliable in its facts and opinions.

Usually, but not in every case, you can identify a journal in these ways:

1. The journal does not have a colorful cover; in fact, the table of contents is often displayed on the cover.
2. No colorful drawings or photography will introduce each journal article, just a title and name of the author.
3. The word *journal* often appears in the title (e.g., *The Journal of Sociology*).
4. The yearly issues of a journal are bound into a book.
5. Usually, the pages of a journal are numbered continuously through all issues for a year (unlike magazines, which are always paged anew with each issue).

Sometimes you may face a bewildering array of articles, and you will wonder which are the best. One way to evaluate a set of articles is with *citation searching*, which is a search for authors who have been cited repeatedly in the literature. For example, one writer located the same name *Kagan, J.* in the bibliographies of three articles. That information signals Kagan's importance to research in this area and suggests the importance of reading Kagan's material (see Figure 7.2).

To see how one student responded to an article, see pages 112–14.

As you search the various bibliographies, mark your bibliography cards with stars or circles each time a particular source is cited. Two or more stars will suggest *must* reading. Three citation indexes will do some of this work for you:

Arts and Humanities Citation Index (AHCI) 1977–date
Science Citation Index (SCI) 1961–date
Social Sciences Citation Index (SSCI) 1966–date

Sponsored Website

The Internet supplies excellent information and some that is questionable in value. You must make judgments about the validity of these materials. On that note, see section 4d for a set of guidelines.

For an online article marked with one student's annotations, see page 116.

Graham, S., & Folkes, V. S. (1990). *Attribution theory: Applications to achievement, mental health, and interpersonal conflict.* Hillsdale, NJ: Erlbaum.

Kagan, J., Kearsley, R. B., & Zelazo, P. R. (1978). *Infancy: Its place in human development.* Cambridge, MA; Harvard University Press.

Levy, D. M. (1937). Studies in sibling rivalry. Research Monographs, *American Orthopsychiatric Association*

Kagan, J. (1984). *The nature of the child.* New York: Basic.

Kagan, J. (1992). Yesterday's premises, tomorrow's promises. *Developmental Psychology, 28,* 990–997.

Kagan J. (1994). *Galen's prophecy: Temperament in human nature.* New York: Basic.

Kagan, J., Rossman, B. L., Day, D., Albert, J., & Phillips, W. (1964). Information processing in the child: Significance of analytic and reflective attitudes. *Psychological Monographs, 78* (Whole No. 578).

Goldsmith, H. H., & Rothbart, M. K., (1992). *Laboratory Temperament Assessment Battery (LABTAB).* Pre- and Locomotor Versions. University of Oregon.

Kagan, J. (1984). *The nature of the child.* New York: Basic Books.

Kochanska, G. (1993). Toward a synthesis of parental socialization and child temperament in early development of conscience. *Child Development, 64,* 325–347.

FIGURE 7.2. From *Child Development,* 1997; author who appears in three different bibliographies

Ask yourself a few questions about any website information:

Is it appropriate to my work?
Is it reliable and authoritative?
Is it sponsored by an institution or organization?

Interview

Interviews with knowledgeable people provide excellent information for a research paper. Whether conducted in person, by telephone, or by e-mail, the interview brings a personal, expert perspective into your work. The key element, of course, is the expertise of the person. For full details about conducting an interview, see section 5a, pages 78–80.

Experiment, Test, or Observation

Gathering your own data for research is a staple in many fields, especially the sciences. An experiment will bring primary evidence into your paper as you explain your hypothesis, give the test results, and discuss the implications of your findings. For a full discussion on conducting scientific investigation, with guidelines and details on format, see section 5d, pages 83–85.

Trade Book

How to Launch a Small Business and *Landscaping with Rocks* are typical titles of nonfiction trade books to be found in book stores, not in a college library (although public libraries often have some holdings in trade books). Designed for commercial consumption, trade books seldom treat with depth a scholarly subject. The problem is that manuscripts for trade books do not go through the rigorous scrutiny by peer review that faces the manuscripts of scholarly books and textbooks. For example, if your topic is "dieting" with a focus on "fad diets," you will find plenty of diet books at the local book store and numerous articles on commercial websites. However, the serious discussions backed by careful research will be found in the journals or at the sponsored websites.

Encyclopedia

By design, encyclopedias contain brief surveys of every well-known person, event, place, and accomplishment. They will serve you well during preliminary investigation, but most instructors prefer that you go beyond encyclopedias in order to cite from scholarly books and journal articles. In addition, encyclopedias offer facts, not the critical perspectives that you can gain from academic scholars. There are some exceptions, of course, because specialized encyclopedias (see pages 38–39) often have in-depth articles by noted scholars.

Popular Magazine

Like trade books, magazines are written rather quickly and the articles seldom face critical review by a panel of experts, so you will need to exercise caution. However, some magazines have a superior quality to others. If your paper concerns, let's say, sports medicine, citing *Atlantic Monthly* or *Scientific Review* in your paper will gain you far higher marks than citing *Sports Illustrated, Sport,* or *NBA Basketball.* In general, college libraries will house magazines with merit in the quality of writing (see pages 112–14).

Newspaper

In the main, newspapers have reporters writing under the pressure of deadlines. Seldom do they have the time for careful research and documentation that you see in a journal article. On occasion, a newspaper will assign reporters to a series of articles on a complex topic. These in-depth analyses have merit. Thus, newspaper articles must be used only after cautionary and critical evaluation.

Listserv

E-mail information via a listserv deserves consideration when the listserv focuses on an academic issue, such as *British Romantic Literature* or more specifically *Shelley's Poetry*. In many cases, listservs originate from a college or scholarly organization. In fact, many instructors establish their own listserv sites for individual classes. Online web courses usually feature a listserv site for exchange of ideas and peer review. These listservs can be a great way to seek out possible topics. What are literature teachers or biologists talking about these days? Rather than a source for facts to quote, use the listserv to generate ideas.

Individual Website

A person's home page, with its various links to other information, provides a publication medium for anybody who presumes to a knowledge they may or may not possess. You can't avoid them because they pop up on various search engines. But you can approach them with caution. For example, one student, investigating the topic "fad diets," searched the Web to find mostly commercial sites that wanted to sell something or home pages that described personal battles with weight loss. On this point see 4b, pages 57–62.

Usenet

Many usenet news groups post information on a site. Like a call-in radio show, they invite opinions from a vast cross section of people, some reliable and some not. In most cases, participants have an anonymous username, rendering their ideas useless for a documented paper.

Internet Chat

Internet chat conversations have almost no value for academic research. In most cases, you don't even know who you are chatting with. Moreover, the conversations are seldom about scholarly issues.

7b Selecting a Mix of Primary and Secondary Sources

Primary sources include novels, speeches, eyewitness accounts, interviews, letters, autobiographies, or the results of original research. Feel free to quote often from a primary source because it has direct relevance to your discussion. If you examine a poem by Dylan Thomas, you must quote the poem. If you examine President George W. Bush's domestic policies on health care, you must quote from White House documents.

Secondary sources are writings *about* the primary sources, *about* an author, or *about* somebody's accomplishments. Examples of secondary sources are a report on a presidential speech, a review of new scientific findings, or an analysis of a poem. A biography provides a secondhand view of the life of a notable person. A history book interprets events. These evaluations, analyses, or interpretations provide ways of looking at original, primary sources.

Do not quote liberally from secondary sources. Be selective. Use a well-worded sentence, not the entire paragraph. Incorporate a key phrase into your text, not eight or nine lines.

For more information about reading key parts of a book, article, or Internet site, see pages 111–16.

The subject area of a research paper determines in part the nature of the source materials. Use the chart on the next page as a guide.

Citing from Primary and Secondary Sources

	Primary Sources	*Secondary Sources*
Literature	Novels, poems, plays, short stories, letters, diaries, manuscripts, auto-biographies, films, videos of live performances	Journal articles, reviews, biographies, critical books about writers and their works
Government Political Science History	Speeches, writings by presidents and others, the *Congressional Record,* reports of agencies and departments, documents written by historic figures	Newspaper reports, news magazines, political journals and newsletters, journal arti-cles, history books
Social Sciences	Case studies, findings from surveys and question-naires; reports of social workers, psychiatrists, and lab technicians	Commentary and evalua-tions in reports, docu-ments, journal articles, and books
Sciences	Tools and methods, exper-iments, findings from tests and experiments, observa-tions, discoveries, and test patterns	Interpretations and discussions of test data as found in journals and books (scientific books, which are quickly dated, are less valuable than up-to-date journals)
Fine Arts	Films, paintings, music, sculptures, as well as re-productions and synopses of these for research pur-poses	Evaluations in journal articles, critical reviews, biographies, and critical books about the authors and their works
Business	Market research and test-ing, technical studies and investigations, drawings, designs, models, memo-randums and letters, com-puter data	Discussion of the busi-ness world in news-papers, business mag-azines, journals, government documents, and books
Education	Pilot studies, term pro-jects, sampling results, tests and test data, sur-veys, interviews, observa-tions, statistics, and com-puter data	Analysis and evaluation of educational experi-mentation in journals, pamphlets, books, and reports

7c Reading All or Part of a Source

Confronted by several books and articles, many writers have trouble determining the value of material and the contribution it will make to the research paper. To save time, be selective in your reading. To serve your reader, cite material that is pertinent to the argument. To avoid the loss of your own voice, do not dump huge blocks of quotation into the paper.

Reading Key Parts of an Article

1. The **title**. Look for the words that have relevance to your topic before you start reading the article. For example, *Children and Parents* may look ideal for child abuse research until you read the subtitle: *Children and Parents: Growing Up in New Guinea.*
2. An **abstract**. Reading an abstract is the best way to ascertain if an essay or book will serve your specific needs. Abstracts are available at the beginning of most printed articles; others are provided by abstracting services (e.g., *Psychological Abstracts*).
3. The **opening paragraphs**. If the opening of an article shows no relevance to your study, abandon it.
4. Each **topic sentence** of paragraphs of the body. These first sentences, even hastily scanned, will give you a digest of the author's main points.
5. The **closing paragraphs**. If the opening of an article seems promising, skim the closing for relevance.
6. **Author credits.** Learn something about the credentials of the author. Magazine articles often provide brief biographical profiles of authors. Journal articles and Internet home pages generally include the author's academic affiliation and some credentials.

Read the entire article only if a quick survey encourages you to investigate further. One student photocopied a political article from the magazine *George*, highlighting key phrases and making marginal comments to fit his research on John F. Kennedy's legacy (see Figure 7.3 on the following pages; a portion of the article has been omitted). Note that he recognizes the bias that the author and the magazine bring into the article. This magazine, after all, was founded by Kennedy's son.

Reading the Key Parts of a Book

A **book** requires you to survey several additional items beyond those listed above for articles:

1. The **table of contents**. A book's table of contents may reveal chapters that pertain to your topic. Often, only one chapter is useful. For example, Richard Ellmann's *Oscar Wilde* has one chapter, "The Age of Dorian," devoted to Wilde's novel *The Picture of Dorian Gray*. If your research focuses on this novel, then the chapter, not the entire book, will demand your attention.

had held national air-raid drills in May. And while the 1950s are celebrated as a booming era, the U.S.–with an economy barely a quarter its current size–entered its fourth recession in seven years in 1960. Moreover, a tenth of its citizens remained in the chains of legal segregation.

Nevertheless, the nation shared a fundamental optimism and a faith in the commonwealth–and Kennedy tapped that feeling. It's hard to conceive how today's candidates might recapture the sense of public purpose Kennedy kindled. Al Gore fairly blares, "Go ahead, ask what your country will do for you," while George W. Bush's slogan might as well be, "Ask what you can do for yourself."

Comparison with Gore and Bush on the sense of "public purpose."

Americans feel the contrast between today's era and Kennedy's. In an exclusive national poll conducted for *George* by the Angus Reid Group, a New York-based opinion research firm, 42 percent of Americans associated "national pride" with the year 1960, but just 23 percent with 2000. Twice as many Americans associated "confidence in government" with 1960 as they did with 2000 (38 percent to 19 percent), and respondents also ranked 1960 high in "faith," "generosity," and "kindness." And while 56 percent of Americans associated "national prosperity" with 2000, compared to only 11 percent who chose 1960, 60 percent also associated "greed" with 2000, in contrast to 8 percent with 1960. The year 2000 also led in the categories of "laziness" and "self-indulgence."

Statistics show the differing attitudes of people in 1960 and in 2000.

So, although the nation faced staggering problems back then, it believed it saw them clearly–and when called to arms by a startlingly fresh leader, proved willing to tackle them. But it was not easy. Forty years ago this summer, in the same city in which the Democrats will nominate Al Gore, Jack Kennedy took command of his party and took his message to the nation after only a week of intense drama. . . .

▬ **FIGURE 7.3, continued**

2. The **book jacket**, if one is available. For example, the jacket to Richard Ellmann's *Oscar Wilde* says:

> Ellmann's *Oscar Wilde* has been almost twenty years in work, and it will stand, like his universally admired *James Joyce*, as the definitive life. The book's emotional resonance, its riches of authentic color and conversation, and the subtlety of its critical illuminations give daz-zling life to this portrait of the complex man, the charmer, the great playwright, the daring champion of the primacy of art.

Such information can stimulate the reading and note-taking from this important book.

3. The **foreword, preface** or **introduction**. An author's preface or intro-duction serves as a critical overview of the entire book, pinpointing the primary subject of the text and the particular approach of this author. For example, Ellmann opens the introduction to *Oscar Wilde* by saying:

> Oscar Wilde: we have only to hear the great name to anticipate that what will be quoted as his will surprise and delight us. Among the

writers identified with the 1890s, Wilde is the only one whom every-one still reads. The various labels that have been applied to the age—Aestheticism, Decadence, the Beardsley period—ought not to conceal that fact that our first association with it is Wilde, refulgent, majestic, ready to fall.

This introduction describes the nature of the book: Ellmann will portray Wilde as the dominating literary figure of the 1890s. A foreword is often written by somebody other than the author. It is often insightful and worthy of quotation.

4. The **index**. A book's index will list names and terminology with page numbers for all items mentioned within the text. For example, the index to *Oscar Wilde* lists about eighty items for *The Picture of Dorian Gray*, among them:

> homosexuality and, 312, 318
> literature and painting in, 312–3l
> magazine publication of, 312, 319, 320
> possible sources for, 311
> underlying legend of, 314–15
> W's Preface to, 311, 315, 322, 335
> W's self-image in, 312, 319
> writing of, 310–14

The index, by virtue of its detailed listing, has determined the relevance of the book to a student's research.

Reading the Key Parts of an Internet Article

The techniques listed for evaluating a periodical article (page 111) will apply also to an Internet article. In addition, examine:

1. The **home page** if there is one. Prefer sites sponsored by universities and professional organizations. Sometimes you may have to truncate the URL to find the home page where such information will be featured. For example, this URL:

> **www.theatlantic.com/unbound/wordpolice/three/**

can be truncated to **www.theatlantic.com/**, which is the magazine's home page.

2. The **hypertext links** to other sites. Their quality can be determined by the domain tag *edu, org, gov.* Be wary of sites that have the tag *com.*

For additional information, see Chapter 4, section 4d, pages 65–66, for guidelines on evaluating Internet sources.

Figure 7.4 displays a sponsored website with marginal notes to crucial information. Examine your Internet articles in like manner.

ISSUES IN SCIENCE AND TECHNOLOGY *online*

Spring 2000

Home

Issue Contents

Search

Back Issues

The Delicate Balance: Environment, Economics, Development

DAVID WESTERN

Conservation in a Human-Dominated World

Forging a tangible connection among environment, development, and welfare is a formidable challenge, given the complex global interactions and slow response times involved. The task is made all the harder by quickening change, including new ideas about conservation and how it can best be done. Present policies and practices, vested in government and rooted in a philosophy that regards humanity and nature as largely separate realms, do little to encourage public participation or to reinforce conservation through individual incentives and civil responsibility. The challenge will be to make conservation into a household want and duty. This will mean moving the focus of conservation away from central regulation and enforcement and toward greater emphasis on local collaboration based on fairness, opportunity, and responsibility. Given encouragement, such initiatives will help reduce extinction levels and the isolation of parks by expanding biodiversity conservation in human-dominated landscapes.

The problems that beset current conservation efforts are daunting. Three factors in particular threaten steady economic and social progress as well as conservation: poverty, lack of access rights linked to conservation responsibilities, and environmental deterioration. Poverty and lack of access rights, especially in Africa, will keep populations growing and will fuel Rwandan-like emigration and political unrest. With short-term survival as its creed, poverty accelerates environmental degradation and habitat fragmentation. The peasant lacking fuel and food will clear the forest to plant crops or will poach an elephant if there is no alternative. So, for example, tropical forests–home to half the world's species–are being lumbered, burned, grazed, and settled. Forest destruction precipitates local wrangles between indigenous and immigrant communities over land and squabbles between North and South over carbon sinks and global warming.

We cannot rely on the trickle-down effect of economic development and liberalism to eradicate poverty, solve access problems, or curb environmental losses–at least not soon. It was, after all, unfettered consumerism in the West that killed off countless animal species, stripped the forests, and polluted the air and water. And the same consumer behavior and commercial excesses are still evident, depleting old-growth forests and fighting pollution legislation every step of the way....

Western addresses the problems of effective conservation.

Instead of expecting the government to handle conservation, people must do it on their own as a civic responsibility.

Poverty must be controlled.

He says consumer behavior has destroyed the environment, and it's human behavior that must change.

FIGURE 7.4. Internet article from *Issues Online*.
Reprinted with permission of National Academy Press. A portion of this article has been omitted.

7d   **Responding to the Sources**

After you find source material relevant to your subject, you must respond in several ways:

1. Read the material.
2. As you read, write notes that record key ideas.
3. Outline the key ideas of an article.
4. Write notations on the margins of photocopied materials.
5. Write a rough summary.
6. Position the source to the best advantage

Selecting Key Ideas for Your Notes

In many instances you may borrow only one idea from a source that you can rephrase into your own words. The passage below shows a portion of a bulletin on air bag safety.

New Rules Proposed by NHTSA
to Reduce Dangers of Air Bags

The National Highway Traffic Safety Administration (NHTSA) is considering new rules to minimize the dangers of air bags to children and small adults, while preserving the lifesaving benefit of the devices.

Calling for a phase-in of smart air bag technology, the proposal also contains more immediate measures such as enhanced warning labels and a reduction in the deployment force of bags.

Smart Technology

"Smart" air bag technology will allow the deployment force of the bag to be determined by factors such as weight or position of the occupant. Development of the technology has been underway for some time, and Mercedes has already introduced a Seimen system which can detect the presence of a child safety seat in the front passenger position and disable the air bag.

Use this idea
in my paper!

Depowering

NHTSA will propose a reduction of between 20–35 percent of the deployment force of air bags until smart technology is in place. The agency believes this action will reduce the incidence of injury and improve performance of air bags for belted occupants including children, individuals with acute medical conditions and small-stature adults, while still providing significant protection for the unbelted occupants.

Options for Owners

NHTSA will also propose allowing dealers to deactivate the air bags of any vehicle owner who requests it, such as families who need to have children in the front seat for medical monitoring purposes, car pools with front-seated children, short-stature individuals who have reasonable concerns about a potential danger. . . .

Rather than copy the entire piece, the researcher read first, related the reading to her thesis and her own outline, and wrote this summary. She had found what she needed from the article.

From "New Rules" page 1

Technology is now being developed for the automatic disabling of an air bag when it detects a child or small adult in the seat.

Outlining the Key Ideas of a Source

You can frame your own outline to capture an author's primary themes; that is, list the main ideas and subtopics to show the hierarchy of issues, to identify parallel parts, and to locate supporting ideas. A quick outline of the "New Rules" article, above, might look like this:

New Rules for Air Bags
    Smart technology
        Detects position
        Detects weight
        Detects child safety seat
    Depowering the bags
        Reduce deployment power
        Make a 20–35 percent reduction
    Give options to owners
        Allow them to deactivate
            For children
            For medical monitoring
            For short people

Such an outline gives the researcher a clear overview of the issues.

Making Notations on Photocopied Materials

Avoid making marks on library books and magazines, but *do* make marginal notes in your own books and magazines or on photocopied materials or printouts. Underline sentences, circle key ideas, ask questions, and react with your own comments.

The passages on pages 117–18 show how students responded to sources.

Writing a Rough Summary

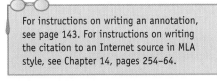

For more help with writing a summary, see section 9e, pages 141–42. To write a précis, which is a more polished form, see section 9f, pages 142–44.

A *summary* condenses into a brief note the general nature of a source. Writing one forces you to grasp the essence of the material. You might even use it in your paper. Note this example of a summary:

From "New Rules" page 1

NHTSA wants smart technology to detect small people in the seats, less power in the air bag, and more options for auto owners to deactivate their air bags.

7e Preparing an Annotated Bibliography

An *annotation* is a summary of the contents of a book or article. A *bibliography* is a list of sources on a selected topic. Thus, an annotated bibliography does two important things: (1) it gives a bibliographic list to all your sources, and (2) it summarizes the contents of each book or article. Writing an annotated bibliography may at first appear to be busywork, but it will help you to evaluate the strength of your sources.

For instructions on writing an annotation, see page 143. For instructions on writing the citation to an Internet source in MLA style, see Chapter 14, pages 254–64.

The annotated bibliography that follows gives a few Internet sources on the issue of school bus safety.

Ashley Barnette
English 1020
July 24, 2000

Annotated Bibliography

National Safety Council. "Child School Bus Rules" 6 Jan. 2000. 22
   July 2000 <http://www.nsc.org/lrs/lib/fs/home/schobus. htm>.
   For some 23 million students nationwide, the school day
   begins and ends with a trip on a school bus. Unfortunately,
   each year many youngsters are injured and several are killed
   in school bus incidents. This article surveys the rules.

United States Department of Transportation. National Highway
   Traffic Safety Administration. "Number of Persons That Can

Safely Sit on a School Bus Seat" 1 Apr. 2000. 22 July 2000 <http://www.nhtsa.dot.gov/people/injury/buses/ pub/numseat.hmp.html>. School bus manufacturers, not federal regulations, determine the maximum seating capacity of a school bus. This document contains NHTSA's recommendation that all passengers be seated entirely within the confines of the school bus seat while the bus is in motion.

–.–.–. "School Bus Safety: Safe Passage for America's   Children" 1 Apr. 2000. 22 July 2000 <http://www.nhtsa. dot.gov/people/injury/buses/schbus/schbus/schbussafe. html>. This publication provides a brief history of the national school bus safety program. Every year, 23.5 million children are transported to and from school and school related activities. Included are behavioral programs and vehicle regulations.

–.–.–. "Seat Belts on School Buses" 1 Apr. 2000. 11 Jan. 2001 <http://www.nhtsa.dot.gov/people/injury/buses/pub/ seatbelt.hmp.html>. This bulletin provides a brief discussion on why seat belts are not required to be on large school buses. A description of the occupant protection system required on school buses, "Compartmentalization," is included.

7f Preparing a Review of the Literature on a Topic

The review of literature presents a set of summaries in essay form for two purposes.

1. It helps you investigate the topic because it forces you to examine and then to show how each source addresses the problem. (*Note:* Do not simply list summaries of the sources without relating each source to your thesis.)
2. It organizes and classifies the sources in some reasonable manner for the benefit of the reader.

The brief review that follows classifies a few sources with respect to three aspects of the need for better school bus safety: the regulations, the risks, and the resolutions. With this analysis, the writer has brought the sources into harmony with the research project. Although only four Internet sources were used, the instructor could see that the project was moving in the right direction. Also, a brief review will usually find its way into the paper's introduction.

To write summaries of your key sources, see sections 9e and 9f, pages 141–44. To blend source material into your survey, see section 11a, pages 159–60. To write the bibliography entries, see Chapter 14, pages 224–76.

Ashley Barnette
English 1020
July 24, 2000

School Bus Safety

Many children are killed or injured each year due to accidents on school buses. Government agencies are addressing this issue with numerous Internet articles. One learns rather quickly that each tragedy might be avoided if the government, bus manufacturers, and local boards of education would take heed of the potential dangers and adopt some simple measures that could assure more safety. The National Safety Council (NSC) explains that "for some 23 million students nationwide, the school day begins and ends with a trip on a school bus" (NSC). Common sense warns us that children deserve the same precautions, if not more so, than what they get in the family car. This review examines a few government sources to identify three aspects of the problem: the regulations, the risks, and the resolutions.

The regulations need more strength even though the National Highway Traffic Safety Administration (NHTSA) states that school bus transportation is one of the safest forms of transportation in the United States. The bulletin "Seat Belts on School Buses" states:

> New school buses must meet safety requirements over and above those applying to other passenger vehicles. These include requirements for improved emergency exits, roof structure, seating and fuel systems, and bus body joint integrity.

While these requirements increase safety for most school bus riders, there is no requirement for something as simple as a seat belt.

The risks apply to children in harm's way. While bus specifications and construction requirements are strong measures to protect the nation's youth, it is actually the school bus manufacturers, not federal regulations, that determine the maximum seating capacity of a school bus ("Number"). Statistics from the NHTSA report, "Since 1984, on the average, 11 passengers per year have died in school bus crashes"

Three resolutions might serve the children. While no one can assure complete and total protection for all children riding school buses, simple measures can protect the young passengers. First, the NHTSA, which has openly said that there is "insufficient reason for a federal mandate for seat belts on large school buses" ("Seat Belts"), should consider the same standards we apply to cars. Next, standards could be established for no more than two students to occupy a 39-inch bus seat. According to one source, manufacturers generally "fit three smaller elementary school age persons" into a typical bus seat ("Number of Person"). Finally, bus monitors could supervise students within the bus and when students exit the bus to control pedestrian fatalities ("School Bus Safety"). Why do we provide crossing guards at intersections near schools, but we let children wander across dangerous highways to catch the bus?

In conclusion, one message should sound from every parent with a school-age child: we need stricter precautions for school bus safety. For the federal government and school bus manufacturers, meeting standards and keeping fatalities to a minimum are essential.

For the bibliography that would normally follow this review article, see the annotated bibliography above, pages 119-20.

YOUR RESEARCH PROJECT

1. Examine your working bibliography to test its validity against the grid on page 103. Do you have enough sources from the upper tier of scholarly works? If not, go in search of journal articles and scholarly books to beef up the list. Do not depend entirely upon Internet articles, even if every one is from a sponsored website.
2. Conduct a citation search (see pages 106-07 for details) on your topic, which will help you identify key people who have written on the subject several times and for different publications.
3. Examine the chart of primary and secondary sources on page 110. Look for your discipline—literature, government, history—and then determine if you are using a mix of primary and secondary sources.
4. Respond to one of your sources by writing two items: (1) a key idea written into one of your notes (see page 112), and (2) an annotated bibliography entry to the source (see pages 119-20).

8

Practicing Academic Integrity

Intellectual property has value just like the cash drawer at a local McDonald's. Yet words are not hard currency and they can't be confined to somebody's cash box. In fact, ideas and theories must be shared if they are to multiply and grow. What's more, federal law gives students limited rights to copy from sources. Nevertheless, the word *plagiarism* raises red flags and frightens some students to the point of stifling research. The purpose of this chapter is to make you comfortable with and knowledgeable about the ethics of research, especially about these matters:

- Using sources to establish your credibility.
- Using sources to place your work in its proper context.
- Honoring property rights.
- Avoiding plagiarism.
- Sharing credit and honoring it in collaborative projects.
- Honoring and crediting electronic sources.
- Seeking permission to publish material on your website.

8a Using Sources to Establish Your Credibility

Research writing is an exercise in critical thinking that reveals your ability to collect ideas and share them with the reader. You will explain not only the subject matter, *religious conservatives*, but also the *literature* of the topic found in articles from the Internet and current periodicals. By announcing clearly the name of a source, you reveal the scope of your reading on the subject and thus your credibility, as in this student's note:

Christianity and political activists

Commenting on the political activities of the Christian coalition within the Republican party, Steven V. Roberts makes this observation in <u>U.S. News and World Report</u>: "These incidents have triggered a backlash among establishment Republicans who fear that religious conservatives are pulling their party too far to the right and undermining their ability to win national elections"(43).

123

This sentence serves the reader, who can identify the political commentator of a national news magazine. It gives clear evidence of the writer's investigation into the subject. It enhances the student's image as a researcher.

8b   Placing the Source in Its Proper Context

Your sources will reflect all kinds of special interests, even biases, so you need to position them within your paper as reliable sources. If you must use a biased or questionable source, tell your reader up front. For example, if you are writing about the dangers of smoking cigarettes, you will find different opinions in a farmer's magazine, a health and fitness magazine, and a trade magazine sponsored by R. J. Reynolds. You owe it to your research and the reader to examine an article for:

- Special interests that might color the report.
- Lack of credentials.
- Unsponsored website.
- Opinionated speculation, especially that found in chat rooms.
- Trade magazines that promote special interests.
- Extremely liberal or extremely conservative positions.

Here's an example of how one student positioned a source for the reader. To see the source, look on pages 112–14.

> The magazine <u>George</u>, which was founded by John F. Kennedy's son, paints an alluring portrait of President Kennedy as a man who made citizens proud to be Americans, unlike candidates Al Gore and George W. Bush in the summer of 2000 (Keating 49–57). However, neither Gore nor Bush had arrived at the seat of power and therefore had no position of strength for their words and actions. It seems somewhat unfair to compare a legend of American politics with two fledgling candidates.

By positioning the material within the context of the report about former President Kennedy, the writer shows that one source, while interesting, has a somewhat biased position.

8c   Honoring Property Rights

If you invent a new piece of equipment or a child's toy, you can get a patent that protects your invention. You now own it. If you own a company, you can register a symbol that serves as a trademark for the products produced. You own the trademark. In like manner, if you write a set of poems and publish them in a chapbook, you own the poems. Others must seek your permission before they can reproduce the poems, just as others must buy your trademark or pay to produce your toy.

The principle behind the copyright law is relatively simple. Copyright begins at the time a creative work is recorded in some tangible form—a written document, a drawing, a tape recording. It does not depend upon a legal registration with the copyright office in Washington, D.C., although published works are usually registered. Thus, the moment you express yourself creatively on paper, in song, on a canvas, that expression is your intellectual property. You have a vested interest in any profits made from the distribution of the work. For that reason, song writers, cartoonists, fiction writers, and other artists guard their work and do not want it disseminated without compensation.

In scholarly work there is seldom compensation, but there is certainly the need for recognition. We do that by providing in-text citations and bibliography entries. As a student you may use copyrighted material in your research paper under a doctrine of *fair use* as described in the U.S. Code, which says:

> The fair use of a copyrighted work ... for purposes such as criticism, comment, news reporting, teaching (including multiple copies for classroom use), scholarship, or research is not an infringement of copyright.

Thus, as long as you borrow for educational purposes, such as a paper to be read by your instructor, you should not be concerned. Just give the source the proper recognition and documentation as explained next in section 8d. However, if you decide to *publish* your research paper on a website, then new considerations come into play (see 8g, "Seeking Permission to Publish Material on Your Website," pages 131–32).

8d Avoiding Plagiarism

First, develop personal note cards full of your own ideas on a topic. Discover how you feel about the issue. Then, rather than copy sources onto your pages of text, try to synthesize the ideas of the authorities with your own thoughts by using the précis and the paraphrase. Rethink and reconsider ideas gathered by your reading, make meaningful connections, and when you refer to a specific source—as you inevitably will—give it credit.

Fundamentally, plagiarism offers the words or ideas of another person as one's own. A major violation is the use of another student's work or the purchase of a "canned" research paper. Also flagrantly dishonest are writers who knowingly copy whole passages into their paper without documentation. But a gray area in plagiarism is a student's carelessness that results in an error. For example, the writer fails to enclose quoted material within quotation marks, yet he or she provides an in-text citation, or the writer's paraphrase never quite becomes paraphrase—too much of the original is left intact. In this area, instruction must step in and help the beginning researcher, for although these cases are not flagrant instances of plagiarism, these errors can mar an otherwise fine piece of research.

Admittedly, double standards exist. Magazine writers and newspaper reporters quote people constantly without documentation. But as an academic writer, you must document original ideas borrowed from source materials. Citations help establish your credibility because you've made it clear who you've read, and readers can see how your ideas came into being. Even

C H E C K L I S T

Documenting Your Sources

- Let a reader know when you begin borrowing from a source by introducing a quotation or paraphrase with the name of the authority.

- Enclose within quotation marks all quoted materials—a key word, a phrase, a sentence, a paragraph.

- Make certain that paraphrased material has been rewritten into your own style and language. The simple rearrangement of sentence patterns is unacceptable.

- Provide specific in-text documentation for each borrowed item, but keep in mind that styles differ for MLA, APA, CBE, and CMS standards.

- Provide a bibliography entry in the "Works Cited" for every source cited in the paper.

then, scholarly documentation differs from field to field; that is, literary papers are written in a different style from scientific papers. In the social sciences a paraphrase does not require a page number. In the applied sciences a number replaces the authority's name, the year, and even the page number. So you will find that standards shift considerably as you move from class to class and from discipline to discipline. The good writer learns to adapt to the changes in the academic standards. Thus, this book devotes separate chapters to MLA, APA, CBE, and CMS styles.

Common Knowledge Exceptions

Common knowledge exceptions exist because you and your reader will share the same perspectives on a subject. For example, if you attend Northern Illinois University, you need not cite the fact that Illinois is known as the "Land of Lincoln," that Chicago is its largest city, or that Springfield is the capital city. Information of this sort requires *no* in-text citation because your Illinois audience will be knowledgeable, as shown in the following example.

> The flat rolling hills of Illinois form part of the great Midwestern Corn Belt. It stretches from its border with Wisconsin in the north to the Kentucky border in the south. Its political center is Springfield in the center of the state, but its industrial and commercial center is Chicago, that great boisterous city camped on the shores of Lake Michigan.

However, a writer in another place and time might need to cite the source of this information. Most writers would probably want to document this next passage.

Early Indian tribes on the plains called themselves <u>Illiniwek</u> (which meant strong men), and French settlers pronounced the name <u>Illinois</u> (Angle 44).

Common knowledge is a matter of the situation. If a student writes about Langston Hughes as part of a classroom project on major poets of the Harlem Renaissance, the student will probably not need to cite the source for general information about the poet's love for Harlem and his pride in his African American heritage.

Here are two more examples:

President George Bush launched the Desert Storm attack against Iraq with the support of allies and their troops from several nations.

Bush demonstrated great mastery in his diplomatic unification of a politically diverse group of allies.

The first probably needs no documentation, but the farther we move in history from that time and place, the more likely will be the need for its documentation. The second could be the writer's thesis and be supported by other material, or it could be written within the context of a political science course that has been discussing these matters, making them common knowledge. Of course, if ideas or words have been taken directly from a source, show that evidence:

Bush demonstrated great mastery in his "diplomatic unification" of a "politically diverse group" of allies (Wolford 37).

Borrowing from a Source Correctly

The next examples in MLA style demonstrate the differences between accurate use of a source and the shades of plagiarism. First is the original reference material; it is followed by the student versions with discussions of their merits.

Original Material

Imagine your brain as a house filled with lights. Now imagine someone turning off the lights one by one. That's what Alzheimer's disease does. It turns off the lights so that the flow of ideas, emotions and memories from one room to the next slows and eventually ceases. And sadly—as anyone who has ever watched a parent, a sibling, a spouse succumb to the spreading darkness knows—there is no way to stop the lights from turning off, no way to switch them back on once they've grown dim. At least not yet.

But sooner than one might have dared hope, predicts Harvard University neurologist Dr. Dennis Selkoe, Alzheimer's disease will shed the veneer of invincibility that today makes it such a terrifying affliction. Medical practitioners, he believes, will shortly have on hand not one but several drugs capable of slowing—and perhaps even halting—the progression of the disease. Best of all, a better understanding of genetic and environmental risk factors will lead to much earlier diagnosis, so that patients will receive treatment long before their brains start to fade. From J. Madeleine Nash, "The New Science of Alzheimer's," *Time* 17 July 2000: 51.

C H E C K L I S T

Common Knowledge Exceptions

- Do not document the source if an informed person would and should know this information, given the context of both writer and audience.

- Do not document the source if you knew the information before reading it in an article or book, unless the wording is distinctive and worthy of quotation.

- Do not document encyclopedia-type information, such as birth date, place of birth, a parent's name, etc.

- Do not document information that has become general knowledge by being reported repeatedly in many different sources (i.e., Michael Jordan holds several NBA scoring records).

Student Version A (needs revision)

Alzheimer's disease is like having a brain that's similar to a house filled with lights, but somebody goes through the house and turns out the lights one by one until the brain, like the house, is dark.

This sentence sounds good, and the reader will probably think so also. However, the writer has borrowed the simile and much of the wording from the original source, so it's not the student's work. In addition, the writer has provided no documentation whatsoever, nor has the writer named the authority. In truth, the writer implies to the reader that these sentences are an original creation when, actually, nothing belongs to the writer.

Student Version B (needs revision)

Alzheimer's is a terrifying disease, for both victim and relatives. However, sooner than we might expect, medical scientists will have available several drugs capable of slowing—and perhaps even halting— the progress of the disease. In addition, earlier diagnosis will mean patients can receive treatment before their brains start to go dark.

This version borrows key words from the original without the use of quotation marks and without a citation. The next version provides a citation, but it too has errors.

Student Version C (needs minor revision)

Alzheimer's is a terrifying disease, but help is on the way. Dr. Dennis Selkoe, a neurologist at Harvard University, predicts that medical practitioners will shortly have on hand several drugs that will slow or stop the progression of the disease (Nash 51).

This version is better. It provides a reference to Dr. Selkoe, who has been cited by Nash. But readers cannot know that the paraphrase contains far too much of Nash's language—words that should be enclosed within quotation marks. Also, the citation to Nash is ambiguous. The next version handles these matters in a better fashion.

Student Version D (Acceptable)

> Alzheimer's is a terrifying disease, but help is on the way. In a recent report in <u>Time</u>, medical reporter Madeleine Nash cites Dr. Dennis Selkoe, a neurologist at Harvard University, who believes that "medical practitioners ... will shortly have on hand not one but several drugs capable of slowing—and perhaps even halting—the progression of the disease" (Nash 51).

This version represents a satisfactory handling of the source material. The writer is acknowledged at the outset of the borrowing, the neurologist is given credit for his ideas, and a key section has been quoted. A correct page citation closes the material. Let's suppose, however, that the writer does not wish to quote directly at all. The following example shows a paraphrased version:

Student Version E (Acceptable)

> Alzheimer's is a terrifying disease, but help is on the way. In a recent report in <u>Time</u>, medical reporter Madeleine Nash cites Dr. Dennis Selkoe, a neurologist at Harvard University, who believes that the scientific community is knocking on the door of a cure or maybe even a set of cures. The goal, according to Nash, is to halt the disease or at least slow its insidious stalking of some of our best and brightest, such as former president Ronald Reagan (Nash 51).

This version also represents a satisfactory handling of the source material. In this case, no direct quotation is employed, the author and the authority are acknowledged and credited, and the entire paragraph is paraphrased in the student's own language. Note: the reference to the former president is not mentioned in the original passage, but such usage is a prime example of "common knowledge" (see pages 126–27).

8e Sharing Credit in Collaborative Projects

Joint authorship is seldom a problem in collaborative writing, especially if each member of the project understands his or her role. Normally, all members of the team receive equal billing and credit. However, it might serve you well to predetermine certain issues with your peer group and the instructor:

- How will the project be judged and grades awarded?
- Will all members receive the same grade?
- Can a nonperformer be dismissed from the group?

- Should each member write a section of the work and everybody edit the whole?
- Should certain members write the draft and other members edit and load it onto a CD or onto the Web?
- Can the group work together via e-mail rather than meeting frequently for group sessions?

Resolving such issues at the beginning can go a long way toward eliminating entanglements and disagreements later on.

The matter of electronic publishing of your collaborative project on the Web raises other legal and ethical questions (see 8g, pages 131–32).

8f   Honoring and Crediting Sources in Online Classrooms

A rapidly growing trend in education is the Web-based course or online course via e-mail. In general, you should follow the fair use doctrine of printed

C H E C K L I S T

Required Instances for Citing a Source

1. An original idea derived from a source, whether quoted or paraphrased. This next sentence requires an in-text citation and quotation marks around a key phrase.

   > Genetic engineering, by which a child's body shape and intellectual ability is predetermined, raises for one source "memories of Nazi attempts in eugenics" (Riddell 19).

2. Your summary of original ideas by a source.

   > Genetic engineering has been described as the rearrangement of the genetic structure in animals or in plants, which is a technique that takes a section of DNA and reattaches it to another section (Rosenthal 19–20).

3. Factual information that is not common knowledge within the context of the course.

   > Genetic engineering has its risks: a nonpathogenic organism might be converted into a pathogenic one or an undesirable trait might develop as a result of a mistake (Madigan 51).

4. Any exact wording copied from a source.

   > Kenneth Woodward asserts that genetic engineering is "a high stakes moral rumble that involves billions of dollars and affects the future" (68).

sources (see page 125), that is, give proper credit and reproduce only limited portions of the original.

The rules are still emerging, and even faculty members are often in a quandary about how to transmit information back and forth. For educational purposes, the rules are pretty slack, and most publishers have made their texts or portions thereof available on the Web. Plus, the copyrights of many works have expired and are therefore free. In addition, many magazines and newspapers have made their online versions of articles available for free.

What you send back and forth with classmates and the instructor has little privacy and even less protection. Rules are gradually emerging for electronic communication. In the meantime, abide by a few common-sense principles:

> Chapters 14–17 provide the bibliography forms in the styles required by MLA, APA, CBE, and CMS. To find examples, see "Bibliography, Internet sources" in the index of this book.

1. Credit sources in your online communications just as you would in a printed research paper, with some variations (see pages 254–64).

   The author, creator, or maintainer of the site
   The title of the electronic article
   The title of the website
   The date of publication on the Web
   The date you accessed the site
   The address (URL)

2. Download images and text into your files only from sites that have specifically granted permission to users.

3. Non-free graphic images and text, especially an entire website, should be mentioned in your text, even paraphrased and quoted in a limited manner, but not downloaded into your file. Instead, link to them or point to them with URL addresses. In that way, your reader can go find the material and count it as a supplement to your text.

4. Seek permission if you download substantive blocks of material. See 8g below if you wish to publish your work on the Web.

5. If in doubt, consult by e-mail with your instructor, the moderator of a listserv, or the author of an Internet site.

8g Seeking Permission to Publish Material on Your Website

If you have your own home page and website, you might wish to publish your papers on the Web. However, the moment you do so, you are *publishing* the work and putting it into the public domain. That act carries responsibilities. In particular, the *fair use* doctrine of the U.S. Code refers to the personal educational purposes of your usage. When you load onto the Internet borrowed images, text, music, or artwork, you are making that intellectual property available to everybody all over the world.

A short quotation to support your argument is probably a fair use. Permission will not be needed; however, seek permission if the amount you borrow is substantial. The borrowing cannot affect the market for the original work, and you cannot misrepresent it in any way. The courts are still refining the law. For example, would your use of three Doonsbury comic strips be substantial? Yes, if you reproduce them in full. Would it affect the market for the comic strip? Perhaps. Follow these guidelines:

> For information on the Fair Use Laws, visit the website to accompany this book at www.ablongman.com/lester.

- Seek permission for copyrighted material that you publish within your Web article. Most authors will grant you free permission. The problem is tracking down the copyright holder.
- If you make the attempt to get permission and if your motive for using the material is *not for profit*, it's unlikely you will have any problem with the copyright owner. The owner would have to prove that your use of the image or text caused the owner financial harm.
- You may publish without permission works that are in the public domain, such as a section of Hawthorne's *The Scarlet Letter* or a speech by the President from the White House.
- Document any and all sources that you feature on your website.
- If you provide hypertext links to other sites, you may need permission to do so. Some sites do not want their address clogged by inquiring students. However, right now the Internet rules on access are being freely interpreted.
- Be prepared for other persons to visit your website and even borrow from it. Decide beforehand how you will handle requests for use of your work, especially if it includes your creative efforts in poetry, art, music, or graphic design.

YOUR RESEARCH PROJECT

1. Conduct an examination of your borrowing from the sources. Have you used direct quotation to reflect the voice of an expert on the subject? Have you used paraphrase to maintain your voice? Double-check every paraphrase to be certain that you have not borrowed the exact wording of the original.
2. Examine your college bulletin and the student handbook. Do they say anything about plagiarism? Do they address the matter of copyright protection?
3. Make an appointment with your writing instructor to review your work to this point. Query the instructor about any problems you face.
4. If you think you might publish your paper on the Web, begin now to seek permission from the authors or copyright holders. In your letter or e-mail, give your name, school, the subject of your research paper, the material you want to borrow, and how you will use it. You might copy or attach the page of your paper in which the material appears.

9

Writing Notes

The primary reason for any scholarly research is to announce and publicize new findings. A botanist explains the discovery of a new strain of ferns in Kentucky's Land between the Lakes. A medical scientist reports the results of cancer research. A sociologist announces the results of a two-year pilot study of Native Americans in the Appalachian region.

Similarly, you will be asked to explain your findings from a geology field trip, disclose research on animal imagery in Robert Frost's poetry, or discuss the results of an investigation into overcrowding of school classrooms. The accurate notes from your personal research will join with your carefully paraphrased notes from experts on the topic to form the support for your thesis. Your goal is to share verifiable information, but others can verify your work only if good records are kept and reported.

Keeping accurate records and writing notes of high quality are essential steps in the research process. As you write, you will depend heavily on the notes. In like manner, your reader will rely on the precision of your information. For example, the inventor Thomas Edison built upon documented research by others. How fortunate he was that his predecessors recorded their experiments and kept good notes.

Thus, note-taking is the heart of research. A few notes of high quality may fill some appropriate places in your first draft. Prepare yourself to write different types of notes—quotations for well-phrased passages by authorities but also paraphrased or summarized notes to maintain your voice. This chapter explains the following types of notes:

Personal notes (9b) that express your own ideas and theories.

Quotation notes (9c) that preserve any distinguished syntax of an authority.

Paraphrase notes (9d) that interpret and restate what the authority has said.

Summary notes (9e) that distill factual data that has marginal value; you can return to the source later if necessary.

Précis notes (9f) that capture the essence of one writer's ideas in capsule form.

Field notes (9g) that record interviews, questionnaire tabulations, laboratory experiments, and other types of field research.

HINT: The Internet offers many articles that you can print or download to a file. Treat these as you would a printed source; that is, develop notes from them that you can transfer into your draft. If you download an article to your files, you can mark passages and transfer them quickly into your notes or draft. See pages 66–69.

9a Creating Effective Notes

Whether you write notes on a computer or by hand, you should keep in mind some basic rules, summarized in the checklist at the bottom of this page.

Honoring the Conventions of Research Style

Your note-taking will be more effective from the start if you practice the conventions of style for citing a source, as advocated by the Modern Language Association (MLA), American Psychological Association (APA), Chicago Manual of Style (CMS), or Council of Biology Editors (CBE) and as shown briefly below and explained later in this book.

MLA: Lawrence Smith states, "The suicidal teen causes severe damage to the psychological condition of peers" (34).

APA: Smith (1997) has commented, "The suicidal teen causes severe damage to the psychological condition of peers" (p. 34).

CMS footnote: Lawrence Smith states, "The suicidal teen causes severe damage to the psychological condition of peers."[3]

CBE number: Smith (4) has commented, "The suicidal teen causes severe damage to the psychological condition of peers."

C H E C K L I S T

Writing Effective Notes

1. Write one item per note to facilitate the shuffling and rearranging of the data as you organize your paper during all stages of organization. Several notes can be kept in a computer file if each is labeled clearly.

2. List the source with name, year, and page for in-text citations.

3. Label each note (for example, "objectivity on television").

4. Write a full note in well-developed sentences.

5. Keep everything (photocopies, scribbled notes) in order to authenticate dates, page numbers, or full names.

6. Label your personal notes with "my idea" or "personal note" to distinguish them from the sources.

Identifying sources, 159–60   Darrel Abel in his third volume of <u>American</u>   Underscoring, A-29–A-30

<u>Literature</u> narrates the hardships of the Samuel Clemens

family in Hannibal, yet Abel asserts that "despite such

Using lower case after that, 174   hardships and domestic grief, which included the deaths

of a brother and sister, young Sam Clemens [Mark Twain]   Interpolations, 177–78

had a happy and reasonably carefree boyhood" (11–12).   Page citations, 160

Single quotation marks 170–71   Abel acknowledges the value of Clemens's "rambling

reminiscences dictated as an 'Autobiography' in his old

Punctuation with quotations, 168–71   age" (12). Of those days Clemens says, "In the small   Ellipses points, 174–77

town . . . <u>everybody</u> [my underlining] was poor, but didn't

know it; and everybody was comfortable, and did know it"

Signaling your underscoring of another's words, 177–78

(qtd. in Abel 12). Clemens felt at home in Hannibal with

One source quotes another, 164–65   everybody at the same level of poverty.

FIGURE 9.1. Conventions of style for writing notes.

Figure 9.1 provides another sample of MLA style with sidebars to direct you to detailed instructions.

Using a Computer for Note-Taking

The computer affects note-taking strategies in several ways:

1. You can enter your notes into the word processor using one of two methods:
   a. Write each note as a separate file in a common directory so that each can be moved later into the appropriate section of your draft by the copy and paste commands.
   b. Write all notes in a single file. Begin each new note with a code word or phrase. Begin writing your paper at the top of the file, which will push the notes down as you write. As necessary, search out specific notes. In other situations you might employ a split screen, or use two windows with your draft in one and your notes in the other.

Note: It might be wise to keep a copy of the original files in case anything gets lost or is deleted while you are arranging materials.

2. You can record the bibliography information for each source you encounter by listing it in a BIBLIO file so that you build the necessary list of references in one alphabetical file. Chapters 14, 15, 16, and 17 give you the correct forms.

> **HINT:** Note-taking programs such as *Take Note!* and bibliography organizers such as *Endnote* can serve you well in this stage of developing your paper. Later, formatting software such as *StyleEase* can help you format the paper as you write it.

Developing Handwritten Notes

Handwritten notes should conform to these additional conventions:

- Write in ink because penciled notes become blurred after repeated shuffling of the cards.
- Use index cards in two sizes, one for notes and one for bibliography entries. This practice keeps the two separate.
- Write on one side of a card because information written on the back may be overlooked. Use the back side, if at all, for personal notes and observations, but mark the front with "OVER."
- Staple together two or more cards that form one note.

9b   Writing Personal Notes

The content of a research paper is not a collection of ideas transmitted by experts in books and articles; it is an expression of your own ideas as supported by the scholarly evidence. Readers are primarily interested in *your* thesis sentence, *your* topic sentences, and *your* personal view of the issues. Therefore, during your research, record your thoughts on the issues by writing plenty of personal notes in your research journal, in your computer files, or on cards. Personal notes are essential because they allow you to:

- Record your discoveries.
- Reflect on the findings.
- Make connections.
- Explore another point of view.
- Identify prevailing views and patterns of thought.

Personal notes should conform to these three standards:

1. The idea on the note is yours.
2. The note is labeled with "my idea," "mine," "personal thought" so that later you can be certain that it has not been borrowed.

3. The note is a rough summary, a sketch of ideas, or preferably, a complete sentence or two.

A sample of a personal note follows:

> Personal thought
> ───────────
> For me, organ donation might be the gift of life, so I have signed my donor card. At least a part of me will continue to live if an accident claims my life. My boyfriend thinks I'm gruesome, but I consider it practical. Besides, he might be the one who benefits, and then what will he say?

9c Writing Direct Quotation Notes

Copying the words of another person is the easiest type of note to write. Quotation notes are essential because they allow you to:

- Capture the authoritative voices of the experts on the topic.
- Feature essential statements.
- Prove that you have researched the subject carefully.
- Offer conflicting points of view.
- Show the dialogue that exists about the topic.

In the process, you will need to follow basic conventions:

1. Select quoted material that is important and well-phrased, not something trivial or something that is common knowledge. NOT "John F. Kennedy was a Democrat from Massachusetts" (Rupert 233) BUT "John F. Kennedy's Peace Corps left a legacy of lasting compassion for the down-trodden" (Rupert 233).

2. Use quotation marks. Do not copy the words of a source into your paper in such a way that readers will think that *you* wrote the material.

3. Use the exact words of the source.

4. Provide an in-text citation to author and page number, like this (Henson 34–35), or give the author's name at the beginning of the quotation and put the page number after the quotation, like this:

> Barnill says, "More than 400 people each month receive the gift of sight through yet another type of tissue donation—corneal transplants. In many cases, donors unsuitable for organ donation are eligible for tissue donation" (2).

5. The in-text citation goes *outside* the final quotation mark but *inside* the period.

6. Try to quote key sentences and short passages, not entire paragraphs. Find the essential statement and feature it; do not force your reader to fumble through a long quoted passage in search of the relevant statement. Make the brief quotation a part of your sentence, in this way:

> Many Americans, trying to mend their past eating habits, adopt functional foods as an essential step toward a more health-conscious future. This group of believers spends "an estimated $29 billion a year" on functional foods (Nelson 755).

7. Quote from both primary sources (the original words by a writer or speaker) and secondary sources (the comments after the fact about original works). The two types are discussed immediately below.

Quoting Primary Sources

Quote from primary sources for four specific reasons:

1. To draw on the wisdom of the original author
2. To let readers hear the precise words of the author
3. To copy exact lines of poetry and drama
4. To reproduce graphs, charts, and statistical data

Cite poetry, fiction, drama, letters, and interviews. In other cases, you may want to quote liberally from a presidential speech, cite the words of a business person, or reproduce original data. As shown in the next example, quote exactly, retain spacing and margins, and spell words as in the original.

For a chart of primary and secondary sources, see 7b, "Selecting a Mix of Primary and Secondary Sources," pages 109–10.

> Images of frustration in Eliot's "Prufrock," 5
>
> ---------------
>
> "For I have known them all already,
>   known them all:—
> Have known the evenings, mornings,
>   afternoons,
> I have measured out my life with
>   coffee spoons;
> I know the voices dying with a
>   dying fall
> Beneath the music of a farther room.
>   So how should I presume?"

Quoting Secondary Sources

Quote from secondary sources for three specific reasons:

1. To display excellence in ideas and expression by experts on the topic.
2. To explain complex material.

3. To set up a statement of your own, especially if it spins off, adds to, or takes exception to the source as quoted.

The overuse of direct quotation from secondary sources indicates either (1) that you did not have a clear focus and copied verbatim just about everything related to the subject, or (2) that you had inadequate evidence and used numerous quotations as padding. Therefore, limit quotations from secondary sources by using only a phrase or a sentence, as shown here:

> The geographical changes in Russia require "intensive political analysis" (Herman 611).

If you quote an entire sentence, make the quotation a direct object. It tells *what* the authority says. Headings on your notes will help you arrange them.

> Geographic changes in Russia
>
> ---------------
>
> In response to the changes in Russia, one critic notes, "The American government must exercise caution and conduct intensive political analysis" (Herman 611).

Blend two or more quotations from different sources to build strong paragraphs, as shown here:

> Functional foods are helping fight an economic battle against rising health care costs. Clare Hasler notes, "The U.S. population is getting older," which means more people are being diagnosed and treated for disease (68). These individuals are putting a huge financial strain on the health care system with their need for expensive antibiotics and hospital procedures. Dr. Herbert Pierson, director of the National Cancer Institute's $20 million functional food program, states, "The future is prevention, and looking for preventive agents in foods is more cost effective than looking for new drugs" (qtd. in Carper xxii).

For additional examples of handling quoted materials, see Chapter 11, pages 159–79.

9d Writing Paraphrased Notes

A paraphrase is the most difficult note to write. It requires you to restate in your own words the thought, meaning, and attitude of someone else. With *interpretation* you act as a bridge between the source and the reader as you capture the wisdom of the source in approximately the same number of words. Use paraphrase for these reasons:

- To maintain your voice in the text of the paper.

- To sustain your style.
- To avoid an endless string of direct quotations.
- To interpret the sources as you rewrite them.

Keep in mind these five rules for paraphrasing a source:

1. Rewrite the original in about the same number of words.
2. Provide an in-text citation to the source (the author and page number in MLA style).
3. Retain exceptional words and phrases from the original by enclosing them within quotation marks.
4. Preserve the tone of the original by suggesting moods of satire, anger, humor, doubt, and so on. Show the author's attitude with appropriate verbs: "Edward Zigler condemns . . . defends . . . argues . . . explains . . . observes . . . defines."
5. Put the original aside while paraphrasing to avoid copying word for word. Compare the finished paraphrase with the original source to be certain that the paraphrase truly rewrites the original and that it uses quotation marks with any phrasing or key words retained from the original.

> **HINT:** When instructors see an in-text citation but no quotations marks, they will assume that you are paraphrasing, not quoting. Be sure that their assumption is true.

Here are examples that show the differences between a quotation note and a paraphrased one.

Quotation

Heredity   Hein 294

Fred Hein explains, "Except for identical twins, each person's heredity is unique" (294).

Paraphrase

Heredity   Hein 294

Fred Hein explains that heredity is special and distinct for each of us, unless a person is one of identical twins (294).

Quotation (more than four lines)

Heredity   Hein 294

Fred Hein clarifies the phenomenon:

Since only half of each parent's chromosomes are

transmitted to a child and since this half represents a

chance selection of those the child could inherit, only twins that develop from a single fertilized egg that splits in two have identical chromosomes. (294)

As shown above, MLA style requires a 10-space indention.

Paraphrase

Heredity   Hein 294

- - - - - - - - - - - - - -

Hein specifies that twins have identical chromosomes because they grow from one egg that divides after it has been fertilized. He affirms that most brothers and sisters differ because of the "chance selection" of chromosomes transmitted by each parent (294).

As shown in the example above, place any key wording of the source within quotation marks.

9e   Writing Summary Notes

You may write two types of summary notes: a quick sketch of material, as discussed here, and the more carefully drawn *précis*, as explained in 9f.

The *summary note* describes and rewrites the source material without great concern for style or expression. Your purpose at the moment will be quick, concise writing without careful wording. If its information is needed, you can rewrite it later in a clear, appropriate prose style and, if necessary, return to the source for revision. Use summary notes for these reasons:

- To record material that has marginal value.
- To preserve statistics that have questionable value for your study.
- To note an interesting position of a source speaking on a closely related subject but not on your specific topic.
- To reference several works that address the same issue, as shown in this example:

The logistics and cost of implementing a recycling program has been examined in books by West and Loveless and in articles by Jones et al., Coffee and Street, and Abernathy.

Success with the summary requires the following:

1. Keep it short. It has marginal value, so don't waste time on fine tuning it.
2. Mark with quotation marks any key phrasing that you cannot paraphrase.
3. Provide documentation to the author and page number. However, a page number is unnecessary when the note summarizes the entire article or book, not a specific passage.

TV & reality   Epstein's book

Now dated but cited by various sources, the 1973 book by Epstein
seems to lay the groundwork for criticism in case after case of
distorted news broadcasts.

This sort of summary might find its way into the final draft, as shown here:

Television viewers, engulfed in the world of communication,
participate in the construction of symbolic reality by their
perception of and belief in the presentation. Edward Jay Epstein laid
the groundwork for such investigation in 1973 by showing in case
after case how the networks distorted the news and did not, perhaps
could not, represent reality.

9f Writing Précis Notes

A précis note differs from the quick summary note. It serves a specific
purpose, so it deserves a polished style for transfer into the paper. It requires
you to capture in just a few words the ideas of an entire paragraph, section,
or chapter. Use the précis for these reasons:

- To review an article or book.
- To annotate a bibliography entry.
- To provide a plot summary.
- To create an abstract.

Success with the précis requires the following:

1. Condense the original with precision and directness. Reduce a long paragraph into a sentence, tighten an article into a brief paragraph, and summarize a book into a page.
2. Preserve the tone of the original. If the original is serious, suggest that
   tone in the précis. In the same way, retain moods of doubt, skepticism,
   optimism, and so forth.
3. Write the précis in your own language. However, retain exceptional
   phrases from the original, enclosing them in quotation marks. Guard
   against taking material out of context.
4. Provide documentation.

Use the Précis to Review Briefly an Article or Book

Note this example of the short review:

On the "Donor Initiative" 1999 website

The National Community of Organ and Tissue Sharing has a website
devoted to its initiatives. Its goal is to communicate the problem; for

example, more than 55,000 people are on the waiting lists. It seeks a greater participation from the public.

For help in preparing a review of literature—brief descriptions of the contents of various articles and books—see pages 120–22.

With three sentences, the writer has made a précis of the entire article.

Use the Précis to Write an Annotated Bibliography

An annotation is a sentence or paragraph that offers explanatory or critical commentary on an article or book. It seldom extends beyond two or three sentences. The difficulty of this task is to capture the main idea of the source.

"Top Ten Myths about Donation and Transplantation." (N.d.). October 10, 2000 http://www.transweb.org/myths/ myths.htm. This site dispels the many myths surrounding organ donation, showing that selling organs is illegal, that matching donor and recipient is highly complicated, and secret back room operations are almost impossible.

For additional examples, see also "Preparing an Annotated Bibliography," pages 119–20.

Use the Précis in a Plot Summary Note

In just a few sentences a précis summarizes a novel, short story, drama, or similar literary work, as shown by this next note:

Great Expectations by Dickens describes young Pip, who inherits money and can live the life of a gentleman. But he discovers that his "great expectations" have come from a criminal. With that knowledge his attitude changes from one of vanity to one of compassion.

Furnish a plot summary in your paper as a courtesy to your readers to cue them about the contents of a work. The précis helps you avoid a full-blown retelling of the plot.

Use the Précis as the Form for an Abstract

An abstract is a brief description that appears at the beginning of an article to summarize the contents. It is, in truth, a précis. Usually, it is written by the article's author, and it helps readers make decisions about reading or skipping the article. You can find entire volumes devoted to

See also page 300 for a student example of an abstract in APA style.

abstracts, such as *Psychological Abstracts* or *Abstracts of English Studies*. An abstract is required for most papers in the social and natural sciences. Here's a sample from Katie Hebert's paper.

Abstract

The functional food revolution has begun! Functional foods, products that provide benefits beyond basic nutrition, are adding billions to the nation's economy each year. So what is their secret? Why are functional foods a hit? Functional foods are suspected to be a form of preventive medicine. This news has made the public swarm and food nutritionists salivate. Consumers hope that functional foods can calm some of their medical anxieties. Many researchers believe that functional foods may be the answer to the nation's prayers for lower health care costs. This paper goes behind the scenes, behind all the hype, in its attempt to determine if functional foods are an effective form of preventive medicine. The paper identifies several functional foods, locates the components that make them work, and explains the role that each plays on the body.

9g Writing Notes from Field Research

You will be expected to conduct field research in some instances. This work will require different kinds of notes kept on charts, cards, note pads, laboratory notebooks, a research journal, or the computer.

If you **interview** knowledgeable people, make careful notes during the interview and transcribe those notes to your draft in a polished form. A tape recorder can serve as a backup to your note-taking.

If you conduct a **questionnaire**, the results will become valuable data for developing notes and graphs and charts for your research paper.

See pages 83–85 for a full discussion of the four parts to a report of empirical research.

If you conduct **experiments, tests, and measurements,** the findings serve as your notes for the "results" section of the report and will give you the basis for the "discussion" section.

YOUR RESEARCH PROJECT

1. Look carefully at each of the sources you have collected so far—sections of books, journal articles, Internet printouts. Try writing a summary or précis of each one. At the same time, make decisions about material worthy of direct quotation and material that you wish to paraphrase or summarize.
2. Decide how you will keep your notes—in a research journal, on handwritten note cards, or in computer files. Note: the computer files will

serve you well because you can transfer them into your text and save typing time.

3. Write various types of notes, that is, write a few that use direct quotations, some that paraphrase, and some that summarize.

4. Conscientiously and with dedication, write as many personal notes as possible. These will be your ideas, and they will establish your voice and position. That is, don't let the sources speak for you; let them support your position.

5. If you have access to *Take Note!* or some other note-taking program, take the time to consider its special features. You can create notes, store them in folders, and even search your own files by key word, category, and reference.

10

Drafting the Paper in an Academic Style

As you draft, your voice should flow from one idea to the next smoothly and logically. You should adopt an academic style, understanding that such a style requires precision but not necessarily long, polysyllabic words that you pull from a thesaurus. Therefore, treat the initial draft as exploratory, one that searches for the exact word, not just a long word. Every discipline has its own specialized words, and part of this exercise is for you to find them and use them effectively. This matter is discussed in more detail on pages 154–55.

Try to present a fair, balanced treatment of the subject. Do not load the paper with favorable citations at the expense of contradictory evidence. In fact, mentioning opposing viewpoints early in a report gives you something to work against and may strengthen the conclusion. Also, the claims made should be supportable. The writer who might say, "Robert Frost exhibits a death wish in many of his poems," must be ready to cite both from the poems and from well-researched biographical data.

A research paper may examine a subject in depth but it also examines your knowledge and the strength of your evidence. You may need to retrace previous steps—reading, researching, and note-taking. Ask your instructor to examine the draft, not so much for line editing but for the big picture, to see if you have met the assignment and not oversimplified the issues.

Be practical

- Write what you know and feel, not what you think somebody wants to hear.
- Pause now and then to rethink the direction of the research project.
- Write portions of the paper when you are ready, not only when you arrive there by outline sequence.
- If necessary, leave blank spots on the page to remind you that more evidence will be required.
- Skip entire sections if you are ready to develop later paragraphs.

Be uninhibited

- Initial drafts must be attempts to get words on the page rather than to create a polished document.
- Write without fear or delay.

Be conscientious about references

- Cite the names of the sources in your text.
- Enclose quotations in your text.
- Supply page numbers to the sources.

Your early draft is a time for discovery. Later, during the revision period, you can strengthen skimpy paragraphs, refine your prose, and rearrange material to maintain the momentum of your argument. Revision techniques are examined in Chapter 13, pages 195–223.

Begin with these tasks:

1. Focus your argument (10a).
2. Refine your thesis sentence (10b).
3. Write a title that identifies your key terms (10c).
4. Begin writing from your notes and outline (10d).

10a Focusing Your Argument

Your writing style in a research paper needs to be factual, but it should also reflect your "take" on the topic. Drafting the paper will happen more quickly if you have focused on the central issue(s). Each paragraph will then amplify upon your primary claim. Your aim or purpose is the key to discovering an argument. Do you wish to persuade, inquire, or negotiate?

Persuasion means that you wish to convince the reader that your position is valid and, perhaps, to ask the reader to take action. For example:

> We need to establish green zones in every city of this country to control urban sprawl and to protect a segment of the natural habitat for the animals.

Inquiry is an exploratory approach to a problem in which you examine the issues without the insistence of persuasion. It is a truth-seeking adventure. For example:

> Many suburban home dwellers complain that deer, raccoons, and other wild animals ravage their gardens, flowerbeds, and garbage cans; however, the animals were there first. Thus, we may need a task force to examine the rights of each side of this conflict.

Negotiation is a search for a solution. It means that you attempt to resolve a conflict by inventing options or a mediated solution. For example:

Suburban neighbors need to find ways to embrace the wild animals that have been displaced rather than voice anger at the animals or the county government. Perhaps green zones and wilderness trails would solve some of the problems; however, such a solution would require serious negotiations with real estate developers who want to use every square foot of every development.

Often, the instructor's research assignment will tell you whether you want to persuade, inquire, or negotiate. But if it doesn't, try to determine early in the process where your research is heading.

> For additional discussion of persuasive techniques, see 1c, pages 3–8.

Maintaining a Focus on Objective Facts and Subjective Ideas

As an objective writer, you will need to examine the problem, make your claim in a thesis statement, and provide supporting evidence. As a subjective writer, you will want to argue with a touch of passion; you must believe in your position on the issues. For this reason, complete objectivity is unlikely for any research paper which puts forth an intellectual argument in the thesis statement (see again pages 29–31). Of course, you must avoid being overly subjective, as by demanding, insisting, and quibbling. Moderation of your voice, even during argument, suggests control of the situation, both emotionally and intellectually.

Your objective and subjective analysis alerts the audience to your point of view in two ways:

Ethical appeal. If you project the image of one who knows and cares about the topic, the reader will recognize and respect your deep interest in the subject and your carefully crafted argument. The reader will also appreciate your attention to research conventions.

Logical appeal. For readers to believe in your position, you must provide sufficient evidence in the form of statistics, paraphrases, and direct quotations from authorities on the subject.

For example, in an examination of *humanitarian aid to foreign countries*, a writer might remain objective by presenting evidence and statistics. Even so, the ethical problem remains close to the surface: People need assistance regardless of the crisis.

10b   Refining the Thesis Sentence

A thesis statement expresses a theory that you hope to support with your evidence and arguments. It is a proposition that you want to maintain, analyze, and prove. It will perform three tasks:

1. Set the argument to control and focus the entire paper.

2. Provide unity and a sense of direction.

3. Specify to the reader the point of the research.

For example, one student started with the topic "exorbitant tuition." He narrowed his work to "tuition fees put parents in debt." Ultimately, he crafted this thesis:

> The exorbitant tuition at America's colleges is forcing out the poor and promoting an elitist class.

Without the focus on the fees and enrollment, the student might have drifted into other areas, confusing himself and his readers.

Using Questions to Focus the Thesis

If you have trouble focusing on a thesis sentence, ask yourself a few questions. One of the answers might serve as the thesis.

- What is the point of my research?

THESIS: A delicate balance of medicine, diet, and exercise can control diabetes mellitus to offer a comfortable life style for millions.

- What do I want this paper to do?

THESIS: The public needs to understand that advertisers who use blatant sexual images have little regard for moral scruples and ordinary decency.

- Can I tell the reader anything new or different?

THESIS: The evidence indicates clearly that most well water in the county is unsafe for drinking.

- Do I have a solution to the problem?

THESIS: Public support for "safe" houses will provide a haven for wives who are abused by their husbands.

- Do I have a new slant and new approach to the issue?

THESIS: Personal economics is a force to be reckoned with, so poverty, not greed, forces many youngsters into a life of crime.

- Should I take the minority view of this matter?

THESIS: Give credit where it is due: Custer may have lost the battle at Little Bighorn, but Crazy Horse and his men, with inspiration from Sitting Bull, won the battle.

- What exactly is my theory about this subject?

THESIS: Because they have certain medicinal powers, functional foods can become an economic weapon in the battle against rising health care costs.

- Will an enthymeme serve my purpose by making a claim in a *because* clause?

THESIS: Sufficient organ and tissue donation, enough to satisfy the demand, remains almost impossible because negative myths and religious concerns dominate the minds of many people.

These sample thesis statements each use declarative sentences that focus the argument toward an investigative issue that will be resolved in the paper's general discussion and conclusion.

For additional commentary on writing the thesis sentence, see pages 29–31 and 91–92.

Using Key Words to Focus the Thesis

Use the important words from your notes and rough outline to refine your thesis sentence. For example, during your reading of several novels or short stories by Flannery O'Connor, you might have jotted down certain repetitions of image, theme, or character. The key words might be *tragic endings, ironic moments of humor, hysteria and passion, human shortcomings,* or other issues that O'Connor explored time and again. These concrete ideas might point you toward a general thesis:

The tragic endings of Flannery O'Connor's stories depict desperate people coming face to face with their own shortcomings.

C H E C K L I S T

Writing the Final Thesis

You should be able to answer "yes" to each question that follows. Does the thesis:

1. Express your position in a full, declarative statement which is not a question, not a statement of purpose, and not merely a topic?
2. Limit the subject to a narrow focus that grows out of research?
3. Establish an investigative, inventive edge to the discovery, interpretation, or theoretical presentation?
4. Point forward to the conclusion?
5. Conform to the title and the evidence you have gathered?

Adjust or Change Your Thesis During Research if Necessary

Be willing to abandon your preliminary thesis if research leads you to new and different issues. For example, one writer began research on child abuse with this preliminary thesis: "A need for a cure to child abuse faces society each day." Investigation, however, narrowed her focus: "Parents who abuse their children should be treated as victims, not criminals." The writer moved, in effect, to a specific position from which to argue that social organizations should serve abusing parents in addition to their help to abused children.

10c Writing an Academic Title

A well-phrased title, like a good thesis sentence, will control your writing and keep you on course. Although writing a final title may not be feasible until the paper is written, the preliminary title can provide specific words of identification to keep you on track. For example, one writer began with this title: "Diabetes." Then, to make it more specific, the writer added another phrase: "Diabetes Management." As research developed and she realized the role of medicine, diet, and exercise for victims, she refined the title even more: "Diabetes Management: A Delicate Balance of Medicine, Diet, and Exercise." Thereby, she and her readers had a clear idea of what the paper was to do, that is, explore methods for managing the disease. Note that long titles are standard in scholarly writing. Consider the following strategies for writing your title.

1. Name a general subject, followed by a colon and a phrase that focuses or shows your slant on the subject.

   Organ and Tissue Donation and Transplantation: Myths, Ethical Issues, and Lives Saved

2. Name a general subject and narrow it with a prepositional phrase.

   Gothic Madness in Three Southern Writers

3. Name a general subject and cite a specific work that will illuminate the topic.

   Analysis of Verbal Irony in Swift's A Modest Proposal

4. Name a general subject, followed by a colon, and followed by a phrase that describes the type of study.

   Black Dialect in Maya Angelou's Poetry: A Language Study

5. Name a general subject, followed by a colon, and followed by a question.

   AIDS: Where Did It Come From?

6. Establish a specific comparison.

   Religious Imagery in N. Scott Momaday's The Names and Heronimous Storm's Seven Arrows

As you develop a title, be sure to avoid fancy literary titles that fail to label issues under discussion.

POOR: "Nutritional Foods"
BETTER: "Nutritional Foods: A Survey"
BEST: "Nutritional Foods: A Powerful Step on the Path of Preventive Medicine"

For placement of the title, see "Title Page or Opening Page," pages 198-99.

10d Drafting the Paper from Your Research Journal, Notes, and Computer Files

To begin writing your research report, you may work systematically through a preliminary plan or outline. You may also begin by writing what you know at the time. Either way, keep the pieces of your manuscript under control: your notes will usually keep you focused on the subject and your thesis statement will control the flow and direction of your argument. Yet you must let the writing find its own way, guided but not controlled by your preliminary plans. Consult also the paradigm (see 6b) that best fits your design.

Writing from Your Notes

Use your notes and research journal to:

- Transfer personal notes, with modification, into the draft.
- Transcribe précis notes and paraphrased materials directly into the text.
- Quote primary sources.
- Quote secondary sources from notes.

Weave source material into the paper to support *your* ideas, not as filler. Your notes will let the essay grow, blossom, and reach up to new levels of knowledge. You can do this in several ways, and you may even have a method beyond the four mentioned here.

Method one requires separate note files within a specially named directory, as explained on pages 135-36. During the drafting stage, you can use the INSERT, COPY, and READ commands to transfer your notes into your text.

Method two assumes that you have placed all your notes within one file. Begin writing your paper in a new file. As you need a note, minimize this text file and maximize your file of notes, or use two windows. Find the note you wish to transfer, highlight it, copy it, and then paste it into your file.

Method three assumes that you have placed all your notes within one file and that you have labeled each with a code word or title. Begin drafting your paper at the top of this file, which will push the notes down as you write. When you need a note, find it, copy it, and paste it into your text.

Method four requires the complete outline on file so that you can enter information onto the screen underneath any of the outline headings as you develop ideas (see Chapter 6 for details on outlining). You can import your notes to a specific location of the outline. This technique allows you to work anywhere within the paper to match your interest of the moment with a section of your outline. In effect, you expand your outline into the first draft of your research paper.

In the initial draft, leave plenty of space as you write. Keep the margins wide, use double-spacing, and leave blank spaces between some paragraphs. The open areas will invite your revisions and additions later on.

When working with pages copied from articles, books, or Internet sites, use caution. You will be tempted to borrow too much. Quote or paraphrase key phrases and sentences; do not quote an entire paragraph unless it is crucial to your discussion and you cannot easily reduce it to a précis. Moreover, any information that you borrow should come from a credible source that has a scholarly or educational basis.

> **HINT:** Drafting a paragraph or two by using different methods of development is one way to build the body of your paper, but only if each part fits the purpose and design of your work. Write a comparison paragraph, classify and analyze one or two issues, show cause and effect, and ask a question and answer it. Sooner than you think, you will draft the body of the paper. See Chapter 12 for detailed discussion of these methods of development.

Writing with Unity and Coherence

Unity refers to exploring one topic in depth to give your writing a single vision. With unity, each paragraph carefully expands upon a single aspect of the narrowed subject. *Coherence* connects the parts logically by:

- Repetition of key words and sentence structures.
- The judicious use of pronouns and synonyms.
- The effective placement of transitional words and phrases (e.g., *also, furthermore, therefore, in addition*, and *thus*).

The next passage reads with unity (it keeps its focus) and coherence (it repeats key words and uses transitions effectively, as indicated).

Talk shows are spectacles and forms of dramatic entertainment; therefore, members of the studio audience are acting out parts in the drama, like a Greek chorus, just as the host, the guest, and the television viewers are actors as well. Furthermore, some sort of interaction with the "characters" in this made-for-television "drama" happens all the time. If we read a book or attend a play, we question the text, we question the presentation, and we determine for ourselves what it means to us.

Writing in the Proper Tense

Verb tense often distinguishes a paper in the humanities from one in the natural and social sciences. MLA style and the footnote style both require the present tense to cite an author's work (e.g., "Patel *explains*" or "the work of Scogin and Roberts *shows*"). The CMS footnote style also asks for present tense.

> APA and CBE styles both require the past tense or present perfect tense to cite an author's work. See Chapter 15, 15b, pages 278–79, and Chapter 17, 17c, pages 340–42.

MLA style requires that you use the present tense for comments by you and by the sources because the ideas and the words of the writers remain in print and continue to be true in the universal present, as shown here:

"It was the best of times, it was the worst of times," writes Charles Dickens about the eighteenth century.

Johnson argues that sociologist Norman Wayman has a "narrow-minded view of clerics and their role in the community" (64).

Use the past tense in a humanities paper only for reporting historical events. In the next example, past tense is appropriate for all sentences except the last:

In 1876 Alexander Graham Bell invented the telephone. Signals, sounds, and music had been sent by wire before, but Bell's instrument was the first to transmit speech. Bell's story is a lesson in courage, one worthy of study by any would-be inventor.

Using the Language of the Discipline

Every discipline and every topic has its own vocabulary. Therefore, while reading and taking notes, jot down words and phrases relevant to your research study. Get comfortable with them so you can use them effectively. For example, a child abuse topic requires the language of sociology and psychology, thereby demanding an acquaintance with:

social worker	maltreatment	aggressive behavior
poverty levels	behavioral patterns	incestuous relations
stress	hostility	battered child
formative years	recurrence	guardians

Similarly, a poetry paper might require such terms as *symbolism, imagery, rhythm, persona*, or *rhyme*. Many writers create a terminology list to strengthen their command of appropriate nouns and verbs. However, nothing will betray a writer's ignorance of the subject matter more quickly than awkward and distorted technical terminology. For example, the following sentence uses big words, but it distorts and scrambles the language:

The enhancement of learning opportunities is often impeded by a pathological disruption in a child's mental processes.

The words may be large, but what does the passage mean? Maybe this:

Education is often interrupted by a child's daydreams.

Using Source Material to Enhance Your Writing

Readers want to see your thoughts and ideas on a subject. For this reason, a paragraph should seldom contain source material only; it must contain a topic sentence to establish a point for the research evidence. Every paragraph should explain, analyze, and support a thesis, not merely string together a set of quotations.

See Chapter 11, pages 159–79, on blending sources into your text.

The following passage cites effectively two different sources in CMS style.

Organ and tissue donation is the gift of life. Each year many people confront health problems due to diseases or congenital birth defects. Tom Taddonia explains that tissues such as skin, veins, and valves can be used to correct congenital defects, blindness, visual impairment, trauma, burns, dental defects, arthritis, cancer, vascular and heart disease.[8] Steve Barnill says, "More than 400 people each month receive the gift of sight through yet another type of tissue donation—corneal transplants. In many cases, donors unsuitable for organ donation are eligible for tissue donation."[9] Barnill notes that tissues are now used in orthopedic surgery, cardiovascular surgery, plastic surgery, dentistry, and podiatry.[10] Even so, not enough people are willing to donate organs and tissues.

This passage illustrates four points. A writer should:

Weave the sources effectively into a whole.
Use the sources as a natural extension of the discussion.
Cite each source separately, one at a time.
Provide footnote numerals for CMS style.

This means you will need to read carefully so that you can select the key ideas and phrasing. It also means you should be accurate and precise.

Writing in the Third Person

Write your paper with third-person narration that avoids "I believe" or "It is my opinion." Rather than saying, "I think objectivity on television is nothing more than an ideal," drop the opening two words and say, "Objectivity on television is nothing more than an ideal." Readers will understand that the statement is your thought. However, attribute human functions to yourself or other persons, not to nonhuman sources:

WRONG   The study considered several findings.
CORRECT   The study reported the findings of several sources.

The study can report its findings, but it can't consider them.

Writing with the Passive Voice in an Appropriate Manner

Instructors often caution young writers against using the passive voice, which is often less forceful than an active verb. However, research writers sometimes need to shift the focus from the actor to the receiver, as shown here:

PASSIVE: Forty-three students of a third-grade class at Barksdale School were observed for two weeks.

ACTIVE: I observed forty-three students of a third-grade class at Barksdale school.

In the examples above, the passive voice is preferred because it keeps the focus on the subject of the research, not the writer. Also, as a general rule, avoid the first person in research papers. Here are additional examples of the effective use of the passive voice:

The soil was examined for traces of mercury.

President Jackson was attacked repeatedly for his Indian policy by his enemies in Congress.

Children with attention disorders are often targeted for drug treatment.

As you see, the sentences place the focus on the soil, the President, and the children.

Placing Graphics Effectively in a Research Essay

Graphics enable you to analyze trends and relationships in numerical data. Use them to support your text. Most computers allow you to create tables, line graphs, or pie charts as well as diagrams, maps, and other original designs. You may also import tables and illustrations from your sources. Place these graphics as close as possible to the parts of the text to which they relate. It is acceptable to use full-color art if your printer will print in colors; however, use black for the captions and date.

See Appendix A, pages A-13–A-16, for help with designing tables, line graphs, illustrations, pie charts, and other visuals.

Place a full-page graphic design on a separate sheet after making a textual reference to it (e.g., "see Table 7"). Place graphic designs in an appendix when you have several complex items that might distract the reader from your textual message.

10e Avoiding Sexist and Biased Language

Racial and gender fairness is one mark of the mature writer. The best writers exercise caution against words that may stereotype any person, regardless of gender, race, nationality, creed, age, or disability. If the writing is precise, readers will not make assumptions about race, age, and disabilities. Therefore, do not freely mention sexual orientation, marital status, ethnic or racial identity, or a person's disability. The following are some guidelines to help you avoid discriminatory language.

Age

Review the accuracy of your statement. It is appropriate to use *boy* and *girl* for children of high school age and under. *Young man* and *young woman* or *male adolescent* and *female adolescent* can be appropriate, but *teenager* carries a certain bias. Avoid *elderly* as a noun; use *older persons*.

Gender

Gender is a matter of our culture that identifies men and women within their social groups. *Sex* tends to be a biological factor (see below for a discussion of sexual orientation).

1. Use plural subjects so that nonspecific, plural pronouns are grammatically correct. For example, do you intend to specify that Judy Jones maintains *her* lab equipment in sterile condition or to indicate that technicians, in general, maintain *their* own equipment?
2. Reword the sentence so that a pronoun is unnecessary:

CORRECT   The doctor prepared the necessary surgical   not his
equipment without interference.

CORRECT   Each technician must maintain the laboratory   not her
equipment in sterile condition.

3. Use pronouns denoting gender only when necessary to specify gender or when gender has been previously established.

Mary, as a new laboratory technician, must learn to maintain her
equipment in sterile condition.

4. The use of *woman* and *female* as adjectives varies, as in *female athlete* or *woman athlete*. Use *woman* or *women* in most instances (e.g., *a woman's intuition*) and use *female* for species and statistics (e.g., *four female subjects, 10 males and 23 females,* or *a female chimpanzee*). The word *lady* has fallen from favor (i.e., avoid *lady pilot*).
5. The first mention of a person requires the full name (e.g., Ernest Hemingway or Joan Didion) and thereafter requires only the use of the surname (e.g., Hemingway or Didion). At first mention, use Emily Brontë,

but thereafter use Brontë, *not* Miss Brontë. In general, avoid formal titles (e.g., Dr., Gen., Mrs., Ms., Lt., or Professor). Avoid their equivalents in other languages (e.g., Mme, Dame, Monsieur).

6. Avoid *man and wife* or *7 men and 16 females.* Keep them parallel by saying *busband and wife* or *man and woman* and *7 male rats and 16 female rats.*

Sexual orientation

The term *sexual orientation* is preferred over the term *sexual prefer-ence.* It is preferable to use the terms *lesbians* and *gay men* rather than *homo-sexuals.* The terms *heterosexual, homosexual,* and *bisexual* can be used to describe both the identity and the behavior of subjects.

Ethnic and racial identity

Some persons prefer the term *Black,* others prefer *African American,* and still others prefer *a person of color.* The terms *Negro* and *Afro-American* are now dated and not appropriate. Use *Black* and *White,* not the lowercase *black* and *white.* In like manner, some individuals may prefer *Hispanic, Latino, Mexican,* or *Chicano.* Use the term *Asian* or *Asian American* rather than *Oriental. Native American* is a broad term that includes *Samoans, Hawaiians,* and *American Indians.* A good rule is to use a person's nation-ality when it is known (*Mexican, Korean, Comanche,* or *Nigerian*).

Disability

In general, place people first, not their disability. Rather than *disabled person* or *retarded child* say *person who has scoliosis* or *a child with Down's syndrome.* Avoid saying *a challenged person* or *a special child* in favor of *a person with _____* or *a child with _____.* Remember that a *disability* is a phys-ical quality while a *handicap* is a limitation that might be imposed by non-physical factors, such as stairs or poverty or social attitudes.

■ YOUR RESEARCH PROJECT

1. Examine your own thesis using the Final Thesis Checklist on page 150. Revise your thesis as necessary.
2. Consider your focus to determine if you will persuade, inquire, negotiate (see pages 147–48) or perhaps use a focus as explained in Chapter 1: eval-uation, definition, proposal, causal argument, analogy, precedence (see pages 3–8).
3. Write an academic title for your paper, one that clearly describes the nature of your work (see pages 151–52).
4. After you draft a significant portion of the paper, review it carefully for each of these items: coherence, proper tense, third-person voice, and the language of the discipline.

Blending Reference Material into Your Writing

Your in-text citations should conform to standards announced by your instructor. This chapter explains the MLA style, as established by the Modern Language Association. It governs papers in English composition, literature, usage, and foreign languages.

The MLA style puts great emphasis upon the writer, asking for the full name of the scholar on first mention but last name only thereafter and last name only in parenthetical citations. Other styles emphasize the timeliness of the year of publication as well as the author. Still other styles use merely a number in order to emphasize the material, not the author or date.

MLA Style, pages 224–76
APA Style, pages 277–309
CMS Footnote Style, pages 310–35
CBE Number Style, pages 337–40

11a Blending Reference Citations into Your Text

As you might expect, writing a research paper carries with it certain obligations. You will need to gather and present source material on the topic and to display those sources prominently in your writing, not hide them. In addition, you will need to provide enough information within your text to identify a source with both a name and a page number. Of course, a page number is not required for nonprint items nor for most Internet sources.

As a general policy, keep citations brief. Remember, your readers will have full documentation to each source on the "Works Cited" page (see Chapter 14).

Making a General Reference without a Page Number

Sometimes you will need no parenthetical citation.

The women of Thomas Hardy's novels are the special focus of three essays by Nancy Norris, Judith Mitchell, and James Scott.

Beginning with the Author and Ending with a Page Number

Introduce a quotation or a paraphrase with the author's name and close it with a page number, placed inside parentheses. Try always to use this standard citation because it indicates the beginning and end of borrowed materials, as shown here:

Herbert Norfleet states that the use of video games by children improves their hand and eye coordination (45).

In the following example, the reader can easily trace the origin of the ideas.

Video games for children have opponents and advocates. Herbert Norfleet defends the use of video games by children. He says it improves their hand and eye coordination and that it exercises their minds as they work their way through various puzzles and barriers. Norfleet states, "The mental gymnastics of video games and the competition with fellow players are important to young children and their physical, social, and mental development" (45).

Putting the Page Number Immediately after the Name

Sometimes, notes at the end of a quotation make it expeditious to place the page number immediately after the name.

Boughman (46) urges car makers to "direct the force of automotive air bags upward against the windshield" (emphasis added).

Putting the Name and Page Number at the End of Borrowed Material

You can, if you like, put cited names with the page number at the end of a quotation or paraphrase.

"Each DNA strand provides the pattern of bases for a new strand to form, resulting in two complete molecules" (Justice, Moody, and Graves 462).

In the case of a paraphrase, you should give your reader a signal to show when the borrowing begins:

One source explains that the DNA in the chromosomes must be copied perfectly during cell reproduction (Justice, Moody, and Graves 462).

NOTE: In MLA style do not place a comma between the name and the page number.

11b Citing a Source When No Author Is Listed

When no author is shown on a title page, cite the title of an article, the name of the magazine, the name of a bulletin or book, or the name of the publishing organization.

> **HINT:** Search for the author's name at the bottom of the opening page, at the end of the article, at an Internet home page, or an e-mail address.

Citing the Title of a Magazine Article

At various foundations of their homes, Americans are threatened by chemistry and its attacks on the human system. The dangers of Chlordane and the problems with Dursban are explored in one article ("Terminating Termites"), but termites just grab the headlines. There are many more dangers lurking in the crevices of the average home.

The Works Cited entry would read:

"Terminating Termites." <u>Southern Living</u> July 2000: 110.

You may shorten magazine titles to a key word for the citation, such as "Selling" rather than the full title, "Selling Products to Young Children." You would then give the full title in the Works Cited entry.

Citing the Title of a Report

One bank showed a significant decline in assets despite an increase in its number of depositors (<u>Annual Report,</u> 2000, 23).

Citing the Name of a Publisher or a Corporate Body

The report by the school board endorsed the use of Channel One in the school system and said that "students will benefit by the news reports more than they will be adversely affected by advertising" (Clarion County School Board 3–4).

11c Identifying Nonprint Sources That Have No Page Number

On occasion you may need to identify nonprint sources, such as a speech, the song lyrics from a compact disk, an interview, or a television program. Since no page number exists, omit the parenthetical citation. Instead, introduce the type of source—i.e., lecture, letter, interview—so that readers do not expect a page number.

> Thompson's lecture defined <u>impulse</u> as "an action triggered by the nerves without thought for the consequences."

> Mrs. Peggy Meacham said in her phone interview that prejudice against young black women is not as severe as that against young black males.

11d   Identifying Internet Sources

The process for citing a Web source is really the same as for citing a print source—the same information should be included if available, and if it's not available, that's a good cue to question the validity of the material. So always try to identify within your text the author of an Internet article.

> Hershel Winthop interprets Hawthorne's stories as the search for holiness in a corrupt Puritan society.

If you can't identify an author, give the article title or website information.

> One website claims that any diet that avoids carbohydrates will avoid some sugars that are essential for the body ("Fad Diets").

In some instances, your instructors may expect you to indicate your best estimate of the scholarly value of a source. For example, the next citation explains the role of the Center for Communications Policy.

> The UCLA Center for Communication Policy, which conducted an intensive study of television violence during 1995, has advised against making the television industry the "scapegoat for violence" by advocating a focus on "deadlier and more significant causes: inadequate parenting, drugs, underclass rage, unemployment and availability of weaponry" (UCLA Television Violence Report 1996).

Here's another example of an introduction that establishes credibility:

> John Armstrong, a spokesperson for Public Electronic Access to Knowledge (PEAK), states:
>
>> As we venture into this age of biotechnology, many people predict gene manipulation will be a powerful tool for improving the quality of life. They foresee plants engineered to resist pests, animals designed to produce large quantities of rare medicinals, and humans treated by gene therapy to relieve suffering.

NOTE: To learn more about the source of an Internet article, as in the case immediately above, learn to search out a home page. The address for Armstrong's article is

<http://www.peak.org/~armstroj/america.html#Aims>

By truncating the address to <http://www.peak.org/> you can learn about the organization that Armstrong represents.

If you are not certain about the credibility of a source, that is, it seemingly has no scholarly or educational basis, do not cite it, or describe the source so that readers can make their own judgments:

An Iowa non-profit organization, the Mothers for Natural Law, says—but offers no proof—that eight major crops are affected by genetically engineered organisms—canola, corn, cotton, dairy products, potatoes, soybeans, tomatoes, and yellow crook-neck squash ('What's on the Market").

11e Omitting Page Numbers to Internet Citations

Omit page numbers to Internet sites:

- You cannot list a screen number because monitors differ.
- You cannot list a page number of a downloaded document because computer printers differ.
- Unless they are numbered in the document, you cannot list paragraph numbers. Besides, you would have to go through and count every paragraph.

C H E C K L I S T

Using Links to Document Internet Sources

If you are publishing your project on your own Web page, you have the opportunity to send your readers to various sites by use of hypertext links (see Chapter 18 for more information). If you do so, follow these guidelines:

1. Activate a link in your document that will correctly send your reader to one of your sources.
2. Identify the link clearly so that the reader will know where the link will take them.
3. Be selective; don't sprinkle links all over your website. You want the reader to stay with you, not wander around on the Internet.
4. Provide a regular Works Cited page at the end of your online article. The links will not substitute for the Works Cited page.

The marvelous feature of electronic text is that it is searchable, so your readers can find your quotation quickly using the FIND or SEARCH feature. Suppose that you have written the following:

> One source advises against making the television industry the "scapegoat for violence" by advocating a focus on "deadlier and more significant causes: inadequate parenting, drugs, underclass rage, unemployment and availability of weaponry" (UCLA Television Violence Report 1996).

A reader who wants to investigate further will find your complete citation on your Works Cited page. There the reader will discover the Internet address for the article. The reader can then find the article via a browser, type in a key phrase (such as *scapegoat for violence*), and use FIND to go to the passage shown above. That's much easier for the reader than counting through forty-six paragraphs.

However, you should provide a paragraph number if the Internet article has numbered its paragraphs. Some academic societies are urging scholars who write on the Internet to number their paragraphs, and that practice may catch on quickly.

> The Insurance Institute for Highway Safety emphasizes restraint first, saying, "Riding unrestrained or improperly restrained in a motor vehicle always has been the greatest hazard for children" (par. 13).

Provide a page number only if you find page numbers buried within brackets here and there throughout an article. These refer to the page numbers of the printed version of the document. In these cases, you should cite the page just as you would a printed source.

> The most common type of diabetes is non-insulin-dependent-diabetes mellitus (NIDDM), which "affects 90% of those with diabetes and usually appears after age 40" (Larson 3).

11f   Citing Indirect Sources

Sometimes the writer of a book or article will quote another person from an interview or personal correspondence, and you will want to use that same quotation. For example, in a newspaper article in *USA Today*, page 9A, Karen S. Peterson writes this passage in which she quotes two other people:

> Sexuality, popularity, and athletic competition will create anxiety for junior high kids and high schoolers, Eileen Shiff says. "Bring up the topics. Don't wait for them to do it; they are nervous and they want to appear cool." Monitor the amount of time high schoolers spend working for money, she suggests. "Work is important, but school must be the priority." Parental

intervention in a child's school career that worked in junior high may not work in high school, psychiatrist Martin Greenburg adds. "The interventions can be construed by the adolescent as negative, overburdening and interfering with the child's ability to care for himself." He adds, "Be encouraging, not critical. Criticism can be devastating for the teen-ager."

Suppose that you want to use the quotation above by Martin Greenburg. You will need to quote the words of Greenburg and also put Peterson's name in the parenthetical citation as the person who wrote the article:

> After students get beyond middle school, they begin to resent interference by their parents, especially in school activities. They need some space from Mom and Dad. Martin Greenburg says, "The interventions can be construed by the adolescent as negative, overburdening and interfering with the child's ability to care for himself" (qtd. in Peterson 9A).

On the Works Cited page, Peterson's name will appear on a bibliography entry, but Greenburg's name will not appear there because Greenburg is not the author of the article.

In other words, you need a double reference that introduces the speaker and includes a clear reference to the book or article where you found the quotation or the paraphrased material. Without the reference to Peterson, nobody could find the article. Without the reference to Greenburg, readers would assume that Peterson had spoken the words.

HINT: Cite the original source if it is readily available rather than use the double reference.

11g Citing Frequent Page References to the Same Work

When you make frequent references to the same novel, drama, or long poem, you need not repeat the author's name in every instance; a specific page reference is adequate, or you can provide act, scene, and line if appropriate.

> When the character Beneatha denies the existence of God in Hansberry's A Raisin in the Sun, Mama slaps her in the face and forces her to repeat after her, "In my mother's house there is still God" (37). Then Mama adds, "There are some ideas we ain't going to have in this house. Not long as I am at the head of the family" (37). Thus Mama meets Beneatha's challenge head on. The other mother in the Younger household is Ruth, who does not lose her temper, but through kindness wins over her husband (79–80).

> **NOTE:** If you are citing from two or more novels in your paper, let's say John Steinbeck's *East of Eden* and *Of Mice and Men,* provide both title (abbreviated) and page unless the reference is clear: (*Eden* 56) and (*Mice* 12–13).

11h Citing Material from Textbooks and Large Anthologies

Reproduced below is a poem that you might find in many literary textbooks.

The Red Wheelbarrow
so much depends
upon

a red wheel
barrow

glazed with rain
water

beside the white
chickens.
          William Carlos Williams

If you quote lines of the poem, and if that is all you quote from the anthology, cite the author and page of the text; then put a comprehensive entry in the Works Cited list.

Text

For Williams, "so much depends" on the red wheel barrow as it sits "glazed with rain water beside the white chickens" (1926–27).

Bibliography Entry

Williams, William Carlos. "The Red Wheelbarrow." The Norton Anthology of American Literature. Ed. Nina Baym et al. New York: Norton, 1999. 1926–27.

Suppose, however, that you also want to quote not only from Williams but from other poems in the textbook. You should make in-text citations to name and page, but your Works Cited entries can be shortened by cross-references to the editors of the anthology.

See pages 234–35 for more details on shortening bibliography entries to an anthology.

Frost, Robert. "The Pasture." Baym et al. 1859.

Sandberg, Carl. "Fog." Baym et al. 1887.

11i   Adding Extra Information to In-text Citations

As a courtesy to your reader, add extra information within the citation. Show parts of books, different titles by the same writer, or several works by different writers. For example, your reader may have a different anthology than yours, so a clear reference "(*Great Expectations* 681; ch. 4)," will enable the reader to locate the passage. The same is true with a reference to "(*Romeo and Juliet* 2.3.65–68)." The reader will find the passage in any edition of Shakespeare's play.

One of Several Volumes

These next two citations provide three vital facts: (1) an abbreviation for the title, (2) the volume used, and (3) the page number.

> In a letter to his Tennessee Volunteers in 1812 General Jackson chastised the "mutinous and disorderly conduct" of some of his troops (Papers 2: 348–49).

> Joseph Campbell suggests that man is a slave yet also the master of all the gods (Masks 1: 472).

Two or More Works by the Same Writer

In this example the writer makes reference to two different novels, both abbreviated. Full titles are *Tess of the D'Urbervilles* and *The Mayor of Casterbridge.*

> Thomas Hardy reminds readers in his prefaces that "a novel is an impression, not an argument" and that a novel should be read as "a study of man's deeds and character" (Tess xxii; Mayor 1).

The complete titles of the two works by Campbell that are referenced in the following example are *The Hero with a Thousand Faces* and *The Masks of God,* a four-volume work.

> Because he stresses the nobility of man, Joseph Campbell suggests that the mythic hero is symbolic of the "divine creative and redemptive image which is hidden within us all [. . .]" (Hero 39). The hero elevates the human mind to an "ultimate mythogenetic zone—the creator and destroyer, the slave and yet the master, of all the gods" (Masks 1: 472).

Several Authors in One Citation

You may wish to make a citation to several different sources that treat the same topic. Put them in alphabetical order to match that of the Works Cited page, or place them in the order of importance to the issue at hand.

> Several sources have addressed this aspect of gang warfare as
> a fight for survival, not just for control of the local turf
> (Robertson 98–134; Rollins 34; Templass 561–65).

Additional Information with the Page Number

> Horton (22, n. 3) suggests that Melville forced the symbolism, but
> Welston (199–248, esp. 234) reaches an opposite conclusion.

Classical prose works such as *Moby Dick* or *Paradise Lost* may appear in two or more editions. Courtesy dictates that you provide extra information to chapter, section, or part so that readers can locate a quotation in any edition of the work. See how this writer handles a reference to *Moby Dick*.

> Melville uncovers the superstitious nature of Ishmael by stressing
> Ishmael's fascination with Yojo, the little totem god of Queequeg
> (71; ch. 16).

11j Punctuating Citations Properly and With Consistency

Keep page citations outside quotation marks but inside the final period, as shown here:

> Smith says, "The benefits of cloning far exceed any harm that might
> occur" (34).

In MLA style, use no comma between the name and the page within the citation—for example, "(Jones 16-17)" *not* "(Jones, 16-17)". Do not use *p.* or *pp.* with the page numbers in MLA style.

Commas and Periods

Place commas and periods inside quotation marks unless the page citation intervenes. The example below shows (1) how to put the mark inside the quotation marks, (2) how to interrupt a quotation to insert the speaker, (3) how to use single quotation marks within the regular quotation marks, and (4) how to place the period after a page citation.

> "Modern advertising," says Rachel Murphy, "not only creates a
> marketplace, it determines values." She adds, "I resist the
> advertiser's argument that they 'awaken, not create desires'" (192).

Sometimes you may need to change the closing period to a comma. Suppose you decide to quote this sentence: "Scientific cloning poses no threat to the human species." If you start your sentence with the quotation, you will need to change the period to a comma, as shown:

> "Scientific cloning poses no threat to the human species," declares Joseph Wineberg in a recent article (357).

However, retain question marks or exclamation marks, and no comma is required:

> "Does scientific cloning pose a threat to the human species?" wonders Mark Durham (546).

Let's look at other examples. Suppose this is the original material:

> The Russians had obviously anticipated neither the quick discovery of the bases nor the quick imposition of the quarantine. Their diplomats across the world were displaying all the symptoms of improvisation, as if they had been told nothing of the placement of the missiles and had received no instructions what to say about them.—From: Arthur M. Schlesinger Jr., *A Thousand Days* (New York: Houghton, 1965) 820.

Punctuate citations from this source in one of the following methods in accordance with MLA style.

> "The Russians," writes Schlesinger, "had obviously anticipated neither the quick discovery of the [missile] bases nor the quick imposition of the quarantine" (820).

> Schlesinger notes, "Their diplomats across the world were displaying all the symptoms of improvisation [. . .]" (820).

> Schlesinger observes that the Russian failure to anticipate an American discovery of Cuban missiles caused "their diplomats across the world" to improvise answers as "if they had been told nothing of the placement of the missiles [. . .]" (820).

Note that the last example correctly changes the capital "T" of "their" to lowercase to match the grammar of the restructured sentence, and it does not use ellipsis points before "if" because the phrase flows smoothly into the text.

Semicolons and Colons

Both semicolons and colons go outside the quotation marks, as illustrated by these three examples.

> Zigler admits that "the extended family is now rare in contemporary society"; however, he stresses the greatest loss as the "wisdom and daily support of older, more experienced family members" (42).

Zigler laments the demise of the "extended family": that is, the family suffers by loss of the "wisdom and daily support of older, more experienced family members" (42).

Brian Sutton-Smith says, "Adults don't worry whether their toys are educational" (64); nevertheless, parents want to keep their children in a learning mode.

The third example shows how to place the page citation after a quotation and before a semicolon.

Question Marks and Exclamation Marks

When a question mark or an exclamation mark serves a part of the quotation, keep it inside the quotation mark. Put the page citation immediately after the name of the source to avoid conflict with the punctuation mark.

Thompson (16) passionately shouted to union members, "We can bring order into our lives even though we face hostility from every quarter!"

Retain questions marks and exclamation marks when the quotation begins a sentence. No comma is required.

"We face hostility from every quarter!" declared the union leader.

Question marks may appear inside the closing quotation mark when they are part of the original quotation; otherwise, they go outside.

The philosopher Brackenridge (16) asks, "How should we order our lives?"

but

Did Brackenridge say that we might encounter "hostility from every quarter"?

Single Quotation Marks

When a quotation appears within another quotation, use single quotation marks with the shorter one.

George Loffler (32) confirms that "the unconscious carries the best of human thought and gives man great dignity, but it also has the dark side so that we cry, in the words of Shakespeare's Macbeth, 'Hence, horrible shadow! Unreal mockery, hence.'"

Remember that the period always goes inside quotation marks unless the page citation intervenes.

George Loffler confirms that "the unconscious carries the best of human thought and gives man great dignity, but it also has the

dark side so that we cry, in the words of Shakespeare's Macbeth,
'Hence, horrible shadow! Unreal mockery, hence'" (32).

11k Indenting Long Quotations

Set off long prose quotations of four lines or more by indenting one inch,
usually two clicks of the tab key, or ten spaces with a typewriter font. Do not
use quotation marks with the indented material. If you quote only one paragraph or the beginning of one, do *not* indent the first line an extra five spaces.
Double space between your text and the quoted materials. Place the parenthetical citation *after* the final mark of punctuation, as shown below.

> The number of people who need transplants continues to increase,
> but the number of donors fails to meet these needs. In 1999 the
> National Organ and Tissue Donation Initiative asserted:
>
> > Approximately 55 people each day receive life-enhancing
> > organ transplants, another 10 people die each day on the
> > national list waiting for a donated organ. In September
> > 1997, more than 55,000 people were on the list, which
> > grows by about 500 every month. Most Americans
> > approve of organ donation, but too few give this gift of
> > life to others. ("Organ")
>
> With the ever increasing number of organ donors needed, why
> don't people give of themselves? The most recognized reason for the
> shortage of donors is directly related to the myths that are
> associated with organ and tissue donation.

If you quote more than one paragraph, indent the first line of all paragraphs an extra three spaces on the typewriter or a quarter inch. However, if
the first sentence quoted does not begin a paragraph in the original source,
do not indent it an extra three spaces.

> Zigler makes this observation:
>
> > With many others, I am nevertheless optimistic that our
> > nation will eventually display its inherent greatness and
> > successfully correct the many ills that I have touched
> > upon here.
> >
> > > Of course, much remains that could and should be
> > done, including increased efforts in the area of family
> > planning, the widespread implementation of Education for
> > Parenthood programs, an increase in the availability of
> > homemaker and child care services, and a reexamination
> > of our commitment to doing what is in the best interest of
> > every child in America. (42)

11l Citing Poetry

Quoting Two Lines of Poetry or Less

Incorporate short quotations of poetry (one or two lines) into your text.

> In Part 3 Eliot's "The Waste Land" (1922) remains a springtime
> search for nourishing water: "Sweet Thames, run softly, for
> I speak not loud or long" (line 12) says the speaker in "The Fire
> Sermon," while in Part 5 the speaker of "What the Thunder
> Said" yearns for "a damp gust / Bringing rain" (73–74).

As the example demonstrates:

1. Set off the material with quotation marks.
2. Indicate separate lines by using a virgule (/) with a space before and after the slash mark.
3. Place line documentation within parentheses immediately following the final quotation mark and inside the period. Do not use the abbreviation *l.* or *ll.*, which might be confused with page numbers; use *lines* initially to establish that the numbers represent lines of poetry and thereafter use only the numbers.

> For complete information, see "Arabic Numerals," pages A-8–A-10).

4. Use Arabic numerals for books, parts, volumes, and chapters of works; acts, scenes, and lines of plays; cantos, stanzas, and lines of poetry.

Quoting Three Lines or More

Set off three or more lines of poetry by indenting ten spaces on the typewriter or one inch (usually two tabs), as shown below. Use double-spaced lines. A parenthetical citation ends the last line of the quotation. If the parenthetical citation will not fit on the last line, place it on the next line, flush with the right margin of the poetry text.

Typewriter:

The king cautions Prince Henry:

> Thy place in council thou has rudely lost,
> Which by thy younger brother is supplied,
> And art almost an alien to the hearts
> Of all the court and princes of my blood.
>
>   (3.2.32–35)

or

Arial font:

The king cautions Prince Henry:

> Thy place in council thou has rudely lost,
> Which by thy younger brother is supplied,
> And art almost an alien to the hearts
> Of all the court and princes of my blood.
>
> (3.2.32–35)

An alternative is to center the indented block of poetry. Refer to act, scene, and lines only after you have established Shakespeare's *Henry IV, Part 1* as the central topic of your study; otherwise, write "(1H4 3.2.32–35)."

Signaling Turnovers for Long Lines of Poetry

See also pages 174–77 for instructions on using ellipsis points to omit phrases and lines from poetry.

When quoting a line of poetry that is too long for your right margin, indent the continuation line three spaces or a quarter inch more than the greatest indentation.

Plath opens her poem with these lines:

> Love set you going like a fat gold watch.
> The midwife slapped your footsoles, and
>   your bald cry
> Took its place among the elements. (lines 1–3)

You may also indent less to make room for the words:

Plath opens her poem with these lines:

> Love set you going like a fat gold watch.
> The midwife slapped your footsoles, and your bald cry
> Took its place among the elements. (lines 1–3)

11m Handling Quotations from a Play

Set off from your text any dialogue of two or more characters. Begin with the character's name, indented one inch (or ten spaces on a typewriter) from the left margin and written in all capital letters. Follow the name with a period, space once, and begin the quotation. Reproduce any extra spacing used in the original; notice the different spacing shown below with the lines of Kreon, which are set to the right. Indent subsequent lines of speech an extra quarter inch or three spaces. Start a new line when the dialogue shifts to another character.

> At the end of <u>Oedipus Rex</u>, Kreon chastises Oedipus, reminding him that he no longer has control over his own life nor that of his children.
>
> OEDIPUS.   Send me from Thebes!
> KREON.   God grant that I may!
> OEDIPUS.   But since God hates me . . .
> KREON.   No, he will grant your wish.
> OEDIPUS.   You promise?
> KREON.   I can not speak beyond my knowledge.
> OEDIPUS.   Then lead me in.
> KREON.   Come now and leave your children.
> OEDIPUS.   No! Do not take them from me!
> KREON.   Think no longer
>   That you are in command here, but rather think
>   How, when you were, you served
>   your own destruction.

11n Altering Initial Capitals in Some Quoted Matter

In general, you should reproduce quoted materials exactly, yet one exception is permitted for logical reasons. Restrictive connectors, such as *that* or *because*, create restrictive clauses and eliminate the need for a comma. Without a comma, the capital letter is unnecessary. In the following example, "The," which is capitalized as the first word in the original sentence, is changed to lowercase because it continues the grammatical flow of the student's sentence.

> Another writer argues that "the single greatest impediment to our improving the lives of America's children is the myth that we are a child-oriented society" (Zigler 39).

Otherwise, write:

> Another writer argues, "The single greatest [. . .]."

11o Omitting Quoted Matter with Ellipsis Points

You may omit portions of quoted material with three spaced ellipsis points set within brackets [. . .]. Observe the following guidelines.

Context

In omitting passages, be fair to the author. Do not change the meaning or take a quotation out of context.

Correctness

Maintain the grammatical correctness of your sentences; that is, avoid fragments and misplaced modifiers. You don't want your readers to misunderstand the structure of the original. When you quote only a phrase, readers will understand that you omitted most of the original sentence.

> Phil Withim recognizes the weakness in Captain Vere's "intelligence and insight" into the significance of his decisions regarding Billy Budd (118).

Omission within a sentence

Use three spaced ellipsis points (periods) to signal material omitted from *within* a sentence:

> Phil Withim objects to the idea that "such episodes are intended to demonstrate that Vere [. . .] has the intelligence and insight to perceive the deeper issue" (118).

Omission at the end of a sentence

See "Brackets," pages 177–78, for additional examples.

If an ellipsis occurs at the end of your sentence, use bracketed points and follow the last bracket with the sentence period and the closing quotation mark.

> R. W. B. Lewis (62) declares that "if Hester has sinned, she has done so as an affirmation of life, and her sin is the source of life [. . .]."

But if a page citation also appears at the end in conjunction with the ellipsis, use three spaced ellipsis points within brackets followed the closing quotation mark, add the page citation within parentheses, and then add the period.

> R. W. B. Lewis declares that "if Hester has sinned, she has done so as an affirmation of life, and her sin is the source of life [. . .]" (62).

Omission at the beginning of a sentence

Most style guides discourage the use of ellipsis points for material omitted from the beginning of a source:

> He states: "[. . .] the new parent has lost the wisdom and daily support of older, more experienced family members" (Zigler 34).

The passage would read better without the ellipsis points (see section 11m):

He states that "the new parent has lost the wisdom and daily
support of older, more experienced family members" (Zigler 34).

Omission of complete sentences and paragraphs

When you quote more than one sentence, your ellipsis points can indicate the type of omission.

Quotation omitting one or more sentences:

Zigler reminds us that "child abuse is found more frequently in a
single (female) parent home in which the mother is working. [. . .] The
unavailability of quality day care can only make this situation more
stressful" (42).

Quotation omitting from the middle of one sentence to the end of one or
more other sentences:

Zigler reminds us that "child abuse is found more frequently in a
single (female) parent home in which the mother is working [. . .]. The
unavailability of quality day care can only make this situation more
stressful" (42).

Quotation omitting from the middle of one sentence to the middle of
another:

Zigler reminds us that "child abuse is found more frequently in a
single (female) parent home in which the mother is working,[. . .] so
the unavailability of quality day care can only make this situation
more stressful" (42).

Omissions in poetry

If you omit a word or phrase in a quotation of poetry, indicate the omission with three or four ellipsis points just as you would with omissions in a prose passage. However, if you omit a complete line or more from the poem, indicate the omission by a line of spaced periods that equals the average length of the lines.

> Do ye hear the children weeping, O my brothers,
>   Ere the sorrow comes with years?
> They are leaning their young heads against their mothers,
> And <u>that</u> cannot stop their tears.
> [. . . . .]
> They are weeping in the playtime of the others,
>   In the country of the free. (Browning 382)

Avoid excessive use of ellipsis points

Many times you can be more effective if you incorporate short phrases rather than quote the whole sprinkled with many ellipsis points. Note how this next passage incorporates quotations without the use of ellipsis.

> The long-distance marriage, according to William Nichols, "works best when there are no minor-aged children to be considered," the two people are "equipped by temperament and personality to spend a considerable amount of time alone," and both are able to "function in a mature, highly independent fashion" (54).

11p Altering Quotations with Parentheses and Brackets

You will sometimes need to alter a quotation to emphasize a point or to make something clear. You might add material, italicize an important word, or use the word *sic* (Latin for *thus* or *so*) to alert readers that you have properly reproduced the material even though the logic or the spelling of the original might appear to be in error. Use parentheses or brackets according to these basic rules.

Parentheses

Use parentheses to enclose comments or explanations that immediately follow a quotation:

> Boughman (46) urges car makers to "direct the force of automotive air bags <u>upward</u> against the windshield" (emphasis added).

Brackets

Use brackets for interpolation, which means to insert new matter into a text or quotation. The use of brackets signals the insertion. Note the following rules.

Use brackets to clarify

> This same critic indicates that "we must avoid the temptation to read it [The Scarlet Letter] heretically" (118).

Use brackets to establish correct grammar within an abridged quotation

> "John F. Kennedy [was] an immortal figure of courage and dignity in the hearts of most Americans," notes one historian (Jones 82).

He states: "[The] new parent has lost the wisdom and daily support of older, more experienced family members" (Zigler 34).

Use brackets to note the addition of underlining

He says, for instance, that the "extended family is now rare in contemporary society, and with its demise the new parent has <u>lost the wisdom</u> [my emphasis] and daily support of older, more experienced family members" (Zigler 42).

Use brackets to substitute a proper name for a pronoun

"As we all know, he [Kennedy] implored us to serve the country, not take from it" (Jones 432).

Use brackets with *sic* to indicate errors in the original

Lovell says, "John F. Kennedy, assassinated in November of 1964 [sic], became overnight an immortal figure of courage and dignity in the hearts of most Americans" (62).

> **NOTE:** Kennedy's assassination occurred in 1963. However, do not burden your text with the use of "sic" for historical matter in which misspellings are obvious, as with: "Faire seemly pleasauance each to other makes."

Use brackets with ellipsis points
See the examples on pages 175–76.

YOUR RESEARCH PROJECT

1. Make a critical journey through your draft with one purpose—to examine your handling of the sources. Have you introduced them clearly so that the reader will know when the borrowing began? Have you closed them with a page citation, as appropriate? Have you placed quotation marks at the beginning and the end of borrowed phrases as well as borrowed sentences?

2. If you have used any Internet sources, look again at the sources to see if the paragraphs on the Internet site are numbered. If so, use the paragraph numbers in your citations; if not, use no numbers—not the numbers on any printout and not paragraph numbers if you must count them.

3. Look at your source material to find a table, graph, figure, or photograph that you might insert into your paper as additional evidence. Then consult pages A-13–A-16 to be certain that you have labeled it correctly.

4. Make a critical journey through your text to be certain that you have made an informed choice about the documentation style you need. Normally, your instructor will inform you. In general, use MLA style for papers in English composition and literature classes; use APA style for papers in the social sciences; use the footnote style for papers in history and the fine arts; use CBE number style for papers in the applied sciences.

12

Writing the Introduction, Body, and Conclusion

The three parts of your paper—the introduction, the body, and the conclusion—each demand special considerations. For most papers, follow the guidelines offered below. However, some scientific papers will demand different elements (see 15a, pages 277-78).

12a Writing the Introduction of the Paper

Use the first few paragraphs of your paper to establish the nature of your study. In brief, the introduction should establish the problem, the body should present the evidence, and the conclusion should arrive at answers, judgments, proposals, and a closure. Most important, let the introduction and body work *toward* a demonstrative conclusion. The introduction should be long enough to establish the required elements described in this checklist.

How you work these essential elements into the framework of your opening will depend upon your style of writing. They need not appear in this order; nor should you cram all these items into a short, opening paragraph. Feel free to write two or three paragraphs of the introduction, letting it run over onto page two, if necessary. When crafting your introduction, use more than one of the techniques described in the following approaches.

Provide the Thesis Statement

Generally, the thesis statement will appear in the final paragraph of the general opening, although it sometimes begins a research paper. For example, this opening features the thesis first:

Thesis —— Shoplifting in stores all over America has reached the point that all shoppers are suspects; each of us is photographed, followed, and watched. The people who use the "five-finger discount" come from all walks of life—the unemployed, sure, but also doctors, lawyers, and even public officials. As a result, clerks in many retail stores look at us with ill will, not friendliness, and they treat us with suspicion, not trust.

C H E C K L I S T

Writing the Introduction

Subject Identify your specific topic, and then define, limit, and narrow it to one issue.

Background Provide relevant historical data. Discuss a few key sources that touch on your specific issue. If writing about a major figure, give relevant biographical facts, but not an encyclopedia-type survey. (See "Provide Background Information," below.)

Problem The point of a research paper is to explore or resolve a problem, so identify and explain the complications that you see. The examples shown below demonstrate this technique.

Thesis Within the first few paragraphs, use your thesis sentence to establish the direction of the study and to point your readers toward your eventual conclusions. (See below, "Opening with Your Thesis Sentence.")

Relate to the Well Known

The next passage will appeal to the popular interest and knowledge of the reader:

Television flashes images into our living rooms, radios invade the confines of our automobiles, and local newspapers flash their headlines to us daily. However, one medium that has gained great popularity and influence within the past decade is the specialized magazine.

— Popular appeal

Provide Background Information

In some instances, trace the historical nature of your topic, give biographical data about a person, or provide a geographic description. A summary of a novel, long poem, or other work can refresh a reader's memory about details of plot, character, and so forth.

To examine the introductions in sample papers by students, see pages 204 and 211.

First published in 1915, <u>Spoon River Anthology</u> by Edgar Lee Masters gives readers candid glimpses into the life of a small town at the turn of the twentieth century. Speaking from beyond the grave, the narrator of each poem gives a portrait of happy, fulfilled people or draws pictures of lives filled with sadness and melancholy.

— Background

This passage offers *essential* background matter, not information that is irrelevant to the thesis. For example, explaining that Eudora Welty was born in Jackson, Mississippi, in 1909 would contribute little to the following opening.

Background —

> In 1941 Eudora Welty published her first book of short stories, *A Curtain of Green*. That group of stories was followed by <u>The Wide Net</u> (1943) and <u>The Bride of the Innisfallen</u> (1955). Each collection brought her critical acclaim, but taken together the three volumes established her as one of America's premier short story writers.

Review the Literature

Cite a few books and articles relevant to the specific issue to introduce some of the literature connected with the topic. This paragraph gives distinction to your introduction because it establishes the scholarship on the subject. It also distinguishes your point of view by explaining the logical connections and differences between previous research and your work.

Review of literature —

> Throughout his novella <u>Billy Budd</u>, Herman Melville intentionally uses biblical references as a means of presenting different moral principles by which people may govern their lives. The story depicts the "loss of Paradise" (Arvin 294); it serves as a gospel story (Weaver 37–38); and it hints at a moral and solemn purpose (Watson 319). The story explores the biblical passions of one man's confrontation with good and evil (Howard 327–328; Mumford 248).

Review the History and Background of the Subject

This opening passage will review the history of the topic, often with quotations from the sources, as shown below in APA style.

Background information —

> Autism, a neurological dysfunction of the brain which commences before the age of thirty months, was identified by Leo Kanner (1943). Kanner studied eleven cases, all of which showed a specific type of childhood psychosis that was different from other childhood disorders, although each was similar to childhood schizophrenia. Kanner described the characteristics of the infantile syndrome as:
>
> 1. Extreme autistic aloneness
> 2. Language abnormalities
> 3. Obsessive desire for the maintenance of sameness
> 4. Good cognitive potential
> 5. Normal physical development
> 6. Highly intelligent, obsessive, and cold parents

Medical studies have reduced these symptoms to four criteria: onset within 30 months of birth, poor social development, late language development, and a preference for regular, stereotyped activity (Rutter, 1978; Watson, 1997; Waller, Smith, and Lambert, 2000). In the United States, autism affects one out of 2,500 children, and is not usually diagnosed until the child is between two and five years of age (Lambert & Smith, 2000).

Take Exception to Critical Views

This opening procedure identifies the subject, establishes a basic view taken by the literature, and then differs with or takes exception with the critical position of other writers, as shown in the following example.

Lorraine Hansberry's popular and successful <u>A Raisin in the Sun</u>, which first appeared on Broadway in 1959, is a problem play of a black family's determination to escape a Chicago ghetto to a better life in the suburbs. There is agreement that this escape theme explains the drama's conflict and its role in the black movement (e.g., Oliver, Archer, and especially Knight, who describes the Youngers as "an entire family that has become aware of, and is determined to combat, racial discrimination in a supposedly democratic land" [34]). Yet another issue lies at the heart of the drama. Hansberry develops a modern view of black matriarchy in order to examine both the cohesive and the conflict-producing effects it has on the individual members of the Younger family.

— Exception to prevailing views

Challenge an Assumption

This passage for the introduction will introduce a well-known idea or general theory in order to question it, analyze it, challenge it, or refute it.

Christianity dominates the religious life of most Americans to the point that many assume that it dominates the world population as well. However, despite the denominational missionaries who have reached out to every corner of the globe, only one out of every four people on the globe is a Christian, and far fewer than that practice their faith.

— Challenge to an assumption

Provide a Brief Summary

When the subject is a novel, long poem, book, or other work that can be summarized, a very brief summary refreshes the memory of the reader.

Ernest Hemingway's novel <u>The Old Man and the Sea</u> narrates the ordeal of an old Cuban fisherman, Santiago, who manages to endure a test of strength when locked in a tug of war with a giant marlin that he hooks and later when he fights sharks who attack his small boat. The heroic and stoic nature of this old hero reflects the traditional Hemingway code.

— Summary

C H E C K L I S T

Avoiding Certain Mistakes in the Opening

- Avoid a purpose statement such as "The purpose of this study is ..." unless you are writing reports of empirical research, in which case you *should* explain the purpose of your study (see Chapter 15, "Writing in APA Style").
- Avoid repetition of the title, which should appear on the first page of the text anyway.
- Avoid complex language or difficult questions that may puzzle the reader. However, general rhetorical questions are acceptable.
- Avoid simple dictionary definitions, such as "Webster defines *monogamy* as marriage with only one person at a time." See page 211 for an acceptable opening that features definition, and see pages 187–88 for ways to define key terminology.
- Avoid humor, unless the subject deals with humor or satire.
- Avoid hand-drawn artwork and comic clip art, unless the paper's subject matter requires it (for example, "The Circle as Advertising Symbol"). *Do* use computer graphics, tables, illustrations, and other designs that are appropriate to your subject.

Or

Alice Walker's The Color Purple narrates the ordeal of a young black girl living in Georgia in the early years of the twentieth — Summary century. Celie writes letters to God because she has no one else to help her. The letters are unusually strong and give evidence of Celie's painful struggle to survive the multiple horrors of her life.

Define Key Terms

Sometimes an opening passage will need to explain difficult terminology, as shown with the following example.

Definition — Black matriarchy, a sociological concept with origins in slavery, is a family situation, according to E. Earl Baughman, in which no husband is present or, if he is present, in which the wife and/or mother exercises the main influence over family affairs (80–81). Hansberry develops a modern view of black matriarchy in order to examine the effects of the dominating mother on the individual members of the Younger family.

Supply Data, Statistics, and Special Evidence

Concrete evidence can attract the reader and establish the subject. For example, a student working with demographic data might compare the birth and death rates of certain sections of the world. In Europe, the rates are almost constant while the African nations have birth rates that are 30 percent higher than the death rates. Such statistical evidence can be a useful tool in many papers. Just remember to support the data with clear, textual discussion. The glossary and appendix in the paper by Katie Hebert, pages 210–23, show how tabulated data can support a report.

To examine methods for adding illustrations and tables, see pages A-13–A-16.

12b Writing the Body of the Research Paper

When writing the body of the paper, you should classify, compare, and analyze the various issues. Keep in mind three key elements, as shown in the checklist.

The length of your paragraphs ought to be from four sentences up to twelve or even fifteen. You can accomplish this task only by writing good topic sentences and by developing them fully. The techniques described in the following paragraphs demonstrate how to build substantive paragraphs for your paper.

C H E C K L I S T

Writing the Body of the Paper

Analysis Classify the major issues of the study and provide a careful analysis of each in defense of your thesis.

Presentation Provide well-reasoned statements at the beginning of your paragraphs, and supply evidence of support with proper documentation.

Paragraphs Offer a variety of development to compare, show process, narrate the history of the subject, show causes, and so forth.

Relate a Time Sequence

Use *chronology* and *plot summary* to trace historical events and to survey a story or novel. You should, almost always, discuss the significance of the events. This first example traces historical events.

Time sequence established —

Following the death of President Roosevelt in April 1945, Harry S. Truman succeeded to the Presidency. Although he was an experienced politician, Truman "was ill prepared to direct a foreign policy," especially one that "called for the use of the atomic bomb to bring World War II to an end" (Jeffers 56). Consideration must be directed at the circumstances of the time, which lead up to Truman's decision that took the lives of over 100,000 individuals and destroyed four square miles of the city of Hiroshima. Consideration must be given to the impact that this decision had on the war, on Japan, and on the rest of the world. Consideration must be directed at the man who brought the twentieth century into the atomic age.

The next passage shows the use of plot summary.

Quick plot summary —

John Updike's "A & P" is a short story about a young grocery clerk named Sammy, who feels trapped by the artificial values of the small town where he lives and, in an emotional moment, quits his job. The store manager, Lengel, is the voice of the conservative values in the community. For him, the girls in swimsuits pose a disturbance to his store, so he expresses his displeasure by reminding the girls that the A & P is not the beach (1088). Sammy, a liberal, believes the girls may be out of place in the A & P only because of its "fluorescent lights," "stacked packages," and "checkerboard green-and-cream-rubber-tile floor," all artificial things (1086).

> **HINT:** Keep the plot summary short and relate it to your thesis, as shown by the first sentence in the passage above. Do not allow the plot summary to extend beyond one paragraph; otherwise, you may retell the entire story. Your task is to make a point, not retell the story.

Compare or Contrast Issues, Critical Views, and Literary Characters

Employ *comparison* and *contrast* to show the two sides of a subject, to compare two characters, to compare the past with the present, or to compare positive and negative issues. The next passage compares and contrasts the differences in forest conservation techniques.

When a "controlled burn" gets out of hand and burns an entire town, defenders of controlled burns have a serious public relations problem. Thus, to burn or not to burn the natural forests in the national parks is the question. The pyrophobic public voices its protests while environmentalists praise the rejuvenating effects of a good forest fire. It is difficult to convince people that not all fire is bad. The public has visions of Smokey the Bear campaigns and mental images of Bambi and Thumper fleeing the roaring flames. Perhaps the public could learn to see beauty in fresh green shoots, like Bambi and Faline as they returned to raise their young. Chris Bolgiano explains that federal policy evolved slowly "from the basic impulse to douse all fires immediately to a sophisticated decision matrix based on the functions of any given unit of land" (22). Bolgiano declares that "timber production, grazing, recreation, and wilderness preservation elicit different fire-management approaches" (23).

— Comparison and contrast

Develop Cause and Effect

Write *cause and effect* paragraphs to develop the reasons for a circumstance or to examine the consequences. An example is shown here which explains not only with cause and effect but also with *analogy*, a metaphoric comparison.

To see how the Hubble Law implies uniform, centerless expansion of a universe, imagine that you want to make a loaf of raisin bread. As the dough rises, the expansion pushes the raisins away from each other. Two raisins that were originally about one centimeter apart separate more slowly than raisins that were about four centimeters apart. The uniform expansion of the dough causes the raisins to move apart at speeds proportional to their distances. Helen Write, in explaining the theory of Edwin Powell Hubble, says the farther the space between them, the faster two galaxies will move away from each other. This is the basis for Hubble's theory of the expanding universe (369).

— Analogy

— Cause and effect

Define Your Key Terminology

Use *definition* to explain and expand upon a complex subject. This next example by student Katie Hebert (see pages 210–23) defines *functional foods.*

Functional foods, as defined by the Australian National Food Authority, are:

Definition ——
> A class of foods that have strong putative metabolic and regulatory (physiological) roles over and above that seen in a wide range of common foods; a class of foods that achieve a defined endpoint that can be monitored (e.g., reduction in blood pressure, reduction in plasma-borne risk markers); and products referred to as special dietary foods. (Head, Record, and King S17)

Explain a Process

Draft a *process* paragraph that explains stage by stage the steps necessary to achieve a desired end.

Blood doping is a process for increasing an athlete's performance on the day of competition. To perform this procedure, technicians drain about one liter of blood from the competitor about 10 months prior to the event. This time allows the "hemoglobin levels to return

Process ——
to normal" (Ray 79). Immediately prior to the athletic event, the blood is reintroduced by injection to give a rush of blood into the athlete's system. Ray reports that the technique produces an "average decrease of 45 seconds in the time it takes to run five miles on a treadmill" (80).

Ask Questions and Provide Answers

Framing a question as a topic sentence gives you the opportunity to develop a thorough answer with specific details and evidence. Look at how a question and answer are used in this example.

Question ——
Does America have enough park lands? The lands now designated as national and state parks, forests, and wild land total in excess of 33 million acres. Yet environmentalists call for additional protected land. They warn of imbalances in the environment. Dean Fraser, in his book, <u>The People Problem</u>, addresses the question of whether we have enough park land:

> Yosemite, in the summer, is not unlike Macy's the week before Christmas. In 1965 it had over 1.6 million visitors; Yellowstone over 2 million. The total area of federal plus state-owned parks is now something like 33 million acres, which sounds impressive until it is divided by the total number of annual visitors of something over 400 million[. . .](33).

> We are running short of green space, which is being devoured by highways, housing projects, and industrial development. — Answer

Cite Evidence from the Source Materials

Citing evidence from the various authorities in the form of quotations, paraphrases, and summaries to support your topic sentences is another excellent way to frame a paragraph. This next passage combines commentary by a critic and a poet to explore Thomas Hardy's pessimism in fiction and poetry.

Several critics reject the impression of Thomas Hardy as a pessimist. He is instead a realist who tends toward optimism.

Thomas Parrott and Willard Thorp make this comment about Hardy in Poetry of the Transition:

> There has been a tendency in the criticism of Hardy's work to consider him as a philosopher rather than as a poet and to stigmatize him as a gloomy pessimist. This is quite wrong. (413) — Evidence from a source

The author himself felt incorrectly labeled, for he writes:

> As to pessimism. My motto is, first correctly diagnose the complaint—in this case human ills—and ascertain the cause: then set about finding a remedy if one exists. The motto of optimists is: Blind the eyes to the real malady, and use empirical panaceas to suppress the symptoms. (Life 383)

Hardy is dismayed by these "optimists" and has little desire to be lumped within such a narrow perspective.

Use a Variety of Other Methods

Many methods exist for developing paragraphs; among them are *description* of a scene in a novel, *statistics* in support of an argument, *historical evidence* in support of a hypothesis, and *psychological theory*. You must make the choices, basing your decision on your subject and your notes. Employ the following methods as appropriate to your project.

- Use *classification* to identify several key issues of the topic, and then use *analysis* to examine each issue in detail. For example, you might classify several types of fungus infections and do an analysis of each, such as athlete's foot, dermatophytosis, and ringworm.
- Use specific *criteria of judgment* to examine performances and works of art. For example, analyze the films of George Lucas by a critical response to story, theme, editing, photography, sound track, special effects, and so forth.

- Use *structure* to control papers on architecture, poetry, fiction, and biological forms. For example, a short story might have six distinct parts that you can examine in sequence.
- Use *location* and *setting* for arranging papers in which geography and locale are key ingredients. For example, examine the settings of several novels by William Faulkner or build an environmental study around land features (e.g., lakes, springs, or sinkholes).
- Use *critical responses to an issue* to evaluate a course of action. For example, an examination of President Harry Truman's decision to use the atomic bomb at the end of World War II would invite you to consider several minor reasons and then to study Truman's major reasons for his decision.
- Dividing the body by important *issues* is standard fare in many research papers. One student examined the major issues of organ and tissue donation (see pages 323–35) and another developed the major issues about nutritional foods (see pages 210–23).

12c Writing the Conclusion of the Research Paper

The conclusion of a research paper should offer the reader more than a mere summary. Use the checklist below to compare against your conclusion.

How you work these elements into your conclusion will depend upon your style of writing. They need not appear in this order; nor should you crowd all the items into one paragraph. The conclusion can extend over several paragraphs and require more than one page. Consider using several of the techniques described in the following approaches.

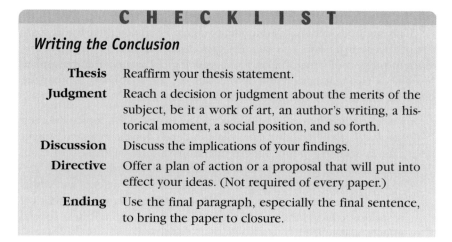

C H E C K L I S T

Writing the Conclusion

Thesis   Reaffirm your thesis statement.

Judgment   Reach a decision or judgment about the merits of the subject, be it a work of art, an author's writing, a historical moment, a social position, and so forth.

Discussion   Discuss the implications of your findings.

Directive   Offer a plan of action or a proposal that will put into effect your ideas. (Not required of every paper.)

Ending   Use the final paragraph, especially the final sentence, to bring the paper to closure.

Restate the Thesis and Reach Beyond It

As a general rule, restate your thesis sentence; however, do not stop and assume that your reader will generate final conclusions about the issues. Instead, establish the essential mission of your study. In the example below, Katie Hebert opens her conclusion by reestablishing her thesis sentence and then moves quickly to her persuasive, concluding judgments.

> Functional foods appear to exert a strong preventive effect on the two diseases that take more American lives than any other— coronary heart disease and cancer. High cholesterol levels cause coronary heart disease, the factor responsible for 24% of the fatalities that occur in the United States (Blumberg 3). Foods high in antioxidants (i.e., Vitamins C, E, and beta-carotene), omega-e fatty acids, and soluble fiber, along with green and black tea have been proven to be an effective form of preventive medicine for individuals at risk of developing coronary heart disease. Second only to coronary heart disease, "cancer is the cause of death in 22% of Americans" (4). Functional foods have exhibited similar strength in the fight for cancer prevention. By incorporating functional foods, such as insoluble fiber, garlic, and green and black tea into the diet, an individual can lower one's risk of being diagnosed with cancer. Although this finding does do not mean one should cancel all future doctor appointments, it has shown that individuals who eat functional foods are a step ahead in the battle for disease prevention.

Thesis restated in the conclusion

Close with an Effective Quotation

Sometimes a source may provide a striking commentary that deserves special placement, as shown by this example.

> W. C. Fields had a successful career that extended from vaudeville to musical comedy and finally to the movies. In his private life, he loathed children and animals, and he fought with bankers, landladies, and the police. Off screen, he maintained his private image as a vulgar, hard-drinking cynic until his death in 1946. On the screen, he won the hearts of two generations of fans. He was beloved by audiences primarily for acting out their own contempt for authority. The movies prolonged his popularity "as a dexterous comedian with expert timing and a look of bibulous rascality," but Fields had two personalities, "one jolly and one diabolical" (Kennedy 990).

Effective quotation

Return the Focus of a Literary Study to the Author

While the body of a literary paper should analyze the characters, images, and plot, the conclusion should explain the author's accomplishments. The following closing shows how one writer focused on the author.

Focus on the author —

As to the issues of the country versus the city and the impact of a market economy, Jonathan Swift advances the conservative position of the early eighteenth century which lamented the loss of the rural, agrarian society, with its adherence to tradition and a stable social hierarchy. His position focused on the social outcomes: unemployment, displacement, and the disenfranchisement of a significant portion of the populace. Unlike his London contemporaries, Swift resided in the economic hinterland of Ireland, so he had a more direct view of the destructive population shifts from rural to urban.

Focus on the author —

Ultimately, Swift's commentary in <u>A Modest Proposal</u> is important because it records a consciousness of a continuing problem, one that worsens with the intensification of the urban rather than rural growth. It continues to plague the twenty-first-century world, from America to Africa and from Russia to Latin America.

Compare the Past to the Present or the Present to the Future

You can use the conclusion to compare the historic past with the contemporary scene. For example, after explaining the history of two schools of treatment for autism, one writer switches to the present, as shown in this excerpt:

Future in contrast to the present —

There is hope in the future that both the cause and the cure for autism will be found. For the present, new drug therapies and behavior modification offer some hope for the abnormal, SIB actions of a person with autism. Since autism is sometimes outgrown, childhood treatment offers the best hope for the autistic person who must try to survive in an alien environment.

Offer a Directive or Solution

After analyzing a problem and synthesizing issues, offer your theory or solution, as demonstrated immediately above in the example in which the writer suggests that "childhood treatment offers the best hope for the autistic person who must try to survive in an alien environment." Note also this closing:

All of the aspects of diabetes management can be summed up in one word: balance. Diabetes itself is caused by a lack of balance of insulin and glucose in the body. In order to restore that balance, a diabetic must juggle medication, monitoring, diet, and exercise. Managing diabetes is not an easy task, but a long and healthy life is very possible when the delicate balance is carefully maintained.

— A directive or solution

Discuss Test Results

In scientific writing (see Chapters 15 and 17), your conclusion, labeled "discussion," will need to explain the ramifications of your findings and to identify any limitations of your scientific study, as shown.

The results of this experiment were similar to expectations, but perhaps the statistical significance, because of the small subject size, was biased toward the delayed conditions of the curve. The subjects were, perhaps, not representative of the total population because of their prior exposure to test procedures. Another factor that may have affected the curve was the presentation of the data. The images on the screen were available for five seconds, and that amount of time may have enabled the subjects to store each image effectively. If the time period for each image were reduced to one or two seconds, there could be lower recall scores, thereby reducing the differences between the control group and the experimental group.

— Test results

C H E C K L I S T
Avoiding Certain Mistakes in the Conclusion

- Avoid afterthoughts or additional ideas. Now is the time to end the paper, not begin a new thought. If new ideas occur to you as you draft a conclusion, don't ignore them. Explore them fully in the context of your thesis and consider adding them to the body of your paper or modifying your thesis. Scientific studies often discuss options and possible alterations that might affect test results (see "Discuss Test Results," above).
- Avoid the use of *thus, in conclusion,* or *finally* at the beginning of the last paragraph. Readers can see plainly the end of the paper.
- Avoid ending the paper without a sense of closure.
- Avoid questions that raise new issues; however, rhetorical questions that restate the issues are acceptable.
- Avoid decorative artwork.

■ YOUR RESEARCH PROJECT

1. Review your opening to determine whether it builds the argument and sets the stage for analysis to come in the body. Consider adding paragraphs like those described on pages 180–85: relate the well known, provide background information, review the literature, review the history of the subject, take exception to prevailing views, challenge an assumption, provide a summary of the issues, define key terms, supply statistical evidence.

2. After finishing the first draft, review the body of your paper. Has your analysis touched on all the issues? Have you built paragraphs of substance, as demonstrated on pages 185–90? Judge the draft against the checklist for the body on page 185.

3. Evaluate your conclusion according to the checklist on page 190. If you feel it's necessary, build the conclusion by these techniques: elaborate on the thesis, use an effective quotation, focus on a key person, compare the past and the present, offer a directive or solution, or discuss test results (see pages 190–93 for a discussion of these techniques).

13

Revising, Proofreading, and Formatting the Rough Draft

Once you have the complete paper in a rough draft, the serious business of editing begins. First, you should revise your paper on a global scale, moving blocks of material around to the best advantage and into the proper format. Second, edit the draft with a line by line examination of wording and technical excellence. Third, proofread the final version to ensure that your words are spelled correctly and the text is grammatically sound.

Ask a classmate to review your draft (see page 197 on peer reviews). Also, ask your instructor to skim through your rough draft and offer suggestions. In every case, you should be ready to conduct more research, abandon unsubstantiated ideas, cut frivolous and repetitive passages, and change long, unnecessary quotations into penetrating short quotations or effective paraphrases.

13a Conducting a Global Revision

Revision can turn a passable paper into an excellent one and change an excellent one into a radiant one. First, revise the whole manuscript by performing the tasks in the checklist.

CHECKLIST

Global Revision

1. Skim through the paper to check its unity. Does the paper maintain a central proposition from paragraph to paragraph?
2. Transplant paragraphs, moving them to more relevant and effective positions.
3. Delete sentences that do not further your cause.
4. Revise your outline to match these changes if you must submit the outline with the paper.

Use the computer during global revision to redesign and realign sentences and paragraphs. Depending on your software, use CUT, PASTE, COPY, and so forth; however, after each move, remember to rewrite and blend the words into your text. Use the FIND command to locate some words and phrases in order to eliminate constant scrolling up and down the screen. Use FIND/REPLACE to change wording or spelling throughout the document.

Revising the Introduction

Examine your opening for the presence of several items:

- Your thesis
- A clear sense of direction or plan of development
- A sense of involvement that invites the reader into your investigation of a problem.

Revising the Body

Use the following bulleted list as a guide for revising each paragraph.

- Cut irrelevant words and phrases, even to the point of deleting entire sentences that contribute nothing to the dynamics of the paper.

- Combine a short paragraph with others, or build one of substance.

- Revise long, difficult paragraphs by dividing them or by using transitions effectively (see "Writing with Unity and Coherence," pages 153–54).

- For paragraphs that seem short, shallow, or weak, add more commentary and more evidence, especially quotations from the primary sources or critical citations from secondary sources.

- Add your own input to paragraphs that rely too heavily on the source materials.

- Examine your paragraphs for transitions that move the reader effectively from one paragraph to the next.

Revising the Conclusion

Examine the conclusion to see it meets these criteria:

- It is drawn from the evidence.
- It is developed logically from the introduction and the body.
- It expresses your position on the issues.
- It examines the implication of the study.

Participating in Peer Review

Part of the revision process for many writers, both students and professionals, is peer review. It has two sides. First, it means submitting your paper to a friend or classmate, asking for their opinions and suggestions. Second, it means reviewing a classmate's research paper. You can learn by reviewing as well as by writing.

Since this task asks you to make judgments, you need a set of criteria. Your instructor may supply a peer review sheet, or you can use the following list. Criticize the paper constructively on each point. If you can answer each question with a *yes*, your classmate has performed well. For those questions that you assign a *no*, you owe it to your classmate to explain what seems wrong. Make suggestions. Offer tips. Try to help!

C H E C K L I S T

Peer Review

1. Are the subject and the accompanying issues introduced early?

2. Is the writer's critical approach to the problem stated clearly in a thesis sentence? Is it placed effectively in the introduction?

3. Do the paragraphs of the body have individual unity? That is, does each one develop an important idea and only one idea? Does each paragraph relate to the thesis?

4. Are sources introduced, usually with the name of the expert, and then cited by a page number within parentheses? Keep in mind that Internet sources will not have page numbers.

5. Is it clear where a paraphrase begins and where it ends?

6. Are the sources relevant to the argument?

7. Does the writer weave quotations into the text effectively while avoiding long quotations that look like filler instead of substance?

8. Does the conclusion arrive at a resolution about the central issue?

9. Does the title describe clearly what your classmate has put in the body of the research paper?

13b Formatting the Paper to MLA Style

The format of a research paper consists of the following parts:

1. Title page
2. Outline
3. Abstract
4. The text of the paper
5. Content notes
6. Appendix
7. Works Cited

Items 4 and 7 are required for a paper in the MLA style; use the other items to meet the needs of your research. *Note:* A paper in APA style (see Chapter 15) requires items 1, 3, 4, and 7, and the order differs for items 5 through 7.

Title Page or Opening Page

A research paper in MLA style does not need a separate title page unless you include an outline, abstract, or other prefatory matter. Place your identification in the upper left corner of your opening page, as shown here.

Howell

Identifying — information

Pamela Howell
English 102c, U of A
May 17, 2000

Creative Marriages

   Judging by recent divorce rates, it would seem that the traditional marriage fails to meet the needs[. . .].

However, if you include prefatory matter, such as an outline, you need the title page with centered divisions for the title, the author, and the course identification.

An Interpretation of Melville's
Use of Biblical Characters
In <u>Billy Budd</u>

by
Doris Singleton

Freshman English II, Section 108b
Dr. Crampton
April 23, 2001

Follow these guidelines for writing a title page in MLA style:

1. Use an inverted pyramid to balance two or more lines.
2. Use capitals and lowercase letters without underlining and without quotation marks. Published works that appear as part of your title will require underlining (books) or quotation marks (short stories). Do not use a period after a centered heading.
3. Place your full name below the title, usually in the center of the page.
4. Employ separate lines, centered, to provide the course information, institution, instructor, date, or program (e.g., Honors Program).
5. Provide balanced, two-inch margins for all sides of the title page.
6. Use your computer to print a border on this page, if you so desire, but not on any other pages.

NOTE: APA style requires a different setup for the title page; see page 300 for an example.

Outline

Print your outline into the finished manuscript only if your instructor requires it. Place it after the title page on separate pages, and number these pages with small Roman numerals, beginning with ii (for example, ii, iii, iv, v) at the top right-hand corner of the page just after your last name (e.g., Spence iii).

For information on writing an outline, see 6c, 96–101, and see also the sample outline on pages 324–25.

Abstract

Include an abstract for a paper in MLA style only if your instructor requires it. (APA style requires the abstract; see 15h, page 299). An abstract provides a brief digest of the paper's essential ideas in about 100 words. To that end, borrow from your introduction, use some of the topic sentences from your paragraphs, and use one or two sentences from your conclusion.

In MLA style, place the abstract on the first page of text (page 1) one double-space below the title and before the first lines of the text. Indent the abstract five spaces as a block, and indent the first line an additional five spaces. Use quadruple spacing at the end of the abstract to set it off from the text, which follows immediately after. You may also place the abstract on a separate page between the title page and first page of text.

For additional discussion of the abstract and examples, see pages 143–44, 211, and 299.

Remember that the abstract is usually read first and may be the *only* part read; therefore, make it accurate, specific, objective, and self-contained (i.e., so that it makes sense alone without references to the main text). Note the example on the following page.

Walker 1

Abstract

Child Abuse: A View of the Victims

This study examines the problems of child abuse, especially the fact that families receive attention after abuse occurs, not before. With abuse statistics on the rise, efforts devoted to prevention rather than coping should focus on parents in order to discover those adults most likely to commit abuse because of heredity, their own childhood, the economy, and other causes of depression. Viewing the parent as a victim, not just a criminal, will enable social agencies to institute preventive programs that may control abuse and hold together family units.   —— Quadruple space

Family troubles will most likely affect the delicate members   —— Text of our society, the children. The recognition of causal elements[. . .].

The Text of the Paper

Double space throughout the entire paper except for the title page (see pages 198–99) and the separation of the abstract from the first line of text (see above). In general, you should *not* use subtitles or numbered divisions for your paper, even if it becomes twenty pages long. Instead, use continuous paragraphing without subdivisions or headings. However, some scientific and business reports require subheads (see Chapters 15 and 17).

If the closing page of your text runs short, leave the remainder of the page blank. Do not write "The End" or provide artwork as a closing signal. Do not start "Notes" or "Works Cited" on this final page of text.

Content Endnotes Page

Label this page with the word "Notes" centered at the top edge of the sheet, at least one double space below your page numbering sequence in the upper right corner. Double space between the "Notes" heading

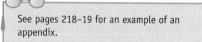

See "Content Notes," pages 316–19, and see also the sample "Notes" page on page 217.

and the first note. Number the notes in sequence with raised superscript numerals to match those within your text. Double space all entries and double space between them.

Appendix

Place additional material, if necessary, in an appendix preceding the "Works Cited" page. It is the logical location for numerous tables and illustrations, computer data, questionnaire results, complicated sta-

See pages 218–19 for an example of an appendix.

tistics, mathematical proofs, or detailed descriptions of special equipment. Double space Appendices and begin each appendix on a new sheet. Continue your page numbering sequence in the upper right corner of the sheet. Label the page "Appendix," centered at the top of the sheet. If you have more than one appendix, use "Appendix A," "Appendix B," and so forth.

Works Cited

Center the heading "Works Cited" one inch from the top edge of the sheet. Continue the page numbering sequence in the upper right corner. Double space throughout. Use the hanging indention; that is, set the first line of each entry flush left and indent subsequent lines five spaces or one half inch.

> For samples and additional information see Chapter 14, "Works Cited," pages 224–76, and the sample bibliography on pages 222–23.

13c Editing Before Typing or Printing the Final Manuscript

The cut-and-paste revision period is complemented by careful editing of paragraphs, sentences, and individual words. Travel through the paper to study your sentences and word choice. Look for ways to tighten and condense. Here is a checklist.

> To review matters of unity and coherence and writing effectively, see 10d, pages 152–56.

C H E C K L I S T

Editing

1. Cut phrases and sentences that do not advance your main ideas or that merely repeat what your sources have already stated.

2. Determine that coordinated, balanced ideas are appropriately expressed and that minor ideas are properly subordinated.

3. Change most of your "to be" verbs (*is, are, was*) to stronger active verbs.

4. Maintain the present tense in most verbs when writing in MLA style, but see also Chapter 15, pages 278–79, for APA style.

5. Convert passive structures to active unless you want to emphasize the subject, not the actor (see page 156).

6. Confirm that you have introduced paraphrases and quotations so that they flow smoothly into your text.

7. Use formal, academic style and be on guard against clusters of little monosyllabic words that fail to advance ideas. Examine your wording for its effectiveness within the context of your subject.

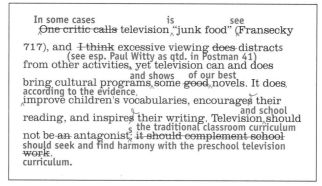

Example of editing on a manuscript page.

Note the editing by one student in Figure 13.1. As shown, the writer conscientiously edited the paragraph, deleted unnecessary material, added supporting statements, related facts to one another, rearranged data, added new ideas, and rewrote for clarity.

Using the Computer to Edit Your Text

Some software programs will examine your grammar and mechanics: look for parentheses that you opened but never closed, find unpaired quotation marks, flag passive verbs, question your spelling, and mark other items for correction. Pay attention to the caution flags raised by this type of program. As a software program examines the style of your manuscript, you should edit to improve stylistic weaknesses. However, edit and adjust your paper by *your* standards with due respect to the computer analysis. Remember, it is your paper, not the computer's. You may need to use some long words and write some long sentences, or you may prefer the passive voice in one particular sentence.

13d Proofreading on the Screen and on the Printed Manuscript

First, proofread your paper on the screen with programs that check spelling, grammar, and style. Also check on screen your formatting, such as double spacing, one-inch margins, running heads, page numbers, and so forth.

Consult "Glossary of Manuscript Style," pages A-1–A-30, for instructions on handling abbreviations, margins, tables, numbering, punctuation, content notes, and other matters.

After editing the text on screen to your satisfaction, print or type a hard copy of the manuscript. You should proofread this final version with great care because the software will not catch every error. Be

C H E C K L I S T

Proofreading

1. Check for errors in sentence structure, spelling, and punctuation.
2. Check for hyphenation and word division. Remember that no words should be hyphenated at the ends of lines. If you are using a computer, turn off the automatic hyphenation.
3. Read each quotation for accuracy. Look, too, for the correct use of quotation marks.
4. Be certain that in-text citations are correct and that each source is listed in the "Works Cited" page.
5. Double-check the format—the title page, margins, spacing, content notes, and many other elements, as explained on pages 198–201, and in the glossary on pages A-1–A-30.

sure that your in-text citations are correct, that you have a bibliography entry for each one, and that the bibliography entries are cited in the correct form.

■ YOUR RESEARCH PROJECT

1. Examine once again the intellectual argument of your first draft. Is your thesis established clearly in the opening and then reaffirmed in the closing?
2. Do the paragraphs of the body develop the evidence systematically to support your claim or thesis? Examine each paragraph for relevance.
3. Examine again your title. Does it meet the criteria set forth in 10c?
4. If you participated in a peer review, consider carefully the recommendations and judgments of your reviewer. There's always a tendency to dismiss words of criticism, but you need to learn that constructive criticism exists at all levels of collegiate and professional life.
5. Read aloud to yourself a portion of the paper. Does it have an academic style? If not, read the sample paragraphs in Chapter 12, pages 180–94. Edit to conform to these examples of style.

Short Literary Research Paper

Shannon Williams accepted the challenge to write a brief literary paper on Langston Hughes using as sources only her textbook and academic Internet sites. While printed library sources are important, the test for Williams was to work from her home computer, drawing from sites at the University of Texas, the University of Illinois at Urbana-Champaign, and Boston Book Review.

Shannon Williams

English 1020

Dr. Lester

April 20, 2000

A title page is not usually required. Just provide your name and course information in the left column, center the title, and begin your text.

Langston Hughes

At the advent of the Harlem Renaissance in the 1920s, the relatively genteel world of American poetry was shaken to its foundations. Strong Black voices, writing with African American rhythms and cadences broke out all over the country. White poetry written by Caucasian artists was no longer the only game in town. Of this remarkable creative outpouring by blacks, one voice rose among all of the rest. This was the voice of Langston Hughes, who inspired and angered both whites and blacks.

The writer introduces Hughes as a controversial figure.

James Mercer Langston Hughes is now widely recognized as an accomplished, world-renowned author. He has been described by Gerald Early, English professor and director of African and Afro-American Studies at Washington University in St. Louis, as the major artistic link between the revolutionary poet, Paul Lawrence Dunbar, and the radical poet, Amiri Baraka. Andrew Jackson considers him a leading African American voice of the twentieth century. In the forty-five years between his first book that was published in 1926 and his death in 1967, he devoted his life to writing and lecturing. Accoding to Michael Meyer, his works include volumes of "poetry, novels, short stories, essays, plays, opera librettos, histories, documentaries, autobiographies, biographies, anthologies, children's books, and translations, as well as radio and television scripts" (1011).

Jackson is a web source, so there is no page number (see pages 162–63).

Meyer is a printed source, so a page number is necessary.

Hughes has several recurring themes in his works that are mainly centered on race relations, racial oppression, racial consciousness, Black pride, and personal dignity. Hughes's poems express vividly different Black sentiments, hopes, aspirations and pride; but most of all, according to Belinda Chow, his poems show "one unifying thread, one origin: the need for more equal treatment between races " [. . .] ("Langston Hughes: Poems"). Unfortunately, to the dissatisfaction of other notable African American poets and critics, Hughes often wrote about black people while writing in the vernacular that was common to "ordinary" African Americans. This particular style of writing was offensive to many African American and White American poets, critics, and intellectuals alike, because they only

The writer confronts one controversial aspect of Hughes— his use of vernacular language in his poetry.

Williams 2

wanted the most positive and refined images of Black life to be presented for the inspection of White audiences (Chow, "Langston Hughes: Poems").

Provide name and abbreviated title for a source that provides two or more works.

Seemingly in retaliation, Hughes penned the essay, "The Negro Artist and the Racial Mountain." The work speaks of Black writers and poets who would, in his opinion, surrender racial pride in the name of a false integration. It spoke of the issues of talented Black writers who would prefer to be considered poets, not Black poets, which meant to Hughes that such Black poets subconsciously wanted to write like White poets. An excerpt from the essay reads:

Long blocks of quotation should be indented 10 spaces, or one inch, from the left margin (MLA style only).

> We younger Negro artists now intend to express our individual dark-skinned selves without fear or shame. If white people are pleased we are glad. If they aren't it doesn't matter. We know we are beautiful. And ugly too [. . .] . If colored people are pleased we are glad. If they are not, their displeasure doesn't matter either. We build our temples for tomorrow, as strong as we know how and we stand on the top of the mountain, free within ourselves.
> (Qtd. in Jackson)

A prime example of Hughes's use of the vernacular that was common to ordinary African Americans is demonstrated in the poem "Red Silk Stockings." The poem reads:

> Put on yo' red silk stockings,
>   Black gal.
> Go out an' let de white boys
> Look at yo' legs.
> Ain't nothin' to do for you, nohow,
> Round this town,
> You's too pretty.
> Put on yo' red silk stockings, gal,
> An' tomorrow's chile'll
> Be a high yaller.
> Go out an' let de white boys
> Look at yo' legs.
>   (Qtd. in Meyer 1022-23)

The writer must show the source of the quotation.

Though many middle-class African Americans considered Hughes's use of the vernacular "an embarrassing handicap and an impediment to social progress," Meyers argues that Hughes was successful "in securing appreciative audiences" among both the African American

Williams 3

and White American communities (1011). In keeping with Hughes's recurring theme of racial consciousness, he penned the poem, "I Too," which effectively demonstrates Hughes's faith in the racial consciousness of African Americans. In this poem, Hughes expresses his desire for African Americans to recognize their personal integrity and beauty while simultaneously urging them to demand respect and acceptance from others (Meyer 1014). The poem reads:

> I, too, sing America.
>
> I am the darker brother.
>
> They send me to eat in the kitchen when
>
> > company comes,
>
> But I laugh,
>
> And eat well,
>
> And grow strong.
>
> Tomorrow,
>
> I'll be at the table
>
> When company comes.
>
> Nobody'll dare
>
> Say to me,
>
> "Eat in the kitchen,"
>
> Then.
>
> Besides,
>
> They'll see how beautiful I am,
>
> And be ashamed—
>
> I, too, am America.
>
> > (Qtd. in Meyer 1014)

One online source reminds us that even at his death in 1967 Hughes was controversial: "Having been considered a dangerous radical in the 1930s, he was now [. . .] rejected by 1960s radicals as part of the problem, rather than part of the solution" ("Langston Hughes: Biography").

Beyond the racial issue, Hughes has an interesting style of writing. He successfully weaves rhythms of jazz and blues into his poetry. This was largely due to his participation in the Harlem Renaissance, a movement that allowed Black artists to express their art through music, verse, and theater in the 1920s (Chow, "A Research Brief"). Hughes spent a lot of time in the blues and jazz clubs of Harlem, New York, and almost immediately, his poetry began to reflect the effective rhythms of the popular music of the Harlem Renaissance.

The writer moves from the racial issue in Hughes's poetry to the role of Hughes in the jazz movement of the Harlem Renaissance.

When a writer has two or more works cited in your paper, add an abbreviated title to the citation.

Williams 4

'The Weary Blues" is a good example of his use of blues in his poetry.
An excerpt of the poem reads:

> Thump, thump, thump, went his foot
>> on the floor.
> He played a few chords then he sang
>> some more
> "I got the Weary Blues
> And I can't be satisfied.
> Got the Weary Blues
> And can't be satisfied
> I ain't happy no mo'
> And I wish that I had died.
>> (Qtd. in Meyer 1019-1020)

His poem "Lenox Avenue: Midnight" is a good example of his use
of jazz rhythms in his poetry. Jazz poetry has been described in
Britannica.com as poetry read to the accompaniment of jazz music
in which "authors attempt to emulate the rhythms and freedom of
the music in their poetry" ("Jazz Poetry"). Hughes often read his
poetry at jazz clubs on Lenox Avenue. One poem, "Lenox Avenue:
Midnight," reads:

> The rhythm of life
> Is a jazz rhythm,
> Honey.
> The gods are laughing at us.
> The broken heart of love,
> The weary, weary heart of pain,
>> Overtones,
>> Undertones,
> To the rumble of street cars,
> To the swish of rain.
> Lenox Avenue,
> Honey.
> Midnight,
> And the gods are laughing at us.
>> (Qtd. in Meyer 1022)

Hughes also effectively incorporates remarkable symbolism in
his poetry. In "The Negro Speaks of Rivers," Hughes pictures
Africa's dusky rivers to show how they "run concurrently with the
poet's soul as he draws spiritual strength as well as individual

The poetry, prose, and fiction of a writer serve as primary evidence in a literary essay just as test results are primary evidence in a scientific study.

The writer moves to another issue—Hughes's use of symbols in his poetry.

Williams 5

identity from the collective experience of his ancestors" (Meyer 1011). According to Arnold Rampersad, author of <u>The Life of Langston Hughes</u>, Hughes demonstrates in "The Negro Speaks of Rivers" his masterful use of symbolism. Rampersad contends that the poem is "suffused with the image of death and simultaneously, the idea of deathlessness." Onwucheka Jemie, author of <u>Langston Hughes: An Introduction to Poetry</u>, has a similar perspective in regard to Hughes's use of symbolism in the poem. Jemie points out in his review of the poem that the images of the rivers are in fact allusions to God's body, and they "participate in his immortality." Jemie goes on to say that the rivers are earthly analogues of eternity, which are deep, continuous, and mysterious.

The conclusion connects Hughes to the modern age; that is, to the rap music of today's musicians.

Hughes, a multi-talented man, was a master of poetry. He was an innovator as he developed a style of poetry that sparked a trend that would continue to be emulated by many poets to come. By his daring, he is one of the fathers of today's rap music. Though he was criticized by many, Hughes endured and proved to be an important literary figure who stood by his beliefs in the need to encourage others to be racially conscious while maintaining a positive self-identity.

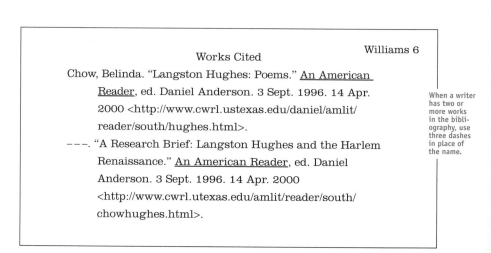

Williams 6

Works Cited

Chow, Belinda. "Langston Hughes: Poems." <u>An American Reader</u>, ed. Daniel Anderson. 3 Sept. 1996. 14 Apr. 2000 <http://www.cwrl.ustexas.edu/daniel/amlit/reader/south/hughes.html>.

---. "A Research Brief: Langston Hughes and the Harlem Renaissance." <u>An American Reader</u>, ed. Daniel Anderson. 3 Sept. 1996. 14 Apr. 2000 <http://www.cwrl.utexas.edu/amlit/reader/south/chowhughes.html>.

When a writer has two or more works in the bibliography, use three dashes in place of the name.

Early, Gerald. Rev. of <u>The Collected Poems of Langston</u>
<u>Hughes</u>, by Arnold Rampersad and David Roessel,
eds. <u>The Boston Book Review</u> May 1995. 14 Apr.
2000 <http://www.bookwire.com/bbr/poetry/
collected-langston-hughes.html>.

Jackson, Andrew [Sekou Molefi Baako]. "James Langston
Hughes." The Red Hot Jazz Archive: A History of
Jazz before 1930. N.d. 14 Apr. 2000
<http:// www.redhotjazz.com/hughes.html>.

"Jazz Poetry." Britannica.com. N.d. 13 Aug. 2000
<http://www.britannica.com/bcom/ab/article/1/
0,5716,1187911110142,00.html>.

Jemie, Onwuchekwa. <u>Langston Hughes: An Introduction</u>
<u>to the Poetry</u>. 1976. Rpt. in <u>Modern American</u>
<u>Poetry</u>. Comp. Cary Nelson. Urbana-Champaign:
U of Illinois, 1999. 14 Apr. 2000
<http://www.english.uiuc.edu/maps/ poets/g_l/
hughes/rivers.html>.

"Langston Hughes: Biography." <u>Literature Online: Poetry</u>
<u>Author Casebooks</u>. N.d. 14 Apr. 2000
<http://longman.awl.com/kennedy/hughes/
biography.html>.

Meyer, Michael, ed. <u>The Bedford Introduction to Literature</u>.
5th ed. Boston: Bedford/St. Martin's, 1999.

Rampersad, Arnold. <u>The Life of Langston Hughes</u>. 1988.
Rpt. in <u>Modern American Poetry</u>. Comp. Cary Nelson.
Urbana-Champaign: U of Illinois, 1999. 14 Apr. 2000
<http:// www.english.uiuc.edu/maps/poets/g_l/
hughes/rivers.htm>.

This entry cites a review article.

This entry cites a pseudonym as well as an archival site.

This entry cites an online encyclopedia.

This entry cites a source reprinted in an online anthology.

This entry cites the literature anthology from which the student drew her poetry examples.

Long Research Paper

Katie Hebert decided to examine the role of certain foods in preventing diseases. She examined a variety of sources, reproduced tables, added content notes as well as in-text citations, and supplemented the text with two appendices.

"Healing Foods": A Powerful Step in the
Way of Preventive Medicine?

Hebert provides
a title page
because an
abstract
separates the
title from
the beginning
of the text.

by

Katie Hebert

English 102
Professor James Stokes
December 5, 2000

Hebert 2

Abstract

The functional food revolution has begun! Functional foods, products that provide benefits beyond basic nutrition, are making billions for the nation's economy each year. So what is their secret, why are functional foods a hit? Functional foods are suspected to be a form of preventive medicine. This news has made the public swarm and food nutritionists salivate. Consumers hope that functional foods can calm some of their medical anxieties. Many researchers believe that functional foods may be the answer to the nation's prayers for lower health care costs. This paper goes behind the scenes, beyond all the hype, in its attempt to determine if functional foods are an effective form of preventive medicine. The paper identifies several functional foods, locates the components that make them work, and explains the role that each plays on the body.

Although medical professionals are just beginning to open their minds and eyes to the medicinal power of food, others have known about food's healing properties for centuries.

The great philosopher Hippocrates, surely a man ahead of his time in 400 BC, wrote, "Let food be thy medicine and medicine be thy food" (qtd. in Hasler, "Their Role,"). Despite a slow onset, the popularity of "healing foods" is alive and growing today. So what exactly are "healing foods"? In their 1999 position report on functional foods, a term synonymous with "healing foods," the American Dietetic Association (ADA) states, "There is no universally accepted definition of functional foods" ("Position" 1278). Yet the Australian National Food Authority does provide a definition:

> A class of foods that have strong putative metabolic and regulatory (physiological) roles over and above that seen in a wide range of common foods; a class of foods that achieve a defined endpoint that can be monitored (e.g., reduction in blood pressure, reduction in plasma-borne risk markers), and products referred to as special dietary foods. (Head, Record, and King 617)

Indent an abstract as a block and separate it from the opening line of text with quadruple spacing.

Early in the essay, the writer defines her concept of 'functional foods.'

Hebert 3

Clare Hasler says that consumers are highly inquisitive about this "miracle medicine" ("Western Perspective" 67). She adds that researchers believe that if the medicinal properties of functional foods can gain the support of clinical evidence, functional foods can become an economic weapon in the battle against rising health care costs. In addition, food scientists believe that functional foods may be a promising addition to the diet of those suffering from deadly disease. As executive director of the Functional Foods for Health Program at the University of Illinois, Hasler claims, "Six of the ten leading causes of death in the United States are believed to be related to diet: cancer, coronary heart disease, stroke, diabetes, atherosclerosis, and liver disease" ("Western Perspective" 66).

Are healing foods an effective form of preventive medicine? The evidence swings toward a positive answer, so a massive industry devoted to "dietary supplements" has begun to amass huge profits. The benefits to people consuming such items as chicken collagen or ginkgo biloba remain unclear. This study will therefore examine the different "healing" components, identify the role that they play on the body, and pinpoint the foods in which they are found.[1]

The writer establishes her primary thesis.

Before examining the medicinal components of functional foods, it is necessary that one understand how functional foods recently rode to the top of the nutritional world. Consumer demand, dietary labeling, and the high cost of health care are just some of the factors responsible for the functional food explosion in the United States (Hasler, "Western Perspective" 66). Many Americans, trying to mend their past nutritional mistakes, see functional foods as an essential step toward a more health conscious future. This nation of believers spends "an estimated $29 billion a year" on functional foods (Nelson 755). The food industry is playing upon the public's sense of guilt by marketing a number of expensive foods that appear to be a form of preventive medicine when in actuality, it is simply a ploy. So how do food companies get away with this? The answer is simple: they slip their product through regulatory loopholes.

The writer explores the loopholes that allow food additives and dietary supplements to become the sweethearts of a massive industry.

The loose regulatory environment of the United States allows functional foods and components to be categorized as "conventional foods, food additives, dietary supplements, medical foods, or foods with special dietary use" ("Position" 1279). Granted, allowing products backed by little or no scientific evidence (i.e., antioxidant-enriched drinks and candies) to leak through regulatory cracks is a definite

When no author is listed, use an abbreviation of the title in the place of the author's name.

Hebert 4

drawback to the system; however, its flexibility has also provided
functional foods of scientific merit with a chance to prove
themselves to consumers. Although the U.S. Food and Drug
Administration (FDA) supports a broad categorization of functional
foods, it recognizes and approves only the most "scientifically
sound" (see Appendix A). Functional foods that are approved by the
FDA carry a nutritional label that explains that the product is "a
tested form of preventive medicine (i.e., increased consumption of
fruits and vegetables results in a decreased risk of cancer and/or
coronary heart disease)" ("Position" 1279). In order for functional
foods to become "FDA approved," the food companies must provide
all the scientific evidence that supports their "risk reduction" claim
in the form of a petition to the FDA ("Position" 1279). But where does
that leave functional foods that have yet to be approved by the FDA?

> A reference to an appendix aids readers.

> The writer uses effectively the question-answer technique for developing her ideas.

The breakthrough for this class of functional foods came in 1994
with the passing of the Dietary Supplement Health and Education Act
(DSHEA) ("Position" 1279). Many of the functional foods in this
category are supported by insubstantial scientific evidence and either
have not yet petitioned the FDA or have petitions pending. Because
the FDA does not back these products (marketed as dietary
supplements), they do not have the advantage of wearing a label that
makes a "risk reduction" claim. But the DSHEA allows dietary
supplements to wear a different type of label, one that shows that the
supplement has a positive effect on the body, for example, Vitamin A
improves eyesight ("Position" 1279). These particular dietary
supplements are set apart from those supported by a FDA approved
health claim by the disclosure[2] that must accompany their label
("Position" 1279). The enactment of the DSHEA has provided
functional foods, caught in this in-between stage, with a chance to
hint of their nutritional value and control a person's medical costs.

> Superscript numerals refer readers to content notes at the end of the paper (see pages 316–19 for how to write content notes).

In truth, many researchers believe that, economically, functional
foods can save the United States billions. Functional foods are
helping fight an economic battle against rising health care costs.
It's common knowledge that the U. S. population is getting older,
which means more people are being diagnosed and treated for a wide
variety of diseases. These individuals place a huge financial strain on
the health care system with their need for expensive antibiotics and
hospital procedures. So many people, consumers and researchers
alike, have turned to functional foods in hopes of finding some sort

Hebert 5

of financial relief. Dr. Herbert Pierson, director of the National Cancer Institute's $20 million functional food program, states, "The future is prevention, and looking for preventive agents in foods is more cost-effective than looking for new drugs" (qtd. in Carper xxii). In addition, substantial reductions in hospital costs were made possible by functional foods (Table 1).

Table 1: Potential Economic Consequences
of Preventive Nutrition

Disease	Reductions based on only hospitalization costs/yr, $
Cardiovascular disease	22 billion
Cancer	1 billion
Cardiovascular birth defects	800 million
Low birth weight	500 million
Neural tube birth defects	70 million
Cataract	2 million

Source: Bendich and Deckelbaum ix.

Based on the evidence shown in Table 1, it is apparent that the functional food industry has reduced the cost of health care, which consequently has made functional foods the most talked about discovery in nutrition today. Some of the medicinal components responsible for making functional foods the hot topic of nutritional headlines include antioxidants, omega-3 fatty acids, and fiber. All three of these functional components are thought to play a role in reducing the risk of somebody being diagnosed with one of the two most fatal diseases in the United States: coronary heart disease and

cancer (Blumberg 4). Antioxidants are components that are highly concentrated in foods rich in Vitamin C, E, and beta-carotene, which fight to prevent the "bad-type" of cholesterol, low-density lipoprotein (LDL), from combining with oxygen free radicals that circulate in the blood (Carper 4-6). Oxygen free radicals are "unstable molecules created from normal metabolic processes or from outside factors [such as] cigarette smoke [. . .]" that if able to undergo an oxidation reaction with LDL cause the cholesterol to become toxic (Carper 3). If the oxidation reaction is successful, receptors from cells, in a

confused attempt to get rid of these toxic molecules, latch on to
the cholesterol and draw it into the cell (Carper 3). The
accumulation of toxic cholesterol within the cells eventually causes
fat deposits to form within the arteries, putting one at risk of
developing heart disease (Carper 3-4).

Antioxidant rich foods work their magic in many different
ways. Foods rich in Vitamin C are known to eliminate oxygen free
radicals from the plasma portion of the blood, whereas Vitamin E
protects cell membranes from bombarding oxygen free radicals
(Carper 4-5). Conversely, beta-carotene uses its antioxidant powers
to find and destroy "a particular type of free radical called singlet
oxygen" (Carper 6). The highest amounts of Vitamin C, E, and
beta-carotene are found in citrus fruits, nuts, vegetable oils, and
deep orange fruits and vegetables, respectively (Margen et al. 112).
Antioxidants are a valuable source of ammunition against high
cholesterol and thus are a functional component that people at risk
of developing heart disease should consume in large doses.

[A portion of the student's text is omitted.]

Although not nearly as pungent, both green and black tea are
reported to work their anticarcinogenic powers in a similar fashion
to that of garlic. The allyl sulfur equivalent in green and black tea
is a polyphenol called catechin (see Glossary). Like the allyl sulfur
compounds of garlic, catechins have a detrimental effect on
nitrosamines, in that "both green tea and black tea have been
reported to block nitrosamine-induced tumorigenesis" (Milner,
"Nonnutritive Components" 144). In addition, catechins are reported
to have antioxidant properties, in that they have the "capacity to
scavenge most oxygen-centered free radicals [. . .]" (Dreosti 654).
These antioxidant polyphenols were shown to "reduce coronary
heart disease mortality" of tea drinkers in Norway, a population in
which "a significant inverse relationship[5] between tea drinking and
plasma cholesterol levels" was observed (Dreosti 653). Although
boxes of green and black tea currently do not display an "FDA
approved" label, tea drinkers reduce their risk of developing
coronary heart disease and some forms of cancer.

Functional foods appear to exert a strong preventive effect on
the two diseases that take more American lives than any other, i.e.,
coronary heart disease and cancer. High cholesterol levels cause

The writer
now draws
conclusions
from her
theories.

Hebert 7

coronary heart disease, the factor responsible for 24% of the fatalities that occur in the United States (Blumberg 3). Foods high in antioxidants (i.e., Vitamin C, E, and betacarotene), omega-3 fatty acids, and soluble fiber, along with green and black tea have been proven to be effective forms of preventive medicine for individuals at risk of developing coronary heart disease. Second only to coronary heart disease, "cancer is the cause of death in 22% of Americans" (Blumberg 4). Functional foods have exhibited similar strength in the fight for cancer prevention.

By incorporating functional foods such as insoluble fiber, garlic, and green and black tea into the diet, individuals can lower their risk of being diagnosed with cancer. Although a person should not cancel all future doctor appointments, this study has shown that individuals who eat functional foods are a step ahead of those that do not in the battle for disease prevention.

Notes

1. Although functional foods are often referred to as "healing foods," there is little evidence that supports the notion that these foods actually heal. Functional foods are better known for their preventive properties (Burros F-5). Therefore, in this paper, functional foods are treated as a type of preventive medicine. In no way, shape, or form should functional foods be perceived as an adequate substitute for antibiotics.

2. Dietary supplements that make such "structure/function" claims display the following label as a warning to consumers: "This statement has not been evaluated by the Food and Drug Administration. This product is not intended to diagnose, treat, mitigate, cure, or prevent any disease." ("Position" 1279).

3. At this time, researchers are not aware of how soluble fiber works with the body to lower the risk of heart disease (Margen et al. 91). Therefore, its properties as a functional food cannot be explained in this paper.

4. All sound scientific research uses statistics to assess the accuracy of study results. The p value is a type of statistic that measures the probability that a study's results were produced by chance alone; stated simply: science played no part in determining the results. A p value of 0.05 is the cut-off point between science and chance, meaning that data with a p value greater than 0.05 most likely was decided by chance alone. On the other hand, if the researchers come up with data that has a p value that is less than 0.05, it is more likely to be a significant piece of data, one that is not the result of chance. From a scientific standpoint, the only credible scientific evidence is that which is supported by a p value that is less than 0.05 (Rosenfield).

5. An inverse relationship is a relationship between two factors that are exact opposites, so that an increase in the concentration of one of the factors triggers a reduction in the other factor. In this example, it is reported that an increase in the consumption of green and black tea causes a reduction in the amount of plasma cholesterol in the body (Rosenfield).

Content notes explain matters not essential within the text. Each has been signaled in the text with a superscript numeral.

Appendix A: A Few Functional Foods

To Show Key Components, Potential Health Benefits, Scientific

Evidence, and Regulatory Classifications

An appendix for charts, graphs, tables, and illustrations eliminates clutter in the text.

Functional Food	Key Component	Potential Health Benefits	Scientific Evidence	Regulatory Classification
Low-fat foods as part of a low-fat diet (e.g., cheese, snack foods, meats, fish, dairy)	Low in total or saturated fat	Reduce risk of cancer Reduce risk of coronary heart disease	Clinical trials	FDA approved health claim
Food con-taining sugar alcohols in place of sugar (gum, candies, beverages, snack foods)	Sugar alcohols	Reduce risk of tooth decay	Clinical trials	FDA approved health claim
Oatmeal, oat bran, whole oat products	Beta glucan soluble fiber	Reduce cholesterol	Clinical trials	FDA approved health claim
Milk— low fat	Calcium	Reduce risk for osteoporosis	Clinical trials	FDA approved health claim
Vegetables and fruits	Vitamins, phyto-chemicals, fiber	Reduce can-cer risk Reduce heart disease risk	Epidemi-ologic studies, animal studies	FDA approved health claim

Hebert 10

Functional Food	Key Component	Potential Health Benefits	Scientific Evidence	Regulatory Classification
Cereal with added folic acid	Folic acid	Reduce risk for neural tube defect	Clinical trials	FDA approved health claim
Juice, pasta, rice, snack bars, and other foods with calcium	Calcium	Reduce risk for osteoporosis	Clinical trials	FDA approved health claim
Psyllium-containing products (e.g., pasta, bread, snack foods)	Psyllium fiber	Reduce risk of coronary heart disease	Clinical trials	FDA approved health claim
Whole-grain bread, high-fiber cereals	Fiber	Reduce risk of certain cancers Reduce risk of heart disease	Clinical trials	Notification of FDA pursuant to FDAMA
Snack foods with echinacea	Echinacea	Dietary support for the immune system	No direct evidence	Food, Drug, and Cosmetic Act (FDCA) structure function claim

<u>Source</u>: "Position" 1280-81.

Hebert 13

Works Cited

Form for an encyclopedia or dictionary.

Anderson, Douglas M., et al. Dorland's Illustrated Medical
　　Dictionary. 1994 ed.

Form for a preface to a book.

Bendich, Adrianne, and Richard J. Deckelbaum. Preface. Preventive
　　Nutrition: The Complete Guide for Health Professionals. Ed.
　　Adrianne Bendich and Richard J. Deckelbaum. Totowa:
　　Humana, 1997. vii-x.

Form for using et al. for a book with multiple authors.

Berube, Margery S., et al. The American Heritage Stedman's Medical
　　Dictionary. 1995 ed.

Form for part of a book.

Blumberg, Jeffrey B. "Public Health Implications of Preventive
　　Nutrition." Preventive Nutrition: The Complete Guide for Health
　　Professionals. Ed. Bendich and Deckelbaum, 1–15.

Bostick, Robert M. "Diet and Nutrition in the Etiology and Primary
　　Prevention of Colon Cancer." Preventive Nutrition: The
　　Complete Guide for Health Professionals. Ed. Bendich and
　　Deckelbaum, 5–75.

Form for a newspaper article.

Burros, Marian. "Hurrah for Cranberries (but You Knew That)."
　　New York Times 6 Oct. 1999, Late ed.: F5.

Carper, Jean. Food Pharmacy Guide to Good Eating. New York:
　　Bantam, 1991.

Claudio, Virginia S., and Rosalinda T. Lagua. Nutrition and Diet
　　Therapy Dictionary. 3rd ed. 1992.

Conner, William E., and Sonja L. Conner. "Omega-3 Fatty Acids
　　from Fish." Preventive Nutrition: The Complete Guide for
　　Health Professionals. Ed. Bendich and Deckelbaum, 225–43.

Form for a journal article.

Dreosti, Ivor E. "Bioactive Ingredients: Antioxidants and Poly-
　　phenols in Tea." Nutrition Reviews 54.11 (1996): 651-57.

Ensminger, Audrey H., et al. "Antioxidant." Foods and Nutrition
　　Encyclopedia. 2nd ed. 1994.

Hasler, Clare M. "Functional Foods: Their Role in Disease
　　Prevention and Health Promotion." Food Technology 52.11
　　(1998): 63-69.

Three hyphens to replace name in second entry.

---. "Functional Foods: The Western Perspective." Nutrition
　　Reviews 54.11 (1996): 6-10.

Head, Richard J., Ian R. Record, and Roger A. King. "Functional
　　Foods: Approaches to Definition and Substantiation."
　　Nutrition Reviews 54.11 (1996): 617.

Hebert 14

Margen, Sheldon, et al. <u>The Wellness Encyclopedia</u>. 1991 ed.

Milner, John A. "Garlic: Its Anticarcinogenic and Antitumorigenic
 Properties." <u>Nutrition Reviews</u> 54.11 (1996): 682-86.

---. "Nonnutritive Components in Foods as Modifiers of the Cancer
 Process." <u>Preventive Nutrition: The Complete Guide for Health
 Professionals</u>. Ed. Bendich and Deckelbaum, 135–69.

Nelson, Nancy J. "Purple Carrots, Margarine Laced With Wood
 Pulp? Nutraceuticals Move Into the Supermarket." <u>Journal of
 the National Cancer Institute</u> 91.9 (May 1999): 755-57.

"Position of The American Dietetic Association: Functional-Foods."
 <u>Journal of the American Dietetic Association</u> 99 (Oct. 1999):
 1278-85.

Rosenfield, Bob. Lecture. College of Natural Resources, Stevens
 Point. 13 Oct. 1999.

Form for an
article in an
edited
anthology.

Form for a
lecture.

14

Works Cited: MLA Style

After writing your paper, you should prepare a Works Cited page to list your reference materials. List only those actually used in your manuscript, including works mentioned within content endnotes and in captions to tables and illustrations. Preparing the Works Cited will be relatively simple if you carefully developed your working bibliography as a computer file (see pages 33–34). It will be difficult only if you have not kept publication data on each source cited in the paper.

Keep in mind that on occasion somebody might use your bibliography for research of their own. A documentation system, such as the MLA style, gives all scholars in the field a consistent way to consult the sources. Inaccurate records might prevent an easy retracing of your steps.

> For examples of Works Cited pages, see pages 208–09 or 222–23. For an example of an annotated bibliography (one with explanatory notes about each source) see pages 119–20.

Select a heading that indicates the nature of your list.

Works Cited for a list of works (books, articles, films, recordings, Internet sources, and so forth) that are quoted or paraphrased in the research paper.

Works Consulted for a list that is not confined to the works cited in the paper.

Annotated Bibliography for a list that includes a description of the contents of each source (see pages 119–120).

Bibliography for a complete listing of all works related to the subject, an unlikely prospect for most research papers unless the topic is very narrow indeed.

Selected Bibliography for a list of readings on the subject.

> For information on other bibliography forms, see the following: APA, Chapter 15; CMS footnote and endnote style, Chapter 16; CBE number style, Chapter 17.

Works pertinent to the paper but not quoted or paraphrased, such as an article on related matters, can be mentioned in a content endnote (see pages 316–19) and then listed in the Works Cited. On this point, see especially the Notes page of the sample paper, page 217.

14a Formatting the Works Cited Page

Arrange items in alphabetic order by the surname of the author, using the letter-by-letter system. Ignore spaces in the author's surname. Consider the first names only when two or more surnames are identical. Note how the following examples are alphabetized letter by letter.

De Morgan, Augustus
Dempsey, William H.
MacDonald, Lawrence
McCullers, Carson
McPherson, James Alan
McPherson, Vivian M.
Saint-Exupéry, Antoine de
St. James, Christopher

When two or more entries that begin with the same name cite coauthors, alphabetize by the last names of the second authors:

Harris, Muriel, and David Bleich
Harris, Muriel, and Stephen M. Fishman

When no author is listed, alphabetize by the first important word of the title. Imagine lettered spelling for unusual items. For example, "#2 Red Dye" should be alphabetized as though it were "Number 2 Red Dye."

The list of sources may also be divided into separate alphabetized sections for primary and secondary sources, for different media (articles, books, Internet sources), for different subject matter (biography, autobiography, letters), for different periods (Neoclassic period, Romantic period), and for different areas (German viewpoints, French viewpoints, American viewpoints).

Place the first line of each entry flush with the left margin and indent succeeding lines one half inch, usually one tab space on the computer or five spaces on a typewriter. Double space the lines. Use one character space after periods and other marks of punctuation.

Set the title "Works Cited" one inch down from the top of the sheet and double space between it and the first entry. A sample is illustrated on the following page.

HINT: Check your instructor's preference before using italics in place of underlining. If in doubt, use underlining because it prevents ambiguity by its distinctive marking of words and titles. However, use italics if you expect to publish on the Web because underlining is reserved there for links.

Works Cited

Campbell, Joseph. <u>The Hero With a Thousand Faces</u>. Cleveland: Meridian, 1956.

– – –. <u>The Masks of God</u>. 4 vols. New York: Viking, 1970.

Dipert, Randall R. "The Mathematical Structure of the World as Graph." <u>Journal of Philosopy</u> 44.7 (1997): 329-58.

Green, Robert R., ed. <u>Human Behavior Theory and Social Work Practice</u>. 2nd ed. New York: Gruyler, 2000.

Levitt, Joseph A. "Dietary Supplement Strategy." Letter. U.S. Food and Drug Administration. 3 Jan. 2000. 20 July 2000 <http://vm.cfsan. fda.gov/dms/ds-strat.html>.

Mickelson, James S., Karen S. Haynes, and Barbara Mikulski. 4th ed. <u>Affecting Change: Social Workers in the Political Arena</u>. Boston: Allyn, 2000.

Rader, Allen, and Ruth Rader. "Freudian Theory: New Developments." Green 212-241.

"A Thought-Provoking Book on the Nation's Social Health." Review of <u>The Social Health of the Nation: How America Is Really Doing</u>, by Marc L. Miringoff, Marque Luisa Miringoff, and Sandra Opdycke. Amazon.com 12 Mar. 2000. 20 July 2000 <http://www.Amazon.com/exec/obidos/ASIn/019513348/ ref=sim_books>.

Western, David. "Conservation in a Human-Dominated World." <u>Issues in Science and Technology Online</u>. Spring 2000. 20 July 2000 <http://www.nap.edu/issues/16.3/western.htm>.

United States Food and Drug Administration. "Dietary Supplement Strategy." 3 Jan. 2000. 20 July 2000 <http://vm.cfsan.fda.gov/ dms/ds-strat.html>.

Index to Bibliographic Models: MLA Style

Index to Bibliographic Models: MLA Style (continued)

14b   Bibliography Form—Books

Enter information for books in the following order. Items 1, 3, and 8 are required; add other items according to the circumstances explained in the text that follows.

1. Author
2. Chapter or part of book
3. Title of the book
4. Editor, translator, or compiler
5. Edition

6. Volume number of book
7. Name of the series
8. Place, publisher, and date
9. Page numbers
10. Number of volumes

The following list in alphabetic order explains and gives examples of the correct form for books.

Author's Name

List the author's name, surname first, followed by given name or initials, and then a period:

Reamer, Frederic G. Social Work Values and Ethics. New York:
    Columbia UP, 1999.

Always give authors' names in the fullest possible form, for example, "Cosbey, Robert C." rather than "Cosbey, R. C." unless, as indicated on the title page of the book, the author prefers initials. However, APA style (see Chapter 15, 288) requires last name and initials only (e.g., Cosbey, R. C.). If you spell out an abbreviated name, put square brackets around the material added:

Lewis, C[live] S[taples].

With pseudonyms you may add the real name, enclosing the addition in brackets.

Twain, Mark [Samuel Clemens].

Omit a title, affiliation, or degree that appears with the author's name on the title page.

If the title page says:	*In the Works Cited use:*
John Morgan, PhD	Morgan, John
Sister Margaret Larson	Larson, Margaret
Sir Hillary Edmunds	Edmunds, Hillary

However, do provide an essential suffix that is part of a person's name:

Justin, Walter, Jr.
Peterson, Robert J., III

Author, Anonymous

Begin with the title. Do not use *anonymous* or *anon.* Alphabetize by the title, ignoring initial articles, *A, An,* or *The.*

The Song of Roland. Trans. Glyn Burgess. New York: Penguin,
    1990.

Author, Anonymous but Name Supplied

Alphabetize by the supplied name.

[Madison, James.] All Impressments Unlawful and Inadmissible.
    Boston: William Pelham, 1804.

Author, Pseudonymous but Name Supplied

Slender, Robert [Freneau, Philip]. <u>Letters on Various and
Important Subjects</u>. Philadelphia: D. Hogan, 1799.

Author, Listed by Initials with Name Supplied

A[lden], E[dmund] K. "Alden, John." <u>Dictionary of American
Biography</u>. New York: Scribner's, 1928. 146–47.

Authors, Two

Sulpy, Doug, and Ray Schweighardt. <u>Get Back: The Unauthorized
Chronicle of the Beatles "Let It Be" Disaster</u>. New York:
St. Martin's, 1997.

Authors, Three

Mickelson, James S., Karen S. Haynes, and Barbara Mikulski.
4th ed. <u>Affecting Change: Social Workers in the Political
Arena</u>. Boston: Allyn, 2000.

Authors, More Than Three

Use "et al.," which means "and others," or list all the authors. See the two
examples that follow:

Lewis, Laurel J., et al. <u>Linear Systems Analysis</u>. New York:
McGraw, 2000.

Balzer, LeVon, Linda Alt Berene, Phyllis L. Goodson, Lois Lauer,
and Irwin L. Slesnick. <u>Life Science</u>. Glenview, IL: Scott, 1990.

Author, Corporation or Institution

A corporate author can be an association, a committee, or any group or
institution when the title page does not identify the names of the members.

Committee on Telecommunications. <u>Reports on Elected Topics in
Telecommunications</u>. New York: Nat. Acad. of Sciences, 2001.

List a committee or council as the author even when the organization is also
the publisher, as in this example:

American Council on Education. <u>Annual Report, 1999</u>.
Washington, DC: ACE, 2000.

Author, Two or More Books by the Same Author

When an author has two or more works, do not repeat his or her name with each entry. Rather, insert three hyphens flush with the left margin, followed by a period. Also, list the works alphabetically by the title (ignoring *a, an,* and *the*), not by the year of publication. In the following example, the *C* of *Chamber* precedes the *G* of *Goblet.*

> Rowling, J. K. <u>Harry Potter and the Chamber of Secrets</u>. New York:
> Scholastic, 1999.
>
> ~~~. <u>Harry Potter and the Goblet of Fire</u>. New York: Scholastic,
> 2000.
>
> ~~~. <u>Harry Potter and the Sorcerer's Stone</u>. New York: Scholastic,
> 1998.

The three hyphens stand for exactly the same name as in the preceding entry. However, do not substitute three hyphens for an author who has two or more works in the bibliography when one is written in collaboration with someone else:

> Bizzell, Patricia. "Opportunities for Feminist Research in the
> History of Rhetoric." <u>Rhetoric Review</u> 11 (1992): 50–58.
>
> ~~~. "<u>The Praise of Folly</u>, The Woman Rhetorician, and Post-
> Modern Skepticism." <u>Rhetoric Society Quarterly</u> 22 (1992):
> 7–17.
>
> Bizzell, Patricia, and Bruce Herzberg. <u>The Rhetorical Tradition:
> Readings from Classical Times to the Present</u>. Boston:
> Bedford-St. Martin's, 1990.

If the person edited, compiled, or translated the work, place a comma after the three hyphens and write *ed., comp.,* or *trans.* before you give the title. This label does not affect the alphabetic order by title.

> Finneran, Richard J. <u>Editing Yeats's Poems</u>. New York: St.
> Martin's, 1983.
>
> ~~~, ed. <u>W. B. Yeats: The Poems</u>. New ed. New York: Macmillan,
> 1983.

Authors, Two or More Books by the Same Authors

When you cite two or more books by the same authors, provide the names in the first entry only. Thereafter, use three hyphens, followed by a period.

> Axelrod, Rise B., and Charles R. Cooper. <u>Reading Critically,
> Writing Well</u>. 5th ed. Boston: St. Martin's, 1999.

---. The St. Martin's Guide to Writing. Short 6th ed. Boston: St.
Martin's, 2001.

Alphabetized Works, Encyclopedias, and Biographical Dictionaries

Treat works arranged alphabetically as you would an anthology or collection, but omit the name of the editor, the volume number, place of publication, publisher, and page numbers. If the author is listed, begin the entry with the author's name; otherwise, begin with the title of the article. If the article is signed with initials, look elsewhere in the work for a complete name. Well-known works, such as the first two examples that follow, need only the edition and the year of publication.

"Kiosk: Word History." The American Heritage Dictionary of the
English Language. 3rd ed. 1992.
Moran, Joseph. "Weather." The World Book Encyclopedia. 1998 ed.

If you cite a specific definition from among several, add *Def.* (Definition), followed by the appropriate number/letter of the definition.

"Level." Def. 4a. The American Heritage Dictionary of the English
Language. 3rd ed. 1992.

Less familiar reference works need a full citation:

"Infections." The American Medical Association Family Medical
Guide. Ed. Charles B. Clayman. New York: Random, 1994.

Place within quotation marks the title to a synopsis or description of a novel or drama, even though the novel or the drama would normally be underscored or italicized.

"Antigone." Masterpieces of World Literature. Ed. Frank N. Magill.
New York: Harper, 1989. 44–46.

Anthology, Component Part

In general, works in an anthology have been published previously and collected by an editor. Supply the names of authors as well as editors. Almost always cite the author first. Many times the prior publication data on a specific work may not be readily available; therefore, use this form:

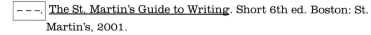

If you use several works from the same anthology, you can shorten the citation by citing the short work and by making cross-references to the larger one; see "Cross-References," pages 234–35.

Bradford, William. "Of Plymouth Plantation." The American
Tradition in Literature. Ed. George Perkins and Barbara
Perkins. 9th ed. New York: McGraw, 1998. 132–40.

Provide the inclusive page numbers for the piece, not just the page or pages that you have cited in the text.

Use the following form if you can quickly identify original publication information. Note that the page numbers in the *New Yorker* were unavailable in the reprint:

> "Soup." <u>New Yorker</u> Jan. 1989: n. pag. Rpt. in Rise B. Axelrod and
>   Charles R. Cooper. <u>The St. Martin's Guide to Writing</u>. Short
>   6th ed. Boston: Bedford, 2001. 132–34.

> Elder, Lonne. "Ceremonies in Dark Old Men." <u>New Black
>   Playwrights: An Anthology</u>. Ed. William Couch Jr. Baton
>   Rouge: Louisiana State UP, 1968. 55–72.

If you cite lines from a drama, such as Aristophanes' *The Birds*, write this kind of entry:

> Aristophanes. <u>The Birds. Five Comedies of Aristophanes</u>.
>   Trans. Benjamin B. Rogers. Garden City, NY: Doubleday,
>   1955. Lines 110–54.

If you cite material from a chapter of one volume in a multivolume set, write an entry like this:

> Child, Harold. "Jane Austen." <u>The Cambridge History of English
>   Literature</u>. Ed. A. W. Ward and A. R. Waller. Vol. 12. London:
>   Cambridge UP, 1927.

Although not required, you may also provide the total number of volumes.

> Saintsbury, George. "Dickens." <u>The Cambridge History of English
>   Literature</u>. Ed. A. W. Ward and A. R. Waller. Vol. 13. New
>   York: Putnam's, 1917. 14 vols.

The Bible

Do not underscore or italicize the word *Bible* or the books of the Bible. Common editions need no publication information, but do underscore or italicize special editions of the Bible.

> The Bible. [Denotes King James version]
> The Bible. The Old Testament. CD-ROM. Bureau Development, 2000.
> The Bible. Revised Standard Version.
> <u>The Geneva Bible</u>. 1560. Facsim. rpt. Madison: U of Wisconsin P,
>   1961.
> <u>NIV [New International Version] Study Bible</u>. Personal Size
>   Edition. N.p.: Zondervan, 1995.

A Book Published before 1900

For older books that are now out of print, you may omit the publisher. Use a comma, not a colon, to separate the place of publication from the year. If it has no date listed, use "n.d." If it has no place mentioned, use "n.p."

Dewey, John. <u>The School and Society</u>. Chicago, 1899.

Chapter or Part of a Book

List the chapter or part of a book on the Works Cited page only when it is separately edited, translated, or written, or when it demands special attention. For example, if you quote from a specific chapter of a book, let's say Chapter 11 of Brian Hall's book, the entry should read:

> If you cite from an anthology or collection, list the title of the specific story, poem, essay, etc. See "Anthology, Component Part," pages 232–33, or "Collection, Component Part," below.

Hall, Brian. <u>Madeleine's World: A Biography of a Three-Year-Old</u>. New York: Houghton, 1997.

Your in-text citation will have listed specific page numbers, so there is no reason to mention a specific chapter, even though it is the only portion of Hall's book that you read.

Classical Works

Homer. <u>The Iliad</u>. Trans. Richmond Lattimore. Chicago: U of Chicago P, 1951.

You are more likely to find a classical work in an anthology, which would require this citation:

Homer. <u>The Odyssey</u>. Trans. Robert Fitzgerald. <u>The Norton Anthology of World Masterpieces</u>. Ed. Maynard Mack, et al. New York: Norton, 1997. 96–336.

Collection, Component Part

If you cite from one work in a collection of works by the same author, provide the specific name of the work and the corresponding page numbers. This next entry cites one story from a collection of stories by the same author:

Kenan, Randall. "Run, Mourner, Run." <u>Let the Dead Bury Their Dead</u>. San Diego: Harcourt, 1992. 163–91.

Cross-References to Works in a Collection

If you are citing several selections from one anthology or collection, provide a full reference to the anthology (as explained on pages 232–33) and then

provide references to the individual selections by providing the author and
title of the work, the last name of the editor of the collection, and the inclusive page numbers used from the anthology.

> Behrens, Laurence, and Leonard J. Rosen. <u>Writing and Reading</u>
> <u>Across the Curriculum</u>. New York: Longman, 2000.
>
> Bettelheim, Bruno. "'Cinderella': A Story of Sibling Rivalry and
> Oedipal Conflicts." Behrens and Rosen 638–45.
>
> Kelley, Karol. "<u>Pretty Woman</u>: A Modern Cinderella." Behrens and
> Rosen 646–55.
>
> Morrison, Toni. "Cinderella's Stepsisters." Behrens and Rosen 638–45.

Note also the following examples in which the first entry refers to the
one that follows:

> Eliot, George. "Art and Belles Lettres." <u>Westminster Review</u>. USA
> ed. April 1856. Partly rpt. Eliot, <u>A Writer's Notebook</u>.
>
> – – –. <u>A Writer's Notebook, 1854–1879, and Uncollected Writings</u>.
> Ed. Joseph Wiesenfarth. Charlottesville: UP of Virginia,
> 1981.

Add an abbreviated title to the cross-reference if you list two or more
works under the editor's name.

> Angelou, Maya. "Uncle Willie." Axelrod and Cooper, Guide 82–86.
>
> Axelrod, Rise B., and Charles R. Cooper. <u>Reading Critically,</u>
> <u>Writing Well</u>. 5th ed. New York: St. Martin's, 1999.
>
> – – –. <u>The St. Martin's Guide to Writing</u>. Short 6th ed. Boston:
> Bedford, 1997.
>
> Forster, E. M. "My Wood." Axelrod and Cooper, Reading 111–14.
>
> Wolff, Tobias. "On Being a Real Westerner." Axelrod and Cooper,
> Guide 33–35.

Edition

Indicate the edition used, whenever it is not the first, in Arabic numerals
("3rd ed."), by name ("Rev. ed.," "Abr. ed."), or by year ("1999 ed.").

> Schulman, Michael, and Eva Meckler. <u>Bringing Up a Moral Child</u>.
> Rev. ed. New York: Doubleday, 1994.

Indicate that a work has been prepared by an editor, not the original author:

> Melville, Herman. <u>Moby Dick</u>. Ed. with intro. by Alfred Kazin.
> 2nd ed. Boston: Houghton, 1956.

If you wish to show the original date of the publication, place the year immediately after the title, followed by a period. Note: the title of an edition in a series is capitalized.

> Hardy, Thomas. <u>Far from the Madding Crowd</u>. 1874. Ed. Robert C.
> Schweik. A Norton Critical Ed. New York: Norton, 1986.

Editor, Translator, Illustrator, or Compiler

If the name of the editor or compiler appears on the title page of an anthology or compilation, place it first:

> Franklin, Phyllis, ed. <u>Profession 1999</u>. New York: Modern
> Language Association, 1999.

If your in-text citation refers to the work of the editor, illustrator, or translator (e.g., "The Ciardi edition caused debate among Dante scholars"), use this form with the original author listed after the work, preceded by the word *By*:

> Ciardi, John, trans. <u>The Purgatorio</u>. By Dante. New York: NAL,
> 1961.
> Kutcher, Ben, illus. <u>The House of Pomegranates</u>. By Oscar Wilde.
> New York: Dodd, 1925.

Refer to one specific illustration in this manner:

> Kutcher, Ben, illus. "The Selfish Giant." <u>The House of
> Pomegranates</u>. By Oscar Wilde. New York: Dodd, 1925. 34.

Otherwise, mention an editor, translator, or compiler of a collection *after* the title with the abbreviations Ed., Trans., or Comp., as shown here:

> Yeats, W. B. <u>The Poems of W. B. Yeats</u>. Ed. Richard J. Finneran.
> New ed. New York: Macmillan, 1983.

List the editor first only if your in-text citation refers to the work of the editor (for example, the editor's introduction or notes). Your in-text citation will give a specific page; for example, a content footnote by David Bevington would be cited in the text as "(Bevington 316n)." The Works Cited entry should then be written as follows:

> Bevington, David, ed. <u>The Complete Works of Shakespeare</u>. 4th ed.
> New York: Harper, 1992.

Encyclopedia and Reference Book

> Ward, Norman. "Saskatchewan." <u>Encyclopedia Americana</u>. 1998 ed.

See also "Alphabetized Works, Encyclopedias,
and Biographical Dictionaries" on page 232
and "Bibliography Form—CD-ROMs,"
pages 264–66.

Introduction, Preface, Foreword, or Afterword

If you are citing the introduction or similar component to a work by
another author, start with the name of the person who wrote the component
you are citing. Give the name of the part being cited, neither underscored nor
enclosed within quotation marks. Place the name of the author in normal
order after the title preceded by the word *By*. Follow with publication information and end with the inclusive page numbers

> Lowell, Robert. Foreword. Ariel. By Sylvia Plath. New York:
>   Harper, 1966. vii–ix.
> Sitwell, Dame Edith. Introduction. Swinburne: A Selection. By
>   Algernon C. Swinburne. London: Weidenfeld, 1960.

If the author of the book has written the prefatory matter, use only the
author's last name after the word *By*.

> Vonnegut, Kurt. Prologue. Jailbird. By Vonnegut. New York:
>   Delacorte, 1979.

Use the form above only if you cite from the prologue and not the main text.

Manuscript Collections in Book Form

> Cotton Vitellius. A.XV. British Museum, London.
> Chaucer, Geoffrey. <u>The Canterbury Tales</u>. Harley ms. 7334. British
>   Museum, London.

See also "Manuscripts (Ms.) and Typescripts
(Ts.)," page 271.

Page Numbers to a Section of a Book

Cite pages to help a reader find a particular section of a book.

See also "Anthology, Component Part,"
pages 232–33.

Knoepfmacher, U. C. "Fusing Fact and Myth: The New Reality of
Middlemarch." This Particular Web: Essays on Middlemarch.
Ed. Ian Adam. Toronto: U of Toronto P, 1975. 55–65.

Play, Classical

Shakespeare, William. Hamlet. Ed. Charles Keen. Rpt. of the 1859
ed. published by Bradbury and Evans, London. London:
Cornmarket Press, 1971.

Today, classical plays are usually found in anthologies, which will require
this form:

Shakespeare, William. Hamlet, Prince of Denmark. The Norton
Anthology of World Masterpieces. Ed. Maynard Mack et al.
New York: Norton, 1997. 1633–1725.

Play, Modern

Contemporary plays may be published independently or as part of a
collection.

Greene, Graham. The Complaisant Lover. New York: Viking, 1959.
Eliot, T. S. The Cocktail Party. The Complete Poems and Plays:
1909–1950. New York: Harcourt, 1952. 295–387.

Poem, Classical

Classical poems are usually translated, so you will often need to list a translator and/or editor. If the work is one part of a collection, show which anthology you used, and give the inclusive page numbers.

Dante. The Divine Comedy. Trans. Lawrence G. White. New York:
Pantheon, 1948.
Dante. Inferno. The Divine Comedy. Trans. John Ciardi.
The Norton Anthology of World Masterpieces. Ed. Maynard
Mack, et al. New York: Norton, 1997. 1017–1142.

If you cite the translator's or editor's preface or notes to the text, put the
name of the translator or editor first. See page 236.

Poem, Modern Collection

Use this form that includes the inclusive page numbers if you cite one
short poem from a collection:

Eliot, T. S. "The Love Song of J. Alfred Prufrock." The Complete
Poems and Plays 1909–1950. New York: Harcourt, 1952. 3–7.

Use this next form if you cite from one book-length poem:

> Eliot, T. S. <u>Four Quartets</u>. <u>The Complete Poems and Plays</u>
>   <u>1909–1950</u>. New York: Harcourt,1952. 115–45.

Do not cite specific poems and pages if you cite several different poems of the collection. Your in-text citations should cite the specific poems and page numbers (see pages 172–73). Your Works Cited entry would then list only the name of the collection.

> Eliot, T. S. <u>The Complete Poems and Plays 1909–1950</u>. New York:
>   Harcourt, 1952.

Publication Information: Place, Publisher, and Date

Indicate the place of publication, the publisher, and the year of publication:

> Schmidgall, Gary. <u>Walt Whitman: A Gay Life</u>. New York: Dutton,
>   1997.

Include the abbreviation for the state or country only if necessary for clarity:

> Morgan, John A. <u>Drama at Stratford</u>. Manchester, Eng.: Wallace,
>   1995.

If more than one place of publication appears on the title page, the first city mentioned is sufficient. If successive copyright dates are given, use the most recent (unless your study is specifically concerned with an earlier, perhaps definitive, edition). A new printing does not constitute a new edition. For example, if the text has a 1940 copyright date and a 1975 printing, use 1940 unless other information is given, such as: "facsimile printing" or "1975 third printing rev."

> Bell, Charles Bailey, and Harriett P. Miller. <u>The Bell Witch: A</u>
>   <u>Mysterious Spirit</u>. 1934. Facsim. ed. Nashville: Elder, 1972.

If the place, publisher, date of publication, or pages are not provided, use one of these abbreviations:

n.p.	No place of publication listed
n.p.	No publisher listed
n.d.	No date of publication listed
n. pag.	No pagination listed

> Lewes, George Henry. <u>The Life and Works of Goethe</u>. 1855. 2 vols.
>   Rpt. as vols. 13 and 14 of <u>The Works J. W. von Goethe</u>. Ed.
>   Nathan Haskell Dole. London: Nicolls, n.d. 14 vols.

Perrine, Laurence. "A Monk's Allegory." <u>A Limerick's Always a
Verse: 200 Original Limericks</u>. San Diego: Harcourt, 1990.
N. pag.

Provide the publisher's name in a shortened form, such as "Bobbs" rather
than "Bobbs-Merrill Co., Inc." A publisher's special imprint name should be
joined with the official name, for example, Anchor-Doubleday, Jove-Berkley, Ace-Grossett, Del Rey-Ballantine, Mentor-NAL.

> Abbreviations to publisher's names are listed on pages A-4–A-5.

Faulkner, William. "Spotted Horses." <u>Three Famous Short Stories</u>.
New York: Vintage-Random, 1963.

Republished Book

If you are citing from a republished book, such as a paperback version of
a book published originally in hardback, provide the original publication date
after the title and then provide the publication information for the book from
which you are citing.

Lowes, John Livingston. <u>The Road to Xanadu: A Study in the Ways
of the Imagination</u>. 1930. New York: Vintage-Knopf, 1959.

Although it is not required, you may wish to explain that the republished
work is a facsimile reprinting.

Hooker, Richard. <u>Of the Lawes of Ecclesiasticall Politie</u>. 1594.
Facsim. rpt. Amsterdam: Teatrum Orbis Terrarum, 1971.

Give facts about the original publication if the information will serve the
reader. In this next example the republished book was originally published
under a different title:

Arnold, Matthew. "The Study of Poetry." <u>Essays: English and
American</u>. Ed. Charles W. Eliot. 1886. New York: Collier,
1910. Rpt. of the General Introduction to <u>The English Poets</u>.
Ed. T. H. Ward. 1880.

Screenplay

Branagh, Kenneth. <u>Hamlet</u> by Shakespeare. Screenplay. New York:
Norton, 1996.

Series, Numbered and Unnumbered

If the work is one in a published series, show the name of the series,
abbreviated, without quotation marks or underscoring, the number of this
work in Arabic numerals (for example, "no. 3," or simply "3"), and a period:

Jefferson, D. W. "'All, all of a piece throughout': Thoughts on
      Dryden's Dramatic Poetry." <u>Restoration Theatre</u>. Ed. J. R.
      Brown and Bernard Harris. Stratford-upon-Avon Studies 6.
      London: Arnold, 1965. 159–76.

Wallerstein, Ruth C. <u>Richard Crashaw: A Study in Style and Poetic
      Development</u>. U of Wisconsin Studies in Lang. and Lit. 37.
      Madison: U of Wisconsin P, 1935.

Sourcebooks and Casebooks

Ellmann, Richard. "Reality." <u>Yeats: A Collection of Critical Essays</u>.
      Ed. John Unterecker. Twentieth Century Views. Englewood
      Cliffs: Prentice, 1963. 163–74.

If you can identify the original facts of publication, include that information also:

Ellmann, Richard. "Reality." <u>Yeats: The Man and the Masks</u>. New
      York: Macmillan, 1948. Rpt. in <u>Yeats: A Collection of Critical
      Essays</u>. Ed. John Unterecker. Twentieth Century Views.
      Englewood Cliffs: Prentice, 1963. 163–74.

> If you cite more than one article from a case-
> book, use cross-references; see pages 234–35.

Title of the Book

Show the title of the work, underscored or italicized, followed by a
period. Separate any subtitle from the primary title by a colon and one space
even though the title page has no mark of punctuation or the card catalog
entry has a semicolon:

Hendrix, Harville, and Helen Hunt. <u>Giving the Love That Heals: A
      Guide for Parents</u>. New York: Pocket, 1997.

If an underscored title to a book incorporates another title that normally
receives underscoring, do not underscore or italicize the incorporated title nor

> See "Titles within Titles," Glossary A, page
> A-28 for additional instructions.

place it within quotation marks. In
the title below, *Absolom and Achi-
tophel* is the incorporated title; it
does not receive underscoring.

Schilling, Bernard N. <u>Dryden and the Conservative Myth: A
      Reading of Absalom and Achitophel</u>. New Haven: Yale UP,
      1961.

Title of a Book in Another Language

In general, use lowercase letters for foreign titles except for the first major word and proper names. Provide a translation in brackets if you think it necessary (e.g., Étranger [*The Stranger*] or Praha [Prague]).

Brombert, Victor. Stendhal et la voie oblique. New Haven: Yale UP,
    1954.

Castex, P. G. Le rouge et le noir de Stendhal. Paris: Sedes, 1967.

NOTE: *Le rouge et le noir* is an incorporated title; thus, it does not receive underscoring; compare with the title immediately below that requires underscoring because there is no title within the title.

Levowitz-treu, Micheline. L'amour et la mort chez Stendhal. Aran:
    Editions due Grand Chéne, 1978.

Translator

List the translator's name first only if the translator's work (preface, foreword, afterword, notes) is the focus of your study.

Condé, Maryse. Segu. Trans. Barbara Bray. New York: Ballantine,
    1982.

Shorey, Paul, trans. Preface. The Republic. By Plato. Cambridge:
    Harvard UP, 1937.

Volumes

If you are citing from only one volume of a multivolume work, provide the number of that volume with information for that volume only. In your text, you will need to specify only page numbers, as in "(Seale 45–46)."

Seale, William. The President's House: A History. Vol. 1.
    Washington, DC: White House Historical Assn., 1986.

Although additional information is not required, you may provide the inclusive page numbers, the total number of volumes, and the inclusive dates of publication.

Daiches, David. "The Restoration." A Critical History of English
    Literature. 2nd ed. Vol. 2. New York: Ronald, 1970. 537–89.
    2 vols.

Wellek, René. A History of Modern Criticism, 1750–1950. Vol. 5.
    New Haven: Yale UP, 1986. 8 vols. 195–92.

If you are citing from two or more volumes of a multivolume work, your in-text citation will need to specify volume and page (2: 320–21); then the Works Cited entry will need to show the total number of volumes, as shown here:

Seale, William. <u>The President's House: A History</u>. 2 vols.
Washington, DC: White House Historical Assn., 1986.

If you are citing from volumes that were published over a period of years, provide the inclusive dates at the end of the citation. Should the volumes still be in production, write *to date* after the number of volumes and leave a space after the hyphen which follows the initial date.

Parrington, Vernon L. <u>Main Currents in American Thought</u>.
3 vols. New York: Harcourt, 1927–32.
Cassidy, Frederic, ed. <u>Dictionary of American Regional English</u>.
3 vols. to date. Cambridge: Belknap-Harvard UP, 1985–.

Handle the reprinting of volumes in this manner:

Seivers, Harry J. <u>Benjamin Harrison: Hoosier Warrior</u>.
3 vols. 1952–68. Rpt. of vol. 1. Newtown CT: American
Political Biography Press, 1997.

If you are using only one volume of a multivolume work and the volume has an individual title, you can cite the one work without mentioning the other volumes in the set.

Crane, Stephen. <u>Wounds in the Rain</u>. <u>Stephen Crane: Tales of War</u>.
Charlottesville: UP of Virginia, 1970. 95–284.

As a courtesy to the reader, you may include supplementary information about an entire edition.

Crane, Stephen. <u>Wounds in the Rain</u>. <u>Stephen Crane: Tales of War</u>.
Charlottesville: UP of Virginia, 1970. Vol. 6 of <u>The University
of Virginia Edition of the Works of Stephen Crane</u>. Ed.
Fredson Bowers. 95–284. 10 vols. 1969–76.

14c Bibliography Form—Periodicals

For journal or magazine articles, use the following order:

1. Author
2. Title of the article
3. Name of the periodical
4. Series number (if relevant)
5. Volume number (for journals)
6. Issue number (if needed)
7. Date of publication
8. Page numbers

These items are explained and shown in the following alphabetized list.

Abstract in an Abstracts Journal

If you have cited from an abstract found in a journal devoted to abstracts, not full articles, begin the citation with information on the original work and then give information on the abstracts journal. Use either item number or page number according to how the journal provides the abstracts.

> Ferguson, Tamara J., and Susan L. Crowley. "Gender Differences
>> in the Organization of Guilt and Shame." Sex Roles
>> 37 (1997): 19–44. Psychological Abstracts 85 (1998):
>> item 4265.

Add the word *Abstract* if the title does not make clear that you have used an abstract, not a full article.

> Gryeh, John H., et al. "Patterns of Adjustment among Children of
>> Battered Women." Journal of Consulting and Clinical
>> Psychology 68 (2000): 84–94. Abstract. PsycINFO 2000–13544.

Use the next form when you cite from *Dissertation Abstracts International* (*DAI*). The page number features A, B, or C to designate the series used: A for Humanities, B for Sciences, C for European dissertations. Before volume 30 (1969) the title was *Dissertation Abstracts*, so use *DA* for those early volumes.

See page 269 for how to cite from the full text of a dissertation. See also "Abstract," page 255, and "Note," page 256.

> Shore, Zandra Lesley. "Girls Reading Culture: Autobiography as
>> Inquiry into Teaching the Body, the Romance, and the
>> Economy of Love." Diss. U of Toronto, 1999. DAI 60 (1999):
>> 1657A.

Author

Show the author's name flush with the left margin, with succeeding lines indented one half inch or five spaces. Enter the surname first, followed by a comma, followed by a given name or initials, followed by a period:

> Smith, Bruce R. "Premodern Sexualities." PMLA 115 (2000):
>> 318–29.

Author, Anonymous

> "The Birthplace of eGovernment." Advertisement. George Aug.
>> 2000: 4–5.

Interview, Published

> Safire, William. Interview. Playboy Nov. 1992: 63+ .

Journal, with All Issues for a Year Paged Continuously

Bartley, William. "Imagining the Future in The Awakening."
College English 62 (2000): 719–46.

Journal, with Each Issue Paged Anew

Add the issue number after the volume number because page numbers alone are not sufficient to locate the article within a volume of six or twelve issues when each issue has separate pagination. Adding the month or season with the year will also serve the researcher.

Naffziger, Douglas W., Jeffrey S. Hornsby, and Donald F. Kuralko.
"A Proposed Research Model of Entrepreneurial Motivation."
Entrepreneurship: Theory and Practice 18.3 (Spring 1994):
29–42.

If a journal uses only an issue number, treat it as a volume number:

Wilson, Katharina M. "Tertullian's De cultu foeminarum and
Utopia." Moreana 73 (1982): 69–74.

Journal, Volume Numbers Embracing Two Years

Some journals that publish only four or six issues a year will bind two years together. Use the form shown in the following example.

Callenbach, Ernest. "The Unbearable Lightness of Leaving."
Film Quarterly 44–45 (Fall 1991): 2–6.

Loose-leaf Collection

If the article is reprinted in an information service that gathers together several articles on a common topic, use this form:

Cox, Rachel S. "Protecting the National Parks." The Environment.
CQ Researcher 16 July 2000: 523+. Washington, DC:
Congressional Quarterly, 2000. No. 23.

If the service reprints articles from other sources, use this next form, which shows original publication data and then information on the SIRS booklet—title, editor, and volume number.

Hodge, Paul. "The Andromeda Galaxy." Mercury July/Aug.
1993: 98 + . Physical Science. Ed. Eleanor Goldstein. Vol. 2.
Boca Raton: SIRS, 1994. Art. 24.

Magazine

With magazines, the volume number offers little help for finding an article. For example, one volume of *Time* (52 issues) will have page 16 repeated

52 times. For this reason, you need to insert an exact date (month and day) for weekly and fortnightly (every two weeks) publications. Do not list the volume and issue numbers.

> Nash, J. Madeleine. "The New Science of Alzheimer's." <u>Time</u>
>   17 July 2000: 51–57.

The month suffices for monthly and bimonthly publications:

> Levingston, Steven. "Steer Clear of These Dangerous Drivers."
>   <u>Reader's Digest</u> July 1997 : 50–55.

Supply inclusive page numbers (202–09, 85–115, or 1112–24), but if an article is paged here and there throughout the issue (for example, pages 74, 78, and 81–88), write only the first page number and a plus sign with no intervening space:

> Cannon, Lou. "Reagan Radiated Happiness and Hope." <u>George</u>
>   Aug. 2000: 58+.

Microform

Some reference sources, such as *NewsBank,* republish articles on microfiche. If you use such a microform, enter the original publication information first and then add the pertinent information about the microform:

> Chapman, Dan. "Panel Could Help Protect Children." <u>Winston-</u>
>   <u>Salem Journal</u> 14 Jan 1990: 14. <u>Newsbank: Welfare and</u>
>   <u>Social Problems</u> 12 (1990): fiche 1, grids A8–11.

Monograph

> Martin, Judith N., Michael L. Hecht, and Linda K. Larkey.
>   "Conversational Improvement Strategies for Interethnic
>   Communication: African American and European American
>   Perspectives." <u>Communication Monographs</u> 61.3 (Sept.
>   1994): 236–55.

Name of the Periodical

Give the name of the journal or magazine in full, underscored or italicized, and with no following punctuation. Omit any introductory article, such as *The*.

> Dooley, Susan. "Music to Your Eyes." <u>Garden Designs</u> Aug./Sept.
>   2000: 20–22.

Notes, Editorials, Queries, Reports, Comments, Letters

Magazines and journals publish many pieces that are not full-fledged articles. Identify this type of material if the title of the article or the name of the journal does not make clear the nature of the material (e.g., "Letter" or "Comment").

> Trainor, Jennifer Seibel, and Deborah Klein. Comment and Response.
>> College English 62 (2000): 767–72.
>
> "Challenges to Intellectual Freedom Rise by Seven Percent."
>> Bulletin. Library Journal 1 March 1994: 13.
>
> Holden, Michael. "Scholarship at Whose Service?"
>> Letter. PMLA 109 (1994): 442–43.
>
> "Where Peacocks Roam." Puzzle. Garden Design Aug./Sept.
>> 2000: 23.

On occasion, an editor or writer will reply to a reader's letter or comment. Identify such a response in this manner:

> Gilbert, Sandra M. Reply to letter of Jerry W. Ward Jr. PMLA 113
>> (1998): 131.

Reprint of a Journal Article

> Simonds, Robert L. "The Religious Right Explains the
>> Religious Right." School Administrator 9 (Oct. 1993): 19–22.
>> Rpt. in Education Digest Mar. 1994: 19–22.

> If the article is reprinted in a loose-leaf collection such as SIRS, see page 245.

Review, in a Magazine or Journal

Name the reviewer and the title of the review. Then write *Rev. of* and the title of the work being reviewed, followed by a comma, and the name of the author or producer. If necessary, identify the nature of the work within brackets immediately after the title.

> Seymour, Jim. "Push Back." Rev. of Pointcast and Backweb
>> [computer software]. PC Magazine Aug. 1997: 93–94.

If the name of the reviewer is not provided, begin the entry with the title of the review.

> "Recent Books." Rev. of Writing as a Road to Self-Discovery, by
>> Barry Lane. CCC 45 (May 1994): 279.

If the review has no title, use this form:

Rogers, Michael. Rev. of <u>Keats the Poet,</u> by Stuart Sperry. <u>Library</u>
<u>Journal</u> 15 Mar. 1994: 105.

If the review is neither signed nor titled, begin the entry with *Rev. of* and
alphabetize the entry under the title of the work reviewed.

Rev. of <u>Anthology of Danish Literature,</u> ed. F. J. Billeskov Jansen and
P. M. Mitchell. <u>Times Literary Supplement</u> 7 July 1972: 785.

As shown in the example above, use an appropriate abbreviation (e.g., *ed.,*
comp., trans.) for the work of someone other than an author.

Series

Between the name of the publication and the volume number, identify a
numbered series with an ordinal
suffix (*2nd, 3rd*) followed by the
abbreviation *ser.* For publications
divided between the original series
and a new series, designate the
series with *os* or *ns*, respectively.

For a serialized article (one that appears in
two or more successive issues of a periodical), see "Serialized Article in a Newspaper or
Periodical," page 252.

Hill, Christopher. "Sex, Marriage and the Family in England."
<u>Economic History Review</u> 2nd ser. 31 (1978): 450–63.

Terry, Richard. "Swift's Use of 'Personate' to Indicate Parody."
<u>Notes and Queries</u> ns 41.2 (June 1994): 196–98.

Special Issue

If you cite one article from a special issue of a journal, you may indicate
the nature of this special issue:

See also "Cross-References to Works in a Collection," pages 234–35.

Ackerman, James. "Leonardo da Vinci: Art in Science." <u>Science and</u>
<u>Culture</u>. Spec. Issue of <u>Daedalus</u> 127.1 (1998): 207–24.

If you cite several articles from the special issue, begin the primary citation with the name of the editor:

Smith, John, ed. Spec. Issue of <u>Daedalus</u> 127.1 (1998): 1–236.

Once that entry is established, cross-reference each article used:

Ackerman, James. "Leonardo da Vinci: Art in Science."
Smith 207–24.

Speech or Address, Published

> Humphries, Alfred. "Computers and Banking." Address to
>   Kiwanis Club, Nashville, TN, 30 Feb. 2000. Rpt. in part
>   Tennessee Monthly 31 Aug. 2000: 33–34.
> United States. President. " Address to Veterans of Foreign Wars."
>   19 Aug. 1974. Rpt. in Weekly Compilation of Presidential
>   Documents 10 (26 Aug. 1974): 1045–50.

Title of the Article

Show the title within quotation marks, ending with a period inside the closing quotation marks:

> Baum, Rosalie Murphy. "Early-American Literature: Reassessing
>   the Black Contribution." Eighteenth Century Studies 27
>   (1994): 533–49.

Title, Omitted

> Berkowitz, David. Renaissance Quarterly 32 (1979): 396–493.

Title, Quotation within the Article's Title

> Ranald, Margaret Loftus. " 'As Marriage Binds, and Blood Breaks' :
>   English Marriage and Shakespeare." Shakespeare Quarterly
>   30 (1979): 68–81.

Title, within the Article's Title

> Dundes, Alan. " To Love My Father All : A Psychoanalytic Study
>   of the Folktale Source of King Lear." Southern Folklore
>   Quarterly 40 (1976): 353–66.

Title, Foreign

> Rebois, Charles "Les effets du 12 juin." Le Figaro Magazine 2
>   juillet 1994: 42–43.
> Stivale, Charles J. "Le vraisemblable temporel dans Le Rouge et
>   le noir." Stendhal Club 84 (1979): 299–313.

See also "Title of a Book in Another Language," page 242.

Volume, Issue, and Page Numbers for Journals

Most journals are paged continuously through all issues of an entire year, so listing the month of publication is unnecessary. For example, page numbers and a volume number are sufficient for you to find an article in *Eighteenth Century Studies* or *English Literary Renaissance*. However, some journals have separate pagination for each issue. If that is the case, you will need to add an issue number following the volume number, separated by a period:

> Cann, Johnson, and Deborah Smith. "Volcanoes of the Mid-ocean
> Ridges and the Building of New Oceanic Crust." <u>Endeavor</u>
> 18.2 (1994): 61–66.

Add the month also to ease the search for the article: "20.5 (Nov. 1954): 4–6."

14d Bibliography Form—Newspapers

Provide the name of the author; the title of the article; the name of the newspaper as it appears on the masthead, omitting any introductory article (e.g., *Wall Street Journal*, not *The Wall Street Journal*); and the complete date—day, month (abbreviated), and year. Omit any volume number.

Provide a page number as listed (e.g., 21, B-6, 14C, D3). For example, *USA Today* uses "6A" but the *New York Times* uses "A6." There is no uniformity among newspapers on this matter, so list the page accurately as an aid to your reader. If the article is not printed on consecutive pages (for example, if it begins on page 1 and skips to page 8), write the first page number and a plus (+) sign.

Newspaper in One Section

> Jonsson, Patrik. "New Racial Climate in Suburban South."
> <u>The Christian Science Monitor</u> 28 July 2000: 1+.

Newspaper with Lettered Sections

> Morrison, Blake. "Sierra Fire Continues Rampage." <u>USA Today</u> 31
> July 2000: 10A.

Newspaper with Numbered Sections

> Jones, Tim. "New Media May Excite, While Old Media Attract."
> <u>Chicago Tribune</u> 28 July 1997, sec. 4: 2.

Newspaper Editorial with No Author Listed

"Legislative Endorsement." Editorial. <u>Tennessean</u> [Nashville] 31
July 2000: 12A.

Newspaper Column, Cartoon, Comic Strip, Advertisement, etc.

Add a description to the entry to explain that the citation refers to something other than a regular news story.

Fisher, Marc. "A Memorial, Yes, But What about the Message."
Column. <u>Washington Post</u> 22 July 2000: B1.

Newspaper Article with City Added

In the case of locally published newspapers, add the city in square brackets.

Powers, Mary. "Finding Advances in the Search for Strep Vaccine."
<u>Commercial Appeal</u> [Memphis] 7 July 1991: C3.

Newspaper Edition or Section

When the masthead lists an edition, add a comma after the date and name
the edition (*late ed., city ed.*), followed by a colon and then the page number.

Lohr, Steve. "Now Playing: Babes in Cyberspace." <u>New York Times</u>
3 Apr. 1998, late ed.: C1 +.

The *New York Times* presents two types of pagination, depending on the
day. On Monday through Saturday, the *New York Times* usually has lettered
sections (*A, B, C,* etc.) with each having separate pagination, such as page C1
through page C24.

Lewin, Tamar. "Boom in Gene Testing Raises Question on Sharing
Results." <u>New York Times</u> 21 July 2000: A1 +.

The Sunday edition of the *New York Times* has numbered sections, individually paged, to cover art, business, travel, and so forth. If you cite from one of
these sections, provide the section number.

Kifner, John. "The Holiest City, the Toughest Conflict." <u>New York
Times</u> 23 July 2000, sec. 4: 1+.

Newspaper in a Foreign Language

Richard, Michel Bole, and Frédéric Fritscher. "Frederick DeKlerk,
l'homme qui a aboli l'apartheid." <u>Le Monde</u> 3 juillet 1991: 1.

Serialized Article in a Newspaper or Periodical

A series of articles, published in several issues under the same general heading, requires identification of the different issues. If each article that you cite has the same author and title, include the bibliographic information in one entry.

> Meserole, Harrison T., and James M. Rambeau. "Articles on
>
> American Literature Appearing in Current Periodicals."
>
> American Literature 52 (1981): 688–705; 53 (1981):
>
> 164–80,348–59.

If each article that you cite has different authors and/or different titles, list each one separately. Indicate the number of this article in the series and give the name of the series. If the series features the same author, alphabetize by the first letters of the titles.

> Thomas, Susan, and Brad Schmitt. "Kids Find Their Fun in
>
> Danger." Tennessean [Nashville] 1 Sept. 1994: 1A+. Pt. 5 of a
>
> 30-day journal. Taking Back Our Kids: An Inner City Diary,
>
> begun 28 Aug. 1994.
>
> – – –. "Little Love, Less Hope, Lost Lives." Tennessean [Nashville]
>
> 28 Aug. 1994: 1A+. Pt. 1 of a 30-day journal. Taking Back
>
> Our Kids: An Inner City Diary.
>
> – – –. "This Is a Horrible Street." Tennessean [Nashville] 29 Aug.
>
> 1994: 1A+. Pt. 2 of a 30-day journal. Taking Back Our Kids:
>
> An Inner City Diary, begun 28 Aug. 1994.

14e Bibliography Form—Government Documents

Since the nature of public documents is so varied, the form of the entry cannot be standardized. Therefore, you should provide sufficient information so that the reader can easily locate the reference. As a general rule, place information in the bibliographic entry in this order (but see below if you know the author, editor, or compiler of the document):

Government
Body or agency
Subsidiary body
Title of document
Identifying numbers
Publication facts

When you cite two or more works by the same government, substitute three hyphens for the name of each government or body that you repeat:

> United States. Cong. House.
>
> – – –. – – –. Senate.
>
> – – –. Dept. of Justice.

Begin with the author's name if known, especially if you cited the name in your text.

Poore, Benjamin Perley, comp. <u>A Descriptive Catalogue of the</u>
<u>Government Publications of the United States, September 5,</u>
<u>1774–March 4, 1881</u>. US 48th Cong., 2nd sess. Misc. Doc. 67.
Washington: GPO, 1885.

Congressional Papers

Senate and House sections are identified by an S or an H with document numbers (e.g., S. Res. 16) and page numbers (e.g., H2345–47).

United States. Cong. Senate. Subcommittee on Juvenile Justice of
the Committee on the Judiciary. <u>Juvenile Justice: A New</u>
<u>Focus on Prevention</u>. 102nd Cong., 2nd sess. S. Hearing
102. Washington, DC: GPO, 1992.
– – –. – – –. – – –. <u>Violent Crime Control Act 1991</u>. 102nd Cong.,
1st sess. S. 1241. Washington, DC: GPO, 1991.

If you provide a citation to the *Congressional Record*, you should abbreviate that title to *Cong. Rec.* and provide only the date and page numbers.

<u>Cong. Rec</u>. 25 Aug. 1994: S12566–75.

Executive Branch Documents

United States. Dept. of State. <u>Foreign Relations of the United</u>
<u>States: Diplomatic Papers, 1943</u>. 5 vols. Washington, DC:
GPO, 1943–44.
– – –. President. <u>Health Security: The President's Report to the</u>
<u>American People</u>. Pr Ex 1.2:H34/4. Washington, DC:
GPO, 1993.

Documents of State Governments

Publication information on state papers will vary widely, so provide sufficient data for your reader to find the document.

<u>1992–1993 Statistical Report</u>. Nashville: Tennessee Board of
Regents, 1994. TBR A-001-92.
<u>Tennessee Election Returns, 1796–1825</u>. Microfilm. Nashville:
Tennessee State Library and Archives, n.d. M-Film JK
5292 T46.
"Giles County." <u>1993–94 Directory of Public Schools</u>. Nashville:
State Dept. of Educ., n.d. 61.

Legal Citations and Public Statutes

Use the following examples as guidelines for developing your citations.

California. Const. Art. 2, sec. 4.

Environmental Protection Agency et al. v. Mink et al.
U.S. Reports, CDX. 1972.

15 U.S. Code. Sec. 78h. 1964.

Illinois. Revised Statutes Annotated. Sec. 16-7-81. 1980.

Noise Control Act of 1972. Pub. L. 92-574. 1972. Stat. 86.

People v. McIntosh. California 321 P.3d 876, 2001-6. 1970.

State v. Lane. Minnesota 263 N. W. 608. 1935.

U.S. Const. Art 2, sec. 1.

14f Bibliography Form—Electronic Sources

New technology makes it possible for you to have access to information

For discussion of the Internet's special format, see pages 54–57.
For making judgments about the validity of Internet sources, see pages 65–66.
For information about the best places to look, see pages 57–62.

at your computer that was only a dream five years ago. The Internet, in particular, opens a cornucopia of information from millions of sources. Other electronic sources are e-mail and databases.

Citing Sources Found on the Internet

Include these items as appropriate to the source:

1. Author/editor name
2. Title of the article within quotation marks, or the title of a posting to a discussion list or forum followed by the words *online posting*, followed by a period
3. Name of the book, journal, or complete work, italicized
4. Publication information

> Place, publisher, and date for books
> Volume and year of a journal
> Exact date of a magazine
> Date and description for government documents

5. Name of the sponsoring institution or organization, if available.
6. Date of your access, not followed by a comma or period
7. URL (Uniform Resource Locator), within angle brackets, followed by a period. If you must divide the URL at the end of a line, break it only after a slash.

NOTE: Do not include page numbers unless the Internet article shows original page numbers from the printed version of the journal or magazine. Do not include the total number of paragraphs nor specific paragraph numbers unless the original Internet article has provided them.

World Wide Web Sites

Titles of books and journals may be shown either in italics or with underlining. They are shown in this section with underlining.

Abstract

Ladouceur, Robert, et al. "Strategies Used with Intrusive Thoughts:
A Comparison of OCD Patients with Anxious and Community
Controls." Journal of Abnormal Psychology 109 (2000).
Abstract. 10 May 2000 <http://www.apa.org/journals/abn/
500ab.html>.

Advertisement

Dessey Creations. "Butterfly in Miami." Advertisement. N.d. 24
Aug. 1999 <http://www.butterflyinmiami.com.add1.htm>.

Anonymous Article

"People: Your Greatest Asset." Human Resources. 15 July 1999.
11 Sept. 2000 <http://netscape/business/ humanresources/>.

Archive or Scholarly Project

British Poetry Archive. Ed. Jerome McGann and David Seaman.
1999. U of Virginia Lib. 19 Aug. 2000
<http://etext.lib.virginia.edu/britpo.html>.
Coleridge, Samuel Taylor. "Kubla Khan." The Samuel Taylor
Coleridge Archive. Ed. Marjorie A. Tiefert. 10 May 1999. U of
Virginia Lib. 15 June 2001 <http://etext.lib.virginia.edu/
stc/Coleridge/poems/Kubla_Khan.html>.

Article from a Scholarly Journal

Miller, B. A., N. J. Smyth, and P. J. Mudar. "Mothers' Alcohol and
Other Drug Problems and Their Punitiveness toward Their
Children." Journal of Studies on Alcohol 60 (1999): 632–42.
28 Sept. 2000 <http://www.ncbi.nlm.hih.gov.htbin>.

Audio Program Online

See the entry for "Sound Clip," page 263.

Cartoon

Adams, Scott. "The Pointy-Haired Boss Wants to See You." Dilbert
15 Aug. 1999. 24 Aug. 2000 <http://umweb2.unitedmedia.com/
comics/dilbert/archive/cal-35.html>.

Chapter or Portion of a Book

Add the name of the chapter after the author's name:

Bramhall, Frank J. "Industrial Home for Girls." Facts and Figures
about Michigan: A Handbook of the State, Statistical,
Political, Financial, Economical, Commercial. c. 1820–1910.
4 Feb. 2001 <http://memory.loc.gov/egi-bin/query/
r?am...m:@field(DOCID+@lit>.

Database Article from a National Vendor

A database is a massive collection of data arranged by discipline and/or subject. For several years, DIALOG was a popular database, but it has been surpassed by the World Wide Web. If you do use DIALOG, provide the name and identifying numbers to the entry:

Bowles, M. D. "The Organization Man Goes to College: AT&T's
Experiment in Humanistic Education, 1953–60." The
Historian 61 (1998): 15+. DIALOG database (#88, IAC
Business A.R.T.S., Item 04993186). 19 May 2000.

NOTE: Databases that use the CD-ROM technology have been surpassed by the World Wide Web. Some libraries still subscribe to CD-ROM databases. Citations drawn from a CD-ROM program require this form:

Grych, John H. "Patterns of Adjustment among Children of
Battered Women." Journal of Consulting and Clinical
Psychology 68 (2000): 84–94. Abstract. PsycINFO. CD-ROM.
Silverplatter. 3 Aug. 2000.

See also pages 264–66 for additional examples.

Database Article at a Library's Online Service with a Listed URL

Most libraries have converted their computer searches to online databases, such as Lexis-Nexis, ProQuest Direct, OBSCOhost, Electric Library, InfoTrac, and others. If the source provides the URL, omit the identifying numbers for the database or the keyword used in the search and include the URL. Here's an example from InfoTrac:

> Lee, Catherine C. "The South in Toni Morrison's <u>Song of Solomon</u>: Initiation, Healing, and Home." <u>Studies in the Literary Imagination</u> 31 (1998): 109–23. Abstract. 19 Sept. 2001 <http://firstsearch.oclc.org/next=NEXTCMD>.

You will know the database is online when you see the full URL at the top or bottom of the printout. Here's a citation to a full-text article found on the Electronic Library:

> Poncet, Dell. "Have a Seat and Take a Breather." <u>Denver Business Journal</u> 51 (2000): 61. 3 Aug. 2000 <http://web.../ purl=rcl_BCPM/_0_A63300991&dyn4!xrn_1_0_A63300991>.

Database Article from an Online Service to Which You Personally Subscribe

Many students research topics from their homes, where they use such services as America Online or Netscape. If the URL is provided, use the form of this next example:

> "Nutrition and Cancer." <u>Discovery Health</u> 1 May 2000. 3 Aug. 2000 <http://www.discoveryhealth.c...Sc000/8096/164609.html>.

Database Article from an Online Service with an Unlisted or Scrambled URL

Two possible forms are available to you when the online service provides no URL: specifying the keyword or the path. If you access the site by using a keyword, provide a citation that gives the name of the service, the date of access, and the keyword:

> Esslin, Martin. "Theater of the Absurd." <u>Grolier Multimedia Encyclopedia</u>. 1995 ed. Netscape. 3 Aug. 2000.
> Keyword: Theater of the Absurd.

If you follow a series of topic labels to reach the article, and no URL is provided, write the word *Path* followed by the sequence of topic labels that you followed to obtain the article. Use a semicolon to separate each topic.

> <u>Kate Chopin: A Re-Awakening</u>. 23 June 1999. PBS. <u>College Webivore</u>. Netscape. 4 Aug. 2000. Path: US Literature; 19th Century; Women Authors; Chopin, Kate (1850–1904).

Database at a Library's Online Service with No URL Listed

On rare occasions you may access online material in the library that has no URL or the URL on your printout is scrambled or incomplete. In such a case, make a citation to the source, then give the name of the database, underlined (if known); the name of the service; the library; and the date of access. If you can easily locate the URL of the service's home page, provide it in angle brackets after your date of access.

> Brezina, Timothy. "Teenage Violence toward Parents as an
> Adaptation to Family Strain: Evidence from a National
> Survey of Male Adolescents." Youth and Society 30 (1999):
> 416–44. MasterFILE Elite. EBSCOhost. Clarksville
> Montgomery County Library, Clarksville, TN. 3 Aug. 2000
> <http://www.ebsco.com>.

E-mail

> Clemmer, Jim. "Writing Lab." E-mail to the author. 24 Aug. 2001.

Encyclopedia Online

> Encyclopaedia Britannica Online. Vers. 99.1. 1994–1999.
> Encyclopaedia Britannica. 19 Aug. 2001 <http://www.eb.com/>.

Refer to a specific article in this manner:

> "Coleridge, Samuel Taylor." Encyclopaedia Britannica Online. Vers.
> 99.1. 1994–99. Encyclopaedia Britannica. 19 Aug. 2001
> <http://www.eb.com/bol/topic?eu=25136&sctn1>.

ERIC Database

Be sure to give the URL even if the ERIC identifying numbers are available (see also "Database Article from a National Vendor," page 256).

> "America's Children: Key National Indicators of Well-Being."
> Federal Interagency Forum on Child and Family Statistics.
> 1999. ERIC ED427897. 15 Sept. 2001 <http://www.goarch.org/
> goa/departments/gotel/online_videos.html#LIGHT>.

Film, Video, or Film Clip Online

> "A Light Still Bright: Video on the Ecumenical Patriarchate of
> Constantinople." The History of the Orthodox Christian
> Church. 1996. GoTelecom Online. 24 Aug. 2001
> <http://www.goarch.org/goa/departments/gotel/
> online_videos.html#LIGHT>.

FTP, Telnet, and Gopher Sites

Kranidiotis, Argiris A. "Human Audio Perception Frequently
Asked Questions." Online posting. 7 June 1994. Human
Audio Perception Discussion Group. 11 Mar. 1997
<ftp:// svr-ftp.eng.cam.ac.uk/pub/com.speech/ingo/
HumanAudioPerception>.

Most FTP, telnet, and gopher sites are now found on the World Wide Web:

"The John Denver Internet FTP Site." Ed. Rory K. Young. 30 July
2000. 4 Aug. 2000 <http://www.austin1.com/JD/index.html>.

Home Page for a Web Site

Since you are not citing a specific article, you can refer to home pages in
your text, not in the bibliography.

Links to several professional sites are listed at the home page of
Frank M. LoSchiavo (http://www.netreach.net/!losh).

However, you might wish to give the reader the address of an academic site,
such as the following:

Dawe, James. Jane Austen Page. 1996–2000. 15 May 2000
<http://www.jamesdawe.com>.

Interview

Strassman, Marc. "Is Journalism Dead?" Interview with Pete
Hamill, author of News Is a Verb. Strassman Files.
BookRadio 1998. 24 Aug. 2000 <http://www.bookradio.com/>.

Journal Article

See "Article from a Scholarly Journal," page 255.

Letter

Strickland, Ruth Ann. Letter to the Editor. New York Times on the
Web 22 Aug. 1999. 24 Aug. 2000 <http://www.nytimes.com/
yr/mo/day/letter/1stric.html>.

Linkage Data (an accessed file)

"What Happens to Recycled Plastics?" Online posting. Lkd. Better
World Discussion Topics at Recycling Discussion Group nd.
18 June 2000 <http://www.betterworld.com/BWZ/9602/
learn.htm>.

Magazine Article Online

Carney, Dan, Mike France, and Spencer E. Ante. "Web Access
Is Becoming a Dicey Issue for Industry and Regulators."
BusinessWeek Online 31 July 2000. 2 Aug. 2000
<http://www.businessweek.com/2000/00_31>.

Manuscript

Ganus, John. "In the Clouds of Isnos: Prologue." Manuscript, 1999.
24 Aug. 2000 <http://www.xenosbooks.com/isnos.html>.

Map

"U. S. Territorial Map 1870." American Historical Atlas: U. S.
Territorial Maps 1775–1920. U of Virginia Lib. 17 June 1996.
24 Aug. 2000 <http://xroals.Virginia.edu/~map/TERRITORY/
187omdp.html>.

MOO, MUD, and Other Chat Rooms

"Virtual Conference on Mary Shelley's The Last Man." Villa Diodati
at EmoryMOO. 13 Sept. 1997. 24 Aug. 2000
<http://www.rc.umd.edu/villa/vc97/Shelley_9_13_97.html>.

Chat rooms seldom have great value, but on occasion you might find
something that you wish to cite; if so, use this form:

"Australia: The Olympics 2000." 30 May 2000 Yahoo! Chat. 30 May
2000 <http://chat.yahoo.com/
?room=Australia::160032654&identitychat>.

Newsgroup, Usenet News, Forum

Link, Richard. "Territorial Fish." Online Posting. 11 Jan. 1997.
Environment Newsgroup. 11 Mar. 2000
<http://www.rec.aquaria.freshwater.misc>.

Add additional data to cite a document that has been forwarded.

Link, Richard. "Territorial Fish." 11 Jan. 1997. Fwd. by
Harvey Blanchard. Online Posting. 1 Mar. 1997.
Environment Newsgroup. 11 Mar. 2000
<http://www.rec.aquaria.freshwater.misc>.

Newsletter

"TSP to Receive HUD Best Practice Award." UIS Weekly 24 July
2000. 30 May 2000 <http://www.uis.edu/~camprel/weekly/
index/pdf>.

Yeager, Joel. "E-mail as a Therapeutic Adjunct in the Outpatient
Treatment of Anorexia Nervosa: Illustrative Case Material
and Discussion of the Issues." Psychinformatics Mar. 2000.
Abstract. 3 May 2000 <http://psychinformatics.org/
newsletter/psinews/features.htm>.

Newspaper Article, Column, Editorial

Firestone, David. "Anonymous Louisiana Slaves Regain
Identity." New York Times on the Web 30 July 2000.
30 July 2000 <http://www.nytimes.com/library/national/
073000la-slaves.html>.

Weisman, Steven R. "A Debate over Wealth, Virtue and Justice."
Editorial. New York Times on the Web. 22 Aug. 1999.
10 May 2001 <http://www.nytimes.com/yr/mo/day/
editorial/wwSun3.html>.

Novel

Lawrence, D. H. "Chapter 1." Lady Chatterly's Lover. 1928.
26 Sept. 2001 <http://bibliomania.com/fiction/dhl/chat/
chat1.html>.

Online Posting for E-mail Discussion Groups

List the Internet site if known; otherwise show the e-mail address of the
list's moderator.

Chapman, David. "Reforming the Tax and Benefit System
to Reduce Unemployment." Online Posting. 25 Feb.
1998. Democracy Design Forum. 27 May 2000
<http://www.democdesignforum.demon.co.uk/
unemp.nexus.html>.

Chapman, David. "Reforming the Tax and Benefit System to
Reduce Unemployment." Online Posting. 25 Feb. 1998.
Democracy Design Forum. 27 May 2000
<chapman@democdesignforumj.demon.co.uk>.

Photo, Painting, Sculpture

MLA style does not require you to label the type of work, as shown in the first example of a photograph. Usually, the text will have established the nature of the work. However, if you feel that clarification is necessary, as in the case of "The Blessed Damozel," which is both a painting and a poem, you may wish to designate the form.

> Farrar, Ray. "Windsor Castle." 1999. 24 Aug. 2001
> <http://www.jrfarrar.demon.co.uk/town/tll.htm>.
>
> Rossetti, Dante. "The Blessed Damozel." 1875–78. Painting.
> Rossetti Archive. U of Virginia Lib. 9 June 1999. 24 Aug.
> 2000 <http://www.engl.virginia.edu/~bpn2f/rossetti/
> tourf.html>.
>
> "Gold Shield, African Coast." African Sculpture. U of
> Pennsylvania Museum. 22 Sept. 1997. 24 Aug. 2000
> <http://www.sas.upenn.edu/AfricanStudies/sculpture/
> gdsld_akan.gif>.

Poem, Song, or Story

> Keats, John. "Ode on a Grecian Urn." Poetical Works. 1884.
> Project Bartleby. 2000 Great Books Online. 10 July 2000
> <http://www.bartleby.edu/126/41.html>.

Report

> Watkins. R. E. "An Historical Review of the Role and Practice of
> Psychology in the Field of Corrections." Report No. R-29.
> Correctional Service of Canada. 1992. 12 Sept 2000
> <http://www.csc-scc.gc.ca/crd/reports/r28e/r28e/htm>.

Serialized Article

> Frank, Laura. "Worker: 'I Didn't Get That at Home.'"
> Tennessean.com 5 Mar. 1997. Part of a series, An
> Investigation into Illnesses around the Nation's Nuclear
> Weapons Sites, begun 9 Feb. 1997. 20 Aug. 2000
> <http://www.tennessean.com/special/oakridge/part3/
> frames/html>.
>
> Thomas, Susan. "Oak Ridge Workers Offered Medical Screening."
> Tennessean.com 21 Jan. 1999. Part of a series, An
> Investigation into Illnesses around the Nation's Nuclear
> Weapons Sites, begun 9 Feb. 1997. 20 Aug. 2000 <http://
> www.tennessean.com/special/oakridge/part3/frames/html>.

Thomas, Susan, Laura Frank, and Anne Paine. "Taking the
Poison." <u>Tennessean.com</u> 9 Feb. 1997. Part of a series,
An Investigation into Illnesses around the Nation's
Nuclear Weapons Sites, begun 9 Feb. 1997. 20 Aug. 2000
<http://www.tennessean.com/special/oakridge/part3/
frames/html>.

Song

See "Poem, Song, or Story," page 262.

Sound Clip or Recording

Nader, Ralph. "Live Webcast with Ralph Nader." Press Club.
NPR Online. 18 July 2000. Audio transcript. 27 July 2000
<http://www.npr.org/programs/npc/000718.rnader.html>.

Speech, Audio Online

See "Sound Clip or Recording," above.

Story

See "Poem, Song, or Story," page 262.

Synchronous Communication

See "MOO, MUD, and Other Chat Rooms," page 260.

Telnet Site

U.S. Naval Observatory. "The Mercury Ion Frequency Standard."
Online Posting. 24 Feb. 1997. 6 Mar. 2000
<telnet: duke.ldgo.columbia.edu/port=23 login ads, set
terminal to 8/N/1>.

See also "Newsgroup, Usenet News, Forum," page 260.

University Posting, Online Article

Siewers, Alf. "Issues Online." Online Posting. July/ Aug. 2000.
U of Illinois at Springfield. 28 July 2000 <http://www.uis.edu/
~ilissues//owl.htm>.

Video

See "Film, Videocassette, or DVD," page 270.

Web Site, General Reference

As long as you are not citing a specific article but merely making reference to a site, provide the address in your text, *not* on the Works Cited page.

Further information about this program can be found at the website for the Department of Psychology at the University of Wisconsin-Parkside (http://www.uwp.edu/academic/psychology).

Working Papers

Cutler, David M. "How Much Should the Tobacco Companies Have
Paid?" Working Paper #00–004, Harvard Business School,
1999–2000. 30 July 2000 <http://www.hbs.edu/units/
marketing/research.htm>.

14g Bibliography Form—CD-ROMs

CD-ROM technology provides information in several different ways, and each method of transmission requires an adjustment in the form of the entry for your Works Cited page.

Full-Text Articles with Publication Information for the Printed Source

Full-text articles are available from national distributors, such as Information Access Company (InfoTrac), UMI-Proquest (Proquest), Silverplatter, or SIRS CD-ROM Information Systems. (*Note:* Most of these sources are also available online.)

See also page 245 for citing SIRS in its loose-leaf form.

Conform to the examples that follow.

DePalma, Antony. "Mexicans Renew Their Pact on the Economy,
Retaining the Emphasis on Stability." New York Times
25 Sept. 1994: 4. New York Times Ondisc. CD-ROM.
UMI-Proquest. Jan. 1995.

Mann, Thomas E., and Norman J. Ornstein. "Shipshape? A
Progress Report on Congressional Reform." Brookings
Review Spring 1994: 40–45. SIRS Researcher. CD-ROM.
Boca Raton: SIRS, 1994. Art. 57.

HINT: Complete information may not be readily available—for example, the original publication date may be missing. In such cases, provide what is available:

Silver, Daniel J. "The Battle of the Books." Rev. of The Western
Canon: The Books and School of the Ages, by Harold Bloom.
Resource/One. CD-ROM. UMI-Proquest. Feb. 1995.

Full-Text Articles with No Publication Information for a Printed Source

Sometimes the original printed source of an article or report will not be provided by the distributor of the CD-ROM database. In such a case, conform to the examples that follow, which provide limited data.

> "Faulkner Biography." Discovering Authors. CD-ROM. Detroit: Gale, 1999.
> "U.S. Population by Age: Urban and Urbanized Areas." 1999 U.S. Census of Population and Housing. CD-ROM. US Bureau of the Census. 2000.

Complete Books and Other Publications on CD-ROM

Cite this type of source as you would a book, and then provide information to the electronic source that you accessed.

> The Bible. The Old Testament. CD-ROM. Parsippany, NJ: Bureau Development, 1999.
> English Poetry Full-Text Database. Re. 2. CD-ROM. Cambridge, Eng.: Chadwyck, 1993.
> "John F. Kennedy." InfoPedia. CD-ROM. N.p.: Future Vision, n.d.
> Poe, Edgar Allan. "Fall of the House of Usher." Electronic Classical Library. CD-ROM. Garden Grove, CA: World Library, 1999.
> Chaucer, Geoffrey. "The Wife of Bath's Tale." Canterbury Tales. CD-ROM facsimile text. Princeton: Films for the Humanities and Sciences, 2000.

Abstracts to Books and Articles Provided by the National Distributors

As a service to readers, the national distributors have members of their staff write abstracts of articles and books if the original authors have not provided such abstracts. As a result, an abstract that you find on InfoTrac and ProQuest may not be written by the original author, so you should not quote such abstracts. You may quote from abstracts that say "Abstract written by the author." Silverplatter databases *do* have abstracts written by the original authors. In either case, you need to show in the Works Cited entry that you have cited from the abstract, so conform to the example that follows, which provides name, title, publication information, the word *abstract,* the name of the database underlined, the medium (CD-ROM), the name of the vendor, and—if available to you—the electronic publication date (month and year).

> Figueredo, Aurelio J., and Laura Ann McCloskey. "Sex, Money, and Paternity: The Evolutionary Psychology of Domestic Violence." Ethnology and Sociobiology 14 (1993): 353–79. Abstract. PsycINFO. CD-ROM. Silverplatter. 12 Jan. 1999.

Encyclopedia Article

For an encyclopedia article on a compact diskette, use the following form:

"Abolitionist Movement." <u>Compton's Interactive Encyclopedia</u>.
　　CD-ROM. The Learning Company, 1999.

Multidisc Publication

When citing a multidisc publication, follow the term *CD-ROM* with the total number of discs or with the disc that you cited from.

<u>Perseus 2.0: Interactive Sources and Studies on Ancient Greece</u>.
　　CD-ROM Disc 3. New Haven: Yale UP, 1996.

14h   Bibliography Form—Other Electronic Sources

Citing a Source That You Access in More Than One Medium

Some distributors issue packages that include different media, such as CD-ROM and accompanying microfiche or a diskette and an accompanying videotape. Cite such publications as you would a complete book on a CD-ROM, with the addition of the media available with this product.

Franking, Holly. <u>Negative Space: A Computerized Video</u>
　　<u>Novel</u>. Vers. 1.0. Diskette, videocassette. Prairie Village:
　　Diskotech, 1990.

Jolly, Peggy. "A Question of Style." <u>Exercise Exchange</u> 26.2 (1982):
　　39–40. <u>ERIC</u>. CD-ROM, microfiche. Silverplatter. Feb. 17,
　　1995. ED236601, fiche 1.

Silver, Daniel J. "The Battle of the Books." Rev. of <u>The Western</u>
　　<u>Canon: The Books and School of the Ages</u>, by Harold Bloom.
　　<u>Resource/One</u>. CD-ROM, microfiche S-637. UMI-Proquest.
　　Feb. 1995.

Chaucer, Geoffrey. "Prologue." <u>Canterbury Tales</u>. Videocassette,
　　CD-ROM facsimile text. Princeton: Films for the Humanities
　　and Sciences, 2000.

Citing a Source Found on a Diskette

Cite a diskette as you would a book, with the addition of the word *Diskette*.

Lester, James D. <u>Grammar: Computer Slide Show</u>. 10 lessons on 4
　　diskettes. Clarksville, TN: Austin Peay State U, 1997.

"Nuclear Medicine Technologist." <u>Guidance Information System</u>.
　　17th ed. Diskette. Cambridge: Riverside-Houghton, 1992.

Citing a Source Found on a Magnetic Tape

Write this entry as you would for a book, with the addition of the words *Magnetic tape*. If relevant, show edition (3rd ed.), release (Rel. 2), or version (Ver. 3).

Statistics on Child Abuse—Montgomery County, Tennessee.
Magnetic tape. Rel. 2. Clarksville, TN: Harriett Cohn Mental
Health Center, 2001.

Citing a Source Found on an Online Database

To cite an online database, such as DIALOG, conform to the style shown in these samples:

Bronner, E. "Souter Voices Concern over Abortion Curb."
Boston Globe 31 Oct. 1990: 1. Online. Dialog. 22 Nov. 1997.
Priest, Patricia Joyner. "Self-Disclosure on Television: The
Counter-Hegemonic Struggle of Marginalized Groups on
'Donahue.'" Diss. New York U, 1990. DAI 53.7 (1993): 2147A.
Dissertation Abstracts Online. Online. Dialog. 10 Feb. 1994.

Material Accessed through E-mail

Electronic mail may be treated as a letter or memo (see page 258). Provide the name of the sender, a title or subject if one is listed, a description of the mail (e.g., "E-mail to Greg Norman"), and the date of transmission.

Taylor, Stephanie. "Mail How-To #1." E-mail to Harned users.
26 Sept. 2000.
Morgan, Melvin S. E-mail to the author. 16 Feb. 2001.

14i Bibliography Form—Other Sources

Advertisement

Provide the title of the advertisement within quotation marks, or the name of the product or company not within quotation marks, the label *Advertisement*, and publication information.

"Sheer Drive." Advertisement. Zurich Financial Services. Time
17 July 2000: 79.
Slim-Fast. Advertisement. CNNLive. 4 Aug. 2000.
Jenkins & Wynne Ford/Mercury. Billboard advertisement.
Clarksville, TN. Aug. 2000.

Art Work

If you actually experience the work itself, use the form shown by the next two entries:

Remington, Frederic. <u>Mountain Man</u>. Metropolitan Museum of Art,
    New York.
Wyeth, Andrew. <u>Hay Ledge</u>. Private Collection of Mr. and Mrs.
    Joseph E. Levine.

If the art work is a special showing at a museum, use the form of this next example.

"Gertrude Vanderbilt Whitney: Printmakers' Patron." Whitney
    Museum of American Art, New York. 22 Feb. 1995.
Mortenson, Ray. "Photographs of Lakes and Ponds in the Hudson
    Highlands." Borden Gallery, New York. 26 Feb. 1995.

Use this next form to cite reproductions in books and journals.

Lee-Smith, Hughie. <u>Temptation</u>. 1991. <u>A History of African-</u>
    <u>American Artists: From 1792 to the Present</u>. Ed. Romare
    Bearden and Harry Henderson. New York: Pantheon, 1993.
Raphael. <u>School of Athens</u>. The Vatican, Rome. <u>The World Book-</u>
    <u>Encyclopedia</u>. 1976 ed.

If you show the date of the original, place the date immediately after the title.

Raphael. <u>School of Athens</u>. 1510–1511. The Vatican, Rome. <u>The</u>
    <u>World Book-Encyclopedia</u>. 1976 ed.

Broadcast Interview

Cooper, John. "Woodrow Wilson." Interview. <u>American Presidents</u>.
    C-SPAN2. 13 Sept. 1999.
Wolfe, Tom. Interview. <u>The Wrong Stuff: American Architecture</u>.
    Dir. Tom Bettag. Videocassette. Carousel, 1983.

Bulletin

Economic Research Service. <u>Demand and Price Situation</u>. Bulletin
    DPS-141, 14 pp. Washington, DC: Department of Agriculture,
    Aug. 1994.
French, Earl. <u>Personal Problems in Industrial Research and</u>
    <u>Development</u>. Bulletin No. 51. Ithaca: New York State School
    of Industrial and Labor Relations, 1993.

Cartoon

If you cannot decipher the name of the cartoonist and cannot find a title, use this form:

Cartoon. New Yorker 12 Sept. 1994: 92.

Sometimes you will have the artist's name but not the name of the cartoon:

Bennett. Cartoon. Christian Science Monitor 28 July 2000: 10.

Some cartoons are reprinted in magazines:

Shill, Bob, and Paul Fell. "Mulch." Cartoon. Rpt. in Editor and
      Publisher 24 Apr. 2000: 49.

Computer Software

Quicken TurboTax Deluxe. Computer software. CD-ROM. N.p.:
      Intuit, 2000.
Compaq Mobile Internet PC Reference Manual. N.p.: Compaq
      Computer Corp. 2000.

Conference Proceedings

Miller, Wilma J., ed. Writing across the Curriculum. Proceedings
      of the Fifth Annual Conference on Writing across the
      Curriculum. Feb. 1995. U of Kentucky. Lexington: U of
      Kentucky P, 1995.

Dissertation, Published

Nykrog, Per. Les Fabliaux: Etude d'histoire littéraire et de
      stylistique mediévale. Diss. Aarhus U, 1957. Copenhagen:
      Munksgaard, 1957.

Dissertation, Unpublished

Shore, Zandra Lesley. "Girls Reading Culture: Autobiography
      as Inquiry into Teaching the Body, the Romance, and the
      Economy of Love." Diss. U or Toronto, 1999.

If you cite only the abstract of a dissertation, see page 244 for the correct form.

Film, Videocassette, or DVD

Cite the title of a film, the director, the distributor, and the year.

Shakespeare in Love. Dir. John Madden. Universal Pictures, 1998.

If relevant to your study, add the names of performers, writers, or producers after the name of the director.

Little Women. Dir. Gillian Armstrong. Screenplay by Robin
    Swicord. Columbia Pictures, 1993.

If the film is a DVD, videocassette, filmstrip, slide program, or videodisc, add the type of medium before the name of the distributor. Add the date of the original film, if available, before the name of the medium.

The Piano. Dir. Jane Campion. Perf. Sam Neil, Holly Hunter, and
    Harvey Keitel. Miramax, 1992. Videocassette. Live Home
    Video, 1995.

There's Something about Mary. Dir. Bobby Farraley and Peter
    Farraley. DVD. 20th Century Fox, 1999.

If you are citing the accomplishments of the director or a performer, begin the citation with that person's name.

Paltrow, Gwyneth. Shakespeare in Love. Dir. John Madden.
    Universal Pictures, 1998.

If you cannot find certain information, such as the original date of the film, cite what is available.

Altman, Robert, dir. The Room. Perf. Julian Sands, Linda Hunt,
    Annie Lennox. Videocassette. Prism.

Interview, Unpublished

For an interview that you conduct, name the person interviewed, the type of interview (e.g., telephone interview, personal interview, e-mail interview), and the date.

Safire, William. Telephone Interview. 5 Mar. 2000.

See "Broadcast Interview," page 268.

Letter, Personal

Weathers, Walter. Letter to the author. 5 Mar. 2000.

Letter, Published

Eisenhower, Dwight. Letter to Richard Nixon. 20 April 1968.
    Memoirs of Richard Nixon. By Richard Nixon. New York:
    Grosset, 1978.

Loose-leaf Collections

If you cite an article from *SIRS, Opposing Viewpoints,* or other loose-leaf
collections, provide the original publication data and then add information
for the loose-leaf volume:

"The Human Genetic Code." Illustration. Facts on File. 29 June
    2000: 437–38.

Hodge, Paul. "The Andromeda Galaxy." Mercury July/Aug. 1993:
    98+. *Physical Science.* Ed. Eleanor Goldstein. Vol. 2. Boca
    Raton: SIRS, 1994. Art. 24.

Cox, Rachel S. "Protecting the National Parks." CQ Researcher.
    16 July 2000: 523+. Washington, DC: Congressional
    Quarterly Inc., 2000.

Manuscripts (Ms.) and Typescripts (Ts.)

Glass, Malcolm. Journal 3, ms. M. Glass Private Papers,
    Clarksville, TN.

Tanner. Ms. 346 Bodleian Library, Oxford, Eng.

Williams, Ralph. Notebook 15, ts. Williams Papers. Vanderbilt U.,
    Nashville.

Map

Treat a map as you would an anonymous work, but add a descriptive
label, such as *map, chart, survey* unless the title describes the medium.

County Boundaries and Names. United States Base Map GE-50,
    No. 86. Washington, DC: GPO, 1987.

Virginia. Map, Chicago: Rand, 2000.

Microfilm or Microfiche

Chapman, Dan. "Panel Could Help Protect Children." Winston-
    Salem Journal 14 Jan. 1990: 14. Newsbank: Welfare and
    Social Problems 12 (1990): fiche 1, grids A8–11.

Jolly, Peggy. "A Question of Style." <u>Exercise Exchange</u> 26.2 (1982):
39–40. ERIC ED2336601, fiche 1.

Tuckerman, H. T. "James Fenimore Cooper." Microfilm. <u>North
American Review</u> 89 (1859): 298–316.

Miscellaneous Materials (Program, Leaflet, Poster, Announcement)

"Earth Day." Poster. Louisville. 23 Mar. 1998.

"Gospel Arts Day." Program. Nashville: Fisk U. 18 June 2000.

Monograph

Tennessee Teachers Group. <u>Kindergarten Practices, 2000</u>.
Monograph 2000-M2. Knoxville: Author, 2001.

See also "Monograph," page 246, for a monograph published in a journal.

Musical Composition

For a musical composition, begin with the composer's name, followed by
a period. Underline the title of an opera, ballet, or work of music identified by
name, but do not underline or enclose within quotation marks the form, number, and key when these are used to identify an instrumental composition.

Mozart, Wolfgang A. Jupiter. Symphony No. 41.

Wagner, Richard. Lohengrin.

Treat a published score as you would a book.

Legrenzi, Giovanni. <u>La Buscha</u>. Sonata for Instruments. <u>Historical
Anthology of Music</u>. Ed. Archibald T. Davison and Willi Apel.
Cambridge, MA: Harvard UP, 1950. 70–76.

Pamphlet

Treat pamphlets as you would a book.

Federal Reserve Board. <u>Consumer Handbook to Credit Protection
Laws</u>. Washington, DC: GPO, 1993.

Westinghouse Advanced Power Systems. <u>Nuclear Waste
Management: A Manageable Task</u>. Madison, PA: Author, n.d.

Performance

Treat a performance (e.g., play, opera, ballet, or concert) as you would a
film, but include the site (normally the theater and city) and the date of the
performance.

Lakota Sioux Indian Dance Theatre. Symphony Space, New York.
18 Feb. 1995.

Oedipus at Colonus. By Sophocles. Trans. Theodore H. Banks.
Pearl Theatre, New York. New York. 8 Feb. 1995.

Sunset Boulevard. By Andrew Lloyd Webber. Dir. Trevor Nunn.
Perf. Glenn Close, George Hearn, Alan Campbell, and Alice
Ripley. Minskoff Theatre, New York. 7 Feb. 1995.

If your text emphasizes the work of a particular individual, begin with the
appropriate name.

Cytron, Sara. "Take My Domestic Partner—Please." Conf. on Coll.
Composition and Communication Convention. Grand Hyatt
Hotel, Washington, DC. 24 Mar. 1995.

Gregory, Dick, comedian. Village Vanguard, New York. 22 Feb.
1995.

Marcovicci, Andrea, cond. "I'll Be Seeing You: Love Songs of World
War II." American Symphony Orchestra. Avery Fisher Hall,
New York. 15 Feb. 1995.

Photocopied Material

Smith, Jane L. "Terms for the Study of Fiction." Photocopy.
Athens, OH. 2001.

Public Address or Lecture

Identify the nature of the address (e.g., Lecture, Reading), include the site
(normally the lecture hall and city), and the date of the performance.

Evans, Nekhena. Lecture. Brooklyn Historical Soc., New York. 26
Feb. 1995.

Freedman, Diane P. "Personal Experience: Autobiographical
Literary Criticism." Address. MLA Convention. Marriott
Hotel, San Diego. 28 Dec. 1994.

Kinnell, Galway. Reading of Smart, Rilke, Dickinson, and others.
Manhattan Theatre Club, New York. 20 Feb. 1995.

Recording on Record, Tape, or Disk

If you are not citing a compact disc, indicate the medium (e.g., audiocassette, audiotape [reel-to-reel tape], or LP [long-playing record]).

"Chaucer: The Nun's Priest's Tale." Canterbury Tales. Narr. in Middle
English by Robert Ross. Audiocassette. Caedmon, 1971.

John, Elton. "This Song Has No Title." <u>Goodbye Yellow Brick Road</u>.
    LP. MCA, 1974.
Reich, Robert B. <u>Locked in the Cabinet: A Political Memoir</u>.
    4 audiocassettes abridged. New York: Random Audio, 1997.
Sanborn, David. "Soul Serenade." <u>Upfront</u>. CD. Elektra, 1992.
Tchaikovsky. <u>Romeo and Juliet</u>. Fantasy-Overture after
    Shakespeare. New Philharmonic Orchestra London. Cond.
    Lawrence Siegel. DVD. Classical Masters, 2000.

Do not underscore, italicize, or enclose within quotation marks a private
recording or tape. However, you should include the date, if available, as well
as the location and the identifying number.

Walpert, Wanda A. Folk Stories of the Smokey Mountains.
    Rec. Feb. 1995. Audiotape. U of Knoxville. Knoxville, TN.
    UTF.34.82.

Cite a libretto, liner notes, or booklet that accompanies a recording as
follows:

Brooks, Garth. Booklet. <u>No Fences</u>. By Garth Brooks. Capital
    Nashville, 1990.

Report

Unbound reports are placed within quotation marks; bound reports are
treated as books:

Coca-Cola Company. <u>2000 Annual Report</u>. Atlanta: Author, 2000.
Linden, Fabian. "Women: A Demographic, Social and Economic
    Presentation." Report. The Conference Board. New York:
    CBS/Broadcast Group, 1973.

Reproductions and Photographs

Blake, William. <u>Comus</u> Plate 4. Photograph in Irene Taylor.
    "Blake's <u>Comus</u> Designs." <u>Blake Studies</u> 4 (Spring 1972): 61.
Michener, James A. "Structure of Earth at Centennial, Colorado."
    Line drawing in <u>Centennial</u>. By Michener. New York:
    Random, 1974. 26.
Snowden, Mary. <u>Jersey Pears</u>. 1982. <u>American Realism: Twentieth
    Century Drawings and Watercolors</u>. New York: Abrams,
    1986. 159.

Table, Illustration, Chart, or Graph

Tables or illustrations of any kind published within works need a detailed label (chart, table, figure, photograph, and so on):

"Financial Indicators: Money and Interest Rates." Table. Economist
    8 July 2000: 105.
"Alphabet." Chart. Columbus: Scholastic, 1994.

Television or Radio Program

If available or relevant, provide information in this order: the episode (in quotation marks), the title of the program (underscored or italicized), title of the series (not underscored nor in quotation marks), name of the network, call letters and city of the local station, and the broadcast date. Add other information (such as narrator) after the episode or program narrated or directed or performed. Place the number of episodes, if relevant, before the title of the series.

"Frankenstein: The Making of the Monster." Great Books. Narr.
    Donald Sutherland. Writ. Eugenie Vink. Dir. Jonathan Ward.
    Learning Channel. 8 Sept. 1993.
"News Headlines." Narr. Sadie Sakleford. Weekend Edition.
    Host Liane Hanson. NPR News. NPR. WPHN, Nashville.
    19 Feb. 1995.
Middlemarch. By George Eliot. Adapt. Andrew Davies. Dir.
    Anthony Pope. Perf. Juliet Aubrey and Patrick Malahide.
    6 episodes. Masterpiece Theatre. Introd. Russell Baker.
    PBS. WCDN, Nashville. 10 Apr.1994.
Nutrition & Aids. Narr. Carolyn O'Neil. CNN. 19 Feb. 1995.
Prairie Home Companion. NPR. WPHN, Nashville. 18 Feb. 1995.
"Some of Our Planes Are Missing." Narr. Morley Safer. Prod. David
    Fitzpatrick. 60 Minutes. CBS WTVF, Nashville. Feb. 19 1994.

Thesis

See "Dissertation, Unpublished," page 269.

Transparency

Sharp, La Vaughn, and William E. Loeche. The Patient
    and Circulatory Disorders: A Guide for Instructors.
    54 transparencies, 99 overlays. Philadelphia: Lorrenzo,
    2001.

Unpublished Paper

Elkins, William R. "The Dream World and the Dream Vision: Meaning and Structure in Poe's Art." Unpublished paper. Little Rock, AR, 2000.

Videocassette

Sister Wendy's Story of Painting: The Renaissance. Videocassette. BBC Video, 1996.

Alice Walker and the Color Purple: Inside a Modern American Classic. Videocassette. Films for the Humanities and Sciences, 1998.

The Gate to the Mind's Eye. A Computer Animation Odyssey. Dir. Michael Boydstein. Music by Thomas Dolly. Videocassette. BMG Video, 1994.

A Portrait of the Artist as a Young Man. By James Joyce. Dir. Joseph Strick. Perf. Bosco Hogan. Videocassette. Mystic Fire Video, 1989.

Thompson, Paul. "W. B. Yeats." Lecture. Videocassette. Memphis U, 2001.

Voice Mail

Warren, Vernon. "Memo on Awards Day." Voice mail to the author. 6 Jan. 2001.

15

Writing in APA Style

Your instructor may require you to write the research paper in APA style, which is governed by the *Publication Manual of the American Psychological Association*. This style has gained wide acceptance in the social sciences, and versions similar to it are used in the biological sciences, business, and the earth sciences. This chapter conforms to the stipulations of the fifth edition of the *Publication Manual of the American Psychological Association*, 2001, with adjustments and updates based on APA's Web page. Research is paramount in the sciences; in fact, the APA style guide says, "No amount of skill in writing can disguise research that is poorly designed or managed." Thus, you will need to execute your project with precision.

15a Writing Theory, Reporting Test Results, or Reviewing Literature

In the sciences you may choose between three types of articles, or your instructor will specify one of these:

- Theoretical articles
- Reports of empirical studies
- Review articles

Theoretical Article

For an example of a theoretical article, see the student paper on pages 300–09, which examines prevailing theories for treating hyperactive children.

The theoretical article draws upon existing research to examine a topic. This type of paper is the one you will most likely write as an underclassman. You will trace the development of a theory or compare theories. Your theoretical analysis will examine the literature to arrive at the current thinking about topics, such as autism, criminal behavior, dysfunctional families, learning disorders, and so forth. It generally accomplishes four things:

1. Identifies a problem or hypothesis that has historical implications in the scientific community.
2. Traces the development and history of the evolution of the theory.
3. Provides a systematic analysis of the articles that have explored the problem.
4. Arrives at a judgment and discussion of the prevailing theory.

Report of an Empirical Study

For additional details about field research, consult Chapter 5, pages 83–85.

When you conduct field research and perform laboratory testing, you will need to report the details of your original research. The report accomplishes these four things:

1. Introduces the problem or hypothesis under investigation and explains the purpose of the work.
2. Describes the method used to conduct the research.
3. Reports the results and the basic findings.
4. Discusses, interprets and explores the implications of the findings.

You will need to work closely with your instructor to accomplish each of these stages.

Review Article

See pages 120–22 for a sample review of literature.

You may be required to write a critical evaluation of a published article or book, or a set of articles on a common topic. Its purpose is to examine the state of current research and to determine if additional work might be in order. It does several things:

1. Defines the problem to clarify the hypothesis.
2. Summarizes the article or book under review.
3. Analyzes the literature to discover strengths and possible weaknesses or inconsistencies in the research.
4. Recommends additional research that might grow logically from the work under review.

15b   Writing in the Proper Tense for an APA Paper

Verb tense is an indicator that distinguishes papers in the humanities from those in the natural and social sciences. MLA style, as shown in previous chapters, requires you to use present tense when you refer to a cited work ("Johnson *stipulates*" or "the work of Elmford and Mills *shows*"). In contrast, APA style requires you to use past tense or present perfect tense ("Marshall *stipulated*" or "the work of Elmford and Mills *has demonstrated*"). The APA style does require present tense when you discuss the results (e.g., *the results confirm* or *the study indicates*) and when you mention established knowledge (e.g., *the therapy offers some hope* or *salt contributes to hypertension*). These passages show the differences in verb tenses for MLA and APA styles.

MLA Style	APA Style
The scholarly issue at work here is the construction of reality. Cohen, Adoni, and Bantz label the construction a social process "in which human beings act both as the creators and products of the social world" (34). These writers identify three categories (34–35).	The scholarly issue at work here is the construction of reality. Cohen, Adoni, and Bantz have labeled the construction a social process " in which human beings act both as the creators and products of the social world" (p. 34). These writers have identified three categories.

APA style, shown on the right, requires that you use the present tense for generalizations and references to stable conditions, but it requires the present perfect tense or the past tense for sources cited (e.g., the sources *have tested* a hypothesis *or* the sources *reported* the results of a test). This next sentence uses tense correctly for APA style:

The danger of steroid use exists for every age group, even youngsters. Lloyd and Mercer (2000) reported on six incidents of liver damage to 14-year-old swimmers who used steroids.

For updates to APA style, consult the association's Internet site: http://www.apa.org/journals/webref.html.

As shown above in the example, use the present tense (*exists*) for established knowledge and the present perfect (*has reported*) or the past tense (*reported*) for a citation.

15c Using In-text Citations in APA Style

APA style uses these conventions for in-text citations.
- Cites last names only.
- Cites the year, within parentheses, immediately after the name of the author. A specific day precedes the year in textual citations, but follows in bibliography entries.
- Cites page numbers with a direct quotation, seldom with a paraphrase.
- Uses "p." or "pp." before page numbers.

Citing Last Name Only and the Year of Publication

An in-text citation in APA style requires the last name of the author and the year of publication.

Devlin (1999) has advanced the idea of combining the social sciences and mathematics to chart human behavior.

If you do not use the author's name in your text, place the name within the parenthetical citation.

One study has advanced the idea of combining the social sciences and mathematics to chart human behavior Devlin (1999).

Providing a Page Number

If you quote the exact words of a source, provide a page number and use "p." or "pp." Place the page number in one of two places: after the year (e.g., 1999, p. B4) or at the end of the quotation.

Devlin (1999) has advanced the idea of "soft mathematics," which is the practice of "applying mathematics to study people's behavior" (p. B4).

Citing a Block of Material

Present a quotation of forty words or more as a separate block, indented five spaces or one half inch from the left margin. (*Note*: MLA style uses ten spaces or one inch). Because it is set off from the text in a distinctive block, do not enclose it with quotation marks. Do not indent the first line an extra five spaces; however, do indent the first line of any additional paragraphs that appear in the block an extra five spaces, that is, ten spaces from the left margin. Set parenthetical citations outside the last period.

Albert (2000) reported the following:

> Whenever these pathogenic organisms attack the human body and begin to multiply, the infection is set in motion. The host responds to this parasitic invasion with efforts to cleanse itself of the invading agents. When rejection efforts of the host become visible (fever, sneezing, congestion), the disease status exists. (pp. 314–315)

Citing a Work with More than One Author

When one work has two or more authors, use *and* in the text but use & in the citation.

Werner and Throckmorton (1999) offered statistics on the toxic levels of water samples from six rivers.

but

It has been reported (Werner & Throckmorton, 1999) that toxic levels exceeded the maximum allowed each year since 1983.

For three to five authors, name them all in the first entry (e.g., Torgerson, Andrews, Smith, Lawrence, & Dunlap, 2001), but thereafter use "et al." (e.g., Torgerson et al., 2001). For six or more authors, employ "et al." in the first and in all subsequent instances (e.g., Fredericks et al., 2001).

Citing More than One Work by an Author

Use lowercase letters (a, b, c) to identify two or more works published in the same year by the same author, for example, "(Thompson, 2000a)" and "(Thompson, 2000b)." Then use "2000a" and "2000b" in your References list. If necessary, specify additional information:

Horton (2000; cf. Thomas, 1999a, p. 89, and 1999b, p. 426)
suggested an intercorrelation of these testing devices. But after
multiple-group analysis, Welston (1998, esp. p. 211) reached
an opposite conclusion.

Citing Indirect Sources

Use a double reference to cite somebody who has been quoted in a book or article. That is, use the original author in the text and cite your source for the information in the parenthetical citation.

In other research, Massie and Rosenthal (1997) studied home
movies of children diagnosed with autism, but determining criteria
was difficult due to the differences in quality and dating of the
available videotapes (cited in Osterling & Dawson, 1998, p. 248).

Citing from a Textbook or Anthology

If you make an in-text citation to an article or chapter of a textbook, casebook, or anthology, use the in-text citation to refer only to the person you cite:

One writer stressed that two out of every three new jobs in this
decade will go to women (Ralph 2000).

The References list will clarify the nature of this reference to Ralph (see "Textbook, Casebook, Anthology," page 289).

Citing Classical Works

If an ancient work has no date of publication, cite the author's name in the text followed by *n.d.* within parentheses.

Sophocles (n.d.) saw psychic emotions as. . .

Cite the year of any translation you have used, preceded by *trans.,* and give the date of the version used, followed by *version.*

Plato (trans. 1963) offered a morality that. . .

Plato's Phaedrus (1982 version) explored. . .

If you know the original date of publication, include it before the date of the translation or version you have used.

In his "The Poetic Principle," Poe (1850/1967) announced the doctrines upon which he built his canon.

> **NOTE:** Entries in your References list need not cite major classical works and the Bible. Therefore, identify in your text the version used and the book, chapter, line, verse, or canto.

In Exodus 24:3–4 Moses erected an altar and "twelve pillars according to the twelve tribes of Israel" (King James Version).

The Epic of Gilgamesh has shown, in part, the search for everlasting life (Part 4).

Homer took great care in describing the shield of Achilles (18:558–709).

Abbreviating Corporate Authors in the Text

Corporate authors may be abbreviated after a first, full reference:

One source has questioned the results of the use of aspirin for arthritis treatment in children (American Medical Association [AMA], 1991).

Thereafter, refer to the corporate author by initials: (AMA, 1991).

Citing an Anonymous Work

When a work has no author listed, cite the title as part of the in-text citation (or use the first few words of the material).

The cost per individual student has continued to rise rapidly ("Money Concerns," 2000, p. 2).

Citing Personal Communications

E-mail, telephone conversations, memos, and conversations do not provide recoverable data, so APA style excludes them from the References list. Consequently, you should cite personal communications in the text only. In so doing, give the initials as well as the last name of the source, provide the date, and briefly describe the nature of the communication.

Arthur Eaves (personal communication, August 24, 2000) described the symptoms of Wilson's disease.

Citing Internet Sources in Your Text

As with MLA style, material from electronic sources presents special problems when you are writing in APA style. Currently, most Internet sources have no prescribed page numbers or numbered paragraphs. You cannot list a screen number because monitors differ. You cannot list the page numbers of a downloaded document because computer printers differ. Therefore, in most cases do not list a page number or a paragraph number. Here are basic rules.

Omit a Page or Paragraph Number The marvelous feature of electronic text is that it is searchable, so your readers can find your quotation quickly with the FIND feature. Suppose that you have written the following:

> The UCLA Television Violence Report (1996) has advised against
> making the television industry the "scapegoat for violence"
> by advocating a focus on "deadlier and more significant causes:
> inadequate parenting, drugs, underclass rage, unemployment
> and availability of weaponry."

A reader who wants to investigate further will find your complete citation in your References list. There the reader will discover the Internet address for the article. After finding the article via a browser, (e.g., *Netscape* or *Internet Explorer*), the investigator can press EDIT, then FIND, and type in a key phrase, such as *scapegoat for violence.* The software will immediately move the cursor to the passage you have quoted from. That is much easier than counting through forty-six paragraphs.

Provide a Paragraph Number If you find an article on the Internet that has numbered paragraphs, by all means supply that information in your citation.

> The Insurance Institute for Highway Safety (1997) emphasizes
> restraint first, saying, "Riding unrestrained or improperly
> restrained in a motor vehicle always has been the greatest hazard
> for children" (par. 13).

> The most common type of diabetes is non-insulin-dependent-diabetes
> mellitus (NIDDM), which "affects 90% of those with diabetes and
> usually appears after age 40" (Larson, 1996, par. 3).

Provide a Page Number In a few instances, you will find page numbers within brackets here and there throughout an article. These refer to the page numbers of the printed version of the document. In these cases, you should cite the page just as you would a printed source. Here is the Internet source with the page numbers within brackets to signal the break between page 17 and page 18:

> What is required is a careful reading of Chekhov's subtext, that elusive
> [pp 17–18] literature that lingers in psychological nuances of the words,
> not the exact words themselves.—Ward

The page number may be included in the citation:

> One source has argued the merits of Chekhov's subtext and its "psychological nuances of the words" (Ward, 2001, p. 18).

World Wide Web Site
Internet Article

Dove (1997) has made the distinction between a Congressional calendar day and a legislative day, noting, "A legislative day is the period of time following an adjournment of the Senate until another adjournment."

"Psychologically oriented techniques used to elicit confessions may undermine their validity" (Kassin, 1997, abstract).

Commenting on Neolithic sites of the Southern Levant in Biblical Archaeologist, Banning (1995) has argued that the "Natufians set the stage for the development of large villages with an increasing reliance on cereal grains and legumes that could be cultivated." Banning's work has shown that small villages often existed for a time only to disappear mysteriously, perhaps because of plagues, invaders, or—most likely—a nomadic way of life.

HyperNews Posting

Ochberg (2000) has commented on the use of algae in paper that "initially has a green tint to it, but unlike bleached paper which turns yellow with age, this algae paper becomes whiter with age."

Online Magazine

BusinessWeek Online (2001) reported that Napster's idea of peer-to-peer computing is a precursor to new web applications, even though the courts might close down Napster.

Government Document

The website Thomas (1997) has provided the four-page outline to the Superfund Cleanup Acceleration Act of 1997, which will provoke community participation, enforce remedial actions, establish liability, and protect natural resources.

Other Internet Sites

E-mail The *Publication Manual of the American Psychological Association* stipulates that personal communications, which others cannot retrieve, should be cited in the text only and not mentioned at all in the bibliography. However, electronic chat groups have gained legitimacy in recent years, so in your text you might wish to give an exact date and provide the e-mail address *only* if the citation has scholarly relevance and *only* if the author has made public the e-mail address with the expressed wish for correspondence.

> One technical writing instructor (March 8, 2000) has bemoaned the inability of hardware developers to maintain pace with the ingenuity of software developers. In his e-mail message, he indicated that educational institutions cannot keep pace with the hardware developers. Thus, "students nationwide suffer with antiquated equipment, even though it's only a few years old" (ClemmerJ@APSU.EDU).

If the e-mail is part of a network or online journal, it *should be* listed in the bibliography. In such cases, use the form shown next under "Listserv" and see the bibliography form on page 294.

Listserv (E-mail Discussion Group)

> Camilleri (May 7, 1999) has identified the book <u>Storyteller</u> for those interested in narrative bibliography.

> Funder (April 5, 1999) has argued against the "judgmental process."

Gopher Site

> In an essay in <u>Electronic Antiquity,</u> Diamond (1993) has explored the issue of psychological blindness in <u>Oedipus Rex:</u>
>> Thus Sophokles [sic] has us ask the question, who is blind? We must answer that Teiresias is physically blind, yet he sees himself and Oidipous' nature. Oidipous [sic] is physically sighted, but he is blind to himself, to his own nature.

NOTE: Maintain any special spelling in the original, as shown above. Signal to the reader that the spelling is original by following the work with *sic* (see page 177).

FTP Sites

> Kranidiotis (1994) has shown in the following graph that perceptually "all the sounds corresponding to the points on the curve have the same intensity: this means that the ear has a large range where it is nearly linear (1000 to 8000 Hz), achieving better results on a little domain."

CD-ROM

<u>Compton's Interactive Encyclopedia</u> (1999) has explained that the Abolition Society, which originated in England in 1787, appears to be the first organized group in opposition to slavery. Later, in 1823 the Anti-Slavery Society was formed by Thomas Fowell Buxton, who wielded power as a member of Parliament.

15d Preparing a Working Draft or Publishing the Manuscript

The American Psychological Association has established a website that, among other things, explains its method for citing Internet sources. Consult this URL:

http://www.apa.org/journals/webref.html

At this site, instructions augment those in the 2001 *Publication Manual of the American Psychological Association,* 5th edition. Also available from APA is a site that answers frequently asked questions about APA style. Consult this URL:

http://www.apa.org/journals/faq.html

The APA style manual is very clear about the margins for bibliography entries. If you are preparing a draft to go to a journal for publication, you should use a paragraph indention and underlining, as shown:

Ante, S. E. (2001, August 14). How the music-sharing phenom began, where it went wrong, and what happens next. <u>BusinessWeek Online.</u> Retrieved August 10, 2000, from the World Wide Web: http://www.businessweek.com/2000/00_33/b3694001.htm.

However, when you write a final document for your instructor, use the hanging indention shown below and throughout this chapter *unless the instructor specifically requests the paragraph indention for your bibliography entries.* Thus, you should use this next form on most occasions as a student:

Ante, S. E. (2001, August 14). How the music-sharing phenom began, where it went wrong, and what happens next. <u>BusinessWeek Online.</u> Retrieved August 13, 2000, from the World Wide Web: http://www.businessweek.com/2000/00_33/b3694001.htm.

This form, with hanging indention, will serve as the default form throughout this chapter. You, too, should use the hanging indention unless informed otherwise.

15e Preparing the References List

Use the title "References" for your bibliography page. Alphabetize the entries and double space throughout. Every reference used in your text should appear in your alphabetical list of references at the end of the paper. Type the first line of each entry flush left, and indent succeeding lines one half inch or five spaces. You may italicize or underscore names of books, periodicals, and volume numbers. Underline the punctuation mark at the end of names and volume numbers. Use the hanging indention, as explained immediately above, for your undergraduate research papers.

Book

> McGraw, P. C. (2000). <u>Life strategies: Doing what works, doing</u>
>   <u>what matters.</u> New York: Hyperion.

List the author (surname first with initials for given names), year of publication within parentheses, title of the book italicized or underscored and with only first word of the title and any subtitle capitalized (but do capitalize proper nouns), place of publication, and publisher. In the publisher's name omit the words *Publishing, Company*, or *Inc.,* but otherwise give a full name: Florida State University Press; Addison, Wesley, Longman; HarperCollins.

List chronologically, not alphabetically, two or more works by the same author, for example, Fitzgerald's 1999 publication would precede his 2000 publication.

> Fitzgerald, R. F. (1999). Water samples. . .
>
> Fitzgerald, R. F. (2000). Controlling. . .

References with the same author in the same year are alphabetized and marked with lowercase letters (a, b, c) immediately after the date:

> Cobb, R. A. (1999a). Circulating systems. . .
>
> Cobb, R. A. (1999b). Delay valves. . .

Entries of a single author precede multiple-author entries beginning with the same surname, without regard for the dates:

> Fitzgerald, R. F. (2000). Controlling. . .
>
> Fitzgerald, R. F., & Smithson, C. A. (1999). Mapping. . .

References with the same first author and different second or third authors should be alphabetized by the surname of the second author:

> Fitzgerald, R. F., & Smithson, C. A. (1999). Mapping. . .
>
> Fitzgerald, R. F., & Waters, W. R. (1999). Micro carbons. . .

Part of a Book

List author, date, chapter or section title, editor (with name in normal order) preceded by "In" and followed by "(Ed.)" or "(Eds.)," the name of the book (underscored or italicized), page numbers to the specific section of the book cited (in parentheses), place of publication, and publisher.

Hill, R. (1999). Repatriation must heal old wounds. In R. L. Brooks (Ed.) When sorry isn't enough (pp. 283–287). New York: New York University.

If no author is listed, begin with the title of the article.

Joseph. (1999). Who was who in the Bible. Nashville: Nelson.

Textbook, Casebook, Anthology

Make a primary reference to the anthology:

Vesterman, W. (Ed.) (1991). Readings for the 21st century. Boston: Allyn & Bacon.

Thereafter, make cross-references to the primary source, in this case to Vesterman. Note: these entries should be mingled with all others in the Reference list in alphabetical order so that cross-references may appear before or after the primary source. The year cited should be the date when the cited work was published, not when the Vesterman book was published; such information is usually found in a headnote, footnote, or list of credits at the front or back of the anthology.

Bailey, J. (1988). Jobs for women in the nineties. In Vesterman, pp. 55–63.

Fallows, D. (1982). Why mothers should stay home. In Vesterman, pp. 69–77.

Steinem, G. (1972). Sisterhood. In Vesterman, pp. 48–53.

Vesterman, W. (Ed.). (1991). Readings for the 21st century. Boston: Allyn & Bacon.

The alternative to the style shown above is to provide a complete entry for every one of the authors cited from the casebook (in which case you do not need a separate entry to Vesterman):

Bailey, J. (1988). Jobs for women in the nineties. In W. Vesterman (Ed.), (1991), Readings for the 21st Century (pp. 55–63). Boston: Allyn & Bacon.

Fallows, D. (1982). Why mothers should stay home. In W. Vesterman (Ed.), (1991), Readings for the 21st century (pp. 69–77). Boston: Allyn & Bacon.

Steinem, G. (1972). Sisterhood. In W. Vesterman (Ed.), (1991), Readings for the 21st century (pp.48–53). Boston: Allyn & Bacon.

Encyclopedia or Dictionary

Kiosk: Word history. (1992). The American heritage dictionary of the American language (3rd ed., 1 vol.). Boston: Houghton Mifflin.

Moran, J. (1998). Weather. World book encyclopedia (1998 ed., Vols. 1–22). Chicago, Field Enterprises.

Book with Corporate Author

American Medical Association .(1998). Essential guide to menopause. New York: Pocket.

Periodical

Journal

List author, year, title of the article without quotation marks and with the first word (and any proper nouns) capitalized, name of the journal underscored or italicized and with all major words capitalized, volume number underscored or italicized, inclusive page numbers *not* preceded by "p." or "pp."

Meinz, E. J. (2000). Experience-based attenuation of age-related differences in music cognition tasks. Psychology and Aging, 15, 297–312.

Full-Text Article Retrieved from InfoTrac, Silverplatter, ProQuest, or Other Server

Wakschlag, L. S., & Leventhal, B. L. (1996). Consultation with young autistic children and their families. Journal of the American Academy of Child and Adolescent Psychiatry, 35, 963–65. Retrieved August 8, 1999, from Expanded Academic Index (No. A18486937)

Magazine

List author, the date of publication (year, month without abbreviation, and the specific day for magazines published weekly and fortnightly (every two weeks), title of the article without quotation marks and with the first word capitalized, name of the magazine underlined with all major words capitalized, the volume number if it is readily available, and inclusive page numbers preceded by "p." or "pp." only if you do not provide the volume number. If a magazine prints the article on discontinuous pages, include all page numbers.

Lakey, S. (2000, September). Privacy, please. Business Nashville, pp. 26, 28, 30.

Cannon, L. (2000, August). Reagan radiated happiness and hope.
George, 5, 58–63, 110–111.

Daily and Weekly Newspapers

List author, date (year, month, and day), title of article with first word and proper nouns capitalized, complete name of newspaper in capitals and underlined, and all discontinuous page numbers preceded by the section number.

Kemper, T. D. (2000, August 11). Toward sociology as a science, maybe. Chronicle of Higher Education, p. B7.

Abstract
Abstract of a Published Article

Rosen, G. (2000). Public school alternatives: The voucher controversy [Abstract]. Current, 423, 3–8.

Abstract of an Unpublished Work

Burton, B. A. (1999). Telling survival stories: Trauma, violence, family and everyday life in an American community [Abstract]. Austin: University of Texas.

Abstract Retrieved from InfoTrac, Silverplatter, ProQuest, or Other Server

Gryeh, J. H., et al. (2000). Patterns of adjustment among children of battered women. Journal of Consulting and Clinical Psychology, 68, 84–94. Retrieved August 15, 2000, from PsychINFO (Abstract No. 20000-13544)

Review

Pompili, T. (2000, September 1). Exchange topples domino [Review of Microsoft Exchange 2000 Server]. PC Magazine, p. 47.

Rapin, L. (1997). Autism [rev. article]. The New England Journal of Medicine, 337, 97–104. Retrieved August 4, 1998, from Expanded Academic Index (Abstract No. A19615909)

Report

McCroskey, J. (2000). Taxation to subsidize the tourism business (No. 2000-K). Golden, CO: Independence Institute.

Nonprint Material

Corcoran, R. L. (2000, May 22). "Interpreting dreams: Subconscious reflections and realities" [Interview]. Macon, GA.

Ford, B., & Ford, S. (Producers). (1998). <u>Couples Dance</u>
<u>Instructional Videos: Robert Royston & Laureen Baldovi</u>
[Videotape]. Antioch, CA: Images in Motion.

<u>Gold Rush 1. 0.</u> (1999). [Computer program]. Columbia, MD:
WisdomBuilder.

Internet Sources

The following information conforms to the instructions of APA. When citing sources in the "References" of your APA-style paper, provide this information if available:

1. Author/editor last name, followed by a comma, the initials, and a period.
2. Year of publication, followed by a comma, then month and day for magazines and newspapers, within parentheses, followed by a period.
3. Title of the article, not within quotations and not underscored, with the first word and proper nouns capitalized, followed by the total number of paragraphs within brackets only if that information is provided. Note: You need not count the paragraphs yourself; in fact, it's better that you don't. This is also the place to describe the work within brackets, as with [Abstract] or [Letter to the editor].
4. Name of the book, journal, or complete work, underscored or italicized, if one is listed.
5. Volume number, if listed, underscored or italicized.
6. Page numbers only if you have that data from a printed version of the journal or magazine. If the periodical has no volume number, use "p." or "pp." before the numbers; if the journal has a volume number, omit "p." or "pp."
7. The word "Retrieved," followed by the date of access, followed by the source (e.g. World Wide Web or Telnet) and a colon.
8. The URL. (URLs can be quite long, but you will need to provide the full data for other researchers to find the source.)

World Wide Web Sites

Article from an Online Journal

Dow, J. (2000). External and internal approaches to emotion:
Commentary on Nesse on mood. <u>Psycoloquy.</u> Retrieved
September 23, 2000, from the World Wide Web:
http://www.cogsci.soton.ac.uk/cgi/psyc/newpsy?3.01

Article from a Printed Journal, Reproduced Online

Bowler, D. M., & Thommen, E. (2000). Attribution of mechanical
and social causality to animated displays by children with
autism. <u>Autism, 4,</u> 147–172. Retrieved September 23, 2000,
from the World Wide Web: http://www.sagepub.co.uk/
journals/details/J*O192.html

Abstract

Parrott, A. C. (2000). Does cigarette smoking cause stress?
[Abstract]. American Psychologist, 55. Retrieved October 13,
2000, from the World Wide Web: http://www.apa.org/jounals/
amp/amp5410817.html

Article from a Printed Magazine, Reproduced Online

Leahy, M. (2000). Missouri's savannas and woodlands.
Missouri Conservationist, 61, Retrieved August 30, 2000,
from the World Wide Web: http://www.conservation.state.mo.us/
conmag/2000/08/l.htm

Nighbert, S. (2000). Where lost things end up. Kudzu, 98, 1.
Retrieved August 19, 2000, from the World Wide Web:
http://www.etext.org/Zines/Kudzu/current/
current-issue-toc.html

Article from an Online Magazine, No Author Listed

Benefits of electric load aggregation. (2000, May). PMA Online
Magazine. Retrieved November 3, 2000, from the World
Wide Web: http://www.retailenergy.com/articles/
loadagg.htm

NOTE: Avoid "p." and "pp." for online articles.

Article from an Online Newspaper

Gallagher, S. (2000, August 11). Fires in west imperil ancient sites.
Atlanta Journal-Constitution Online. Retrieved August 11,
2000, from the World Wide Web: http://www.accessatlanta.com/
partners/ajc/epaper/editions/today/

Shopping in palm of the hand is making its holiday debut. (2000,
November 11) New York Times on the Web. Retrieved
November 11, 2000, from the World Wide Web:
http://www1.nytimes.com/

Bulletins and Government Documents

Murphy, F. L., M.D. (2000). The beneficial effects of fish oil on
coronary heart disease. Preventive Health Center. Retrieved
October 19, 2000, from the World Wide Web:
http://www.mdphc.com/nutrition/
beneficial-effects-of-fish-oil.htm

U.S. Cong. Senate. (1999, February 3). A bill to amend the Indian
Gaming Regulator Act. Senate Bill 339. Retrieved October 8,
2000, from the World Wide Web: http://thomas.loc.gov/
cgibin/bdquery

HyperNews Posting

Forster, A. (2000, May 18). The best paper of all. Recycling Discussion Group. Retrieved November 5, 2000, from the World Wide Web: http://www.betterworld.com/ BVvDiscuss/get/recycleD/26.html

Linkage Data (a File Accessed from Another File)

Nelder, C. (2000) Envisioning a sustainable future. Lkd. Better world discussion topics at recycling discussion group. Retrieved August 17, 2000, from the World Wide Web: http://www.betterworld.com/BWZ/9610/coverl.htm

Other Internet Sites

Gopher Site

Major, W. E. (2000). Nichols on Aristophanes' novel forms: The political role of drama [Review of the book Aristophanes' novel forms: The political role of drama]. Retrieved September 30, 2000, from gopher://gopher.lib.virginia.edu/ 00/alpha/bmcr/vOO/0002-18%09%09%2B

Pasricha, A. (2000, August 6). India floods. Voice of America. Retrieved October 6, 2000, from gopher://gopher.voa.gov/ 00/newswire/sun/INDIA-FLOODS~/~09 %09%2B

Listserv (E-mail Discussion Group)

Fitzpatrick, B.T. (2000, November 5). Narrative bibliography. Retrieved November 8, 2000, from e-mail: bryanfitzpatrick @mail.csu.edu

News Groups

Haas, H. (2000, August 5). Link checker that works with cold fusion. Fogo archives. Retrieved August 25, 2000, from Usenet: impressive.net/archives/fogo/ 200000805113615.AI4381@w3.org

Telnet Site

U. S. Naval Observatory. The mercury ion frequency standard. Retrieved March 6, 1999, from Telnet: 192.5,41.239/ duke.ldgo.columbia.edu /port=23 login ads, set terminal to 8/N/1

FTP Site

Kranidiotis, A. A. (1994, June 7). Human audio perception frequently asked questions. Retrieved March 11, 1997, from FTP: svr-ftp.eng.cam.ac.uk/pub/comp.speech/info/ HumanAudioPerception

CD-ROM Material

Material cited from a CD-ROM requires different forms. If you are citing from an abstract on CD-ROM, use this form:

Abstract

Figueredo, A. J., & McCloskey, L. A. (1993). Sex, money, and
paternity: The evolutionary psychology of domestic
violence [CD-ROM]. Ethnology and Sociobiology, 14,
353–79. Abstract from: Silverplatter File : PsychINFO
Item: 81-3654.

Encyclopedia Article

African American history: Abolitionist movement (2000).
Encarta encyclopedia. [CD-ROM]. Redmond, WA: Microsoft
Corporation.

Full-Text Article

Firestone, D. (2000, August 10). The south comes of age on
religion and politics [CD-ROM]. New York Times. p. A-17.
Article from UMI-ProQuest file: New York Times Online
Item 3602-108.

Wessel, D. (1995, February 2). Fed lifts rates half point, setting
four-year high [CD-ROM]. Wall Street Journal, p. A2+.
Article from UMI-ProQuest file: Wall Street Journal
Ondisc Item 34561.

15f Variations on the APA Style for Other Disciplines in the Social Sciences

Use APA style as explained in 15a–15f for these disciplines:

Education
Geography
Home Economics
Physical Education
Political Science

Alternative styles may be used for papers in Linguistics and Sociology, as explained next.

Linguistics

In-Text Citation

In-text citations for linguistic studies include almost always a specific page reference to the work along with the date, separated by a colon, for example,

"Jones 1993: 12–18" or "Gifford's recent reference (1994: 162)." Therefore, follow basic standards for the name and year system (see pages 279-86) with a colon to separate the year and the page numbers.

References List

As shown below, label the list "References" and alphabetize the entries. Use full names for authors if available. Place the year immediately after the author's name. For journal entries, use a period rather than a colon or comma to separate volume and page. There is *no* underlining. Linguistic journals are abbreviated (e.g., Lg. for Linguistics); others are not. A sample list follows.

References

Aristar, A. 1994. Review of typology and universals, by William Croft. Lg. 70.172–175.

Beal, Carole R., & Belgrad, Susan L. 1990. The development of message evaluation skills in young children. Child Development 61.705–13.

Birner, Betty J. 1994. Information status and word order: An analysis of English inversion. Lg. 70.233–259.

De Boysson-Bardies, Bénédicte, and Vihman, Marilyn M. 1991. Adaptation to language: Evidence from babbling and first words in four languages. Lg. 67.287–319.

Burnam, Tom. 1988. A misinformation guide to grammar. Writer's Digest 68.36–39.

Chomsky, Noam. 1965. Aspects of the theory of syntax. Cambridge, MA: MIT Press.

- - - - -. 1975. Reflections on language. New York: Pantheon.

Jacobsson, Bengt. 1988. Should and would in factual that-clauses. English Studies 69.72–81.

Ross, John R. 1967. Constraints on variables in syntax. MIT dissertation.

Singer, Murry, Arthur C. Graesser, and Tom Trabasso. 1994. Minimal or global interference during reading. Journal of Memory and Language 33.421–41.

NOTE: The form of these entries conforms in general to that advocated by the Linguistic Society of America, LSA Bulletin, No. 71 (December 1976), 43–45, the December issue annually, and to the form and style practiced by the journal *Language*.

Sociology and Social Work

In-Text Citation

Use the name and year system as explained above in 15c, pages 279-86.

Reference List

Use the format shown below, which duplicates the style of the *American Journal of Sociology*, or use APA style. This style is very similar to MLA style except that the date follows the author.

References

Berezin, Mabel. 1994. "Cultural Form and Political Meaning:
State-subsidized Theater, Ideology, and the Language of Style
in "Fascist Italy." American Journal of Sociology 99:
1237–1286.

Dowrick, Stephanie. 1994. Intimacy and Solitude. New York:
Norton.

Epstein, Edwin M. 1980. "Business and Labor under the Federal
Election Campaign Act of 1971." Pp. 107–151 in Parties,
Interest Groups, and Campaign Finance Laws, edited by
Michael J. Malbin. Washington, D.C.: American Enterprise
Institute for Public Policy Research.

Gest, Ted. 1994. "Crime's Bias Problem." U. S. News & World
Report July 25: 31–32.

15g Formatting an APA Paper

Three types of papers exist in this discipline: theoretical articles, reports of empirical studies, and review articles (as explained in section 15a). Each requires a different arrangement of the various parts of the paper.

Theoretical Paper

The theoretical paper should be arranged much like a typical research paper, with the additional use of subheads to divide the sections. The subheads often describe the contents of the various sections (see the sample paper by Gena Messersmith, pages 300-09).

The introduction should:

- Establish the problem under examination.
- Discuss its significance to the scientific community.
- Provide a review of the literature (see pages 120-122 for more information).
- Quote the experts who have commented on the issue.
- Provide a thesis sentence that gives your initial perspective on the issue.

The body of the theoretical paper will need to:

- Trace the various issues.
- Establish a past to present perspective.
- Compare and analyze the various aspects of the theories.
- Cite extensively from the literature on the subject.

The conclusion of the theoretical paper will need to:

- Defend one theory as it grows from the evidence in the body.
- Discuss the implications of the theory.
- Suggest additional work that might be launched in this area.

Report of Empirical Research

The general design of a report of original research, an empirical study, should conform to the general plan shown here. The subheads are usually *methods, results,* and *discussion.* The introduction needs no subhead.

The introduction should:

- Establish the problem or topic to be examined.
- Provide background information, including a review of literature on the subject.
- Give the purpose and rationale for the study, including the hypothesis that serves as the motivation for the experiment.

The body of the report of empirical research should:

- Provide a methods section for explaining the design of the study with regard to subjects, apparatus, and procedure.
- Offer a results section for listing in detail the statistical finding of the study.

The conclusion of a report of empirical research should:

- Interpret the results and discuss the implications of the findings in relation to the hypothesis and to other research on the subject.

Review Article

The review article is usually a shorter paper because it examines a published work or two without extensive research on the part of the writer of the review.

The introduction of the review should:

- Identify the problem or subject under study and its significance.
- Summarize the article or articles under review.

The body of the review should:

- Provide a systematic analysis of the article, its findings, and the apparent significance of the results.

The conclusion of the review should:

- Discuss the implications of the findings and make judgments as appropriate.

15h   Writing the Abstract

You should provide an abstract with every paper written in APA style. An abstract is a quick but thorough summary of the contents of your paper. It is read first and may be the only part read, so it must be:

1. *Accurate* in order to reflect both the purpose and content of the paper.
2. *Self-contained* so that the abstract (a) explains the precise problem and defines terminology, (b) describes briefly both the methods used and the findings, and (c) gives an overview of your conclusions, but see item 4 below.
3. *Concise and specific* in order to remain within a range of 80 to 150 words.
4. *Nonevaluative* in order to report information, not to appraise or assess the value of the work.
5. *Coherent and readable* in a style that uses an active, vigorous syntax and that uses the present tense to describe results (e.g., *the findings confirm*) but the past tense to describe testing procedures (e.g., *I attempted to identify*).

For theoretical papers, the abstract should include:

- The topic in one sentence, if possible.
- The purpose, thesis, and scope of the paper.
- A brief reference to the sources used (e.g., published articles, books, personal observation).
- Your conclusions and the implications of the study

For a report of an empirical study, the abstract should include the four items listed above for theoretical papers with the addition of three more:

- The problem and hypothesis in one sentence, if possible.
- The subjects (e.g., species, number, age, type).
- The method, including procedures and apparatus.

15i   Sample Paper in APA Style

The following paper demonstrates the format and style of a paper written to the standards of APA style. The paper requires a title page that establishes the running head, an abstract, in-text citations to name and year of each source used, and a list of references.

The paper by Gena Messersmith that follows grew out of her love for her daughter, who suffers with attention deficit hyperactivity disorder. Messersmith frames her essay as a theoretical argument about the use of medication with children who have ADHD. Marginal notes will remind you of format rules for a paper in APA style.

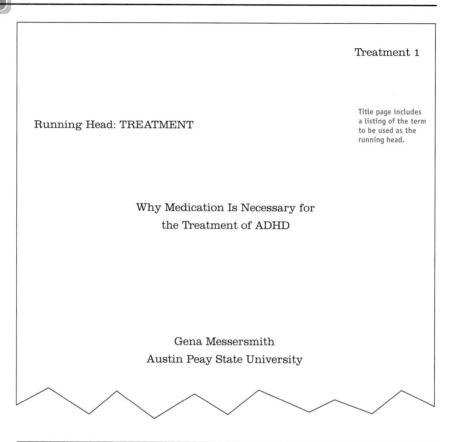

Treatment 1

Running Head: TREATMENT

Title page includes a listing of the term to be used as the running head.

Why Medication Is Necessary for
the Treatment of ADHD

Gena Messersmith
Austin Peay State University

Treatment 2

Rules for writing the abstract are explained in 15h, page 299.

Abstract

This report deals with the issues facing children who are diagnosed with Attention Deficit Hyperactivity Disorder (ADHD) and why medication is the best treatment for this disorder. Respected authorities in the field state over and over again that medication is the only known solution to the treatment of this disorder. The Journal of the American Medical Association, The American Medical Association of General Psychiatry, and The National Institute of Mental Health are just a few who support the use of medication in the treatment of ADHD. These institutions have done research and have scientific backing to show that the use of medication is more effective in the treatment of ADHD than any other two components combined. Even with such credentials backing medication, there is still rampant ignorance regarding the use of medication for children with ADHD, and the report has addressed these issues as well. Also included are interviews and prepared statements from people who either have ADHD or have children with ADHD.

The abstract should include the purpose, the thesis or hypothesis, a reference to the sources, and the implications of the study.

Treatment 3

Why Medication Is Necessary for
the Treatment of ADHD

Attention Deficit Hyperactivity Disorder, hereinafter referred
to as "ADHD," has been labeled "a neurological condition (probably
genetic in origin) where the sufferer has a very reduced ability to
maintain attention without distraction, control of doing or saying
something due to impulsivity and lack of appropriate forethought,
and control over the amount of physical activity appropriate to the
situation" (Berkshire Group 2000). The Berkshire group reported
that although many of us may suffer from some or all of these
symptoms occasionally, for a person with ADHD, these symptoms
are pervasive and debilitating, making day-to-day functioning
almost impossible. This report intends to show that ADHD is not
only a real problem facing many children but that many children do
not get the proper treatment to include medication to help them
overcome the obstacles ADHD places before them. Though contrary
to popular opinion, ADHD is actually under-diagnosed. Therefore,
this report will deal with the following issues:

- 1 in 20 children have ADHD and only 1 in 50 are treated for it.
- Medication and lifestyle changes are the answers for these
  children.
- These childen can adversely affect their families and family
  unity.

For several decades most clinical professionals operated under
the fallacious notions that ADHD was caused by brain injuries or
poor parenting; that children would outgrow it by adolescence;
that stimulant medications would be effective only with children
(not with adults and older adolescents) and only on school days;
and that ADHD children would benefit from a diet free of certain
food additives and sugar—all despite the absence of any set of
findings in the scientific literature to support such claims
(Barkley, 1995). This observation only covers some of the rumors
and misconceptions associated with ADHD and the use of
medication for the problem. It is not uncommon for people on the
street to say, "children are over-medicated"; "if parents did their jobs
we wouldn't need all this medication"; "teachers just want all
children to behave like robots"; and "they get on that medication
and walk around like zombies." There are even parents who have
ADHD children who will not admit anything is wrong with their

---

In general,
use verbs
in the past
tense or
the present
participle.

The authors of
some articles
might be an
organization
or association.

Explain your
purpose in
the opening.
See pages
297–298.

Bulleted lists
are a good
element for
reports in the
sciences.

The author
provides a
brief history
of the
treatment
for ADHD.

Here the
author
establishes
clearly the
authority of
the source.

child. However, speaking as a mother of an ADHD child, most parents of ADHD children know fairly quickly that their child is different, and they experience difficulties not normally associated with a normal, happy 5- 6- 7- or 8-year-old. In April of 1998 the Journal of the American Medical Association (JAMA) published a thorough study of extensive research on ADHD and its treatment. They concluded that ADHD tends to be under-identified even though office visits continue to increase (Goldman, Genel, Bayman, and Slanetz, 1998). The article observed, "1 in 20 children are treated in this country for ADHD but the evidence shows that 1 in 50 children have ADHD" (p. 1102).

Zito et al. (1999) have concluded that the 1990s showed a "substantial increase in physician visits for ADHD among youths with three quarters of these office visits involving prescription of psychotherapeutic medications for ADHD treatment." The increase in medication for children, however, has caused one expert to warn that very little data exist on the safety and effectiveness of the stimulants, antidepressants, clonidine, and mood stabilizers (Hoagwood, 1999, cited in Zito).

Case Studies

An interview with Sam Jones (fictitious name used to protect his identity), a 35-year-old white male in good health with a charming personality, revealed the effects of not receiving treatment for ADHD. Jones is an Army Chief Warrant Officer 3 stationed at Fort Campbell, Kentucky. He figured out on his own that he was ADHD as an adult. He agreed to a private interview, and said, in part:

> I always knew I was different—that something was wrong—but my teachers, my parents and my friends just wanted to believe I was stupid and a troublemaker. Nothing was further from the truth. I was a kid with dreams and I wanted to make my parents happy, but I was always in trouble while my siblings were perfect—a very hard thing to deal with as a child. I'm still not very close with my family even now.

Jones's story is tragic but true. Teachers, parents, and peers often just see the ADHD child as a troublemaker or a problem child. These children never reach their full potential, whereas they could if treated properly. Jones wanted to go to the Air Force Academy but

Normally, writers should not bring themselves into their papers, but Messersmith's experience qualifies her as an expert on the topic.

Zito et al. is a set of six authors, so the plural verb is correct. Data also takes a plural verb

Interviews may serve as primary evidence in a scientific report.

Indent as a block a quotation of forty or more words.

Treatment 5

his grades from middle school and high school were too poor. He always dreamed of being an astronaut, and the Air Force Academy is the perfect start for the astronaut program. Unfortunately, Jones could not focus in school and therefore received bad grades. Is Sam Jones a failure? Absolutely not. He has overcome many obstacles to become a success story. But one can also ask, did Sam reach his full potential? The answer is unequivocally "No." The truly tragic aspect of this story is that Jones is just one of many who experience these same types of things. Medication could have helped Jones.

There is also the case study of a young boy who would go to a dry well he named Horrace ("Feeding Horrace," 1999). He would dump his report cards and bad secrets from school into Horrace. He felt he had nowhere to turn. He felt so out of touch as a child because he was labeled "lazy and stupid" by his teachers, friends and parents. He says in his article, "You feel so different and out of touch with everyone really. So much [is] centered around school. It is hard to be a square peg when there are nothing but classrooms with round holes out there" ("Feeding Horrace," 1999).

Case studies serve as primary evidence in a science report.

Then we have the case study of June, who has a son with ADHD, and through him she discovered her own ADHD condition ("The Two of Us," 1999). She says his problems really started when he began kindergarten. She goes on to say, "His motives and reactions were totally misunderstood by the "color-in-the-lines" public school authorities" ("The Two of Us," 1999). She talks about all the problems, disappointments, and low self-esteem involved until she and her son both found a good counselor and proper medication. There is also the description by a mother, Kim Boykin, of her son ("Unscathed," 1999). She states the same problems as the other stories, i.e., her son was always daydreaming in class, he could remember intimate details about people but not what they said, yet her son really wanted to be good and learn but could not control his behavior.

The main problem arising from these case studies is that many more such stories exist because there are children not getting the help they so need and deserve.

Side heads are standard for science reports.

Why Medicine Is Necessary: A Review of the Literature

Barkley (1995) has argued for medication and behavioral therapy, citing the NIMH's Multimodal Treatment Study of Children with Attention Deficit Hyperactivity Disorder, which "found that medication alone, or medication in combination with

A review of the leterature is a vital part of research reports. See pages 120–22 for more details and an example essay.

intensive behavioral therapy, [is] significantly superior to other types of treatment" (pp. 251-252). Copeland and Love (1991, p. 125) place the illness in the correct perspective with this analogy:

> Just as glasses correct vision, medication alters the neurochemical imbalances causing the ADHD symptoms. Some doctors have compared the use of medications for attention disorders with the use of insulin for diabetes. Medication for ADHD allows the child to function with a more normal brain chemistry, just as insulin helps a diabetic function with better blood chemistry.

Palmer (1999), head of the pediatric center at Fort Campbell's Blanchfield Army Hospital, reported in a private interview that ADHD was comparable to his being without his glasses. He said, "I can still drive a car without my glasses, but not very well, and I will probably have an accident. Children with ADHD who have no medication can still look like other children but they are probably on their way to having problems." He stated that children with ADHD who were on medication could still misbehave, but at least the choice was theirs—because without medication there is no choice.Many experts in the field have agreed that medication can be a huge help to people with ADHD. Dr. Russell Barkley, Directory of Psychology and Professor of Psychiatry and Neurology at the University of Massachusetts Medical Center, has said, "Medication is probably the most widely publicized, most hotly debated treatment for ADHD. As a whole, hundreds of studies conducted indicate that stimulants, antidepressants, and clonidine (a drug used to treat high blood pressure in many adults) can be of great help to those with ADHD" (p. 249). Goldman et al. (1998) recommended the use of methylphenidate, but Baughman (1999) has said that the report by Goldman et al. has done a disservice and argues that methylphenidate "has no positive effect on learning but can impair it."

The Neurology

Alex (1996) reported:

> The lower portion of the brain contains an area known as the Reticular Activating System. It keeps the higher brain centers alert and ready for input. There is some evidence that this area is not working properly in ADHD, and that the

Treatment 7

brain is, in effect, 'going to sleep.' Hyperactivity is really the brain's attempt to generate new stimulation to maintain alertness. See Figure 1.

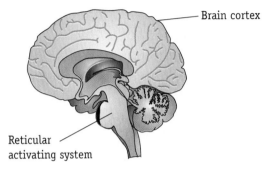

Brain cortex

Reticular activating system

The use of tables and illustrations is important in the writing of science reports. See pages A13–A-16 for explanations and examples.

Figure 1: Reprinted with permission from "Activation by Attention of the Human Reticular Formation and Thalamic Intralaminar Nuclei" by Shigeo Kinomura et al., Science (1996 January 26); 271: 512–515. ©1996 by American Association for the Advancement of Science.

Two Myths Surrounding the Medicine

Myth 1: Stimulant Drugs Are Dangerous and Should Not Be Taken by Any Child. Barkley (1995) has reported:

> During the 1980's an inaccurate and, regrettably, successful media propaganda campaign against the use of stimulants, particularly Ritalin (methylphenidate), with children was waged by a fringe religious group, causing a dramatic decline in the prescribing of this medication in 1987-1989." (p. 251)

Unfortunately, many people still believe that Ritalin and other medications are dangerous and that parents and teachers merely want to drug their children. This simply is not the case.

Myth 2: Stimulants Just Cover Up "the Real Problem" and Do Not Deal Directly with the Root Causes of the Child's ADHD. Barkley (1995) said, "The stimulants deal directly with the part of the brain that is underactive and gives rise to the outward symptoms of ADHD" (p. 251). Again many people within our society

Papers written in APA style require the p or the pp for citing the page(s).

believe that medication is not the answer to dealing with ADHD. However, if your child were diabetic, would you not give him or her insulin? If your child needed glasses to see, would you not buy them? Why, then, do people resist giving medication prescribed by a doctor, normally a psychiatrist or a pediatrician, to a child with ADHD? Because myths and superstitions are a very difficult thing to overcome.

Is Medication the Only Solution?

Medication is not the only solution but is one of the necessary solutions. However, simply using medication alone will not solve the problem. Parents must also have their child in counseling, and the parents must be willing to learn new behavior techniques to deal with their ADHD child.

> Once an attention disorder has been diagnosed, there are
> many treatment options for you to consider and many
> decisions to be made. The range of treatment approaches
> include: medical management; educational intervention;
> attention to diet, nutrition, allergies and environmental
> toxins; behavior management strategies; counseling and
> family therapy; cognitive therapy; and social skills
> training, among others (Copeland & Love, 1991, p. 119).

This advice plainly shows that dealing with an ADHD child is not easy, and although most parents would prefer not to have to use medication, "the one approach which appears consistently to have been the most helpful is the use of stimulant medication. (Copeland & Love, 1991, p. 123). Even though medication is effective, the other approaches are necessary as well.

The Impact ADHD Children Have on Their Families

"The family raising a child with ADHD encounters an immense task—keeping the family unit as normal as possible with a child who does not conform or meet expectations, yours and society's" (Alexander-Roberts, 1994, p. 173). Parents and their child have good days and bad (on this point see the online article by Berkshire, 2000). Parents know the limitations of their ADHD children and in most cases have been dealing with these limitations for years. Routine and balance are critical to maintain a healthy, happy family, but if your child is ADHD, this child will constantly keep

Treatment 9

your family off a routine and out of balance. Running to Wal-Mart or going to visit grandma, or even a trip to the park can never be a spur of the moment thing with an ADHD child. These trips should be well planned in advance. Another problem frequently faced by parents of an ADHD child is well intentioned but hurtful advice from relatives, particularly grandparents. Although grandparents are usually well meaning, unless they themselves have parented a child with special needs, they are probably not qualified to give much advice. Even the parents themselves are quite surprised when "feelings of resentment and loss of self-esteem often develop" within their own psyche (Alexander-Roberts, 1994, p. 174).

Marital stress is another huge issue facing the family of an ADHD child. "I thought that there would never be a time that we wouldn't be discussing our son's problems and how to manage it and him" said Mary from Troy, New York (cited in Alexander-Roberts, 1994, p. 182). This is true for most families dealing with a special needs child. The parents find themselves overwhelmed with the problems created by this disorder. It is very difficult to step back from your child's problems and the tension these problems have created and move your life in a positive manner. Most parents would love to just take a time-out from parenting, which is not always easy to do, even if only for a few hours. The problem with taking the necessary time-out from parenting is that often there is no one willing to watch your child for you. As we all know in this day and age, even families with children who have no particular problems are often burned out and stressed to their limits, but parents with ADHD children are even doubly so. The problems can seem almost insurmountable at times.

What Becomes of these Children When They Mature?

Children with ADHD need high self-esteem and need to be encouraged to look to the future with high expectations— particularly those struggling just to get through grade school. These children need to be told "If you can hang on until adulthood, the odds shift dramatically in your favor. . . . This is true, of course, if their self-esteem has remained intact" (Copeland & Love, 1991, p. 275). If this can be done, many ADHD children will grow up to be the Van Goghs, Robin Williamses, and/or Hemingways of the future.

APA style does not require brackets to enclose the ellipsis points.

Treatment 10

The conclusion of a science report should usually discuss the implications of the study

Conclusion

Medication, behavior therapy, counseling, and understanding are the keys to overcoming the effects of ADHD. Our children are our future; therefore, we must now invest in them. It is time to stop the bickering over whether or not ADHD really exists and why it does. The job now is to help children with ADHD overcome the obstacles in their way, help teachers and schools understand the problem, and support the parents and physicians who desperately attempt to help these children. As shown in this report, there is significant if not overwhelming scientific evidence to support ADHD as a real threat to our children's future, but proper medication can ease the burden on parents, help children to perform in school, and ease them into maturity without trauma.

Treatment 11

The form for a book in APA style is explained on pages 288–90.

Many articles on the World Wide Web do not list an author. Use this form to indicate an anonymous writer.

References

Alexander-Roberts, Colleen. (1994). The ADHD parenting handbook. Dallas, Texas.

[Anonymous]. (1999). Feeding Horrace. Retrieved August 11, 2000, from the World Wide Web:http://www.lehigh.edu/~rjv2/ essayl.html

[Anonymous]. (1999). The two of us. Retrieved August 11, 2000, from the World Wide Web: http://www.lehigh.edu/~rjv2/ essay3.html

[Anonymous]. (2000) What is AD/HD? Berkshire AD/HD Research Group. Retrieved August 11, 2000, from the World Wide Web: http://www/btintemet.com/ ~black.ice/addnet/wotsadd.html

Alex, Neil. (1999). The neurology of ADHD. ADHD Owner's Manual. Retrieved August 11, 2000, from the World Wide Web: http://www.edutechsbs.com/adhd/00010.htm

Treatment 12

Barkley, Russell A. (1995). Taking charge of ADHD. New York: London.

Baughman, F. A. (1999). Treatment of attention-deficit/hyperactivity
    disorder [Letter to the editor]. JAMA, 281. Retrieved August 11,
    2000, from the World Wide Web:
    http://jama.ama-assn.org/issues/ v28In16/full/jlt0428-4.html

Boykin, K. (1999). Unscathed. Retrieved August 11, 2000, from the
    World Wide Web: http://www.lehigh.edu/~rjv2/essay3.html

Cohen, M. D. (1999). Letter to the editor of the Washington Post.
    Retrieved August 11, 2000, from the World Wide Web:
    http://www.chadd.org/news /press12071999.htm

Copeland, E. D., & Love, V. A. (1996). Attention, please!: A
    comprehensive guide for successfully parenting children with
    attention disorders and hyperactivity. Rev. ed. Atlanta: Georgia
    Books.

Goldman, L. S., Genel, M., Beyman, R. J., & Slanetz, P. J. (1998).
    Diagnosis and treatment of attention-deficit-hyperactivity
    disorder in children and adolescents. JAMA, 124, 1100-1107.

Jones, S. [pseudonym] (1999). Interview. Clarksville, TN.

Kinomura et al. (1996). The neurology of ADHD. Science, 271,
    512–515. Retrieved August 11, 2000, from the World Wide Web:
    http://www.edutechsbs.com/adhd/00010.htm

Palmer, R. (2000, March 11). Interview. Fort Campbell, KY.

Zito, J. M, Safer, D. J., dosReis, S., Magder, L. S., Gardner, J. F.,
    & Zarin, D. A. (1999). Psychotherapeutic medication patterns
    for youths with attention-deficit/hyperactivity disorder.
    Pediatrics and Adolescent Medicine, 153. Retrieved August 11,
    2000, from the World Wide Web: http://archpedi.ama-assn.org/
    issues/ v153n12 /full/poa9044.html

You may
specify the
type of article
by describing
it within
brackets.
See page 291.

The form
for citing
Internet
articles is
explained
on pages
292–94.

Use this
form for an
interview or
for a person
who wishes
to remain
anonymous.

16

CMS Style: Using Footnotes or Endnotes

The fine arts and some fields in the humanities (but not literature) use traditional footnotes or endnotes, which should conform to standards set by *The Chicago Manual of Style* (CMS), 14th ed., 1993. In the CMS system, you place superscript numerals within the text (like this[15]) and place documentary footnotes on corresponding pages.

The discussion below assumes that notes will appear as footnotes; however, some instructors accept endnotes, that is, all notes appear together at the end of the paper, not at the bottom of individual pages.

> If you wish to group all your notes into one list, see the instructions in 16e, page 316.

There are two types of footnotes or endnotes: one will document your sources with bibliographic information, but the other can discuss related matters, explain your methods of research, suggest related literature, provide biographical information, or offer other information that is not immediately pertinent to your discussion.

If available, use the footnote or endnote feature of your software. It will not only insert the raised superscript number in the text but also will keep your footnotes arranged properly at the bottom of each page or keep your endnotes in a correct list. In most instances, the software will insert the superscript numeral,

> To see examples of content footnotes as opposed to documentation notes, see pages 316–19.

but it will not write the note automatically; you must type in the essential data in the correct style.

Usually, a "Works Cited" page is *not* necessary because essential data appears in the footnotes; however, some instructors may ask for one at the end of your paper; if so, see 16i, page 322.

16a Inserting a Superscript Numeral in Your Text

Use Arabic numerals typed slightly above the line (like this[12]) to indicate a footnote or endnote. In both Microsoft Word and Wordperfect, go to Font and select Superscript, or go to Insert and select Footnote. Place the superscript numeral at the end of quotations or paraphrases, with the number following immediately without a space after the final word or mark of punctuation, as in this sample:

> Colonel Warner soon rejoined his troops despite severe pain. He wrote in September of 1864: "I was obliged to ride at all times on a walk and to mount my horse from some steps or be helped on. My cains [sic] with which I walked when on foot were strapped to my saddle."[6]
> Such heroic dedication did not go unnoticed, for the Washington Chronicle cited Warner as "an example worthy of imitation."[7] At Gettysburg Warner's troops did not engage in heavy fighting and suffered only limited casualties of two dead and five wounded."[8]

The use of "[sic]" indicates exact quotation, even to the point of typing an apparent error. Footnotes contain the authority's name, so you can omit the name in the text. Endnotes will be at the back of your paper, so you should usually include a source's name in your text. The first example below implies a source that will be found in the footnote; the second expresses the name in the text.

Implied Reference

> The organic basis of autism is generally agreed upon. Three possible causes for autism have been identified: behavioral syndrome, organic brain disorder, or a range of biological and psychosocial factors." [9]

Expressed Reference

> Martin Rutter has acknowledged that the organic basis of autism is generally agreed upon. Rutter named three possible causes for autism: behavioral syndrome, organic brain disorder, or a range of biological and psychosocial factors." [10]

16b Formatting and Writing the Footnotes

Place footnotes at the bottom of pages to correspond with superscript numerals (see immediately above). Some papers will require footnotes on almost every page. Follow these conventions:

1. **Spacing.** In academic papers not intended for publication, footnotes are commonly typed single spaced and placed at the foot of the page, usually with extra space between the notes. Drafts and manuscripts intended for publication in print or on the Web should have all notes double spaced and placed together at the end of the paper. The student example on pages 326–35 shows single-spaced footnotes. A "Notes" page with double-spaced endnotes can be found on page 316.

2. **Indention.** Indent the first line of the note five spaces or one half inch (usually one click of the tab key).

3. **Numbering.** Number the footnotes consecutively throughout the entire paper with an indented number, a period, and space, as shown throughout this chapter.

4. **Placement.** Collect at the bottom of each page all footnotes to citations made on that page.

5. **Distinguish footnotes from text.** Separate footnotes from the text by triple spacing or, if you prefer, by a twelve-space bar line from the left margin. Most word processing programs insert the line for you.

6. **Footnote form.** Basic forms of notes should conform to the following guidelines.

Book

List the author, followed by a comma, the title underlined or in the italics font, the publication data within parentheses (city: publisher, year), followed by a comma and the page numbers. Publisher's names are spelled out in full but the words *Company* or *Inc.* are omitted. Unless ambiguity would result, the abbreviations "p." and "pp." may be omitted.

1. Frederick G. Reamer, <u>Social Work Values and Ethics</u> (New York: Columbia University Press, 1999), 20–23.

List two authors without a comma between their names:

2. Doug Sulpy and Ray Schweighardt, <u>Get Back: The Unauthorized Chronicle of the Beatles "Let It Be" Disaster</u> (New York: St. Martin's Press, 1997), 18.

List three authors separated by commas. Reference to an edition follows the title or the editors, if listed (see footnote 6 below).

3. James S. Mickelson, Karen S. Haynes, and Barbara Mikulski, <u>Affecting Change: Social Workers in the Political Arena</u>, 4th ed. (Boston: Allyn and Bacon, 2000), 340–41.

For more than three authors, use "et al." after mention of the lead author:

4. Lauel J. Lewis et al., <u>Life Science</u> (Glenview, IL: Scott, Foresman, 1990), 65.

For a subsequent reference to an immediately preceding source, use "Ibid." in the roman typeface, not in italics and not underscored:

5. Ibid.

See page 315 for further details about subsequent references and the use of Latinate phrases.

Collection or Anthology

6. William Bradford, "Of Plymouth Plantation," in <u>The American Tradition in Literature</u>, ed. George Perkins and Barbara Perkins, 9th ed. (New York: McGraw Hill, 1998), 132–40.

Journal Article

7. Tamara J. Ferguson and Susan L. Crowley, "Gender Differences in the Organization of Guilt and Shame," <u>Sex Roles</u> 37 (1997): 19–44.

Magazine Article

8. Madeleine J. Nash, "The New Science of Alzheimer's," <u>Time</u>, 17 July 2000, 51–57.

Newspaper Article

9. Blake Morrison, "Sierra Fire Continues Rampage," USA Today, 31 July 2000, 10A.

10. John Kifner, "The Holiest City, the Toughest Conflict," New York Times, 23 July 2000, sec. 4, p. 1.

NOTE: The "p." is necessary to distinguish the 4 from the 1.

Review Article

11. Jim Seymour, "Push Back," review of Pointcast and Backweb [computer software], PC Magazine, August 1997, 93–94.

16c Writing Footnotes for Electronic Sources

To cite electronic sources, *The Chicago Manual of Style* uses brackets to identify the nature of the electronic source, gives the date of when the material was first cited or published or accessed, and provides an electronic address. The models below show these requirements. Adjust your sources accordingly.

Scholarly Project

12. British Poetry Archive, ed. Jerome McGann and David Seaman (Univ. of Virginia Library, 1999) [manuscripts online]; available from http://etext.lib.virginia.edu/britpo.html.

Journal Article Online

13. B. A. Miller, N. J. Smyth, and P. J. Mudar, "Mothers' Alcohol and Other Drug Problems and Their Punitiveness toward Their Children," Journal of Studies on Alcohol 60 (1999): 632–42 [journal online]; available from http://www.ncbi.nlm.hih.gov.htbin.

Database not on the World Wide Web

14. M. D. Bowles, "The Organization Man Goes to College: AT&T's Experiment in Humanistic Education, 1953–1960," The Historian 61 (1998): 15 [database online]; accession no. 88, IAC Business A.R.T.S., Item 04993186; available from DIALOG Information Services, Palo Alto, Calif.

Article from an Online Service

15. "Nutrition and Cancer," Discovery Health 1 May 2000 [journal online]; available from http://www.discoveryhealth.c... Sc000/8096/164609.html.

Book Online

16. D. H. Lawrence, <u>Lady Chatterly's Lover</u>, 1928 [book online]; available from http://bibliomania.com/fiction/dhl/chat.html.

CD-ROM Source

17. Aurelio J. Figueredo and Laura Ann McCloskey, "Sex, Money, and Paternity: The Evolutionary Psychology of Domestic Violence," <u>Ethnology and Sociobiology</u> 14 (1993): 355, PsychINFO [CD-ROM]; available from Silverplatter.

Electronic Bulletin Board

18. Horace Munford, "Teen Violence" [electronic bulletin board] (Knoxville [cited 3 Aug. 2000]); available from munfordh@ut.edu.

E-mail

Since e-mail is not retrievable, do not document with a footnote or bibliography entry. Instead, mention the nature of the source within your text by saying something like this:

Walter Wallace argues that teen violence stems mainly from the breakup of the traditional family (e-mail to the author).

16d Writing Subsequent Footnote References

After a first full footnote, references to the same source should be shortened to the author's name and page number. When an author has two works mentioned, employ a shortened version of the title, such as "3. Jones, *Paine*, 25." In general, avoid Latinate abbreviations such as *loc. cit.* or *op. cit.*; however, whenever a note refers to the source in the immediately preceding note, you may use "Ibid." alone or "Ibid." with a page number, as shown below. If the subsequent note does not refer to the one immediately above it, do not use "Ibid." Instead, repeat the author's last name (note especially the difference between notes 4 and 6):

3. Jerrold Ladd, <u>Out of the Madness: From the Projects to a Life of Hope</u> (New York: Warner, 1994), 24.

4. Ibid., 27.

5. Michael Schulman and Eva Meckler, <u>Bringing Up a Moral Child</u>, rev. ed. (New York: Doubleday, 1994), 221.

6. Ladd, 24.

7. Ibid., 27.

NOTE: Single space footnotes, but double space between the notes.

16e | Writing Endnotes rather than Footnotes

With the permission of your instructor, put all your notes together as a single group of endnotes to lessen the burden of typing the paper. Most computer software programs will help you with this task by inserting the superscript numerals in the text and organizing the endnotes consecutively at the end of the text, not at the bottom of each page. Follow these conventions:

- Begin notes on a new page at the end of the text.
- Entitle the page "Notes," centered, and placed two inches from the top of the page.
- Triple space between the heading and the first note.
- Indent the first line of each note one half inch or five spaces; number the note, followed by a period.
- Double space endnotes.

Conform to the following example.

Notes

1. Jerrold Ladd, <u>Out of the Madness: From the Projects to a Life of Hope</u> (New York: Warner, 1994), 24.

2. Ibid., 27.

3. Michael Schulman and Eva Meckler, <u>Bringing Up a Moral Child</u>, rev. ed. (New York: Doubleday, 1994), 221.

4. W. V. Quine, <u>Word and Object</u> (Cambridge, MA: MIT Press, 1966), 8.

5. Schulman and Meckler, 217.

6. Abraham J. Heschel, <u>Man Is Not Alone: A Philosophy of Religion</u> (New York: Farrar, Straus, and Young, 1951), 221.

7. Ladd, 24.

8. Ibid., 27.

9. Quine, 9–10.

10. Ladd, 28.

16f | Writing Content Notes

As a general rule, put important matters in your text. Use a content note to explain research problems, conflicts in the testimony of the experts, matters of importance that are not germane to your discussion, interesting tidbits, credit to people and sources not mentioned in the text, and other matters that might interest readers.

> **HINT:** After you have embedded most of your computer files into your draft, check the remaining files to find appropriate material for a few content endnotes.

Content notes should conform to these rules:

1. Content notes are *not* documentation notes. A full citation to any source mentioned in the note will appear elsewhere, in a documentation note or in the References or Works Cited list.

See the sample paper on pages 326–335 for its use of superscript numerals, and see page 217 for an example of content endnotes.

2. Content notes may be placed on a separate page following the last page of text, but generally they are mixed among the documentation footnotes or endnotes.

3. Content footnotes should be single spaced, like documentation footnotes. Content endnotes, however, should be double spaced.

4. Unless ambiguity might result without them, do not use "p." or "pp." with page numbers.

The samples below demonstrate various types of content endnotes.

Related Matters not Germane to the Text

1. The problems of politically correct language are explored in Adams, Tucker (4–5), Zalers, and also Young and Smith (583). These authorities cite the need for caution by administrators who would impose new measures on speech and behavior. Verbal abuse cannot be erased by a new set of unjust laws. Patrick German offers several guidelines for implementing an effective but reasonable program (170–72).

Blanket Citation

2. On this point see Giarrett (3–4), de Young (579), Kinard (405–07), and Young (119).

3. Cf. Campbell (<u>Masks</u> 1: 170–225; <u>Hero</u> 342–45), Frazer (312), and Baird (300–344).

NOTE: "Cf." means "compare."

Literature on a Related Topic

4. For additional study of the effects of alcoholics on children, see especially the <u>Journal of Studies on Alcohol</u> for the article by Wolin et al. and the bibliography on the topic by Orme and Rimmer (285–87). In addition, group therapy for children of alcoholics is examined in Hawley and Brown.

Major Source Requiring Frequent In-text Citations

5. All citations to Shakespeare are to the Parrott edition.

6. Dryden's poems are cited from the California edition of his <u>Works</u> and documented in the text with first references to each poem listing volume, page, and lines and with subsequent references citing only lines.

Reference to Source Materials

7. Cf. James Baird, who argues that the whiteness of Melville's whale is "the sign of the all-encompassing God" (257). Baird states: "It stands for what Melville calls at the conclusion of the thirty-fifth chapter of <u>Moby-Dick</u> 'the inscrutable tides of God'; and it is of these tides as well that the great White Whale himself is the quintessential emblem, the iconographic representation" (257).

8. On this point see also the essay by Patricia Chaffee in which she examines the "house" as a primary image in the fiction of Eudora Welty.

Explanation of Tools, Methods, or Testing Procedures

9. Water samples were drawn from the identical spot each day at 8 a.m., noon, 4 p.m., and 8 p.m. with testing done immediately on site.

10. The control group continued normal dietary routines, but the experimental group was asked to consume nuts, sharp cheeses, and chocolates to test acne development of its members against that of the control group.

11. The initial sample was complete data on all twins born in Nebraska between 1920 and 1940. These dates were selected to provide test subjects 60 years of age or older.

NOTE: A report of an empirical study in APA style would require an explanation of tools and testing procedures in the text under "Methods." See 15g, page 298.

Statistics

See also "Figures and Tables," pages A-13–A-16.

12. Database results show 27,000 pupil-athletes in 174 high schools with grades 0.075 above another group of 27,000 non-athletes at the same high schools. Details on the nature of various <u>reward structures</u> are unavailable.

Acknowledgments for Assistance or Support

13. Funds to finance this research were graciously provided by the Thompson-Monroe Foundation.

14. This writer wishes to acknowledge the research assistance of Pat Luther, graduate assistant, Physics Department.

Variables or Conflicts in the Evidence

15. Potlatch et al. included the following variables: the positive acquaintance, the equal status norm, the various social norms, the negative stereotypes, and sexual discrimination (415–20). However, racial barriers cannot be overlooked as one important variable.

16. The pilot study at Dunlap School, where sexual imbalance was noticed (62 percent males), differed sharply from test results of other schools. The male bias at Dunlap thereby caused the writer to eliminate those scores from the totals.

16g Using the CMS System for Papers in the Humanities

Several disciplines in the humanities—history, philosophy, religion, and theology—use footnotes or endnotes. The following list demonstrates the format for the types of notes you might need to write for papers on religion or history. They are shown as endnotes, which should be double spaced.

Sample Page of Notes to a Paper on a Religious Topic

Notes

1. Stephanie Dowrick, <u>Intimacy and Solitude</u> (New York: Norton, 1994), 23–27.

2. Jo Ann Hackett, "Can a Sexist Model Liberate Us? Ancient Near Eastern 'Fertility' Goddesses," <u>Journal of Feminist Studies in Religion</u>, 5 (1989): 457–58.

3. Claude Levi-Strauss, <u>The Savage Mind</u> (Chicago: University of Chicago Press, 1966), chap. 9, esp. p. 312.

4. Ibid., 314.

5. E. E. Evans-Pritchard, <u>Theories of Primitive Religion</u> (Oxford: Clarendon Press, 1965), chap. 2.

6. Evans-Pritchard, <u>Nuer Religion</u> (Oxford: Clarendon Press, 1956), 85.

7. Evans-Pritchard, <u>Primitive Religion</u>, 46.

8. P. T. Humphries, "Salvation Today, Not Tomorrow," Sermon (Bowling Green, KY: First Methodist Church, 2000).

9. Rom. 6:2.

10. 1 Cor. 13:1–3.

11. The Church and the Law of Nullity of Marriage, Report of a Commission Appointed by the Archbishops of Canterbury and York in 1949 (London: Society for Promoting Christian Knowledge, 1955), 12–16.

Sample Page of Notes to a History Paper

Notes

1. Richard Zacks, History Laid Bare: Love, Sex, and Perversity from the Ancient Etruscans to Warren G. Harding (New York: HarperCollins, 1994), 34.

2. Thomas Jefferson, Notes on the State of Virginia (1784), ed. William Peden (Chapel Hill: University of North Carolina Press, 1955), 59.

3. Ralph Lerner, Revolutions Revisited: Two Faces of the Politics of Enlightenment (Chapel Hill: University of North Carolina Press, 1994), 56–60.

4. Encyclopedia Britannica: Macropaedia, 1974 ed., s.v. "Heidegger, Martin."

NOTE: "s.v." means sub verbo, or "under the word."

5. Henry Steele Commager, The Nature and Study of History, Social Science Seminar Series (Columbus, Ohio: Merrill, 1965), 10.

6. Department of the Treasury, "Financial Operations of Government Agencies and Funds," Treasury Bulletin (Washington, D.C.: GPO, June 1974), 134–41.

7. Constitution, Art. 1, sec. 4.

8. Great Britain, Coroner's Act, 1954, 2 & 3 Eliz. 2, ch. 31.

9. State v. Lane, Minnesota 263 N. W. 608 (1935).

10. Papers of Gen. A. J. Warner (P-973, Service Record and Short Autobiography), Western Reserve Historical Society.

11. Ibid., clipping from the Washington Chronicle.

12. Gregory Claeys, "The Origins of the Rights of Labor: Republicanism, Commerce, and the Construction of Modern Social Theory in Britain, 1796–1805." Journal of Modern History 66 (1994): 249–90.

13. Lerner, 54–55.

16h Using the CMS System for Papers in the Fine Arts

Several disciplines in the fine arts—art, dance, music, theater—use footnotes or endnotes. The following list demonstrates the format for the types of notes you might need to write for topics that treat the fine arts.

Notes

1. Natasha Staller, "Melies' 'Fantastic' Cinema and the Origins of Cubism," <u>Art History</u> 12 (1989): 202–39.

2. There are three copies of the papal brief in the archives of the German College, now situated on Via S. Nicola da Tolentino. The document is printed in Thomas D. Culley, <u>Jesuits and Music</u> (Rome and St. Louis, 1979), 1: 358–59.

3. Staller, 214.

4. Denys Hay, ed., <u>The Age of the Renaissance</u> (New York, 1967), 286.

5. Aristophanes, <u>The Birds</u>, in <u>Five Comedies of Aristophanes</u>, trans. Benjamin B. Rogers (Garden City, N.Y.: Doubleday, 1955), 1.2.12–14.

6. Jean Bouret, <u>The Life and Work of Toulouse Lautrec</u>, trans. Daphne Woodward (New York: Abrams, n.d.), 5.

7. Cyrus Hoy, "Fathers and Daughters in Shakespeare's Romances," in <u>Shakespeare's Romances Reconsidered</u>, ed. Carol McGinnis Kay and Henry E. Jacobs (Lincoln: University of Nebraska Press, 1978), 77–78.

8. Lionello Venturi, <u>Botticelli</u> (Greenwich, Conn.: Fawcett, n.d.), plate 32, p. 214.

NOTE: Add "p." for page only if needed for clarity.

9. Cotton Vitellius MSS, A., 15. British Museum.

10. <u>Ham</u>. 2.3.2.

11. George Henry Lewes, Review of "Letters on Christian Art," by Friedrich von Schlegel, <u>Athenaeum</u> No. 1117 (1849): 296.

12. Ron Stoppelmann, "Letters," <u>New York</u>, 23 August 1982, 8.

13. <u>World Book Encyclopedia</u>, 1976 ed., s.v. "Raphael."

14. <u>Last Tango in Paris</u>, United Artists, 1972.

15. Wolfgang A. Mozart, <u>Jupiter</u>, Symphony No. 41.

16. William Blake, <u>Comus</u>, a photographic reproduction in Irene Taylor, "Blake's <u>Comus</u> Designs," <u>Blake Studies</u> 4 (Spring, 1972): 61, plate 4.

17. Lawrence Topp, <u>The Artistry of Van Gogh</u> (New York: Matson, 1983), transparency 21.

18. Eric Sevareid, <u>CBS News</u> (New York: CBS-TV, 11 March 1975); Media Services Videotape 1975-142 (Nashville: Vanderbilt Univ., 1975).

19. Zipperer, Daniel, "The Alexander Technique as a Supplement to Voice Production," <u>Journal of Research in Singing</u> 14 (June 1991): 1–40.

16i Writing a Bibliography Page

In addition to footnotes or endnotes, you may be requested to supply a separate bibliography page that lists sources used in developing the paper. Use a heading that represents its contents, such as "Selected Bibliography," "Sources Consulted," or "Works Cited."

If you write completely documented footnotes, the bibliography is redundant. Check with your instructor before preparing one because it may not be required. Separate the title from the first entry with a triple space. Type the first line of each entry flush left; indent the second line and other succeeding lines five spaces or one half inch. Alphabetize the list by last names of authors. Double space the entries. List alphabetically by title two or more works by one author. The basic forms are shown below.

For a Book

Mapp, Alf J., Jr. <u>Thomas Jefferson: A Strange Case of Mistaken Identity</u>. New York: Madison, 1987.

For a Journal Article

Aueston, John C. "Altering the Course of the Constitutional Convention." <u>Yale Law Journal</u> 100 (1990): 765–783.

For a Newspaper

Stephenson, D. Grier, Jr. "Is the Bill of Rights in Danger?" <u>USA Today</u> 12 May 1991: 82+.

16j Sample Research Paper in the CMS Style

The essay that follows demonstrates the format and documentation style that you should use for a research paper when the instructor asks that you use footnotes or CMS style. If permitted, you may use endnotes rather than footnotes.

Organ and Tissue Donation and Transplantation:
Myths, Ethical Issues, and Lives Saved

By
Adele Gelvin

English Composition 122
Instructor Pam Berns
24 November 2000

Place no number on the title page, but do count it in the sequence of pages as page *i*. The outline will be numbered *ii* and *iii* in lower-case Roman numerals. The text will have Arabic numbers beginning on the first page of the text.

ii

Outline

For help
with writing
an outline,
see pages
96–99.

Thesis: Sufficient organ and tissue donation, enough to satisfy the demand, remains almost impossible because negative myths and religious concerns dominate the minds of many people.

I. Organ and tissue donation is the gift of life.

   A. Initiatives are supported by the government, churches, and private organizations.

   B. Organs that can be successfully transplanted include the heart, lungs, liver, kidneys, and pancreas.

   C. Tissues that can be transplanted successfully include bone, corneas, skin, heart valves, veins, cartilage, and other connective tissues.

   D. The process of becoming a donor is easy.

   E. Many people receive organ and tissue transplants each year, but still many people die because they did not receive the needed transplant.

This writer
uses the
sentence
outline;
others might
use phrases.
See pages
97–99.

II. Many myths mislead people into believing donation is bad and dangerous.

   A. The fire of these myths is the horror story: "I heard about this guy who went to a party, and he woke up the next morning in a bathtub full of ice. His kidneys were stolen for sale on the black market."

   B. Another fear is early death by the doctors: "If I'm in an accident and the hospital knows I want to be a donor, the doctors won't try to save my life!" is another well-circulated myth.

   C. Safeguards assure one's safety against theft of organs or mismanagement by medical personnel.

   D. The legal process sometimes has loopholes that worry surviving relatives.

The sentence
outline can
launch the
drafting of
the paper.
See pages
98–99.

III. Some myths center on the ethical questions: "My religion does not approve of donation."

   A. The New York Regional Transplant Program has published the views of major religions on the subject of organ donation and transplantation.

B. The published evidence shows variations in the specifics of church responses, but all major religions permit, allow, and support transplantation and organ donation.

IV. The evidence and data demonstrate the dire need for donors.

A. The United Network for Organ Sharing (UNOS) provides data to inform potential donors and patients awaiting transplants of the success rates as well as the number of people on the waiting lists.

B. Descriptions of the people on the waiting list give further understanding to the scope of the situation.

C. The shortage of organ donors is constantly being addressed, and legislation is paving the way for more donations.

D. The need extends up and down the economic spectrum, from the very rich to the poor.

V. Organ and tissue donation is ultimately a subject that must be considered by each individual adult.

A. Everyone should discuss the issue of organ and tissue donation with his or her family so that family members know and understand the person's wishes.

B. Many myths hinder the decision of the individual, as well as the family, when it comes to making the final decision about donating body parts.

C. The decision each person makes with his or her family will help make things easier in the future when a decision has to be made.

1

Organ and Tissue Donation and Transplantation:

Myths, Ethical Issues, and Lives Saved

Issues dealing with the ethical practices of organ and tissue donation and transplantation are forever entering people's minds. However, "Organ and tissue transplantation is proven to extend and enhance lives."[1] Many myths lead people to think otherwise, but if one person's life could be saved, would you be the one to help save it? Donating organs or tissues to save a person's life could be the greatest thing a person might do at their own death to help another person appreciate a long, happier life. Organ and tissue donation is an option that every person is eligible to pursue, but few people actually accept the option. The reasons for lack of donation can be attributed to many myths that haunt the practice of organ and tissue donation and transplants. The question, "Is it ethical?" also concerns many people. The initiative joins goverment, churches, and private organizations to promote donation. As vice president, Al Gore said the message to Americans is very simple: "Share your life; share your decision."[2] In her congressional testimony, Donna Shalala, former Secretary of Health and Human Services, said:

> We have come a long way from the pioneering days of organ transplanation. The Organ Transplant Act, and related changes to the Medicare law, provided for national policies and required transplant hospitals to abide by the rules of the national network. The network's primary goal is to ensure that all Americans in need have an equal opportunity to receive an organ transplant, consistent with sound medical judgment, regardless of who they are or where they live and choose to live.[3]

1. "Be a Partner: Join the National Community of Organ and Tissue Sharing," The Organ and Tissue Donation Initiative, 1999 [article online]; available from http://www.organdonor.gov/initiative/default.htm.

2. Al Gore, "Remarks," Organ and Tissue Donation Initative, 1997 [article online]; available from http://www.organdonor.gov/initiative/veep.htm.

3. Donna E. Shalala, Testimony on Organ Donation Allocation, 18 June 1998 [congressional testimony online]; available from Electric Library, keywords: organ donation.

2

She added, "Increasing organ donation is our most important policy goal."[4] One transplant surgeon, Robert Higgins, has said, "We are able to provide stabilizing care and hold out the promise of a continued active life through transplantion. To many of us, the only barrier appears to be lack of available organs."[5] Even the American Bar Association has joined the crusade, saying, "ABA member attorneys are trusted advisors to their clients. Through organ/tissue donation, attorneys can help clients bequeath the gift of life."[6]

The gift of life! Each year many people confront health problems, and organ transplants give these people the chance to live a somewhat normal life. Organs that can be successfully transplanted include the heart, lungs, liver, kidneys, and pancreas.[7] Tissues that can be transplanted successfully include bone, corneas, skin, heart valves, veins, cartilage, and other connective tissues.[8] These tissues are used to correct congenital defects, blindness, visual impairment, trauma, burns, dental defects, arthritis, cancer, and vascular and heart disease.[9] "More than 400 people each month receive the gift of sight through yet another type of tissue donation: corneal transplants. In many cases, donors unsuitable for organ donation are eligible for tissue donation."[10] Tissue grafts are becoming widely used in different medical fields, such as orthopedic surgery, cardiovascular surgery, plastic surgery, dentistry, and podiatry.[11] The advances in technology dealing with the science of organ and tissue transplants are making it easier for people to decide they are going to be a part and give of themselves.

---

4. Ibid.

5. Robert S. D. Higgins, "Increasing Organ Supply for Transplant Patients," 15 April, 1999 [congressional testimony online]; available from Electric Library, keywords: organ donation.

6. Steve Barnhill, "A Legacy for Life—Becoming an Organ or Tissue Donor," American Bar Association, 1994 [article online]; available from http://www.actec.org/pubinforARK/legacy.html.

7. Ibid.

8. Tom Taddonio, "What Kinds of Tissue Can Be Donated?" Transweb at the Univ. of Michigan, 2000 [article online]; available at http://www.transweb.org.

9. Ibid.

10. Barnhill, ibid.

11. Ibid.

Ibid. refers to the immediately preceding note.

3

Even so, not enough people will donate organs and tissues, yet the process of becoming a donor is easy. Carrying a signed donor card or a driver's license that says YES to organ and tissues donation allows for donation. Carrying a signed donor card alone does not guarantee donation because the family of the deceased person has to give the final consent, and if they do not know the feelings of the relative, his or her wishes may not be granted. Discussing the decision to donate organs with family members will make them feel confident in giving their consent when the time comes.[12]

Many people receive organ and tissue transplants each year, but still many people die because they did not receive the needed transplant. The number of people who need transplants continues to increase, but the number of donors fails to meet these demands. According to the National Organ and Tissue Donation Initiative:

> Approximately 55 people each day receive life-enhancing organ transplants; another 10 people die each day on the national list waiting for a donated organ. In September 1997, more than 55,000 people were on the list, which grows by about 500 every month. Most Americans approve of organ donation, but too few give this gift of life to others.[13]

The writer ends the opening part of her essay with a quotation to reinforce her thesis.

With the ever increasing number of organ donors needed, why don't people give of themselves? The most recognized reason for the shortage of donors is directly related to the myths that are associated with organ and tissue donation. People are willing to believe what they hear from the inexperienced and uneducated when there would be more benefits for everyone if they would actually research the issues themselves. "The Centers for Disease Control has estimated that no more than 15 percent of the 20,000 persons who might serve as organ donors actually do so."[14]

---

12. UNOS, "Organ Shortage," United Network for Organ Sharing, 1999 [article online]; available from http://www.unos.org/patients/need_shortage.htm.

13. Ibid.

14. Arthur L. Caplan and Daniel H. Coelho, eds., <u>The Ethics of Organ Transplants: The Current Debate</u>. (New York: Prometheus Books, 1998), 143.

Many myths mislead people into believing donation is bad and unethical. The first of these myths is "I heard about this guy who went to a party and woke up the next morning in a bathtub full of ice. His kidneys were stolen for sale on the black market."[15] According to the United Network of Organ Sharing, nothing like this has ever happened, and there are numerous reasons why this would not happen. The first reason is that it is illegal to sell organs in the United States, as stated in Public Law 98-507.[16] Second, the process of matching donors and recipients as well as the complexity of the surgery is something that could not be easily performed in secrecy.[17] It seems obvious that highly skilled medical professionals are required to carry out these procedures. This myth is a prime example of scare tactics that keep people on edge. The myths let other people's view on the subject get in the way of rational thinking and reasoning.

Part II of her outline is now explored: myths that mislead.

"If I'm in an accident and the hospital knows I want to be a donor, the doctors won't try to save my life!"[18] That is another well-circulated myth. This will not happen because two different teams of doctors are in charge of each of these areas. The team in the emergency room will do everything they can to save their patient's life; only after all lifesaving efforts have failed will the organ procurement organization (OPO) be contacted.[19]

The writer works her way through the various myths that affect the public.

If a patient dies from causes other than head injuries, the OPO will be contacted, they will abide by the family's wishes, and the transplant team will be notified. When dealing with a situation such as brain death, the primary-care doctor has a more difficult decision. Some patients recover after severe head injuries, while others do not. Those who are declared brain dead have some organs that can be used in transplants, but other organs might be "sacrificed" in trying to save the person's life.[20] For a patient to be declared brain

---

15. "Myths," Organ and Tissue Donation Initiative, n.d. [online article]; available from http:organdonor.gov/myth.html.

16. UNOS, ibid.

17. Ibid.

18. "Myths," ibid.

19. Ibid.

20. Jeff Punch, "Myths about Organ Donors Not Receiving Good Medical Care," Transweb at the Univ. of Michigan, 2000 [article online]; available from http://www.transweb.org/qa/qa_txt/faq_donor_care.html.

5

dead, many conditions must be satisfied, and radiological testing can determine lack of blood flow to the brain, normal body temperature, normal blood pressure, and others.[21] Many safeguards assure that there will not be any bias, so the patient has every chance of survival. After a person's death, the OPO is contacted, but nothing will be done until OPO has the consent of the dead person's family. After consent, the donation process begins. This is a long process, but the doctors will never neglect a person's safety in order to use the organs to save another patient's life. It is not ethical, and the hospital would be faced with legal suits.

The legal process sometimes has loopholes that worry surviving relatives. The laws explaining organ and tissue donation are rather vague, and there is no explicit way of giving permission or denying permission for the use of organs.[22] Some of the laws are stated so that the organs can be taken legally as long as the deceased has not declined the donation of his/her organs, even if he or she never actually agreed to organ donation.[23] Dealing with issues of this sort makes people believe their wishes will not be granted, so why should they even make their wishes known to anyone else? The process of organ and tissue donation and transplant is an ethical procedure as long as the physicians uphold the family's wishes.

With a shortage of organs, the doctors see life when a person dies. Viable organs exist in that person's body, and there should be no reason for them to go to waste when they can be used to save another person's life. Sometimes doctors let this thinking get in their way, and the doctor takes a legal risk every time he or she takes the organs of a deceased patient without proper consent. It does not happen often, but we can understand how a doctor can see life while the family sees only death.

Part III of the writer's outline is now developed: ethical issues.

Some myths center on the ethical issue: "My religion does not approve of donation." In actuality most organized religions support donation, believing it is a generous act that is the individual's

---

21. Ibid.

22. R. M. Veatch and J. B. Pitt, "The Myth of Presumed Consent: Ethical Problems in New Organ Procurement Strategies," in Caplan and Coelho, 173.

23. Ibid., 174-75.

choice.[24] The New York Regional Transplant Program published views of major religions on the subject of organ donation and transplantation.[25] Baptists believe donation is an act of charity, and the church leaves the decision to donate up to the individual. For Catholics, says Gallagher, the "transplants are acceptable by the Vatican and donation is encouraged as an act of charity." Lutherans believe "donation contributes to the well-being of humanity and is 'an expression of sacrificial love for a neighbor in need.' They call on 'members to consider donating organs' and to make any necessary family and legal arrangements, including the use of a signed donor card."[26] The United Methodist Church states:

> The United Methodist Church recognizes the life-giving benefits of organ and tissue donation, and thereby encourages all Christians to become organ and tissue donors by signing and carrying cards or driver's licenses, attesting to their commitment of such organs upon their death, to those in need, as a part of their ministry to others in the name of Christ, who gave His life that we might have life in its fullness.[27]

The examples show variations in the specifics, but most major religions permit, allow, and support transplantation and organ donation. Therefore, no one should state that he or she cannot donate due to their religion because most religions approve.

The evidence and data demonstrate the dire need for donors. The UNOS provides data to inform potential donors and recipients of the success rates, as well as the number of people waiting for specific organs. Over time, transplants have become more successful, so the number of people on the waiting list has increased. For example, the number of living kidney donors is less than 5,000 but there are nearly 36,000 people on the waiting list for kidneys.[28] Many

Part IV of the writer's outline is developed: evidence of the need for organ and tissue donors.

---

24. "Myths," ibid.

25. Christin Gallagher, "Does My Religion Approve of Organ Donation?" Transweb at the Univ. of Michigan, 2000 [article online]; available at http://www.transweb.org/qa/qa/_txt /faq_religion.html.

26. Ibid.

27. Cited in Gallagher, ibid.

28. UNOS, ibid.

7

cadaveric kidneys are saved, but an extensive matching process must be performed and no method is available to determine when a cadaveric kidney will be available for transplant due to a waiting period that varies from a few weeks to a number of years.[29] Many people die while waiting for a kidney transplant, and this fate also faces others who need a variety of organs. The number of donors cannot keep up with the number of patients waiting in line for transplant.[30]

Statistics about the people on the waiting list give further understanding to the scope of the situation. UNOS collects data on different organ transplants and the number of people on the waiting list. The most recent information available is from January 1, 1999, to March 31, 1999. According to the information on the cadaveric kidney waiting list for the entire United States, 41,905 people were on the waiting list at the beginning of the period, and 5,171 people were added to the list by the end of the period.[31] Within the three months, 1,914 kidneys were transplanted and 790 people were removed from the list for other reasons, so the final number of people on the waiting list at the end of the three-month period was 42,680.[32] These numbers are tremendous when considering ratio of recipients to the total on the waiting list.

Statistics of 1998 show the problem in more detail. A total of only 5,485 cadaveric transplant donors were available during 1998. During this time 9,270 kidneys, 4,339 livers, 1,218 pancreases, 2,389 hearts, and 1,301 lungs were transplanted.[33] More than one organ was used from some of the donors, which explains why some transplants were greater in number than the total number of donors.

The shortage of organ donors is constantly being addressed, and legislation is paving the way for more donations. Currently in the United States the Uniform Anatomical Gift Act has been passed in some form in all states.[34] "This statute gives all competent adults

---

29. Ibid.

30. Ibid.

31. Ibid.

32. Ibid.

33. Ibid.

34. Aaron Spital, "Mandated Choice for Organ Donation: Time to Give It a Try," in Caplan and Coelho, 147-53.

8

legal authority to decide for themselves whether or not they wish to become organ donors after their death."[35] Even though this is stated in the Uniform Anatomical Gift Act, many times the law is ignored. It does not matter whether or not the deceased wished to be an organ donor because the family must give the final consent, and nearly 50 percent of them say "no." They do not grant the wishes of the deceased and deny his or her organs to be used for transplant.[36]

Currently, work is being done to change the system to honor the wishes of the deceased with no family consent involved, unless otherwise stated as a stipulation on the initial documentation.[37] This type of documentation would make the process easier for the family, especially in the time of sudden death. The extra burden of making the decision would be gone. The decision would have been made, documented, and would have to be honored by the physicians. This method provides an ethical way of approaching the subject.

Incidentally, in a recent poll, over sixty percent of the adult population would choose to donate their organs after death if they were given the option and their wishes followed. Another thirteen percent were undecided, but might say "yes" if the system was changed to a mandatory decision and followed through with what the individual desired.[38]

Another piece of legislation would increase donations. Legislation could be enacted to make it mandatory for physicians to inquire about the donation of organs with the family of deceased individuals. According to Arthur Caplan, this law would decrease the number of people on the waiting list for transplants. It would ease the awkwardness of the physicans who must confront the patient's family about the ordeal. This legislation would mandate it. Everyone would be informed and could be prepared; the surviving relatives would be prepared because they would know that the physician had to ask permission for donations.[39]

---

35. Ibid., 147.

36. Ibid., 147-48.

37. Ibid., 148-49.

38. Spital, ibid., 151.

39. Arthur Caplan, "Ethical and Policy Issues in the Procurement of Cadaver Organs for Transplantation," in Caplan and Coelho, 142-46.

9

The need for organs and tissue extends up and down the economic spectrum. For example, the creator of <u>Peanuts</u>, Charles Schultz, waited in Ward 7 East in Mt. Sinai Hospital in New York City for a new heart that he needed badly.[40] One of his new, close friends in the ward received news that a heart had been found for her. Doris Napoli was the woman; she had been waiting for a heart for nearly five months, and finally her prayers had been answered.[41] When the other residents heard this, including Schultz, they had mixed emotions of joy and self-pity because they all wanted to be in her shoes and be given the gift of life. The playing field was level; Schultz, although wealthy, had to wait his turn. Eventually, Schultz received his chance. The success rate has increased, and after one life has ended, another can be helped and extended.

The writer moves toward her conclusion. See pages 180–94 for help with writing the three parts of a paper— the introduction, body, and conclusion.

Organ and tissue donation is ultimately a subject that must be considered by each individual adult. You, like everyone, should discuss the issue of organ and tissue donation with your family so that the relatives know and understand your wishes. As mentioned above, many things must be considered when you are determining whether or not you want to be an organ and tissue donor after you are deceased. Many myths hinder the decision of the individual, as well as the family. When a family is placed in the position of making a decision on whether or not to donate a loved one's organs at the time of death, there is added tension.[42] However, if they know how you felt, they will not make a wrong decision or feel confused.

In the end, nearly all of the myths are things people have created because they were afraid of actually giving of themselves to help save someone else's life. When a person no longer has anything to offer in life and his or her duties have been fulfilled here on earth, why not donate organs and tissues to help someone else to enjoy their time on earth just a little bit longer? With organ

Footnote 42 is an example of a content footnote, not a documentation note. See page 316–19 for details and examples of content notes.

---

40. Dateline NBC, "Transplant: Waiting for the Gift of Life," 12 Nov. 1999 [television transcript online]; available from http://www.msnbc.com/new/316967.asp?cp1=1#BODY.

41. Ibid.

42. The same burden is placed on a family when no funeral and burial plans have been arranged. It would be easy for an older person to preplan and even prepay the funeral and its expenses.

10

and tissue donation, you increase the quantity of life, but above that
you increase the quality of life for the person who received your
donated organ or tissue. The person who receives the transplant
will always be grateful for someone giving of himself or herself
to save them. The decision each person makes with his or her family
will help make things easier in the future when a final decision
has to be made.

CBE Style for the Natural and Applied Sciences

The Council of Biology Editors, now named the Council of Science Editors, has established two separate forms for citing sources in scientific writing. One is the **Citation-Sequence** (C-S) system for writing in the applied sciences, such as chemistry, computer science, mathematics, physics, and health. This system uses numbers in the text rather than a name and year. The other is the **Name-Year** system for use in the biological and earth sciences.

Citation-Sequence
The original description (3) contained precise taxonomic detail that differed with recent studies (4–6).

Name-Year
The original description (Roberts 1999) contained precise taxonomic detail that differed with recent studies (McCormick 2000a, 2000b, and Tyson and others 1999).

There are advantages and disadvantages to each system. The C-S system saves space, and the numbers make minimal disruption to the reading of the text. But the C-S system seldom mentions names, so readers must refer to the bibliography for the names of authors. Also, any disruption in the numbering sequence late in the composition may necessitate a renumbering of all references in the text and the bibliography.

The Name-Year system mentions authors' names in the text with the year to show timely application and historical perspective. Citations can be deleted or added without difficulty. But a long string of citations in the text can be more disruptive than numbers. In truth, the decision is usually not yours to make. The individual disciplines in the sciences have adopted one form or the other, as shown in the following chart.

Guide by Discipline

Agriculture, Name and Year, 17c and 17d
Anthropology, Name and Year, 17c and 17d
Archaeology, Name and Year, 17c and 17d
Astronomy, Name and Year, 17c and 17d

Biology, Name and Year, 17c and 17d
Botany, Name and Year, 17c and 17d
Chemistry, Number, 17a and 17b
Computer Science, Number, 17a and 17b
Engineering, Number, 17a and 17b
Geography, Name and Year, 17c and 17d
Geology, Name and Year, 17c and 17d
Health, Number, 17a and 17b
Mathematics, Number, 17a and 17b
Medicine, Number, 17a and 17b
Nursing, Number, 17a and 17b
Physics, Number, 17a and 17b
Zoology, Name and Year, 17c and 17d

17a Writing In-Text Citations with Numbers

The Citation-Sequence system features numbers to identify the sources. Use this style with these disciplines: chemistry, computer science, engineering, mathematics, physics, and the medical sciences (medicine, nursing, and general health). In simple terms, it requires an in-text *number*, rather than the year, and a list of "Cited References" that are numbered to correspond to the in-text citations.

After completing a list of references, assign a number to each entry. Use one of two methods for numbering the list: (1) arrange references in alphabetic order and number them consecutively (in which case the numbers will appear in random order in the text), or (2) number the references consecutively as you put them into your text, interrupting that order when entering references cited earlier.

The number serves as the key reference to the source, as numbered in the "Cited References." Conform to the following regulations:

1. Place the number within parentheses (1) or brackets [2] or as a raised index numeral, like this.[5] A name is not required and is even discouraged, so try to arrange your wording accordingly. Full information on the author and the work will be found in the references list.

It is known (1) that the DNA concentration of a nucleus doubles during interphase.

A recent study [1] has raised interesting questions related to photosynthesis, some of which have been answered [2].

In particular, a recent study[1] has raised many interesting questions related to photosynthesis, some of which have been answered.[2]

2. If the sentence uses the authority's name, add the number after the name.

Additional testing by Cooper (3) includes alterations in carbohydrate metabolism and changes in ascorbic acid incorporation into the cell and adjoining membranes.

3. If necessary, add specific data to the entry:

"The use of photosynthesis in this application is crucial to the environment" (Skelton,[8] p 732).

The results of the respiration experiment published by Jones (3, Table 6, p 412) had been predicted earlier by Smith (5, Proposition 8).

17b Using Numbers with Bibliography Entries

Supply a list of references at the end of your paper. Number it to correspond to sources as you cite them in the text. An alternate method is to alphabetize the list and then number it. Label the list "Cited References." The form of the entries should duplicate the examples shown below. Use the hanging indent style, indenting the lines evenly after the first line.

Book

Provide a number and then list the author, title of the book, place of publication, publisher, year, and total number of pages (optional).

1. Gehling E. The family and friends' guide to diabetes: Everything you need to know. New York: Wiley; 2000.

Article in a Journal

Provide a number and then list the author, the title of the article, the name of the journal, the year and month if necessary, volume number and issue number if necessary, and inclusive pages. The month or an issue number is necessary for any journal that is paged anew with each issue.

2. Bolli GB, Owens DR. Insulin glargine. Lancet 2000; 356:443–444.

Internet Articles and Other Electronic Publications

At the end of the citation, add an availability statement and the date you accessed the material. Use the form in number 4 for an article published on the Web. Use the form in number 5 for a periodical article that has been reproduced on the Web. Number 4 is online and number 5 is a printed journal [serial online].

4. [Anonymous]. Diabetes insipidus. Amer. Acad. of Family
   Physicians [online] 2000. Available from http://www.aafp.org/
   patientinfo/insipidu.html. Accessed 2000 Aug 8.
5. Roberts S. The diabetes advisor. Diabetes Forecast [serial online]
   2000;53:41–42. Available from http://www.diabetes.org/
   diabetesforecast/00August/default.asp. Accessed 2000 Aug 8.

Magazine and Newspaper Article

Add a specific date and, for newspapers, cite a section letter or number.

6. Schlosberg S. The symptoms you should never ignore. Shape
   2000 Aug:136.
7. [Anonymous]. FDA approval of drug gives diabetics a new choice.
   Los Angeles Times 2000 Aug 2; Sect A:4.

Proceedings and Conference Presentations

After supplying a number, give the name of the author or editor, the title of the presentation, name of the conference, type of work (report, proceedings, proceedings online, etc.), name of the organization or society, the date of the conference, and the place. If found on the Internet, add the URL and the date you accessed the information.

8. Ashraf H, Banz W, Sundberg J. Soyful luncheon: Setting a
   healthful table for the community [abstract]. In: Crossing
   Borders: Food and Agriculture in the Americas. Proceedings
   online of the Assn. for the Study of Food and Society; 1999 June
   3–6; Toronto(ON). Available from http://www.acs.ryerson.ca/
   foodsec/foodsec/papers.html. Accessed 2000 Aug 8.

Article from a Loose-leaf Collection

9. [Anonymous]. No-till farming shows skeptics the advantages of giving up the plow. CQ Researcher 1994; 4:1066.

> For a sample of a "Cited References" page using the number system, see page 351.

17c Writing In-Text Citations with Name and Year

The CBE Name-Year style applies to these disciplines:

Agriculture	Anthropology	Archaeology
Astronomy	Biology	Botany
Geography	Geology	Zoology

When writing research papers in accordance with the Name-Year system, conform to the following rules:

1. Place the year within parentheses immediately after the authority's name:

Smith (1999) ascribes no species-specific behavior to man. However, Adams (2000) presents data that tend to be contradictory.

2. If you do not mention the authority's name in your text, insert the name, year, and even page numbers within the parentheses:

One source found some supporting evidence for a portion of the questionable data (Marson and Brown 2000, pp 23–32) through point bi-serial correlation techniques.

3. For two authors, employ both names in your text and in the parenthetical citation:

Torgerson and Andrews (2000)

or

(Torgerson and Andrews 2000)

NOTE: Unlike APA style, the CBE style does not use "&."

For three or more authors, use the lead author's name with "and others."

NOTE: CBE style prefers English terms and English abbreviations rather than Latin words and abbreviations, such as *et al.*

IN THE TEXT: Torgerson and others (2000)
IN THE PARENTHETICAL CITATION: (Torgerson and others 2000)

4. Use small letters (a,b,c) to identify two or more works published in the same year by the same author, for example, "Thompson (2001a)" and "Thompson (2001b)." Then use "2001a" and "2001b" in your "Cited References" list (see item 5 immediately below for an example).

5. If necessary, supply additional information:

Horton (2000a, 2000b; cf. Thomas, 1999, p 89) suggests an intercorrelation of these testing devices. But after multiple-group analysis, Welston (1999, esp. p 211) reached an opposite conclusion.

6. In the case of reference to a specific page, separate the page number from the year with a comma and a space. Do not use a period after the "p" or "pp."

Jones stated, "These data of psychological development suggest that retarded adolescents are atypical in maturational growth" (2000, p 215), and Jones attached the data which were accumulated during the study.

Jones (1994) found that "these data of psychological development suggest that retarded adolescents are atypical in maturational growth" (p 215).

Long quotations are set off from the text in an indented block without quotation marks:

Albert (1994) found the following:

> Whenever these pathogenic organisms attack the human body and begin to multiply, the infection is set in motion. The host responds to this parasitic invasion with efforts to cleanse itself of the invading agents. When rejection efforts of the host become visible (fever, sneezing, congestion), the disease status exists. (pp 314–315)

7. Punctuate the citations according to the following stipulations:

Use a comma followed by a space to separate citations of different references by the same author or authors in same-year or different-year references:

Supplemental studies (Johnson 1999a, 1999b, 2000) have shown . . .

Supplemental studies (Randolph and Roberts 1999, 2000) have shown . . .

Use a comma to separate author names accompanied by initials in citations with two or more authors:

(Roberts SL, Rudolph CB, and others 1999)

Use a semicolon followed by a space to separate citations to different authors:

Supplemental studies (Smith, 1999 ; Barfield 1989, 1997 ; Barfield and Smith 1998 ; Wallace 2000) have shown …

17d Using Name and Year with Bibliography Entries

Alphabetize the reference list and label it "Cited References." Double space the entries and use the hanging indention. When there are two to ten authors, all should be named in the reference list. When there are eleven or more authors, the first ten are listed, followed by "and others." If the author is anonymous, insert "[Anonymous]." Place the year immediately after the author's name.

Article in a Journal

List the author, year, article title, journal title, volume number, and inclusive pages. Add an issue number for any journal that is paged anew with each issue.

Lyons-Johnson D. 1998. Deep-rooted safflower cuts fertilizer
    losses. Agr. Research 46:17.

Book

List the author, year, title, place of publication, publisher, and total number of pages (optional).

Gershuny G, Smillie J. 1999. The soul of soil: A soil-building guide
    for master gardeners and farmers. White River Junction, Vt.:
    Chelsea Green. 173 p.

Internet Articles and Other Electronic Publications

Add at the end of the citation an availability statement as well as the date you accessed the material.

Ramsel RE, Nelson LA, Wicks GA. 1999. Ecofarming: No-till
    ecofallow proso millet in winter wheat stubble. NebGuide
    [online]. Available from http://www.ianr.unl.edu/pubs/
    FieldCrops/g835.htm. Accessed 2000 Aug 8.

Journal Article Reprinted on the Internet

Provide original publication data as well as the Internet address and the date you accessed the material. Label it as a *serial online.*

Barbieri PA, Rozas HR, Andrade FH, Echeverria HE. 2000.
    Row spacing effects at different levels of nitrogen availability
    in maize [abstract]. Agron. J. [serial online]; 92:283–287.
    Available from http://link.springer-ny.com/link/service/journals/
    10087/bibs/0092002/00920283.html. Accessed 2000 Aug 8.

Magazine and Newspaper Article

Add a specific date and, if listed, a section letter or number.

Haag E. 1997 March. Farewell to fallow. Farm Journal 121:E-4.

Cowen RC. 1996 June 11. No-till farming can reduce nitrogen
pollution. Christian Science Monitor 88:14.

Proceedings and Conference Publications

Give author, date, title of the presentation, name of conference, type of
work (report, proceeding, proceedings online, etc.), name of the organization or society, and place of the conference. If found on the Internet, add the
URL and the date of your access.

Ashraf H, Banz W, Sundberg J. 1999 June 3–6. Soyful luncheon:
Setting a healthful table for the community [abstract]. In:
Crossing Borders: Food and Agriculture in the Americas.
Proceedings online of the Association for the Study of Food
and Society; Toronto (ON). Available http://www.acs.ryerson.ca/
~foodsec/foodsec/Papers.html. Accessed 2000 Aug 8.

Article from a Loose-leaf Collection

[Anonymous]. 1994. No-till farming shows skeptics the advantages
of giving up the plow. CQ Researcher 4:1066.

17e Arranging the Cited References List by Name and Year

The list of references should be placed in alphabetical order, as shown next.
See page 351 for a list arranged by numbers.

Cited References

Barbieri PA, Rozas HR, Andrade FH, Echeverria HE. 2000.
Row spacing effects at different levels of nitrogen availability
in maize [abstract]. Agron. J. [serial online]; 92:283–287.
Available from http://link.springer-ny.com/link/service/
journals/10087/bibs/0092002/00920283.html. Accessed
2000 Aug 8.

Cowen RC. 1996 June 11. No-till farming can reduce nitrogen
pollution. Christian Science Monitor 88:14.

Gershuny G, Smillie J. 1999. The soul of soil: A soil-building guide
for master gardeners and farmers. White River Junction, Vt.:
Chelsea Green. 173 p.

Haag E. 1997 March. Farewell to fallow. Farm Journal 121:E-4.

Lyons-Johnson D. 1998. Deep-rooted safflower cuts fertilizer
losses. Agr. Research 46:17.

17f   Sample Paper Using the CBE Number System

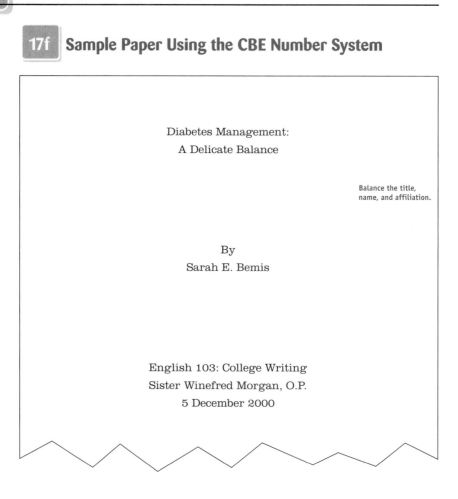

Diabetes Management:
A Delicate Balance

Balance the title,
name, and affiliation.

By
Sarah E. Bemis

English 103: College Writing
Sister Winefred Morgan, O.P.
5 December 2000

ii

Abstract

An abstract
of 100–200
words states
the purpose,
scope, and
major findings
of the report.
Put the
abstract on a
separate page.

Diabetes affects approximately 11 million people in the United States alone, leading to 350,000 deaths per year and $20,273 billion in medical costs. Two types, I and II, have debilitating effects. The body may tolerate hyperglycemia for a short time, but severe complications can occur, such as arterioscleroses, heart disease, nerve damage, and cerebral diseases. New drugs continue to improve the life style of a person with diabetes, but controlling blood sugar requires three elements working together—medication, diet, and exercise. This study examines the importance of each of the three. Patients need a controlled balance of the medication, diet, and exercise program.

1

Diabetes Management: A Delicate Balance

Diabetes is a disease that affects approximately 11 million people in the United States alone. Diabetes and its complications lead to approximately 350,000 deaths per year and cost the nation $20,273 billion per year in medical care, in the direct cost of complications, and in the indirect costs of loss of productivity related to the disease (1). The condition can produce devastating side effects and a multitude of chronic health problems. For this reason, it can be very frightening to those who do not understand the nature and treatment of the disease. Diabetes currently has no known cure, but it can be controlled. Diabetes research has made great advancements in recent years, but the most important insights into the management of this disease are those which seem the most simplistic. By instituting a healthy, balanced lifestyle, most persons with diabetes can live free of negative side effects.

Diabetes mellitus, according to several descriptions, is a disorder in which the body cannot properly metabolize glucose or sugar. The body's inability to produce or properly use insulin permits glucose to build up in the bloodstream. The excess sugar in the blood, or hyperglycemia, is what leads to the side effects of diabetes (2,3,4).

There are actually two types of diabetes. Type 1, or juvenile diabetes, is the name given to the condition in which the pancreas produces very little or no insulin. It is normally discovered during childhood but can occur at any age (3). Adult onset, or Type II diabetes, occurs when the pancreas produces usable insulin, but not enough to counteract the amount of glucose in the blood. This often results from obesity or poor diet.

In both Type I and Type II diabetes, the problem has been identified as hyperglycemia (5). This build up of glucose in the bloodstream leads to a number of dangerous side effects. The initial effects and indicators of hyperglycemia are frequent urination, intense thirst, increased hunger and fatigue. When glucose begins to build up in the blood, the kidneys begin to filter out the excess sugar into the urine. The amount of glucose the kidneys can filter varies with each person. In this process, all the water in the body's tissues is being used to produce urine to flush glucose from the kidneys. This is what leads to the intense thirst and frequent urination associated with hyperglycemia (5).

Use a number to register the use of a source.

The thesis or hypothesis is expressed at the end of the introdution.

Scientific writing requires careful definition, as shown here.

More than one source can be listed for one idea or concept.

Causal analysis, as shown here, is a staple of scientific writing.

2

Because the body lacks the insulin needed to allow glucose into the cells, the glucose cannot be processed to produce energy. The cells signal the brain that they are not getting sugar and this causes hunger. However, no matter how much a victim of hyperglycemic diabetes eats, the cells will not be producing energy (6).

Refer to the sources with the past tense verb or the present participle.

It has been shown (4) that with hyperglycemia the kidneys try to compensate for the excess of sugar and lack of energy. While the kidneys attempt to filter the sugar from the blood, the liver tries to produce energy by burning fat and muscle to produce ketones, a protein that the body attempts to burn in place of glucose. Ketones do not provide the energy the body requires but do produce chemicals toxic to the body. When too many ketones are present in the blood, ketoacidosis occurs (4).

In addition to the number, you may mention the names of your sources.

Guthrie and Guthrie (1) have demonstrated that ketoacidosis is a condition caused by high levels of hydrogen in the blood. This leads initially to a high blood pH, depleted saline fluids and dehydration. If untreated it can lead to a shut down of the central nervous system, coma or even death. In fact, many diabetes-related deaths are caused by ketoacidosis that has reached a comatose state. Ketoacidosis is characterized by frequent urination, dry mouth, extreme thirst, headache, rapid and deep respiration, increased heart rate, nausea, vomiting, disorientation and lethargy (1).

Consumer Reports on Health (4) has reported that hyperglycemia can cause other, more subtle, side effects. Because the body is not receiving the nourishment it requires, a victim of hyperglycemic diabetes often experiences poor tissue growth and repair. This can cause problems with growth and development in children and wound healing in adults as well as children. It has also been reported (7) that the immune system is also affected and that victims experience infection more often and more severely than a person without diabetes. Other conditions that frequently occur in conjunction with hyperglycemia in its early stages are depression and chronic fatigue (8). Many patients who experience hypoglycemia have difficulties controlling gain and loss of weight as well.

Both the names of the authors and the reference number may appear within the parentheses.

It has been shown (Guthrie and Guthrie 1) that the body may tolerate hyperglycemia over a short time period. However, if untreated, it leads to other chronic and often fatal health conditions. Arterioscleroses occurs in hyperglycemic diabetics over time, resulting in decreased circulation and eyesight. This also may lead

3

to heart disease, angina and heart attack, the most prevalent causes of death among diabetics (1). Also common is diabetic neuropathy, a degeneration of the nerves. This condition causes pain and loss of function in the extremities (1).

A person with diabetes is also at risk for many cerebral diseases. Both the large and small cerebral arteries of victims are prone to rupture, which can cause cerebral hemorrhage, thrombosis or stroke. Blockages in the carotid arteries can decrease blood flow to the brain, causing episodes of lightheadedness and fainting (1, pp 201-202).

You may add page numbers to the reference as a courtesy to the reader.

Diabetic nephropathy occurs when the kidneys are overloaded with glucose. Eventually, they begin to shut down. The kidneys of a person with uncontrolled diabetes are also susceptible to infection, resulting in decreased kidney function (1).

With all the complications victims experience, the outlook for a long and healthy life does not seem good for those diagnosed with the disease. However, all of these effects can be reduced, delayed, and even prevented with proper care and control. By monitoring blood sugar and reacting accordingly with medication, by special diets, and by exercise and a controlled lifestyle, persons with diabetes can avoid these serious health conditions (Brancati and others 9).

The first aspect of diabetes care is blood sugar monitoring and medication. The two go hand in hand in that the patient must have the appropriate type and dosage of medication and must know blood sugar values and patterns in order to determine the correct regimen. Two main types of monitoring are necessary for diabetes control. Patients must perform home glucose monitoring on a daily basis. Advancements in this area in recent years have made this relatively effortless. Several glucose monitoring kits are available to the general public. These consist of a small, electronic machine that measures the amount of glucose in the blood, as well as the equipment necessary to obtain a small sample. With such equipment, patients can test and record blood sugars several times per day. This gives both short-term and long-term information by which they and their physicians can determine insulin dosages and meal plans.

Process analysis, as shown here, is often part of scientific writing.

In addition to daily monitoring, victims should visit their physician regularly. Doctors usually perform a test called a hemoglobin AIC, which gives a better indication of blood sugar control over a longer period of time than a home test. This should be

4

done approximately every ninety days, as that is the time period over which blood cells are renewed. This test along with consideration of daily glucose values can help the physician determine overall control and effectiveness of the patient's routine. Regular visits also give the physician an opportunity to monitor the general health of the patient, including circulation, eyesight, infections, and organ infections.

The writer explores control element number one: methods of administering medication.

The treatment of diabetes usually involves medication. Since Type I diabetics produce very little or no insulin, insulin injections will always be necessary. For Type II, the treatment may be strictly dietary, dietary with oral hypoglycemic agents, or insulin therapy.

When insulin therapy is required, it is very important that the appropriate type and dosage are implemented. Many types of insulin are available. The main distinction among these types is in their action time, onset, peak-time, and duration. Different types of insulin begin to act at different rates. They also continue to act for different periods of time and hit peak effectiveness at different intervals (1). This is why it is important to have records of blood sugars at regular intervals over several weeks. From this it can be determined when and what type of insulin is needed most. Once it is determined what insulin regimen is appropriate, the patient must follow it closely. Routine is very important in controlling diabetes.

Patients with diabetes now have a few options when it comes to injection method. One may chose traditional manual injection, an injection aid, or an insulin pump. Injection aids can make using a needle easier and more comfortable or actually use air pressure to inject. The insulin pump is a device that offers convenience as well as improved control. The pump is a small battery-operated device that delivers insulin 24 hours a day through a small needle worn under the skin. The pump contains a computer chip which controls the amount of insulin delivered according to the wearer's personalized plan (10). The pump is meant for patients who do not wish to perform multiple injections but are willing to test blood sugars frequently. The pump can help patients who have some trouble controlling their blood sugars by providing insulin around the clock. It also provides an element of freedom for persons with busy schedules.

Some Type II patients can control the disease with a combination of diet, exercise and an oral hypoglycemic agent. These drugs themselves contain no insulin. They traditionally lower blood

glucose levels by stimulating the pancreas to produce insulin (1). 5
Therefore, they are only appropriate for a patient whose pancreas is
still producing some insulin. Diabetes research has advanced in
recent years, however. Some new drugs may be coming available in
the new millennium. Creators of the pharmaceuticals are able to
increase sensitivity to insulin and suppress the secretion of
hormones that raise blood sugar. A number of new drugs that are
aimed at taking the place of insulin therapy are currently in the
final stages of research and development. Glucovance has been
advanced as a valuable new medication (11). For now, the oral
medications that are available can aid in keeping better control
when properly paired with an effective diet and exercise plan.

> While it is important to have the proper medication, the
backbone of diabetes management is the meal plan. By making wise
choices in eating, persons with diabetes can reduce stress on the
body and increase the effectiveness of their medication. The basis of
a good meal plan is balanced nutrition and moderation. Eating a
low fat, low sodium, low sugar diet is the best way for a diabetic
to ensure longevity and health. It is important for everyone to eat
balanced meals on a routine schedule. For victims of diabetes, it can
help in blood sugar control and in preventing heart disease and
digestive problems.

The writer now explores control element number two: methods of diet management.

> Two established meal plans are recommended for patients:
the Exchange Plan and carbohydrate counting (12, 13). Both are
based on The Diabetes Food Pyramid (Nutrition). The Food Pyramid
divides food into six groups. These resemble the traditional four
food groups, except that they are arranged in a pyramid in which
the bottom, or largest, section contains the foods that should be
eaten most each day. The top, or smallest, section contains the foods
that should be eaten least, if at all. With any diabetic meal plan,
the patient should eat a variety of foods from all the food groups,
except the sweets, fats, and alcohol group.

> The Exchange Plan provides a very structured meal plan.
Foods are divided into eight categories, which are more specific than
those of the Food Pyramid. A dietician or physician determines a
daily calorie range for the patient and, based on that range, decides
how many servings she or he should eat from each category per
meal. Portion sizes are determined and must be followed exactly. The
patient then has the option to either choose foods that fit into the

6

groups recommended for each meal or exchange foods from one group for foods from another.

Another meal plan patients can utilize is carbohydrate counting. This plan is less structured and gives the patient more flexibility in making meal choices. It also involves less planning. Once again, food is categorized, but into only three groups. The largest food group, carbohydrates, encompasses not only starches, but dairy products, fruits, and vegetables as well. The dietician or physician again assigns a calorie range. With this plan, however, only the number of carbohydrates per meal are assigned, and even this is flexible. This plan is recommended for those who know how to make balanced meal choices but need to keep track of their food intake. Once again, portion sizes are important, and the patient must remember to eat the recommended amount of foods from each pyramid category (5, 11, 12).

The writer now explores control element number three: methods of exercise.

The final element in successfully managing diabetes is exercise. It has been shown (14) that exercise can help stimulate the body to use glucose for energy, thus taking it out of the blood. Diabetic patients need regular exercise programs that suit their personal needs. Something as simple as a walking routine can significantly reduce blood glucose levels (14). Some patients may require as little as a fifteen-minute per day walk, while some may need a more involved workout. In each case, an exercise schedule works with meal plans, medication, and lifestyle. Also crucial to the success of an exercise routine is close monitoring of blood sugar. If glucose levels are too high or too low, exercise will have negative effects.

All of the aspects of diabetes management can be summed up in one word: balance. Diabetes itself is caused by a lack of balance of insulin and glucose in the body. In order to restore that balance, a person with diabetes must juggle medication, monitoring, diet, and exercise. Managing diabetes is not an easy task, but a long and healthy life is very possible when the delicate balance is carefully maintained.

7

Cited References

1. Guthrie DW, Guthrie RA. Nursing management of diabetes mellitus. New York: Springer, 1991.

2. [Anonymous]. Diabetes insipidus. American Academy of Family Physicians. Available from http://www.aafp.org/patientinfo/insipidu.html. Accessed 2000 Aug 10.

3. Clark CM, Fradkin JE, Hiss RG, Lorenz RA, Vinicor F, Warren-Boulton E. Promoting early diagnosis and treatment of type 2 diabetes. JAMA 2000;284:363-365.

4. [Anonymous]. Do you know your blood-sugar level? Consumer Reports on Health 2000;12(7):1-4.

5. Gehling E. The family and friends' guide to diabetes: Everything you need to know. New York: Wiley, 2000.

6. Schlosberg S. The symptoms you should never ignore. Shape 2000 Aug;19:136-142.

7. Espenshade JE. Staff Manual For Teaching Patients About Diabetes Mellitus. Chicago: Amer. Hospital Assn., 1979.

8. Roberts SS. The diabetes advisor. Diabetes Forecast 2000;53:41-42. Available from http://www.diabetes.org/diabetesforecast/00August/default.asp. Accessed 2000 Aug 8.

9. Brancati FL, Kao WHL, Folsom AR, Watson RL, Szklo M. Incident type 2 diabetes mellitus in African American and white adults. JAMA 2000;283:2253-2259.

10. Schwartz S, Hitchcock J. Is pumping for you? Diabetes Monitor 1999. Available from http://www.diabetesmonitor.com/slidemain.htm. Accessed 2000 Aug 11.

11. [Anonymous]. Glucophage. Diabetes Healthsource. 2000. Available from http://www.glucophage.com. Accessed 2000 Aug 11.

12. Nurses' Clinical Library. Endocrine Disorders. Springhouse, PA: Springhouse, 1984.

13. Eades MR, Eades MD. Protein Power. New York: Bantam, 1996.

14. [Anonymous]. Exercise. American Diabetes Association. 2000. Available from http://www.diabetes.org/exercise. Accessed 2000 Aug 11.

Citations on this page demonstrate the citation-sequence method, as explained on pages 338–40. For details on the year-date system, see pages 342–43.

18

Preparing Electronic Research Projects

This chapter suggests ways to create and publish your research electronically. It begins with the easiest—putting a word-processed research paper on a floppy disk for your instructor—and moves to the most difficult—designing a website and releasing the paper onto the Internet. This chapter will give you a sense of the possibilities of electronic research papers.

Creating your research paper electronically has a number of advantages:

- **It's easy.** Creating electronic research papers can be as simple as saving a file, and your school probably has resources for publishing your paper electronically.

- **It offers multimedia potential.** Unlike paper documents, electronic documents enable you to include anything available in a digital form—including text, illustrations, sound, and video.

- **It can link your reader to more information.** Your readers can click a hyperlink to access additional sources of information. (A hyperlink or link is a highlighted word or image that, when clicked, lets readers jump from one place to another—for example, from your research paper to a website on your subject.)

18a Getting Started

Before you decide to create your research paper electronically, consider three questions:

1. **What support does your school provide?** Most institutions are making investments in technology and the personnel to support it. Investigate how your college will help you publish in an electronic medium.
2. **Is electronic publishing suitable for your research paper?** Ask yourself what your readers will gain from reading an electronic text rather than the traditional paper version. Will an electronic format really help you get your ideas to readers?

3. **What form will it take?** Electronic research papers appear generally in one of the following forms:

- A word processed document (see section 18b)
- An electronic slide show (see section 18c)
- A website (see section 18d)

Each of these forms can be researched and produced using traditional methods, but the writing and presentation will differ.

18b Using Word Processing

The easiest way to create an electronic document is by using word processing programs such as Microsoft Word® or Corel WordPerfect® and then distributing your report in its electronic form rather than printing it out. (See Figure 18.1 for an example of such a research paper.)

Most popular word processing programs include tools for handling features like these:

- **Graphics.** Word processors can accommodate graphics in a variety of formats, including .gif and .jpg (see the graphic in Figure 18.1 for an example; see section 18f, pages 360-61, for more information on graphic formats).
- **Sound and video.** Word processors can include several common audio and video clip formats. Usually, the reader has to click on an icon to activate the clip (see the sound link in Figure 18.1).
- **Hyperlinks.** Readers can click to go to a website on the Internet for further reading (see the underlined hyperlink in the text of Figure 18.1).

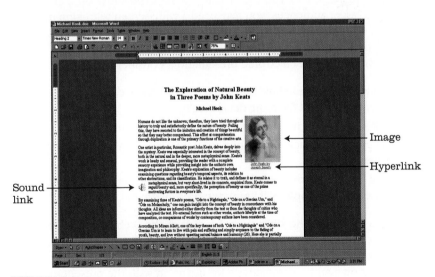

FIGURE 18.1
Word-processed research paper.

The advantages of using a word processor to create an electronic research paper are considerable. Using a word processor is familiar; you probably already use one to create your traditional research papers. It's also flexible; most word processors give you more control over format and design than a typewriter would. However, using a word processor to create your electronic research paper has two disadvantages: The computer file created by your word processor can become very large if you include graphics, sound, and video. Also, to read your paper, people must own the same word processing software and sometimes even the same version of the software. Nevertheless, a word processor works well in a classroom or computer laboratory that shares the same software.

18c Building Electronic Presentations

If you plan an oral presentation, an electronic slide show can help illustrate your ideas. Electronic presentations differ from word-processed documents in that each page, or slide, comprises one computer screen. By clicking, you can move to the next slide (see Figure 18.2).

The most common programs for creating electronic presentations are Microsoft PowerPoint® and Corel Presentations®. Both help you create a series of slides for presentation on your computer screen or through a projector to a large screen. These programs allow you to include graphics, sound, and other elements. More complex, stand-alone presentations with multimedia animation—designed for distribution on CD-ROM or through the Internet—can be created with programs such as Macromedia Director® and Hyperstudio®.

For small audiences you can usually present the show on a computer screen. For larger audiences, you may need a wide-screen television or a data projector. Check with your instructor or school technology specialist to find out what presentation equipment is available.

As you create your electronic presentation, consider these tips:

- Since each slide can hold only limited information, condense the content of each slide and fill in the details orally.
- Use the slide show to support your oral presentation.
- If appropriate, include graphics from your research project in your slide show.
- End the slide show with a carefully designed closing slide or an empty slide so that people will know the presentation is finished.

If you distribute the slide show by disk or the Web, you will probably need to adjust the presentation by adding more information to the slides because your oral commentary will be unavailable to the viewer—or you can record your own audio commentary for inclusion with the presentation.

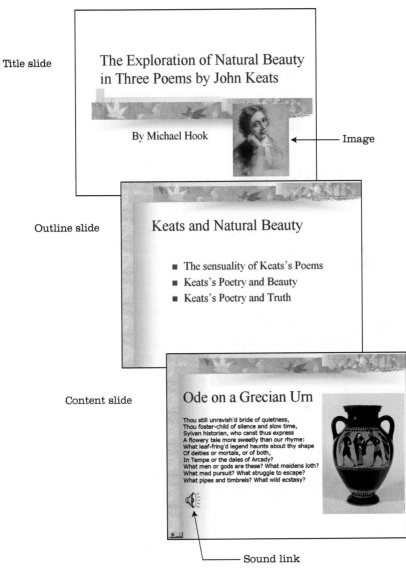

Title slide

Outline slide

Content slide

Sound link

FIGURE 18.2
Research paper slide presentation.

18d   Research Paper Web Pages and Sites

A website can be an exciting and flexible way to convey your research. It's also the easiest way to get your work out to a large audience. Like an electronic presentation, a research paper website can include graphics, sound, and video.

For more information on building web pages and sites, see the NCSA Beginner's Guide to HTML at http://www.ncsa.uiuc.edu/general/internet/www/ htmlprimer.html.

Creating a web page or a website involves collecting or making a series of computer files—some that contain the basic text and layout for your pages, and others that contain the graphics, sounds, or video that goes in your pages. These files are assembled together automatically when you view them in a web browser.

Creating a Single Web Page

If you want to create a single web page from your research paper, the easiest but most limited method is to save your word-processed research paper in HTML (Hyper Text Markup Language, the computer language that controls what websites look like). Different word processing programs perform this process differently, so consult your software's help menu for specific instructions.

When the word processing software converts your document to HTML, it also converts any graphics you've included to separate graphics files. Together, your text and the graphics can be viewed in a web browser like any other web page (see Figure 18.3).

Your research paper will look somewhat different in HTML format than in its word-processed format. In some ways, HTML is less flexible than word processing, but you can still use word processing software to make changes to your new HTML-formatted paper.

NOTE: The reader will need to scroll down the screen to continue to read the document.

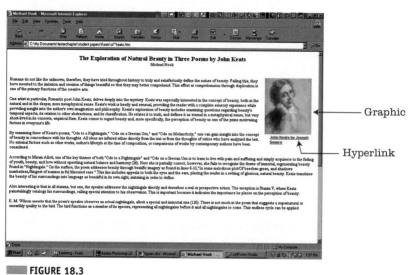

FIGURE 18.3
Single web page research paper.

Creating a Website with Multiple Pages

A multiple-page website allows you to assemble a large number of shorter pages, which are easy for readers to access and read (see Figure 18.4). It requires careful planning and organization.

Research paper home page

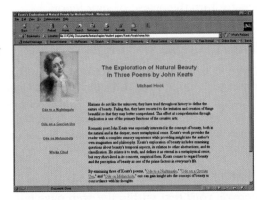

Text page

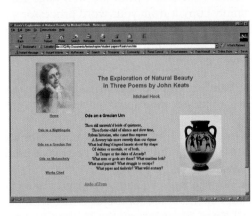

References or works cited page

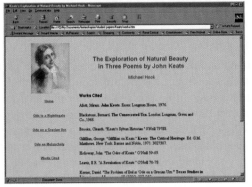

FIGURE 18.4

Three pages from a sample research paper website.

Creating a multipage website means creating one web page after another—you repeat the basic process to create each page, and you add links between the pages so readers can navigate easily from one to the next. Start with a home page that includes a title, a basic description of your project, and an index with hyperlinks to the contents of your site. Navigational elements, such as links to the home page and other major pages of your site, provide a way for readers to "turn the pages" of your report.

Using an Editor to Create Web Pages

The easiest way to create your pages is with a web page editor such as Microsoft FrontPage®, Adobe Page Mill®, or Netscape Composer®. These programs work differently, but they all do the same thing—create web pages. Using them is like using a word processor: you enter or paste in text, insert graphics or other multimedia objects, and save the file to disk.

Importing, Entering, and Modifying Text

You can create your text within the web page editor or outside it. To import text, simply copy it from your word processor and paste it into your web page editor. You can also specify fonts, font sizes, font styles (like bold), alignment, lists with bullets, and numbered lists. Here are a few tips for entering text into a web page:

- **Use bold rather than underlining for emphasis and titles.** On a website, links are underlined, so any other underlining will cause confusion.
- **Do not use tabs.** HTML does not support tabs for indenting the first line of a paragraph. You also won't be able to use hanging indents for your bibliography.
- **Do not double space.** The web page editor automatically single spaces lines of text and double spaces between paragraphs.
- **Make all lines flush left** on the Works Cited page; HTML does not support the hanging indentions.

Citing Your Sources in a Web Research Paper

If you are using MLA, APA, or CBE styles, include parenthetical citations in the text itself and create a separate web page for references. Remember to include such a page in your plans. Do not put footnotes at the bottom of each of your web pages. Instead, use endnotes and create a separate page that holds all the notes, just as you would have a separate page for the Works Cited or References pages. Create each note number in the text as a link to the notes page so readers can click on the number to go to the note. Remember to have a link on the notes page or Works Cited page to take the reader back again to the text.

18e Planning Electronic Research Papers

Because creating an electronic research paper can be more complicated than creating a traditional paper, it's important to plan your project carefully.

Creating a Plan for Your Research Paper

The following questions will help you think through the planning of your project.

- **Assignment.** Does your instructor have specific requirements for this assignment you should keep in mind?
- **Project description.** What topic will you be writing on?
- **Purpose.** What are your reasons for creating an electronic project? Are you going to blend photographs of the 1960s with an essay on the Civil Rights Movement? Or provide audio examples in an essay on John F. Kennedy's speeches?
- **Audience.** Are you writing for the instructor, or will there be a broader audience such as classmates or readers on the Web?
- **Format.** Will your research paper be a word-processed document, an electronic presentation, or a website?
- **Multimedia content.** What information, other than text, will you present? Do you have the tools available to scan or import multimedia?
- **Structure.** How will you organize your document?

Designing Your Electronic Research

Reading any kind of electronic document can be difficult for the reader unless you take special care in designing it. Aim for the following:

- **A consistent look and feel.** Make your research paper look very consistent throughout. Presentation software usually includes ready-made templates that help you to create a consistent look and feel (see Figure 18.2, which uses a ready-made template design for a presentation).
- **A subtle design.** It's easy to create a website or presentation that includes all the bells and whistles—but such documents are hard to navigate and even harder to read. Avoid distractions like blinking text, garish colors, or unnecessary animations (see Figure 18.4 for an example of a subtly designed website).

> For more information on website design, see the Yale CAIM WWW Style Guide at http://info.med.yale.edu/caim/manual/contents.html.

- **Ease of navigation.** Include consistent navigation tools so readers can see where they are and where they can go next (see the navigation links in Figure 18.1).
- **Legibility.** Because readers often access electronic documents through a computer screen, legibility is important. Make the contrast between your text and background colors strong enough that readers can see the text easily. Avoid using italic fonts, which are difficult to see on a computer screen.

18f | Using Graphics in Your Electronic Research Paper

Graphics will give your electronic text some exciting features that are usually foreign to the traditional research paper. They go beyond words on a printed page to pictures, sound, video clips, animation, and a vivid use of full-color art.

 Decorative graphics make the document look more attractive but seldom add to the paper's content. Most clip art, for example, is decorative.

 Illustration graphics provide a visual amplification of the text. For example, a picture of John Keats would reinforce and augment a research paper on the British poet.

 Information graphics, such as charts, graphs, or tables, provide data about your topic.

Graphic File Formats

Graphics are usually files that take up a lot of file space, but you can save them as either JPEGs or GIFs to make them smaller. In fact, websites can use only graphics saved in these formats. Both formats compress redundant information in a file, making it smaller while retaining most of the image quality. You can recognize the file format by looking at the extension to the file name—GIFs have the extension .gif, and JPEGs have the extension .jpg or .jpeg. GIF stands for Graphical Interchange Format, which develops and transfers digital images. JPEG stands for Joint Photographic Experts Group, which compresses color images to smaller files for ease of transport.

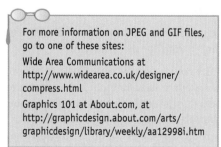

For more information on JPEG and GIF files, go to one of these sites:

Wide Area Communications at http://www.widearea.co.uk/designer/compress.html

Graphics 101 at About.com, at http://graphicdesign.about.com/arts/graphicdesign/library/weekly/aa12998i.htm

In general, JPEGs work best for photographs and GIFs work best for line drawings. To save a file as a GIF or JPEG, open it in an image-editing program like Adobe Photoshop® and save the file as one of the two types (for example, keats.jpg or keats.gif).

For information on securing permission for borrowed material on your website, see Chapter 8, pages 131-32.

When the graphic is ready, you can insert it into your electronic research paper. Programs usually have specific menu commands for inserting graphics; refer to your user documentation to find out how to do so.

You can also borrow images from clip art or other websites (with proper documentation, of course). To borrow an image, go to the site with your web browser, right-click on the image you want, and left-click on "Save image as …" to put it on your hard drive. You can then insert the image into your research paper.

Creating Your Own Digital Graphics

Making your own graphics file is complex but rewarding. It adds a personal creativity to your research paper. Use one of the following techniques:

- **Use a graphics program,** such as Macromedia Freehand® or Adobe Illustrator®. With such software you can create a graphic file and save it as a JPEG or GIF.
- **Use a scanner** to copy your drawings, graphs, photographs, and other matter. Programs such as Adobe Photoshop and JASC Paintshop Pro are useful for modifying scanned photographs.
- **Create original photographs with a digital camera.** Digital cameras usually save images as JPEGs, so you won't need to convert the files into a usable format.

As long as you create JPEG files or GIF files for your graphics, you can transport the entire research paper to a website.

18g Using Sound and Video in Your Electronic Research Paper

Because it usually requires additional hardware and software, working with sound and video can be complicated. It also makes your research paper large and difficult to compress and transfer. Before attempting to use digital audio or video, check into your own resources as well as that of your instructor and school. Many institutions have invested heavily in multimedia technology, while others have not.

A detailed discussion of digital audio and video is beyond the scope of this chapter, but the Web holds a wealth of information on the subject.

For information on digital audio and video, see the following websites.

Builder.com, at http://www.builder.com/graphics

Webmonkey's digital audio tutorial, at http://hotwired.lycos.com/webmonkey/multimedia/audio_mp3/

Webmonkey's digital video tutorial, at http://hotwired.lycos.com/webmonkey/multimedia/video

18h Delivering Your Electronic Research Paper to Readers

Follow your instructor's requirements for delivering your electronic research paper, or use one of the techniques in the following checklist.

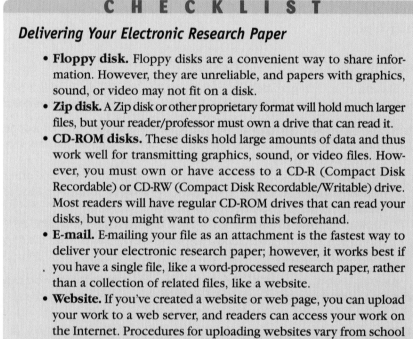

C H E C K L I S T

Delivering Your Electronic Research Paper

- **Floppy disk.** Floppy disks are a convenient way to share information. However, they are unreliable, and papers with graphics, sound, or video may not fit on a disk.
- **Zip disk.** A Zip disk or other proprietary format will hold much larger files, but your reader/professor must own a drive that can read it.
- **CD-ROM disks.** These disks hold large amounts of data and thus work well for transmitting graphics, sound, or video files. However, you must own or have access to a CD-R (Compact Disk Recordable) or CD-RW (Compact Disk Recordable/Writable) drive. Most readers will have regular CD-ROM drives that can read your disks, but you might want to confirm this beforehand.
- **E-mail.** E-mailing your file as an attachment is the fastest way to deliver your electronic research paper; however, it works best if you have a single file, like a word-processed research paper, rather than a collection of related files, like a website.
- **Website.** If you've created a website or web page, you can upload your work to a web server, and readers can access your work on the Internet. Procedures for uploading websites vary from school to school and server to server; work closely with your instructor and Webmaster to perform this process successfully. Regardless of what method you choose, be sure to follow your instructor's directions and requirements.

■ YOUR RESEARCH PROJECT

1. If you are interested in producing an electronic research paper, consult with your instructor for advice and to learn about institutional support.
2. Begin by building a basic model with word processing, one that might include graphics and other elements as described in 18f.
3. If the assignment includes an oral presentation, consider building a slide show as described in 18c.
4. Try building a web page and then a website. Talk with your instructor before uploading it to the Web.
5. Make yourself comfortable about your knowledge of technical terms like floppy disk, Zip disk, CD-ROM, e-mail, and website. (See pages A-18–A-20 of the glossary, Appendix A, for an explanation of common Internet terminology.)

APPENDIX A
Glossary of Manuscript Style

The alphabetical glossary that follows will answer most of your miscellaneous questions about matters of form, such as margins, pagination, dates, and numbers. For matters not addressed below, consult the index, which will direct you to appropriate pages elsewhere in this text.

Abbreviations

Employ abbreviations often and consistently in notes and citations, but avoid them in the text.

> **HINT:** When drafting your text, abbreviate long titles, difficult names, or hard-to-spell terms (e.g., Tess for *Tess of the D'Urbervilles* or T for tourniquet); be certain that you expand the abbreviation with your software's FIND and REPLACE mode before printing the final copy.

In your works-cited entries, but not in your text, always abbreviate these items:

- technical terms (anon., e.g., diss.)
- institutions (acad., assn., Cong.)
- dates (Jan., Feb.)
- states (OH or CA)
- names of publishers (McGraw, UP of Florida).

> See also "Names of Persons," page A-21, for comments on the correct abbreviations of honorary titles.

Abbreviations for Technical Terms and Institutions

abr.	abridged
AD	*anno Domini,* "in the year of the Lord"; precedes numerals with no space between letters, as in "AD 350"
anon.	anonymous
art., arts.	article(s)
assn.	association
assoc.	associate, associated

BC	"before Christ"; follows numerals; no space between letters, as in "500 BC"
bk., bks.	book(s)
ca., c.	*circa,* "about"; used to indicate an approximate date, as in "ca. 1812"
cf.	*confer,* "compare" (one source with another); not, however, to be used in place of "see" or "see also"
ch., chs., **chap., chaps.**	chapter(s)
col., cols.	column(s)
comp.	compiled by or compiler
diss.	dissertation
doc.	document
ed., eds.	editor(s), edition, or edited by
e.g.	*exempli gratia,* "for example"; preceded and followed by a comma
enl.	enlarged, as in "enl. ed."
esp.	especially, as in "312–15, esp. 313"
et al.	*et alii,* "and others"; "John Smith et al." means John Smith and other authors
etc.	*et cetera,* "and so forth"
et pas.	*et passim,* "and here and there" (see "passim")
et seq.	*et sequens,* "and the following"; "9 et seq." means page nine and the following page; compare "f." and "ff."
f., ff.	page or pages following a given page; "8f." means page eight and the following page; but exact references are sometimes preferable, for example, "45–51, 55, 58" instead of "45ff." Acceptable also is "45+."
fig.	figure
fl.	*floruit,* "flourished"; which means a person reached greatness on these dates, as in "fl. 1420–50"; used when birth and death dates are unknown.
ibid.	*ibidem,* "in the same place," i.e., in the immediately preceding title; see 16d.
i.e.	*id est,* "that is"; preceded and followed by a comma
illus.	illustrated by, illustrations, or illustrator
infra	"below"; refers to a succeeding portion of the text; compare "supra." Generally, it is best to write "see below"
intro., introd.	introduction, introduced by
loc. cit.	*loco citato,* "in the place (passage) cited"
ms., mss.	manuscript(s), as in "Cf. the mss. of Glass and Ford"
n., nn.	note(s), as "23, n. 2" or "51 n."
narr.	narrated by
n.d.	no date (of publication)
no., nos.	number(s)
n.p.	no place (of publication), or no publisher
ns	new series
op. cit.	*opere citato,* "in the work cited"
p., pp.	page(s); do not use "ps." for "pages"
passim	"here and there throughout the work," e.g., "67, 72, et passim," but also acceptable is "67+"
proc.	proceedings

pseud.	pseudonym
pt., pts.	part(s)
rev.	revised, revised by, revision, review, or reviewed by
rpt.	reprint, reprinted
sec(s).	section(s)
ser.	series
sess.	session
sic	"thus"; placed in brackets to indicate an error has been made in the quoted passage and the writer is quoting accurately; see example on page 178.
St., Sts.	Saint(s)
st., sts.	stanza(s)
sup.	*supra,* "above"; used to refer to a preceding portion of the text; it is just as easy to write "above" or "see above"
suppl.	supplement(s)
s.v.	*sub voce, sub verbo,* "under the word or heading"
trans., tr.	translator, translated, translated by, or translation
ts., tss.	typescript, typescripts
viz.	*videlicet,* "namely"
vol., vols.	volume(s) (e.g., "vol. 3")
vs., v.	versus, "against"; used in citing legal cases

Abbreviations for Days and Months

Sun.	Jan.	July
Mon.	Feb.	Aug.
Tues.	Mar.	Sept.
Wed.	Apr.	Oct.
Thurs.	May	Nov.
Fri.	June	Dec.
Sat.		

Abbreviations for States and Geographical Names

AL	Alabama	IN	Indiana
AK	Alaska	IA	Iowa
AZ	Arizona	KS	Kansas
AR	Arkansas	KY	Kentucky
CA	California	LA	Louisiana
CO	Colorado	ME	Maine
CT	Connecticut	MD	Maryland
DE	Delaware	MA	Massachusetts
DC	District of Columbia	MI	Michigan
FL	Florida	MN	Minnesota
GA	Georgia	MS	Mississippi
GU	Guam	MO	Missouri
HI	Hawaii	MT	Montana
ID	Idaho	NE	Nebraska
IL	Illinois	NV	Nevada

NH	New Hampshire		SC	South Carolina
NJ	New Jersey		SD	South Dakota
NM	New Mexico		TN	Tennessee
NY	New York		TX	Texas
NC	North Carolina		UT	Utah
ND	North Dakota		VT	Vermont
OH	Ohio		VI	Virgin Islands
OK	Oklahoma		VA	Virginia
OR	Oregon		WA	Washington
PA	Pennsylvania		WV	West Virginia
PR	Puerto Rico		WI	Wisconsin
RI	Rhode Island		WY	Wyoming

Abbreviation of Publishers' Names

Use the shortened forms below as guidelines. Some of these publishers no longer exist, but their imprints remain on copyright pages of the books.

Abrams	Harry N. Abrams, Inc.
Addison	Addison, Wesley, Longman
ALA	American Library Association
Allen	George Allen and Unwin Publishers, Inc.
Allyn	Allyn and Bacon, Inc.
Barnes	Barnes and Noble Books
Basic	Basic Books
Beacon	Beacon Press, Inc.
Bobbs	The Bobbs-Merrill Co., Inc.
Bowker	R. R. Bowker Co.
Cambridge UP	Cambridge University Press
Clarendon	Clarendon Press
Columbia UP	Columbia University Press
Dell	Dell Publishing Co., Inc.
Dodd	Dodd, Mead, and Co.
Doubleday	Doubleday and Co., Inc.
Farrar	Farrar, Straus, and Giroux, Inc.
Free	The Free Press
Gale	Gale Research Co.
GPO	Government Printing Office
Harcourt	Harcourt Brace Jovanovich, Inc.
Harper	Harper and Row Publishers, Inc.
HarperCollins	HarperCollins Publishers, Inc.
Harvard UP	Harvard UP
Heath	D. C. Heath and Co.
Holt	Holt, Rinehart, and Winston, Inc.
Houghton	Houghton Mifflin Co.
Indiana UP	Indiana University Press
Knopf	Alfred A. Knopf, Inc.
Lippincott	J. B. Lippincott Co.
Little	Little, Brown, and Co.
Longman	Addison, Wesley, Longman
Macmillan	Macmillan Publishing Co., Inc.
McGraw	McGraw-Hill, Inc.

MIT P	The MIT Press
MLA	Modern Language Association
Norton	W. W. Norton and Co., Inc.
Oxford UP	Oxford University Press
Prentice	Prentice-Hall, Inc.
Putnam's	G. P. Putnam's Sons
Random	Random House, Inc.
St. Martin's	St. Martin's Press, Inc.
Scott	Scott, Foresman and Co.
Scribner's	Charles Scribner's Sons
Simon	Simon and Schuster, Inc.
State U of New York P	State University of New York Press
U of Chicago P	University of Chicago Press
UP of Florida	University Press of Florida
WashingtonSquare P	Washington Square Press

Abbreviation of Biblical Works

Use parenthetical documentation for biblical references in the text—that is, place the entry within parentheses immediately after the quotation, for example:

> After the great flood God spoke to Noah: "And I will establish my
> covenant with you; neither shall all flesh be cut off any more by the waters
> of a flood; neither shall there any more be a flood to destroy the
> earth" (Gen. 9.11).

Do not italicize or underline titles of books of the Bible. Abbreviate books of the Bible, except some very short titles such as Ezra and Mark.

Acts	Acts of the Apostles	Lev.	Leviticus
1 and 2 Chron.	1 and 2 Chronicles	Mal.	Malachi
Col.	Colossians	Matt.	Matthew
1 and 2 Cor.	1 and 2 Corinthians	Mic.	Micah
Dan.	Daniel	Nah.	Nahum
Deut.	Deuteronomy	Neh.	Nehemiah
Eccles.	Ecclesiastes	Num.	Numbers
Eph.	Ephesians	Obad.	Obadiah
Exod.	Exodus	1 and 2 Pet.	1 and 2 Peter
Ezek.	Ezekiel	Phil.	Philippians
Gal.	Galatians	Prov.	Proverbs
Gen.	Genesis	Ps. (Pss.)	Psalm(s)
Hab.	Habakkuk	Rev.	Revelation
Hag.	Haggai	Rom.	Romans
Heb.	Hebrews	1 and 2 Sam.	1 and 2 Samuel
Hos.	Hosea	Song of Sol.	Song of Solomon
Isa.	Isaiah	1 and 2 Thess.	1 and 2 Thessalonians
Jer.	Jeremiah	1 and 2 Tim.	1 and 2 Timothy
Josh.	Joshua	Zech.	Zechariah
Judg.	Judges	Zeph.	Zephaniah
Lam.	Lamentations		

Abbreviations for Literary Works
Shakespeare

In parenthetical documentation, use italicized or underscored abbreviations for titles of Shake-spearean plays, as shown in this example:

> Too late, Capulet urges Montague to end their feud, "O brother Montague, give me thy hand" (*Rom.* 5.3.296).

Here is a complete list of abbreviations for Shakespeare's plays:

Ado	Much Ado About Nothing	Mac.	Macbeth
Ant.	Antony and Cleopatra	MM	Measure for Measure
AWW	All's Well That Ends Well	MND	A Midsummer Night's Dream
AYL	As You Like It	MV	Merchant of Venice
Cor.	Coriolanus	Oth.	Othello
Cym.	Cymbeline	Per.	Pericles
Err.	The Comedy of Errors	R2	Richard II
Ham.	Hamlet	R3	Richard III
1H4	Henry IV, Part 1	Rom.	Romeo and Juliet
2H4	Henry IV, Part 2	Shr.	The Taming of the Shrew
H5	Henry V	TGV	Two Gentlemen of Verona
1H6	Henry VI, Part 1	Tim.	Timon of Athens
2H6	Henry VI, Part 2	Tit.	Titus Andronicus
3H6	Henry VI, Part 3	Tmp.	Tempest
H8	Henry VIII	TN	Twelfth Night
JC	Julius Caesar	TNK	The Two Noble Kinsmen
Jn.	King John	Tro.	Troilus and Cressida
LLL	Love's Labour's Lost	Wiv.	The Merry Wives of Windsor
Lr.	Lear	WT	Winter's Tale

Use italics or underscoring for these abbreviations of Shakespeare's poems:

Luc.	The Rape of Lucrece
PhT	The Phoenix and the Turtle
PP	The Passionate Pilgrim
Son.	Sonnets (but "Sonnet 14")
Ven.	Venus and Adonis

Chaucer

Use the following abbreviations in parenthetical documentation. Italicize the book but not the individual tales:

CkT	The Cook's Tale	NPT	The Nun's Priest's Tale
ClT	The Clerk's Tale	PardT	The Pardoner's Tale
CT	The Canterbury Tales	ParsT	The Parson's Tale
CYT	The Canon's Yeoman's Tale	PhyT	The Physician's Tale
FranT	The Franklin's Tale	PrT	The Prioress's Tale
FrT	The Friar's Tale	Ret	Chaucer's Retraction
GP	The General Prologue	RvT	The Reeve's Tale
KnT	The Knight's Tale	ShT	The Shipman's Tale
ManT	The Manciple's Tale	SNT	The Second Nun's Tale
Mel	The Tale of Melibee	SqT	The Squire's Tale
MerT	The Merchant's Tale	SumT	The Summoner's Tale
MilT	The Miller's Tale	Th	The Tale of Sir Thopas
MkT	The Monk's Tale	WBT	The Wife of Bath's Tale
MLT	The Man of Law's Tale		

Other Literary Works

Wherever possible in your in-text citations, use the initial letters of the title. A reference to page 18 of Melville's *Moby Dick: The White Whale* could appear as: (*MD* 18). Use the following italicized abbreviations as guidelines:

Aen.	*Aeneid* by Vergil	*Il.*	*Iliad* by Homer
Ag.	*Agamemnon* by Aeschylus	*Inf.*	*Inferno* by Dante
Ant.	*Antigone* by Sophocles	*MD*	*Moby Dick* by Melville
Bac.	*Bacchae* by Euripides	*Med.*	*Medea* by Euripides
Beo.	*Beowulf*	*Nib.*	*Nibelungenlied*
Can.	*Candide* by Voltaire	*Od.*	*Odyssey* by Homer
Dec.	*Decameron* by Boccaccio	*OR*	*Oedipus Rex* by Sophocles
DJ	*Don Juan* by Byron	*PL*	*Paradise Lost* by Milton
DQ	*Don Quixote* by Cervantes	*SA*	*Samson Agonistes* by Milton
Eum.	*Eumenides* by Aeschylus	*SGGK*	*Sir Gawain and the*
FQ	*Faerie Queene* by Spenser		*Green Knight*
Gil.	*Gilgamesh*	*SL*	*Scarlet Letter* by Hawthorne
GT	*Gulliver's Travels* by Swift		

Abbreviation of Scientific Words

A	ampere	mA	milliampere
Å	angstrom	mEq	milliequivalent
AC	alternating current	meV	million electron volts
a.m.	ante meridiem	mg	milligram
°C	degree Celsius	min	minute
Ci	curie	ml	milliliter
cm	centimeter	mm	millimeter
cps	cycles per second	mM	millimolar
dB	decibel (specify scale)	mmHg	millimeters of mercury
DC	direct current	mmol	millimole
deg/s	degrees per second	mol wt	molecular weight
dl	deciliter	mph	miles per hour (convert
°F	degree Fahrenheit		to metric)
g	gram	ms	millisecond
g	gravity	MΩ	megohm
hr	hour	N	newton
Hz	hertz	ns	nanosecond
in.	inch	p.m.	post meridiem
IQ	intelligence quotient	ppm	parts per million
IU	international unit	psi	pound per square inch
kg	kilogram		(convert to metric)
km	kilometer	rpm	revolutions per minute
kph	kilometers per hour	s	second
kW	kilowatt	S	siemens
L	liter	V	volt
m	meter	W	watt

Accent Marks

When you quote, reproduce accents exactly as they appear in the original. You may need to use the character sets embedded within the computer software (see "Character Sets," page A-12). Add the marks with a pen if your typewriter or word processor does not support them.

"La tradición clásica en españa," according to Romana, remains strong and vibrant in public school instruction (16).

Acknowledgments

Generally, acknowledgments are unnecessary. Nor is a preface required. Use a superscript reference numeral to your first sentence and then place any obligatory acknowledgments or explanations in a content endnote (see also page 316–19):

> 1. I wish here to express my thanks to Mrs. Horace A. Humphrey for
> permission to examine the manuscripts of her late husband.

NOTE: Acknowledge neither your instructor nor typist for help with your research paper, though such acknowledgments are standard with graduate theses and dissertations.

Ampersand

MLA style: Avoid using the ampersand symbol (&) unless custom demands it (e.g., "A & P"). Use *and* for in-text citations in MLA style (e.g., Smith and Jones 213–14).

APA style: *Do use* "&" within APA citations (e.g., Spenser & Wilson, 1994, p. 73) but not within the text (Spenser and Wilson found the results in error.)

Annotated Bibliography

An annotation describes the essential details of a book or article. Place it just after the facts of publication. Follow these suggestions:

1. Explain the main purpose of the work.
2. Briefly describe the contents.
3. Indicate the possible audience for the work.
4. Note any special features.
5. Warn of any defect, weakness, or suspected bias.

Provide enough information in about three sentences for a reader to have a fairly clear image of the work's purpose, contents, and special value. Turn to section 7e, pages 119–20, to see a complete annotated bibliography.

Arabic Numerals

The scholarly associations require Arabic numerals whenever possible: for volumes, books, parts, and chapters of works; acts, scenes, and lines of plays; cantos, stanzas, and lines of poetry.

Use Arabic figures to express all numbers 10 and above (such as 154, 1,269, the 15th test, the remaining 12%). Write as Arabic numerals any numbers below 10 that cannot be spelled out in one or two words (e.g., 3 $^1/_4$ or 6.234).

For inclusive numbers that indicate a range, give the second number in full for numbers through 99 (e.g. 3–5, 15–21, 70–96). In MLA and CMS styles, with three digits or more give only the last two in the second number, unless more digits are needed for clarity (e.g. 98–101, 110–12, 989–1001, 1030–33, 2766–854). In APA and CBE styles, with three digits or more give all numbers (e.g., 110–112, 1030–1033, 2766–2854).

Place commas between the third and fourth digits from the right, the sixth, and so on (e.g., 1,200 or 1,200,000). Exceptions are page and line numbers, addresses, the year, and zip codes (e.g., page 1620, at 12116 Nova Road, in 1985, or New York, NY 10012).

Use the number *1* in every case for numbers, not the lowercase *l* or uppercase *I*, especially if you are typing on a word processor or computer.

Numbers Expressed as Figures in Your Text

Use figures in your text according to the following examples:

- All numbers 10 and above:

  the subjects who were 25 years (*but* a twenty-five-year-old woman)
  the collection of 48 illustrations

- Numbers that represent ages, dates, time, size, score, amounts of money, and numerals used as numerals:

> ages 6 through 14
> AD 200 *but* 200 BC
> in 1991–92 *or* from 1991 to 1992, *but not* from 1991–92
> 32–34 *or* pages 32–34 *but not* pp. 32–34
> lines 32–34 *but not* ll. 32–34
> page 45, *but not* the forty-fifth page
> March 5, 1991, *or* 5 March 1991, *but not* both styles
> 1990s *or* the nineties
> six o'clock or 6:00 p.m.
> 6% *but* use "six percent" in discussions with few numbers
> 7 pounds
> $9.00 or $9
> 4 feet
> scores in the 92–96 percentile
> from 1965 through 1970

- Statistical and mathematical numbers:

> 6.213
> 0.5 *but not* .5
> consumed exactly 0.45 of the fuel

- Numbers that precede units of measurement:

> a 5-milligram tablet
> use 7 centimeter of this fluid

- Numbers below 10 grouped with higher numbers:

> 3 out of 42 subjects
> tests 6 and 13
> *but* 15 tests in three categories (Tests and categories are different groups; they are not being compared.)

Numbers Expressed in Words in Your Text

Spell out numbers in the following instances:

- Numbers less than 10 that are not used as measurements:

> three students
> he is one who should know
> a group of six professors
> six proposals
> three-dimensional renderings

- Numbers less than 10 that are grouped with other numbers below 10:

> five sessions with six examinations in each session
> the fifth of eight participants

- Common fractions:

> one fifth of the student population
> eighty-eight errors
> thirty-four times
> a one-third majority

- Any number that begins a sentence:

> Thirty participants elected to withdraw.

- The numbers *zero* and *one* when used alone:

  zero-base budget planning
  a one-line paragraph
  one response *but* 1 of 15 responses

- References to centuries:

  twentieth century
  twentieth-century literature

Numbers as Both Words and Figures

Combine words and figures in these situations:

- Back to back modifiers:

  twelve 6-year-olds or 12 six-year-olds, *but not* 12 6-year olds

- Large numbers:

  an operating budget of 4 million

Numbers in Documentation

Use numbers with in-text citations and Works Cited entries according to the following examples:

(<u>Ham</u>. 5.3.16–18)
(<u>Faust</u> 2.140)
(2 Sam. 2.1–8)
(Fredericks 23–24) (MLA style)
(Fredericks, 1995, pp. 23–24) (APA and CBE style)
2 vols.
Rpt. as vols. 13 and 14
MS CCCC 210
102nd Cong., 1st sess. S. 2411
16 mm., 29 min., color
Monograph 1962-M2
College English 15 (Winter 1995): 3–6 (MLA style)
Memory and Cognition, 3, 562–590 (APA style)
J. Mol. Biol. 1995;149:15–39 (CBE style)
Journal of Philosophy 29 (1995): 172–89 (footnote style)

Asterisks

Do not use asterisks (*) for tables, content notes, or illustrations (see page A-15). Use numbers for tables and figures (e.g., Table 2 or Figure 3) and use letters for content notes (see 16f, pages 316–19).

Bible

Use parenthetical documentation for biblical references in the text (e.g., 2 Chron. 18.13). Do not underline the titles of books of the Bible. For abbreviations, see page A-5.

Borders

Computers offer you the opportunity for building borders around pages, paragraphs, and graphic designs. Use this feature with restraint. Place the title page within a full page border if you like, but *not* pages of your text. Use a border with a fill pattern, if desired, for graphs, charts, highlighted text, and other material that deserves special emphasis.

Bullets and Numbers for Lists

Computers supply several bullet and number formats (circle, square, diamond, triangle, number, letter) for lists:

- Observation 1: Kindergarten class
- Observation 2: First grade class
- Observation 3: Second grade class

Capitalization

Capitalize Some Titles

For books, journals, magazines, and newspapers in MLA and CMS styles, capitalize the first word, the last word, and all principal words, including words that follow hyphens in compound terms (e.g., French-Speaking Islands). Do not capitalize articles, prepositions that introduce phrases, conjunctions, and the *to* in infinitives when these words occur in the middle of the title (e.g., *The Last of the Mohicans*). For titles of articles and parts of books, capitalize as for books (e.g., "Writing the Final Draft" or "Appendix 2"). If the first line of the poem serves as the title, reproduce it exactly as it appears in print (anyone lived in a pretty how town).

NOTE: APA and CBE styles capitalize only the first word and proper names of reference titles (including the first word of subtitles). Study the appropriate style for your field as found in Chapters 14–17.

Capitalize after a Colon

When a *complete* sentence follows a colon, MLA style skips one space and does *not* capitalize the first word; APA style also skips one space but *does* capitalize the first word after the colon.

MLA style:

The consequences of this decision will be disastrous: each division of the corporation will be required to cut twenty percent of its budget within this fiscal year.

APA style:

They have agreed on the outcome: Informed subjects perform better than do uninformed subjects.

Capitalize Some Compound Words

Capitalize the second part of a hyphenated compound word only when it is used in a heading with other capitalized words:

Low-Frequency Sound Equipment

but

Low-frequency sound distortion is caused by several factors.

Capitalize Trade Names

Use capitals for trade names, such as: Pepsi, Plexiglass, Dupont, Tommy, Corvette, Xerox

Capitalize Proper Names

Capitalize proper names used as adjectives *but not* the words used with them.

Einstein's theory   Salk's vaccine

Capitalize Specific Departments or Courses

Capitalize the specific names of departments or courses, but use lowercase when they are used in a general sense.

> Department of Psychology *but* the psychology department
>
> Psychology 314 *but* an advanced course in psychology

Capitalize Nouns Used before Numerals or Letters

Capitalize the noun when it denotes a specific place in a numbered series.

> during Test 6   we observed Group C
>
> as shown in Table 5   see Figure 2

However, do *not* capitalize nouns that name common parts of books or tables followed by numerals.

> chapter 12   page ix   column 14

Character Sets

Most computers provide characters that are unavailable on your keyboard. These are special letters, signs, and symbols, such as ®, Σ, â, and ⟶ The software instructions will help you find and utilize these marks and icons.

Clip Art

Pictures, figures, and drawings are available on many computers, but avoid the temptation to embed them in your document. Clip art, in general, conveys an informal, sometimes comic effect, one that is inappropriate to the serious nature of most research papers.

Copyright Law

"Fair use" of the materials of others is permitted without the need for specific permission as long as your purpose is noncommercial, for criticism, scholarship, or research. Under those circumstances, you can quote from sources and reproduce artistic works within reasonable limits. The law is vague on specific amounts that can be borrowed, suggesting only the "substantiality of the portion used in relation to the copyrighted work as a whole." In other words, you should be safe in reproducing the work of another as long as the portion is not substantial.

To protect your own work, keyboard in the upper right corner of your manuscript, "Copyright ©_____ by _____." Fill the blanks with the year and your name. Then, to register a work, order a form from the U.S. Copyright Office, Library of Congress, Washington, D.C. 20559.

Corrections

Because the computer can produce a printed copy quickly, you should make all proofreading corrections before printing a finished manuscript. With a typed paper, however, you may make corrections neatly using correction fluid, correction paper, or tape to cover and type over any errors. Add words or short phrases directly above a line, not in the margins. Keep such corrections to a minimum; retype pages that require four or more corrections. Do not strike over a letter, paste inserts onto the page, write vertically in the margins, or make handwritten notes on the manuscript pages.

Covers and Binders

Most instructors prefer that you submit manuscript pages with one staple in the upper left corner. Unless required, do not use a cover or binder.

Dates

See Arabic Numerals, pages A-8–A-10.

Definitions

For definitions and translations within your text, use single quotation marks without intervening punctuation, for example:

The use of <u>et alii</u> ("and others") has diminished in scholarly writing.

Endnotes for Documentation of Sources

An instructor or supervisor may prefer traditional superscript numerals within the text and documentation notes at the end of paper. If so, see Chapter 16, pages 311-12 and 316.

Etc. (*et cetera*)

Avoid using this term, which means "and so forth," by completing the list or by writing "such as," "for example," or "including" before the list to indicate a partial list. ("Several colors are being tested, including yellow, rust, and burnt orange.")

Figures and Tables

A table is a systematic presentation of materials, usually in columns. A figure is any nontext item that is not a table: e.g., a blueprint, chart, diagram, drawing, graph, photo, photostat, map, and so on. Use graphs appropriately. A line graph serves a different purpose than a circle (pie) chart, and a bar graph plots different information than a scatter graph. Figure A.1 shows a sample of a figure.

Tables are a systematic presentation of materials, usually in columns. A table is shown in Figure A.2.

Your figures and tables should conform to the following guidelines:

- Present only one kind of information in each figure or table, and make it as simple and as brief as possible. Frills and fancy artwork may distract the reader.

- Place small figures and tables within your text; place large figures, sets of figures, or complex tables on separate pages in an appendix (see pages 218-19).

- Place the figure or table as near to your textual discussion as possible, but it should not precede your first mention of it.

- In the text, explain the significance of the figure or table. Describe the figure or table so that your reader may understand your observations without reference to the figure or table, but avoid giving too many numbers and figures in your text. Refer to figures and tables

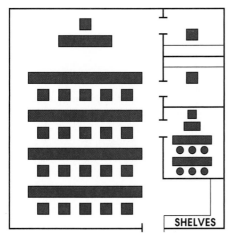

▨**FIGURE A.1**
Sample illustration in a paper.

Figure 4: Audio Laboratory with Private
Listening Rooms and a Small Group Room

SHELVES

Table 1

Response by Class on Nuclear Energy Policy

	Freshmen	Sophomores	Juniors	Seniors
1. More nuclear power	150	301	75	120
2. Less nuclear power	195	137	111	203
3. Present policy is acceptable	87	104	229	37

FIGURE A.2
Sample table in a paper.

by number ("Figure 5") or by number and page reference ("Table 4, 16"). Do not use vague references (such as "the table above," "the following illustration," or "the chart below").

- Write a caption for the figure or table so that your reader can understand it without reference to your discussion. Place the caption *above* a table but *below* a figure, flush left, in full capital letters or in capitals and lowercase, but do not mix forms in the same paper. An alternative is to place the caption on the same line with the number (see Figure A.4.)

- Number figures consecutively throughout the paper with Arabic numbers, preceded by "Fig." or "Figure." (e.g., "Figure 4"). Place the figure number and the caption *below* the figure, as shown in Figures A.3 and A.4.

- Number tables consecutively throughout the paper with Arabic numerals, preceded by "Table" (e.g., "Table 2"). Place the number designation flush left, one double space *above* the table.

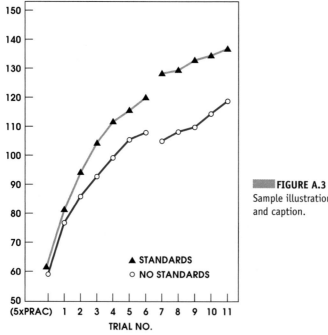

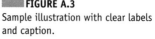
FIGURE A.3
Sample illustration with clear labels and caption.

Figure 6: Mean Number of Matches by Subject with and without Standard (by Trial). Source: Lock and Bryan (289).

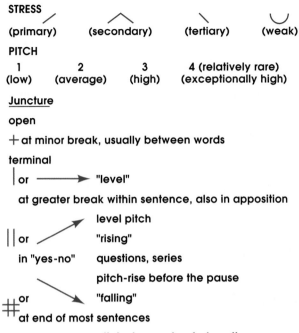

STRESS

/ (primary)   ∧ (secondary)   \ (tertiary)   ∪ (weak)

PITCH

1   2   3   4 (relatively rare)
(low)   (average)   (high)   (exceptionally high)

<u>Juncture</u>

open

+ at minor break, usually between words

terminal

| or ⟶ "level"

at greater break within sentence, also in apposition

‖ or ↗ level pitch
"rising"

in "yes-no"   questions, series

pitch-rise before the pause

or ↘ "falling"

at end of most sentences

pitch-drop, voice fades off

Figure 9: Phonemes of English. Generally this figure follows the Trager-Smith system, used widely in American linguistics. Source: Anna H. Live (1066).

FIGURE A.4
Sample illustration with explanatory caption.

- Insert a caption or number for each column of a table, centered above the column or, if necessary, inserted diagonally or vertically above it.

- When inserting an explanatory or reference note, place it below the table or figure; then use a lowercase letter as the identifying superscript, not an Arabic numeral (see Figures A.5 and A.6).

- Sources are abbreviated as in-text citations, and full documentation must appear in the Works Cited list.

Table 2[a]

Mean Sources of Six Values Held by College Students According to Sex

All Students		Men		Women	
Pol.	40.61	Pol.	43.22	Aesth.	43.86
Rel.	40.51	Theor.	43.09	Rel.	43.13
Aesth.	40.29	Econ.	42.05	Soc.	41.62
Econ.	39.45	Soc.	37.05	Econ.	36.85
Soc.	39.34	Aesth.	36.72	Theor.	36.50

[a]Carmen J. Finley, et al. (165).

FIGURE A.5
Sample table with in-text citation of source.

Table 3

Inhibitory Effects of Sugars on the Growth of Clostribium Histoylticum (11 Strains) on Nutrient Agar

Sugar added 2%	Aerobic incubation (hr)		Anaerobic incubation (hr)	
	24	48	24	48
None	11[a]	11	11	11
Glucose	0	0	11	11
Maltose	0	0	11	11
Lactose	1	1	11	11
Sucrose	3	6	11	11
Arabinose	0	0	0	0
Insotil	0	0	11	11
Xylose	0	0	0	0
Sorbitor	2	7	11	11
Manitol	9	10	11	11
Rhamnose	0	0	11	11

Source: Nishida and Imaizumi (481).

[a]No. of strains that gave rise to colonies in the presence of the sugar.

FIGURE A.6

Sample table with in-text citation and notes.

Footnotes for Documentation

If your instructor requires you to use footnotes, see Chapter 16, pages 310-15, for discussion and examples.

Fonts

Most computers offer a variety of typefaces. Courier (Courier), the typewriter font, is always a safe choice, but you may use others, such as a nonserif typeface like Ariel (**Ariel**) or a serif typeface like Times Roman (**Times Roman**). Use the same font consistently throughout for your text, but shift to different fonts if desired for tables, illustrations, and other matter.

Foreign Cities

In general, spell the names of foreign cities as they are written in original sources. However, for purposes of clarity, you may substitute the English version of the name, or provide both versions with one in parentheses.

Köln (Cologne)   Braunschweig (Brunswick)

München (Munich)   Praha (Prague)

Foreign Languages

Underscore or italicize foreign words used in an English text:

> Like his friend Olaf, he is aut Caesar, aut nihil, either overpowering perfection or ruin and destruction.

Do not underscore or italicize quotations of a foreign language:

> Obviously, he uses it to exploit, in the words of Jean Laumon, "une admirable mine de themes poetiques."

Do not underscore or italicize titles of foreign magazine or journal articles, but do underline the names of the magazines or journals:

> Arrigoitia, Luis de. "Machismo, folklore y creación en Mario Vargas Llosa." Sin nombre 13.4 (1983): 19–25.

Do not underscore or italicize foreign words of places, institutions, proper names, or titles that precede proper names:

> Racine became extremely fond of Mlle Champmeslé, who interpreted his works at the Hotel de Bourgogne.

For titles of French, Italian, and Spanish works, capitalize the first word, the proper nouns, but not adjectives derived from proper nouns:

> La noche de Tlatelolco: Testimoniosde historia oral

and

> Realismo y realidad en la narrativa argentina

Titles of German works: capitalize the first word, all nouns, and all adjectives derived from names of persons:

> Über die Religion: Reden an die Gebildeten unter ihren Verächtern

Graphics

If they will contribute in a demonstrable way to your research study, you may create graphic designs and import them into your document. Computer software offers various methods for performing this task. See "Figures and Tables," pages A-13–A-16, for basic rules; see also the paper by Katie Hebert, pages 210-23, for examples.

Headers and Footers

The software of your computer will automatically insert your name and the page number at the top, right margin of each page for MLA style (see pages 204–09 for examples). Use a "numbering" or a "header" command to set an automatic numbering sequence. For APA style you will need a shortened title and page number (see page 300 for an example). Footers are seldom used.

Headings

Begin every major heading on a new page of your paper (title page, opening page, notes, appendix, works cited or references). Center the heading in capital and lowercase letters one inch from the top of the sheet. Use a double space between the heading and your first line of text. (APA style also requires double spaces between headings and text.) Number *all* text pages, including those with major headings. (See also "Spacing," page A-27.) Most papers will need only major headings (A-level), but the advent of desktop publishing makes it possible for some research papers to gain the look of professional typesetting. Use the following guidelines for writing subheads in your paper.

Writing a Research Paper	←	**A heading,** centered
Writing the First Draft	←	**B heading,** flush left with capital letters on each major word
Revising and editing the manuscript	←	**C heading,** flush left with only the first word capitalized
Proofreading. Every researcher…	←	**D heading,** run-in head, underscored or italicized, that begins a paragraph

Hypertext Link

See Internet Terminology, below.

Hyphenation

Do not hyphenate words at the end of lines. If necessary, turn off your computer's automatic hyphenation command. See also "Punctuation," pages A-24–A-25.

Indention

Indent paragraphs 5 spaces or a half inch. Indent long quotations (4 lines or more) 10 spaces or one inch from the left margin. If you quote only one paragraph, do not indent the first line more than the rest. However, if you quote two or more paragraphs, indent the first line of each paragraph an extra three spaces or a quarter inch (see also page 171). Indent entries of the works cited five spaces on the second and succeeding lines. Indent the first line of content foot-notes five spaces. Other styles (APA or CBE) have different requirements (see Chapter 6, pages 287–95 and Chapter 17, pages 338–40).

Internet Terminology

The following terms are fairly standard in matters of the Internet.

address The route or path for access. The World Wide Web address includes a domain name, a directory, and a file name (see pages 54-57). An e-mail address consists of a log-in name and a domain name.

application A computer program that per-forms a function within an *operating system.* That is, a word processing program like *Wordperfect* is an application. *Windows* is the operating system.

ASCII American Standard Code for Informa-tion Interchange, which is a common way to exchange data. It changes *Word* or *Wordper-fect* into a standard text.

asynchronous Messages do not depend on timing; it is common to e-mail. (see also syn-chronous)

bandwidth The width of Internet cables determines transmission of data. Regular phone lines and a modem limit the band-width, usually measured in *bits*. The goal is for a big bandwidth with fiber-optic high-speed data transmission.

bit Binary digit, which is the smallest unit of digital or computerized data.

bookmark A way of marking your favorite Internet sites for easy recall.

Boolean operators *And, or,* and *not* are the most popular terms for limiting and defining a search (see pages 63-65 for more detail).

browser A software program, like *Netscape Navigator* and *Microsoft Internet Explorer,* that allows you to explore the Internet.

byte A set of *bits,* usually eight *bits,* to rep-resent a single character, like a letter or a mark of punctuation.

CD-ROM A compact disk for storing data in read-only memory (see also RAM).

chat room An Internet site where multiple users communicate with each other in real time by using the keyboard or, increasingly, by audio and video.

database Information stored in categories that can be sorted and retrieved in various ways.

domain name The name assigned to a specific site, such as *www.bn.com* (which is the domain name for Barnes and Noble books).

download The method for copying or moving a file from a host to your local computer.

ethernet A universal connector by which computers on a network can be connected to the Internet.

FAQ Frequently asked questions with answers on a Internet site to prevent repeated questions on the same subject.

flame Angry e-mail messages that make a verbal assault on another person; also an angry debate by users.

FTP File transfer protocol that permits the transfer of files (see pages 70-71).

GIF Graphical Interchange Format, which develops and transfers digital images.

Gopher A menu-based software that interacts with other computers or organizations for accessing files on the Internet. It was popular prior to the World Wide Web.

hit A request by a client to a server to send a file. Thus, servers claim, "We received 72,000 hits at this site in January."

home page The starting point (first page) of a series of linked documents at a website.

HTML Hypertext Markup Language, which is a system of tags in Web files to provide formatting instructions.

HTTP Hyper Text Transfer Protocol serves to transfer hypertext files between remote computers via the Internet with the help of the browser software.

hypertext A document that contains links to other documents by using the tag provided by http; simply a signal, a "hot key" within a text that links a keyword or phrase to another document. You will need such links on your Internet site.

Internet An international network that connects millions of computers via dedicated telecommunications lines. See also World Wide Web.

IRC Internet Relay Chat, which allows multiple users to log in at the same time.

JPEG Joint Photographic Experts Group, which is a digital format for compressing color images to smaller files for ease of transport.

LAN Local Area Network which links a group of computers to a central computer, known as the LAN server.

linkrot A condition that occurs with hypertext links that get removed so that files disappear; a URL cannot find them.

listserv A discussion group in which messages are distributed to all members of the group by e-mail (see page 71).

log in/log out Connecting to a computer, especially one that requires a user ID and a password.

modem Short for modulator-demodulator, a device that connects the computer via a telephone line to the Internet and other communication links.

MOOs and MUDs Multiple Object Oriented and Multiple User Dimension, virtual-reality programs which are used for synchronous conferencing and some distance education applications (see also pages 17 and 71–72).

MPEG Motion Pictures Expert Group, which names a compression format for DVD and audio.

netiquette Net etiquette, which is a set of unwritten, commonsense guidelines for behavior on a shared network.

newsgroup A discussion group that chats via electonic media on a shared topic of interest.

operating system The basic software that a computer uses to interpret data from your keyboard or mouse, such as MS-DOS, Windows, and the Mac internal system. It runs programs and applications. It also reads to and from disks and hard drives.

Pixel Picture element; the smallest unit in a digital image, appearing as a mere dot on the computer screen. A 100 by 200 image is 100 pixels wide and 200 pixels high.

PPP Point-to-Point Protocol, which provides connections to the Internet and allows computers to use Internet protocols via a modem.

protocol Rules for performing various tasks on the Internet; allows computers to talk to one another (see HTTP).

RAM Random Access Memory, a temporary memory storage unit so that your typing, for example, is placed in an active area in the computer's memory chips. When you exit the program or turn off the computer, you clear the RAM; thus, the need to save your information regularly.

search engine The program that searches the contents of files in an indexed database, such as *AltaVista* and *Lycos*.

server A host computer that allows the sharing of files between various computers on the network.

spam Unwanted e-mail messages that are similar to junk mail.

spider A program that autonomously travels from server to server and indexes the contents of public files. Also called Web walkers, Web crawlers, and worms, they enable a search engine to find files that match a request (see pages 57–59).

synchronous It means "at the same time," and refers to real-time conversations, such

as those by telephone, Internet chat, and MUDs.

telnet An Internet protocol that permits a person to access directly the files and programs of a remote computer (see pages 70-71).

upload Transferring your files to a remote server, such as "uploading to the Internet."

URL Uniform Resource Locator, the address that allows you to connect to sites on the Internet (see pages 54-57).

virus A self-replicating computer program that infects a system and causes harm to the operating system, disks, or files.

WWW World Wide Web, the vast system that organizes files on the Internet and which you access by means of your browser.

zine An electronic magazine, usually focused on a special topic for a select audience.

Italics

If your word-processing system and your printer will reproduce italic lettering, use it. Otherwise, show italics in a typed manuscript by underscoring (see also "Underscoring," pages A-29–A-30).

Length of the Research Paper

A reasonable length for a student research paper is ten pages, but setting an arbitrary length is difficult. The ideal length for your work will depend on the nature of the topic, the reference material available, the time allotted to the project, and your initiative as the researcher and writer. Your instructor or supervisor may set definite restrictions concerning the length of your paper. Otherwise, try to generate a paper of 2,000 to 3,000 words, about ten typewritten pages, excluding the title page, outline, endnotes, and Works Cited pages. *Tip:* When you run the spell checker, the final window usually gives the total number of words.

Margins

A one-inch margin on all sides is recommended. Place your page number one-half inch down from the top edge of the paper and one inch from the right edge. Your software will provide a ruler, menu, or style palette that allows you to set the margins. *Tip:* If you develop a header, the running head may appear one inch from the top, in which case your first line of text will begin one and one-half inches from the top.

Monetary Units

Spell out monetary amounts only if you can do so in no more than two words. Conform to the following.

> $10 *or* ten dollars
> $14.25 *but not* fourteen dollars and twenty-five cents
> $4 billion *or* four billion dollars
> $10.3 billion *or* $10,300,000,000
> $63 *or* sixty-three dollars
> The fee is one hundred dollars ($100) *or* the fee is one hundred (100) dollars

two thousand dollars *or* $2,000
thirty-four cents

In business and technical writing that frequently uses numbers, use numerals with appropriate symbols.

$99.45   6@15.00   £92

Names of Persons

As a general rule, first mention of a person requires the full name (e.g., Ernest Hemingway or Margaret Mead) and thereafter requires only usage of the surname, such as Hemingway or Mead. (APA style uses last name only.) Omit formal titles (Mr., Mrs., Dr., Hon.) in textual and note references to distinguished persons, living or dead. Convention suggests that certain prominent figures require the title (e.g., Lord Byron, Dr. Johnson, Dame Edith Sitwell) while others, for no apparent reason, do not (e.g., Tennyson, Browne, and Hillary rather than Lord Tennyson, Sir Thomas Browne, and Sir Edmund Hillary). Where custom dictates, you may employ simplified names of famous persons (e.g., use Dante rather than the surname Alighieri and use Michelangelo rather than Michelangelo Buonarroti). You may also use pseudonyms where custom dictates (e.g., George Eliot, Maxim Gorky, Mark Twain). Refer to fictional characters by names used in the fictional work (e.g., Huck, Lord Jim, Santiago, Capt. Ahab).

Numbering

Pagination

Use a header to number your pages in the upper right corner of the page. Depending on the software, you can create the head with the "numbering" or the "header" feature. It may appear one-half inch or a full inch down from the top edge of the paper and one inch from the right edge. Precede the number with your last name unless anonymity is required, in which case you may use a shortened version of your title rather than your name, as in APA style (see page 300). Otherwise, type the heading and then triple space to your text.

Use lowercase Roman numerals (ii, iii, iv) on any pages that precede your text. If you have a separate title page, count it as a page "i," but do not type the number on the page. You *should* put a page number on your opening page of text, even if you include course identification (see page 204).

Numbering a Series of Items

Within a sentence, incorporate a series of items into your text with parenthetical numbers or lowercase letters:

College instructors are usually divided into four ranks: (1) instructors, (2) assistant professors, (3) associate professors, (4) full professors.

Present longer items in a list with numbers or bullets:

College instructors are divided into four ranks:

1. Full professors generally have fifteen or more years of experience, have the Ph.D. or other terminal degree, and have achieved distinction in teaching and scholarly publications.

2. Associate professors. . .

Paper

Print on one side of white bond paper, sixteen- or twenty-pound weight, $8\frac{1}{2}$ by 11 inches. Use the best quality paper available; avoid erasable paper. Staple the pages of the manuscript together. Do not enclose the manuscript within a cover or binder unless your instructor asks you to do so.

Percentages

Use numerals with the percent symbol (3%); otherwise, use numerals only when they cannot be spelled out in one or two words.

> percent *not* per cent
> one hundred percent *but* 150 percent
> a two-point average *but* a 2.5 average
> one metric ton *but* 0.907 metric ton or 3.150 metric tons
> forty-five percent *but* 45.5 percent *or* 45.5%

In business, scientific, and technical writing that requires frequent use of percentages, write all percentages as numerals and use the percent symbol: 100%, 12%.

Proofreader Marks

Be familiar with the most common proofreading symbols so that you can correct your own copy or mark your copy for a typist. Some of the most common proofreading symbols are shown on the facing page.

Punctuation

Consistency is the key to punctuation. Careful proofreading of your paper for punctuation errors will generally improve the clarity and accuracy of your writing.

Apostrophe

To form the possessive of singular nouns, add an apostrophe and *s* (e.g., the typist's ledger). Add only the apostrophe with plural nouns ending in *s* (e.g., several typists' ledgers). Use the apostrophe and *s* with singular proper nouns of people and places even if the noun ends in an *s* (e.g., Rawlings's novel, Arkansas's mountains, *but* the Rawlingses' good fortune). Exceptions are the names of *Jesus* and *Moses* (e.g. Jesus' scriptures, Moses' words) and hellenized names of more than one syllable ending in *es* (e.g., Euripides' dramas). Use apostrophes to form the plurals of letters (e.g., a's and b's) but not to form the plural of numbers or abbreviations (e.g., ACTs in the 18s and 19s, the 1980s, sevens, three MDs).

Brackets

Use brackets to enclose phonetic transcription, mathematical formulas, and interpolations into a quotation. Interpolation is the insertion of your words into the text of another person (see section 11p, pages 177–78, for examples).

Use brackets to enclose parenthetical material inside parentheses:

> The escape theme explains the drama's racial conflict (see esp. Knight, who describes the Younger family as one that opposes "racial discrimination in a supposedly democratic land" [34]).

or

> Consult the tables at the end of the report (i.e., the results for the experimental group [$n = 5$] are also listed in Figure 3, page 16.)

In addition, use brackets to present fractions in equations:

> $a = [(1 + b)/x]^{1/2}$

To present fractions in a line of text, use a slash mark (/) and parentheses first ( ), then brackets [( )], and finally braces{[( )]}.

Common Proofreading Symbols

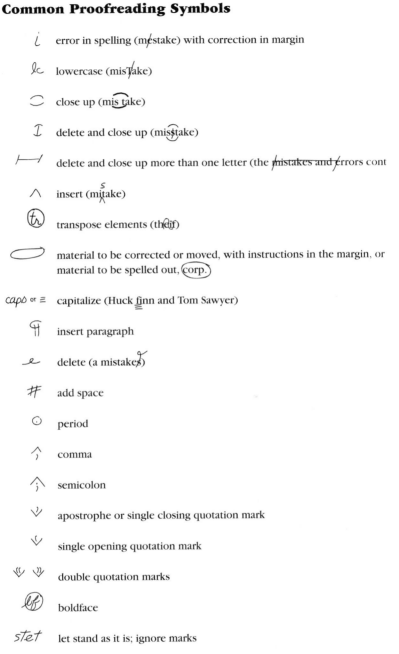

ı̇   error in spelling (m/stake) with correction in margin

lc   lowercase (misᴛake)

⌒   close up (mis take)

𝓘   delete and close up (mis͜take)

⊢—⊣   delete and close up more than one letter (the ~~mistakes and ~~errors cont

∧   insert (mi⌃take)

⟨tr⟩   transpose elements (th⟨eir⟩)

⟨⎯⎯⟩   material to be corrected or moved, with instructions in the margin, or material to be spelled out, ⟨corp.⟩

caps or ≡   capitalize (Huck f̲i̲nn and Tom Sawyer)

⌐P   insert paragraph

ℓ   delete (a mistake⟋)

add space

⊙   period

⟨;⟩   comma

⟨;⟩   semicolon

⋎   apostrophe or single closing quotation mark

⋏   single opening quotation mark

⋎ ⋎   double quotation marks

⟨bf⟩   boldface

stet   let stand as it is; ignore marks

Colons

Use colons to introduce examples or further elaboration on what has been said in the first clause. Semicolons join independent clauses. (For proper use of colons and semicolons within quotations, see 11j, pages 169-70; for usage within documentation, see 14b, pages 228–43.) Skip only one space after the colon or semicolon. Do not capitalize the first word after a colon or semicolon, but see page A-11 if you are following the APA style. Do not use a colon where a semicolon is appropriate for joining independent clauses. Here a colon is used to introduce an elaboration or definition:

> Weathers reminds us of crucial differences in rhetorical profiles that no
> writer should forget[:] colloquial wording differs radically from formal
> wording and a plain texture of writing differs greatly from a rich texture.

Commas

Use commas between items listed in a series of three or more, including before the *and* and *or* that precedes the last item. For example:

> Reader (34)[,] Scott (61)[,] and Wellman (615–17) agree with Steinbeck on
> this point.

The comma follows a parenthesis if your text requires the comma:

> How should we order our lives, asks Thompson [(22–23),] when we face
> "hostility from every quarter"?

The comma goes inside single quotation marks as well as double quotation marks:

> Such irony is discovered in Smith's article, "The Sources of Franklin's
> 'The Ephemera[,'"] but not in most textual discussions.

Dashes

Use dashes to set off special parts of the text that require emphasis. On a computer, use the character set, which will give you an unbroken line. Otherwise, type two hyphens with no blank space before or after, as shown here:

> Two issues [—] slow economic growth and public debt [—] may prevent an early
> recovery for the banking industry.

Exclamation Marks

Exclamation marks make an emotional ending to a sentence. They should be avoided in research writing. A forceful declarative sentence is preferable.

Hyphens

Use hyphens to divide the syllables of words. Both MLA style and APA style discourage division of words at the end of a line, asking instead that you leave the lines short, if necessary, rather than divide a word. If you are using a word-processing program with automatic hyphenation, you can usually disengage it.

   If you must use hyphenation, always double-check word division by consulting a dictionary. Do not hyphenate proper names. Avoid separating two letters at the end or beginning of a line (for example, use "depend-able," not "de-pendable").

When using hyphenated words, follow a few general rules.

- Do not hyphenate unless the hyphen serves a purpose: *a water treatment program* but *a water-powered turbine.*

- Compound adjectives that *precede* a noun usually need a hyphen, but those that follow do not: *same-age children* but *children of the same age.*

- When a common base serves two or more compound modifiers, omit the base on all except the last modifier, but retain the hyphens on every modifier: *right- and left-hand margins* and *5-, 10-, and 15-minute segments.*

- Write most words with prefixes as one word: *overaggressive, midterm, antisocial, postwar.* But there are exceptions: *self-occupied, self-paced, self-protection, post–1980.* Consult a dictionary regularly to resolve doubts on such narrow problems as *anti-Bush* but *antisocial.*

- Use a hyphen between pairs of coequal nouns: *scholar-athlete* or *trainer-coach.*

Parentheses

Use parentheses to enclose words and numbers in your text in the following situations:

- In-text citations:

  Larson (23–25) and Mitchell (344–45) report. . .

- Independent matter:

  The more recent findings (see Figure 6) show. . .

- Headings for a series:

  The tests were (1). . .(2). . .and (3). . .

- First use of an abbreviation:

  The test proved reaction time (RT) to be. . .

Periods

Use a period to signal the end of complete sentences of the text, endnotes, footnotes, and most bibliography entries. APA style uses no period after the URL address. Use one space after a period. When periods are used between numbers to indicate related parts (e.g., 2.4 for act 2, scene 4), use no space. The period normally follows the parenthesis. (The period is placed within the parenthesis only when the parenthetical statement is a complete sentence, as in this instance.) See also Section 11o, pages 174–77, for explanation of the period in conjunction with ellipsis points.

Quotation marks

Use quotation marks to enclose quotations used as part of your text, except for long indented quotations because the indentation signals the use of a quotation. Quotations require proper handling to maintain the style of the original; they also require precise documentation (see examples and discussions in 11a, pages 159-60).

In addition, use quotation marks for titles of articles, essays, short stories, short poems, songs, chapters of books, unpublished works, and episodes of radio and television programs.

Use quotation marks for words and phrases that you purposely misuse, misspell, or use in a special sense:

The "patrons" turned out to be criminals searching for a way to launder their money.

However, a language study requires underscoring or italics for all linguistic forms (letters, words, and phrases) that are subjects of discussion (for example, "The word *patron*"). Use quotation marks around parenthetical translations of words or phrases from another language:

> Jose Donoso's El jardin de al lado, "The Garden Next Door," dramatizes an artistic crisis that has ethical and political implications.

Use single quotation marks for definitions that appear without intervening punctuation (e.g., *nosu* 'nose'). In other cases use quotation marks for foreign phrases and sentences and single quotation marks for your translation/definition.

> It was important to Bacon that the 1625 collection appear in France as "un oeuvre nouveau" 'a new work' (14:536).

Semicolons

Use semicolons to join two distinct independent clauses:

> Weathers reminds us of crucial differences in rhetorical profiles that no writer should forget; the writer who does forget may substitute colloquial wording where formal is appropriate or may use a plain texture where rich texture is needed.

Roman Numerals

Use capital Roman numerals for titles of persons (Elizabeth II) and major sections of an outline (see pages 96-99). Use lowercase Roman numerals for preliminary pages of text, as for a preface or introduction (iii, iv, v). Otherwise, use Arabic numerals (e.g., Vol. 5, Act 2, Ch. 16, Plate 32, 2 Sam. 2.1–8, or *Iliad* 2.121–30), *except* when writing for some instructors in history, philosophy, religion, music, art, and theater, in which case you may need to use Roman numerals (e.g., III, Act II, I Sam. ii.1–8, *Hamlet* I.ii.5–6). Here is a list of Roman numerals:

Number	Units	Tens	Hundreds
1	i	x	c
2	ii	xx	cc
3	iii	xxx	ccc
4	iv	xl	cd
5	v	l	d
6	vi	lx	dc
7	vii	lxx	dcc
8	viii	lxxx	dccc
9	ix	xc	cm

Thus, xxi equals 21, cx equals 110, and clv equals 155.

Running Heads

Repeat your last name in the upper right corner of every page just in front of the page number (see the sample paper, pages 210-23). APA style requires a short title at the top of each page just above the page number or on the same line as the page number (see "Short Titles in the Text").

Short Titles in the Text

Use abbreviated titles of books and articles mentioned often in the text after a first, full reference. For example, after initial usage *Backgrounds to English as Language* should be shortened to *Backgrounds* in the text, notes, and in-text citations (see also page 167) but not in the bibliography entry. Mention *The Epic of Gilgamesh* and thereafter use *Gilgamesh* (*Note*: Be certain to italicize the abbreviation when referring to the work).

Slang

Avoid the use of slang. When using it in a language study, enclose in double quotation marks any words to which you direct attention. Words used as words, however, require underlining (see page A-29).

Spacing

As a general rule, double space everything—the body of the paper, all indented quotations, and all reference entries. Footnotes, if used, should be single-spaced, but endnotes should be double spaced (see pages 312–15). APA style (see pages 277–309) double spaces after all headings and separates text from indented quotes or from figures by double spacing; however, APA advocates quadruple spacing above and below statistical and mathematical expressions.

Space after punctuation according to these stipulations:

- Use one space after commas, semicolons, and colons (see also "Capitalize after a Colon," page A-11).

- Use one space after punctuation marks at the end of sentences.

- Use one space after periods that separate parts of a reference citation (see pages 228–43).

- Do not use space before or after periods within abbreviations (i.e., e.g., a.m.).

- Use one space between initials of personal names (M. C. Bone).

- Do not use a space before of after a hyphen (a three-part test) *but* use one space before and after a hyphen used as a minus sign (e.g., a - b + c) and one space before but none after a hyphen for a negative value (e.g., -3.25).

- Do not use a space before or after a dash (the evidence—interviews and statistics—was published).

Spelling

Spell accurately. Always use the computer to check spelling if the software is available. When in doubt, consult a dictionary. If the dictionary says a word may be spelled in two separate ways, be consistent in the form employed, as with *theater* and *theatre*, unless the variant form occurs in quoted materials. Use American (as opposed to English) spelling throughout.

Statistical and Mathematical Copy

Use the simplest form of equation that can be made by ordinary mathematical calculation. If an equation cannot be reproduced entirely by keyboard, type what you can and fill in the rest with ink. As a general rule, keep equations on one line rather than two:

$(a + b)/(x + y)$

APA style requires quadruple line spacing above and below an equation.

Superscript Numerals

On a computer, use the appropriate keys as explained in the software manual or in the "Help" index. If necessary, place the number with slash marks (e.g., "the end of the sentence./3/"). At a typewriter, create a raised numeral by turning the roller of the typewriter so that the Arabic numeral strikes about half a space above the line, like this.[14] (See also 16a, pages 311-12.)

Table of Contents

A table of contents is unnecessary for undergraduate research papers, but *do* write a table of contents for a graduate thesis or dissertation (see "Theses and Dissertations"). Many computers will develop a table of contents.

Theses and Dissertations

The author of a thesis or dissertation must satisfy the requirements of the college's graduate program. Therefore, even though you may use MLA style or APA style, you must abide by certain additional rules with regard to paper, typing, margins, and introductory matter such as title page, approval page, acknowledgment page, table of contents, abstract, and other matters. Use both the graduate school guidelines and this book to maintain the appropriate style and format.

Titles within Titles

For a title to a book that includes another title indicated by quotation marks, retain the quotation marks.

> O. Henry's Irony in "The Gift of the Magi"

For a title of an article within quotation marks that includes a title to a book, as indicated by underlining, retain the underlining or use italic lettering.

> "Great Expectations as a Novel of Initiation"
> "*Great Expectations* as a Novel of Initiation"

For a title of an article within quotation marks that includes another title indicated by quotation marks, enclose the title of the shorter work within single quotation marks.

> "A Reading of O. Henry's 'The Gift of the Magi'"

For an underscored title to a book that incorporates another title that normally receives underscoring, do not underscore or italicize the incorporated title nor place it within quotation marks.

> *Interpretations of* Great Expectations
> Using Shakespeare's Romeo and Juliet in the Classroom

Typing

Submit the paper in printed or typed form. Print on only one side of the page. In addition to the Courier font (traditional with typewriters), you may use the clear, legible typefaces supported by computer software (Helvetica, Times Roman, Bodoni, and others). Use no hyphens at the ends of lines. Avoid widows and orphans, which are single lines at the top or the bottom of the page; some computers will help you correct this problem. Use special features—boldface, italics, graphs, color—with discretion. The writing, not the graphics, will earn the credits and the better grades. You are ultimately responsible for correct pagination and accuracy of the manuscript. See also "Revising, Proofreading, and Formatting the Rough Draft," pages 195–221.

Underscoring

Titles

Use italic type or underlining for titles of the following types of works:

Type of work	Example
aircraft	*Enola Gay*
ballet	*The Nutcracker*
book	*Earthly Powers*
bulletin	*Production Memo 3*
drama	*Desire Under the Elms*
film	*Treasure of the Sierra Madre*
journal	*Journal of Sociology*
magazine	*Newsweek*
newspaper	*The Nashville Banner*
novel	*The Scarlet Letter*
opera	*Rigoletto*
painting	*Mona Lisa*
pamphlet	*Ten Goals for Successful Sales*
periodical	*Scientific American*
play	*Cat on a Hot Tin Roof*
poem	*Idylls of the King* (only if book length)
radio show	*Grand Ole Opry*
recording	*The Poems of Wallace Stevens*
sculpture	*David*
ship	*Titanic*
short novel	*Billy Budd*
symphony	Beethoven's *Eroica* (*but* Beethoven's Symphony no. 3 in A, to identify form, number, and key)
television	*Tonight Show* (program title, not a single episode)
yearbook	*The Pegasus*

In contrast, place quotation marks around the titles of shorter works, such as articles, essays, chapters, sections, short poems, stories, songs, lectures, sermons, reports, and individual episodes of television programs.

Use italics for the title of a shorter work only if it is separately published, such as a long essay, poem, or story. However, these items are usually published in an anthology or collection, in which cases you would italicize the title of the anthology or collection.

Do not italicize titles of sacred writings (Genesis or Old Testament), series (The New American Nation Series), editions (Variorum Edition of W. B. Yeats), societies (Victorian Society), courses (Greek Mythology), divisions of a work (preface, appendix, canto 3, scene 2), or descriptive phrases (Nixon's farewell address or Clinton's White House years).

Individual Words for Emphasis

The use of underscoring to emphasize certain words or phrases is discouraged. A better alternative is to position the key word in such a way as to accomplish the same purpose. For example:

> Expressed emphasis: Perhaps an answer lies in <u>preventing</u> abuse, not in makeshift remedies after the fact.
>
> Better: Prevention of abuse is a better answer than makeshift remedies after the fact.

Some special words and symbols require italics or underlining.

- Species, genera, and varieties:

  <u>Penstemon caespitosus</u> subsp. <u>thompsoniae</u>

- Letter, word, or phrase cited as a linguistic sample:

  the letter <u>e</u> in the word <u>let</u>

- Letter used as statistical symbol and algebraic variable:

  trial <u>n</u> of the <u>t</u> test or <u>C</u>(3, 14) = 9.432

Word Division

Avoid dividing any word at the end of a line. Leave the line short rather than divide a word (see "Hyphens").

APPENDIX B
Finding Sources for a Selected Discipline

Each disciplinary section that follows is divided into two parts. The first, labeled *library*, lists reference books to be found primarily in your library's reference room, and many of these are now available online or on CD-ROM through the library's network, but usually not from your home computer. The second part, labeled *Internet*, shows a few references that are available outside the university network on the World Wide Web using a browser such as *Netscape* or *Internet Explorer*. By no means is this a definitive list; it merely serves as a launching pad for your investigation. The list cannot be up-to-date nor all inclusive simply because the Web is growing rapidly. Nevertheless, these sites, in addition to the ones found by your keyword and subject searches, will launch your investigation of printed sources in the library and Internet resources. We have listed those disciplines most used by first-year students for research. Keep in mind that a keyword search will find these Internet sites even if the Universal Resource Locator (URL) has changed. Once your search begins, you will open many doors to source materials.

HINT: Truncating the Address

If you have problems accessing a particular site, try truncating the address; that is, cut items from the end. For example, if you have trouble accessing this address:

http://www.emory.edu/WHSC/medweb.medlibs.html

try cutting it to:

http://www.emory.edu

Then, within this main page of the website, you can go in search of the medical files.

Anthropology
Library

Abstracts in Anthropology. Farmingdale: Baywood, 1970–date. Allows you to read the abstract before making an in-depth study of the full article.

Anthropological Literature. Pleasantville: Redgrave, 1979–date. An index to scholarship in all aspects of anthropological research.

The Dictionary of Anthropology. Ed. T. J. Barfield. New York: Blackwell, 1997. Explains the terminology.

Internet

Annual Reviews: Anthropology. <http://anthro.AnnualReviews.org/> Has a search engine that enables you to search for specific reviews.

WWW Virtual Library: Anthropology <http://vlib.anthrotech.com/> A comprehensive search engine into issues and topics in anthropology.

Western Connecticut State University: Anthropology Internet Resources <http://www.wcsu.edu/socialsci/antres.html> Features resource links to culture, physical anthropology, native Americans, and miscellaneous.

Art and Art History
Library

Art Index. New York: Wilson, 1929–date. Indexes most art journals, such as *American Art Journal, Art Bulletin,* and *Artforum.* Look also for *Wilson Art Abstracts* and *Wilson Art Full Text.*

Bibliographic Guide to Art and Architecture. Boston: Hall, 1977–date. Annually. Provides a set of bibliographies on most topics to get your research started.

Dictionary of Art. 34 vols. Ed. J. Turner. New York: Grove's, 1996. A definitive encyclopedia of definitions, biographies, illustrations, and bibliographies.

Internet

The Art History Research Centre <http://art-history.concordia.ca/AHRC/splash.htm> Provides well-selected links to search engines, library catalogs, periodical indexes, online art collections, and other web resources.

The Metropolitan Museum of Art <http://www.metmuseum.org> Provides a virtual tour of the Metropolitan, the largest American art museum. It includes over 3,500 items from their collections, providing images, descriptions, and history.

The Parthnet <http://home.mtholyoke.edu/~klconner/parthenet.html> Gives you information on ancient and classical art, the treasures of the Renaissance, nineteenth-century American works, impressionism, and many other periods. Also links you to major museums and their collections.

World Wide Arts Resources <http://wwar.world-arts-resources.com> Provides an artist index as well as an index to exhibits, festivals, meetings, and performances.

WebLouvre <http://sunsite.unc.edu/wm/> Enables you to visit the painting exhibits, sculptures, auditorium, and miscellaneous exhibits, such as the medieval art collection. It even includes a short tour of Paris.

Astronomy
Library

The Cambridge Atlas of Astronomy. Ed. Jean Audouze and Guy Israel. New York: Cambridge UP, 1994. The atlas provides many maps, illustrations, and graphic explanations to serve both the beginner and the advanced scholar.

The Chronological Encyclopedia of Discoveries in Space. Ed. Robert Zimmerman. Westport, CT: Greenwood Press, 2000. An up-to-date guide to all of the important discoveries down through the ages.

Dictionary of Astronomy. Chicago: Fitzroy Dearborn, 1997. A good place to start because of its comprehensive coverage of key ideas, theories, and terminology.

Encyclopedia of Space Exploration. Ed. Joseph A. Angelo Jr. New York: Facts on File, 2000. Gives you rapid insight into major events, explorations, and equipment.

The Extraterrestrial Encyclopedia: An Alphabetical Reference to All Life in the Universe. Ed. David J. Darling. New York: Times Books, 2000. A good up-to-date starting point for discovering the theories and evidence on life forms in the universe.

The International Encyclopedia of Astronomy. Ed. Patrick Moore. New York: Orion, 1987. Launch your search here by paging through the encyclopedia for ideas and topics that grab your attention.

Internet

American Astronomical Society <http://www.aas.org> Gives you the *Astrophysical Journal,* providing articles, reviews, and educational information. Also links to other astronomical websites.

Extrasolar Planets Encyclopaedia <http://cfa-www.harvard.edu/planets/> Sponsored by the Paris Observatory, Meudon, France, the site contains information on extra solar planets. It includes an overview of detection methods and the search for habitable planets, and contains a catalog and a database of articles and reports on extra solar planets as well as links to other astronomy related sites.

Mount Wilson Observatory <http://www.mtwilson.edu> This site takes you into the Mount Wilson Observatory for outstanding photography of the universe and for online journals, documents, agencies, and activities in astronomical science.

The Northern Lights Planetarium, Norway <http://www.uit.no/npt/homepage-npt.en.html> This site takes you into the planetarium, displays the northern lights in vivid colors, and enables you to research such topics as *Aurora Borealis.*

The Universe at Our Doorstep <http://neptune.cgy.oanet.comp> This site links you to NASA programs, such as the space station, the shuttle program, or Project Galileo. It provides maps of the planets, views of Earth from many different angles, and plenty of planetary information.

Athletics and Physical Education
Library

Guide to Information Sources in the Physical Sciences. Ed. David Stern. Englewood, CO: Libraries Unlimited, 2000. The best starting point to find research sources in physical education.

Intercollegiate Athletics and the American University: A University President's Perspective. James J. Dunderstadt. Ann Arbor: U of Michigan P, 2000. Provides an evaluation of the current status of athletic programs.

Physical Education Index. Cape Giradeau, MO: BenOak, 1978–date. Indexes most topics in athletics, sports medicine, and athletics.

Physical Fitness and Sports Medicine. Washington, DC: GPO, 1978–date. Has a good index to most issues, current theories, and training methods.

Internet

ESPNET Sports Zone <http://espnet.sportzone.com> This site, provided by the ESPN sports network, gives up-to-date sports information as well as behind-the-scene articles.

Outside Online <http://outside.starwave.com:80> This website is devoted to outdoor sports such as biking, skiing, backpacking, and camping, with reviews of current sports and equipment.

Sportsline USA <http://www.sportsline.com/index.html> This site focuses on professional sports, such as auto racing, baseball, golf, and many others. Its Newsroom page provides news, photographs, and links to other sites.

SPORTQuest <http://www.sportquest.com> This site is a searchable directory of links to thousands of selected sites dealing with eighty different sports and related topics. Although some of the information is accessible only through paid subscriptions, the links to free information on the Web about individual sports and their teams, history, rules, and events are good.

Biology
Library

Biological Abstracts. Philadelphia: Biosis, 1926–date. Begin work here in order to read abstracts before you search out the full article at the library's computer. Look also for *Biosis, Biosis Previews, Basic Biosis, Pubmed,* and *Agricola.*

Biological and Agricultural Index. New York: Wilson, 1964–date. A subject index sends you quickly to important articles in biology, agriculture, and related fields.

Encyclopedia of Bioethics. Ed. Warren T. Reich. Rev. ed. 5 vols. New York: Macmillan, 1995. An excellent source for finding a topic on a contemporary issue.

Henderson's Dictionary of Biological Terms. Ed. Eleanor Lawrence. 11th ed. New York: Wiley, 1995. A standard reference tool in the field; consult it for terminology and precise meanings.

Internet

BioOnline <http://www.bio.com/os/start/home.html> An excellent online journal with feature articles and research news. Good spot for searching out a research topic.

BioNetbook <http://www.paseur.fr/recherche/BNB/bnb-en.html> Furnishes you with an Internet search engine that will take you to more than 400 bibliographies and more than 900 resources.

ICE Biblionet <http://ice.ucdavis.edu/biblio/biology.html#biology.> This site, sponsored by the Information Center for the Environment (ICE) at the University of California, Davis, has many links to sources in biology.

Business
Library

Business Information Sources. Ed. L. M. Daniells. 3rd ed. Berkeley: U of California P, 1993. A selective guide arranged by subject area with recommended reference sources.

Business Periodicals Index. New York: Wilson, 1958–date. Indexes most journals in the field, such as *Business Quarterly, Business Week, Fortune, Journal of Business,* and many others. Look also on the library's network for *Reference USA, Business Dateline,* and *Business and Company.*

Business Publications Index and Abstracts. Detroit: Gale, 1983–date. Annually. A place to launch your search on almost any topic related to business.

International Business Information: How to Find It, How to Use It. 2nd ed. Phoenix, AZ: Oryx, 1997. A good source for listing key references, with tips on using the source effectively.

Internet

All Business Network <http://www.all-biz.com> This site provides a search engine to businesses with relevant information for newsletters, organizations, news groups, and magazines.

Finance: The World Wide Web Virtual Library <http://www.cob.ohio-state.edu/dept/fin/overview.html> The Finance Department of Ohio State University has established a site that will link you to hundreds of articles and resource materials on banks, insurers, market news, jobs, and miscellaneous data for students.

Internet Sources for U.S. Corporate Industrial and Economic Information <http://libweb.uncc.edu/ref-bus/buselec.htm> This site provides links to American business, company, industry, and career information websites sponsored by industrial organizations, individual companies, the U.S. government, and commercial firms which provide at least some information at no charge.

Nijenrode Business Webserver <http://www.nigenrode.nl/nbr/index.html> This site serves primarily students and faculty at business schools, with a search engine that finds news, business journals, career opportunities in accounting, banking, finance, marketing, and other related fields.

Chemistry
Library

How to Find Chemical Information: A Guide for Practicing Chemists, Teachers, and Students. Ed. R. E. Maizell. 2nd ed. New York: Wiley, 1987. A detailed overview of selected sources in chemistry. Good explanations of how to use major sources.

Chemical Abstracts. Easton, PA: ACS, 1907–date. Weekly. Indexes such journals as *Applied Chemical News, American Chemical Society Journal, Chemical Bulletin,* and many more. Provides you with a good abstract if your library does not house the journal.

Concise Encyclopedia of Chemical Technology. Ed. Raymond Kirk and Donald Othmer. New York: Wiley, 2001. Begin here if you need clear explanation of terminology, theories, and issues.

World of Chemistry. Ed. Robyn V. Young and Suzanne Sessine. Farmington Hills, MI: Gale, 1999. A general text that offers you a comprehensive look at issues, theories, and new findings. Will help you find a topic.

Internet

Chemistry Bibliographies <http://www.lib.washington.edu/Subject/Chemistry> The University of Washington maintains this site with a catalog to chemistry books, an index to chemistry articles, and a list of electronic journals on chemistry.

Chemistry 2000 <www.ch.cam.ac.uk/ChemSitesUK.html> Maintained by Cambridge University, this site provides 2,000 of the best chemistry sites around the world.

Hot Articles Directory <http://pubs.acs.org/hotartcl/index.html> Sponsored by the American Chemical Society, this site takes you to recent research of hot interest by reproducing articles from many chemical journals, such as *Chemical and Engineering News, Inorganic Chemistry,* and *Biochemistry.*

Communication and Speech

Library

The Corporate Communication Bible. Robert L. Dilenschneider. Beverly Hills, CA: New Millenium Books, 2000. A standard in the field that provides ideas, issues, and controversies in the contemporary networks of communication.

Data and Computer Communications. William Stallings. New York: Prentice-Hall, 1999. Surveys the field of data communications, such as digital signaling and encoding formats.

Digital Communication: Fundamentals of and Applications. Bernard Sklar. New York: Prentice-Hall, 2001. A recent book that serves as a beginner's guide to the new digital age.

The Literary Adviser: Selected Reference Sources in Literature, Speech, Language, Theater, and Film. Thomas P. Slavens. Phoenix: Oryx, 1985. Has a good list of sources for issues and themes in speech/communication.

Internet

Communication Resources on the Web <http://alnilam.ucs.indiana.edu:1027/sources/comm.html> This large database takes you to resources and websites on associations, book reviews, bibliographies, libraries, media, information

science programs, and departments of communication in various universities.

LINKS to Communication Studies Resources <http://www.lib.uiowa.edu/gw/comm/index.html> An excellent starting point for accessing academic and other reputable websites in media and communications studies. Some of the topics covered include gender, ethnicity, and race in mass communication, speeches and speech makers, and visual rhetoric.

Computer and Internet Technology

Library

Encyclopedia of Computer Science and Technology. Ed. J. Belzer. 22 vols. New York: Dekker, 1975–91. Supplement 1991–date. A comprehensive source for launching your investigation.

Applied Science and Technology Index. New York: Wilson, 1958–date. Indexes articles in *Byte, PC Computing,* and the more technical journals, such as *The Computer Journal* or *Computers in Industry.*

Computer Literature Index. Phoenix: ACR, 1971–date. Indexes the articles on computer science in a timely fashion with periodic updates.

Internet

Byte Magazine <http://www.byte.comp> This site provides the major print articles from *Byte* magazine with product information on computer products, such as Netscape or Wordperfect.

Internet Society <http://www.isoc.org/indextxt.html> This site is supported by the companies, agencies, and foundations that launched the Internet and that keep it functioning. It gives you vital information with articles from the ISOC Forum newsletter.

OCP's Guide to Online High Tech Resources <http://ocprometheus.org> With a search engine that performs keyword searches, this site brings you a wealth of full-text articles, online magazines, technical documents, and web links to high-tech issues.

Virtual Computer Library <http://www.utexas.edu/computer/ucl> This site gives you access to academic computing centers at the major universities as well as an index to books, articles, and bibliographies.

Current Events
Library

The Concise Encyclopedia of Democracy. Ed. Eleanora Von Dehsen. Washington, DC: Congressional Quarterly, 2000. A comprehensive survey of key issues and topics on current events that have affected democracy during recent centuries.

CQ's Resource Guide to Modern Elections: An Annotated Bibliography 1960–1996. Ed. Fenton S. Martin and Robert Goehlert. Washington, DC: CQ Press, 1999. The *Congressional Quarterly* provides an index to elections in the second half of the century.

Encyclopedia of Modern Separatist Movements. Ed. Christopher Hewitt and Tom Cheetham. Santa Barbara, CA: ABC-CLIO, 2000. A survey and guide to issues and themes on separatist movements in the modern age.

Encyclopedia of Nationalism. Ed. Alexander Moty. Academic Press, 2000. A good place to begin research on issues that affect the nation and nationalist movements.

Liberalism versus Conservatism: A Bibliography with Indexes. Ed. Francois B. Gerard. Huntington, NY: Nova, 2000. An effective index to the issues and conflicts of the liberals/conservatives and democrats/republicans.

Readers' Guide to Periodical Literature. New York: Wilson, 1900–date. This source indexes hundreds of current-event magazines. It will usually carry you to several magazine articles on topics of current interest.

Internet

Gallup Organization <http://www.gallup.com> The Gallup Organization is one of the oldest, most trusted public opinion polling groups in the country. Their site provides data from their opinion polls, indexed by subject, as well as information on their methods.

New York Times on the Web <http://www.nytimes.com> This sites presents current news of the day from the print edition, with compilations of articles on Arts and Leisure, Travel, and other special features.

Trib.com—The Internet Newspaper <http://www.trib.com> This site is an online newspaper with complete articles on news, weather, and sports from around the world, with links to Reuter's, the Associated Press, and other wire services.

USA Today <http://www.usatoday.com> This online version of *USA Today* contains sections on news, life, money, sports, and special features. An index gives access to previous articles, and a search engine takes you to specific articles on your chosen subject.

Wall Street Journal <http://www.wsj.com> This online edition features headlines and some articles from the print edition, with a classroom edition for secondary school students and teachers.

Education
Library

Education: A Guide to Reference and Information Sources. 2nd ed. Englewood, CO: Libraries Unlimited, 2000. Lists a variety of sources, with each one described and evaluated.

Encyclopedia of Educational Research. Ed. M. C. Alkin. 7th ed. 4 vols. New York: Free Press, 2000. Provides a wealth of up-to-date information on the status of research in education.

Education Index. New York: Wilson, 1929–date. Indexes articles in such journals as *Childhood Education, Comparative Education, Education Digest, Journal of Educational Psychology,* and many more.

Internet

Chronicle of Education <http://chronicle.merit.edu> This site gives you "Academe This Week" from *The Chronicle of Education*, a weekly printed magazine about education on the undergraduate and graduate levels. You will need to be a subscriber to gain full access.

Educom <http://educom.edu> This site has full-text online articles, with a focus on educational technology in its *Educom Review*, a focus on information technology in *Edupage*, and general news from *Educom Update*.

Edweb <http://edweb.cnidr.org:90> This site focuses on educational issues and resource materials for grades K–12 with articles on web education, web history, and web resources.

Online Educational Resources <http://quest.arc.nasa.gov/OER> This site by

NASA provides an extensive list of educational articles and documents on everything from the space shuttle to planetary exploration.

ERIC (Educational Resource and Information Center) <http://ericir.syr.edu/ithome> ERIC is considered the primary source of research information for most educators. It contains about 1 million documents, available by a keyword search, on all aspects of teaching and learning, lesson plans, administration, bibliographies, and almost any topic related to the classroom.

Environmental Science
Library

Encyclopedia of Biodiversity. 5 vols. Ed. S. A. Levin. San Diego: Academic, 2000. Provides a comprehensive view of current work in the field.

Encyclopedia of Environmental Analysis and Remediation. 8 vols. New York: Wiley, 1998. An excellent source for the beginning of your research on environmental issues.

World Resources. Oxford: Oxford UP, 1986–date. Contains chapters on conditions and trends in the environment worldwide. Also provides statistical tables.

Ecological Abstracts. Norwich, UK: Geo Abstracts, 1974–date. Gives you a chance to examine the brief abstract before reading the complete article.

Environment Abstracts Annual. New York: Bowker, 1970–date. Provides abstracts to the major articles in the field.

The Environmental Index. Ann Arbor, MI: UMI, 1992–date. Indexes numerous journals in the field, including *Environment, Environmental Ethics, Journal of Applied Ecology,* and others.

Internet

Ecology, Biodiversity and the Environment <http://www.conbio.rice.edu/vl/browse> This site is sponsored by the Center for Conservation Biology. It consists primarily of an index of links to other websites in categories such as endangered species, global sustainability, and pollution.

Envirolink <http://envirolink.org> This site has a search engine that allows access to environmental articles, photographs, action alerts, organizations, and additional web sources.

Medicine and Global Survival <http://www.healthnet.org/MGS/MGS.html> This online journal features articles on environmental destruction, overpopulation, infectious diseases, the consequences of war, and, in general, the health of the globe. It provides links to other journals, newsletters, and government documents that explore environmental issues.

Scorecard <http://www.scorecard.org> Sponsored by the Environmental Defense Fund, the site provides national and state data on environmental pollution and toxins. It also provides coverage of relevant news stories and maps.

Geography
Library

Companion Encyclopedia of Geography. Ed. Richard J. Huggett, M. E. Robinson, and Ian Douglas. New York: Routledge, 1996. A good starting point for research in the field; provides a broad spectrum of topics that might provoke your interest.

Geographical Abstracts. Norwich, UK: Geo Abstracts, 1972–date. Look here for a quick overview of various articles on your subject; then search out appropriate full-text articles.

Geographers: Bio-Bibliographical Studies. Ed. T. W. Freeman et al. London: Mansell, 1977–date. Annually. Offers biographies of leading figures in the field as well as bibliographies by subject.

Illustrated Encyclopedia of Mankind. 22 vols. Freeport, NY: Marshall Cavendish, 1989. A massive work that has been a standard in the field for some time. Use it to motivate your interest in a topic.

Modern Geography: An Encyclopedic Survey. Ed. Gary S. Dunbar. New York: Garland, 1991. A good starting point because it introduces in clear prose the various issues that geographers face today.

Internet

Current Geographical Publications <http://leardo.lib.uwm.edu/cgp/page2.html?> Has a great index to regional studies by the staff at the University of Wisconsin–Milwaukee. Gives analyses of recent publications.

Social Sciences: Geography <http://www.lib.washington.edu/subject/Geography/dr/elbib.html> Maintained by the University of Washington, this site provides articles as well as links to major geography sites.

Bibliographies: Geography, History <http://bubl.ac.uk/link/types/biblio0.htm> Provides a good subject index that lists many other bibliographies in geography.

Geology
Library

Bibliography and Index of Geology. Alexandria, VA: American Geological Institute, 1933–date. Monthly with annual indexes. Using this subject index will take you quickly to excellent scholarly articles on your subject.

Challinor's Dictionary of Geology. 6th ed. New York: Oxford UP, 1986. Begin here to discover the precise terminology needed in your textual discussions.

Encyclopedia of Earth Sciences. 2 vols. Ed. E. J. Dasch. New York: Macmillan, 1996. Offers a general introduction to the various topics worthy of research and investigation.

Publications of the Geological Survey. Washington, DC: GPO, 1979. The Government Printing Office keeps this index up-to-date with regular supplements.

Internet

West's Geology Directory <http://www.soton.ac.uk/~imw> Provides an index to over 200 web pages devoted to geology. Its massive directory has direct links to geological field guides and bibliographies.

GeoRef Preview Database <http://agi.dominoasp.com/agc/GeoPrev.nsf/subject> Provides an early preview of articles not yet published. Has a good index.

Geology Library <http://www.library.nwu.edu/geology> Maintained by Northwestern University, this site provides links to many important sources in geology.

Geosciences Indexes, Abstracts, Bibliographies, and Table of Content Services <http://info.lib.uh.edu/indexes/geosci.htm> This site at the University of Houston provides a wealth of information and links to abstracting services and bibliographies.

Health and Medicine
Library

Black's Medical Dictionary. 39th ed. Lanham, MD: Barnes and Noble, 1999. A standard in the field and essential to researchers in medicine.

Cumulated Index Medicus. Bethesda, MD: U.S. Department of Health and Human Services, 1959–date. An essential starting point for most papers in medical science.

Cumulated Index to Nursing and Allied Health Literature. Glendale, CA: CINAHL, 1956–date. Nursing students depend on this index to *Cancer Nurse, Journal of Practical Nursing, Journal of Nursing Education*, and many more journals. May be listed as *CINAHL* on the library's network; look there also for *PubMed* and *Health and Wellness*.

Encyclopedia of Human Nutrition. 3 vols. San Diego, CA: Academic, 1999. A good starting point for a paper on nutrition issues.

Sports Injuries Sourcebook. Detroit: Omnigraphics, 1999. A place to begin in this relatively new area of research.

General Science Index. New York: Wilson, 1978–date. Indexes 100 science journals, including *American Journal of Public Health, Health, JAMA, The Physician, Sportsmedicine*, and many others.

Internet

Global Health Network <http://www.pitt.edu/HOME/GHNet.html> This site provides you with access to documents in public health as provided by scholars at the World Health Organization, NASA, the Pan American Health Organization, and others. It links you to agencies, organizations, and health networks.

Healthfinder <http://www.healthfinder.gov> The site provides access to "reliable consumer health and human services information" online, including full-text publications, databases, websites, and libraries. It contains links to over 550 other sites and some 500 full-text documents.

Martindale's Health Science Guide <http://www-sci.lib.uci.edu/HSG/HSGuide.html> This giant database gives you access to several medical centers for online journals and documents in medicine, nursing, nutrition, public health, medical law, and veterinary work.

Medweb: Medical Libraries <http://www.emory.edu/WHSC/medweb.medlibs.html> Emory University provides a site that connects you with medical libraries and their storehouses of information. It also gives links to other health related websites.

National Institutes of Health <http://www.nih.gov> NIH leads the nation in medical research, so this site provides substantive information on numerous topics, from cancer and diabetes to malpractice and medical ethics. It provides links to online journals for the most recent news in medical science.

History
Library

America: History and Life. Santa Barbara, CA: ABC-CLIO, 1964–date. A well-indexed source to articles and bibliographies.

American National Biography. 24 vols. New York: Oxford, 1999. The place to start for a study of most historical figures in American history.

Dictionary of American History. 8 vols. New York: Scribner's, 1976 with a 1996 supplement. Although dated, this encyclopedia is a well-documented, scholarly source on the people, places, and events in U.S. history. Includes brief bibliographies to recommended sources.

Goldentree Bibliographies in History. A series of books published in different years by different publishers on specific time periods in American history (e.g., *Manifest Destiny and the Coming of the Civil War, 1840–1861*).

Historical Abstracts. Santa Barbara, CA: ABC-CLIO, 1955–date. Provides abstracts for a quick overview of historical issues and events worldwide.

Recently Published Articles. Washington: American Historical Association, 1976–date. Indexes articles in *American Historical Review, Journal of American History, Journal of the West,* and many others.

Internet

Archiving Early America <http://earlyamerica.com> This site displays eighteenth-century documents in their original form for reading and downloading, such as the Bill of Rights and the speeches of Washington, Paine, Jefferson, and others.

History Best Information on the Net (BIOTN) <http://vweb.sau.edu/bestinfo/Majors/History/hisindex.htm> A history reference resource covering American history, ancient and medieval history, church and Christian history, and European history. In addition, there are sections devoted to historical documents, images, maps, and methods.

Humanities Hub <http://www.gu.edu.au/gwis/hub.hom.html> This site provides resources in the humanities and social sciences, with links to anthropology, architecture, cultural studies, film, gender studies, government, history, philosophy, sociology, and women.

The Humbul Gateway <http://info.ox.ac.uk/departments/humanities/international.html> This site provides historical resources, references, libraries, and bulletin boards, with links to downloadable texts.

Language and Literature
Library

Contemporary Authors. Detroit: Gale, 1962–date. An excellent set of biographies and critical overviews on most major authors. Updated articles on some authors keep it current.

Dictionary of Literary Biography. Detroit: Gale, 1978–date (in progress). Already comprising more than 130 volumes, this excellent, well-documented encyclopedia is the best source for finding background information and selected bibliographies on individual authors.

Essay and General Literature Index. New York: Wilson, 1900–date. The best source for finding individual essays that might be buried within a book's contents.

Humanities Index. New York: Wilson, 1974–date. A valuable work that indexes all of the major literary magazines and journals. The comprehensive index will usually help you find several articles on your literary topic. May be listed as *Wilson Humanities Index.*

MLA International Bibliography of Books and Articles on the Modern Languages and Literatures. New York: MLA, 1921–date. The best overall index to major literary figures, literary issues, and language topics. May be listed on the library's network as *MLA Bibliography.*

Oxford English Dictionary. 2nd ed. Ed. J. A. Simpson et al. 20 vols. New York: Oxford UP, 1989. The definitive dictionary for language students.

Internet

Electric Library <http://www.elibrary.com> This site provides access to the full text of articles in many magazines and newspapers. Thus, it's a good place to begin research.

Electronic Text Center <http://etext.lib.virginia.edu> This site provides the full-text versions for a vast collection of pieces of literature.

The English Server <http://english-server.hss.cmu.edu> Carnegie Mellon University provides academic resources in the humanities, including drama, fiction, film, television, and history, with the added bonus of calls for papers and a link for downloading freeware and shareware.

Literature Directory <http://web.syr.edu/~fjzwick/sites/lit.html> This site provides a directory, with links, to specific pieces of literature.

Netlibrary <http://www.netlibrary.com> This site provides a vast collection of full-text stories, poems, novels, and dramas. Search by title or author and then read the text online or print it out. Requires completing a free membership form.

Online Literary Criticism Collection <http://www.ipl.org/ref/litcrit> This site, part of the Internet Public Library project, provides links to criticism of U.S. and British literary works. It may be searched by author, title, or time period.

Project Gutenberg <http://promo.net/pg> This site provides literary texts in the public domain that can be downloaded via FTP and that are divided into three divisions: light literature such as fables, heavy literature such as *The Scarlet Letter*, and reference works.

Voice of the Shuttle <http://humanitas.ucsb.edu> For the language or literary scholar, this site gives a massive collection of bibliographies, textual criticism, news groups, and links to classical studies, history, philosophy, and other related disciplines.

Mathematics
Library

Biographical Dictionary of Mathematicians. 4 vols. New York: Scribner's, 1991. If your topic concerns the history of mathematics or its key personalities, begin with this research tool.

Encyclopedia of Mathematics. 10 vols. Norwell, MA: Reidel/Kluwer, 1988–date (in progress). A place to learn the basics and gain an introductory view of issues, theories, and history of the field.

General Science Index. New York: Wilson, 1978–date. Covers about 100 science periodicals, including *American Mathematical Monthly* and *Mathematics Magazine.*

Mathematical Reviews. Providence: American Mathematical Society, 1940–date. The premier source for discovering the literature of mathematics. Begin your research here.

Internet

Bibliographies <http://www.math.ufl.edu/math/biblio.html> This site at the University of Florida provides a collection of bibliographies with links to bibliographies, online journals, and articles.

Bibliographies in Mathematics <http://www.ira.uka.de/bibliography/math/> Although sponsored by Universite Karlsruhe, this list is in English with an excellent list of bibliographies and hot keys to link you quickly to a multitude of sites.

Mathematics Indexes, Abstracts, Bibliographies, and Table of Content Services <http://info.lib.uh.edu/indexes/math.htm> Links you to many sites, including a math database.

Math WWW: Bibliography <http://euclid.math.fsu.edu/Science/Biblo.html> Provides a massive index to authors, with good links to Internet sources.

Music
Library

Bibliographic Guide to Music. Boston: Hall, 1976–date. Annually. Provides an excellent subject index to almost every topic in the field of music. Will give you the bibliographic data to several articles on most topics in the field.

Music Article Guide. Philadelphia: Information Services, 1966–date. Indexes music education and instrumentation in such journals as *Brass and Wind News, Keyboard, Flute Journal,* and *Piano Quarterly.*

Music Index. Warren, MI: Information Coordinators, 1949–date. Indexes music journals such as *American Music Teacher, Choral Journal, Journal of Band Research,* and *Journal of Music Therapy.*

The New Grove Dictionary of Music and Musicians. Ed. S. Sadie. 20 vols. New York: Macmillan, 1986. This mammoth work will provide you with information on almost every topic related to music. A good place to find technical definitions.

Internet

Bibliography of Music <http://www.music.indiana.edu/~1631/bibmusic> The Indiana School of Music sponsors this site with excellent links to musical concepts and instruments, such as *Band, Bassoon, Brass*.

Music Bibliographies <http://www.ithaca.edu/library/music/music_bibliography.html> Ithaca College provides an excellent site with links to bibliographies on scores and librettos, and other sites.

Music/Bibliographies <http://www.inform.umd.edu/EdRes/Topic/music/bibliographies.html> This site at the University of Maryland offers links to many music bibliographies, including unusual sites, such as bibliographies of baseball music, Bob Dylan sites, and computer music.

Popular American Music of the Twentieth Century <http://www.pratt.lib.md.us/slrc/far/musiclinks.html> The Pratt Library in Baltimore offers a site that features links to music libraries, orchestra sites, music societies, and music programs.

Philosophy
Library

Cambridge Dictionary of Philosophy. 2nd ed. Ed. R. Audi. New York: Cambridge, 1999. This recently updated dictionary provides an excellent base for launching your investigation into philosophical issues.

Philosopher's Index: A Retrospective Index. Bowling Green, OH: Bowling Green U, 1967–date. Indexes philosophy articles in journals such as *American Philosophical Quarterly, Humanist, Journal of the History of Ideas, Journal of Philosophy,* and many more.

Routledge Encyclopedia of Philosophy. 10 vols. Ed. E. Craig. New York: Routledge, 1999. The most comprehensive, authoritative, and up-to-date reference work in the field.

Internet

The American Philosophical Association <http://www.oxy.edu/apa.html> This site provides articles, bibliographies, software, a bulletin board, gopher server, and links to other philosophical sites containing college courses, journals, texts, and newsletters.

Episteme Links: Philosophy Resources on the Internet <http://www.epistemelinks.com/> An easy to use site with links to sites containing philosophical topics, traditions, and time periods as well as biographies, full-text works, and related sites on individual philosophers, movements, and works.

Physics
Library

Current Physics Index. New York: American Institute of Physics, 1975–date. Indexes most articles in physics journals such as *Applied Physics, Journal of Chemical Physics, Nuclear Physics,* and *Physical Review*.

Encyclopedia of Physics. 2nd ed. New York: VCH, 1991. An excellent introduction to the field and a good place to begin searching for a workable topic.

Macmillan Encyclopedia of Physics. 4 vols. Ed. J. S. Rigden. New York: Macmillan, 1996. Almost every topic is covered in this comprehensive study of terms, theories, explorations, and laws of physics.

Physics Abstracts. Surrey: Institute of Electrical Engineers, 1898–date. Once you have your topic in mind, look here to find any abstracts to articles that touch on your subject.

Internet

Internet Pilot to Physics <http://www.lib.washington.edu/subject/physic/dr/elbib.html> The library at the University of Washington maintains this excellent site that indexes and provides links to Internet articles listed by subject.

Physics Indexes, Abstracts, Bibliographies, and Table of Content Services <http://info.lib.uh.edu/indexes/physics.htm> This site at the University of Houston will help you launch a search into physics topics and link you to excellent sites.

PhysicsWeb <http://physicsweb.org/
resources/search/phtml> This site provides an excellent search engine that links
you to Internet sites in physics by organizations, country, and field of interest.

Political Science
Library

ABC: Pol Sci. Santa Barbara: ABC-CLIO,
1969–date. Indexes the tables of contents
of about 300 international journals in the
original language.

GPO. Look on your library's network for this
database to the resources of the U.S.
Government Printing Office. Corresponds
to the print version, *Monthly Catalog of
the Government Printing Office.* Has
search engine and links to more than
400,000 records.

International Political Science Abstracts.
Oslo: International Political Science
Assn., 1951–date. Comprehensive, worldwide coverage of more than 600 periodicals with abstracts in English.

*Introduction to United States Information
Sources.* Ed. J. Morehead. 6th ed. Little-
ton, CO: Libraries Unlimited, 1999.
Covers all forms of information sources
(books, periodicals, databases) for
research on American politics and government, international relations, and the
study of foreign governments.

PAIS International in Print. New York: PAIS,
1915–date. Indexes government publica-
tions and such journals as *Annals of the
American Academy of Political and
Social Science* and *International Studies
Quarterly.*

Internet

Fedworld <http://
www.fedworld.gov> This site gives you
links to websites of government departments as well as lists of free catalogs. It
links you to the Internal Revenue Service
and other government agencies.

FindLaw Internet Legal Resources <http://
www.findlaw.com> This source has links
to a legal subject index, statutes and laws
of federal, state, and local governments,
judicial opinions and case law, law schools,
law journals and reviews, U.S. federal
government resources, law libraries, legal
associations, and international resources.

Library of Congress <http://www.lcweb.
loc.gov> This site provides the Library of

Congress catalog online for books by
author, subject, and title. It also links you
to historical collections and research tools.

Thomas <http://thomas.loc.gov> This site
gives you access to congressional legislation and documents indexed by topic, by
bill number if you have it, and by title. It
also allows you to search the Congressional Record, the Constitution, and other
government documents. It links you to
the House, Senate, Government Printing
Office, and General Accounting Office.

White House Web <http://
www.whitehouse.gov> This site provides
a graphical tour, messages from the president and vice president, and accounts of
life at the White House. Visitors to this site
can leave a message for the president in
the guest book.

Political Science Resources on the Web
<http://www.lib.umich.edu/libhome/
Documents.center/polisci.html> This site
at the University of Michigan is a vast
data file on government information—
local, state, federal, foreign, and international. It is a good site for political theory
and international relations, with links to
dissertations, periodicals, reference
sources, university courses, and other
social science information.

Psychology
Library

*Corsini Encyclopedia of Psychology and
Behavioral Science.* Ed. W. E. Craighead
and C. B. Nemerov. 3rd ed. 4 Vols. New
York: Wiley, 2000. A scholarly introduction
to all aspects of psychology with an extensive bibliography in the index volume.

Encyclopedia of Psychology. 8 vols. New
York: Oxford, 2000. The most comprehensive basic reference work in the field;
published under the auspices of the
American Psychological Association.

Psychological Abstracts. Washington, DC:
APA, 1927–date. Provides brief abstracts
to articles in such psychology journals as
*American Journal of Psychology, Behav-
ioral Science, Psychological Review,* and
many more. On the library's network,
look for *PsycINFO.*

Internet

Clinical Psychology Resources
<http://www.psychologie.uni-bonn.de/
kap/links_20.htm> This site features arti-

cles on assessment, behavior, disorders, psychotherapy, and other related issues. It has links to online journals and psychology organizations. It provides a keyword index to articles and books.

PsychREF: Resources in Psychology on the Internet <http://maple.lemoyne.edu/~hevern/psychref.html> This is an award-winning guide and index to researching psychology on the Web. Its focus provides resources for research in psychology, academic skill development, and academic advisement issues such as graduate school or career planning.

PsychWeb <http://www.gasou.edu/psychweb/psychweb.htm#top> This site features a collection of articles from *Psychiatric Times*, reports from the National Institutes of Health, information from universities, and links to psychology journals and other sites on the Internet. It includes, online, Freud's *The Interpretation of Dreams*.

Religion
Library

The Catholic Periodical and Literature Index. New York: Catholic Library Assn., 1934–date. Indexes the annual literature on Catholic issues and church matters.

Humanities Index. New York: Wilson, 1974–date. Indexes religious journals such as *Church History, Harvard Theological Review,* and *Muslim World.*

Index of Articles on Jewish Studies. Jerusalem: Jewish National and University Library Press, 1969–date. Indexes the major religious journals on Jewish issues.

Religion: Index One: Periodicals, Religion and Theological Abstracts. Chicago: ATLA, 1949–date. Indexes religious articles in such journals as *Biblical Research, Christian Scholar, Commonweal, Harvard Theological Review,* and many others.

Who's Who in Religion. Chicago: Marquis, 1975–date. Provides a compendium of the most notable people in religious issues.

Internet

Comparative Religion <http://weber.u.washington.edu/~madin> This comprehensive site gives references and resources to all religions and religious studies and religious organizations.

Finding God in Cyberspace <http://www.fontbonne.edu/libserv/fgic/fgic.htm> A website which links to Internet resources for scholars and students of religious studies. This is a well-balanced, secular site which serves as a good starting point for online religious research.

Vanderbilt Divinity School <http://www.library.vanderbilt.edu/divinity/homelib.html> This source gives you references to and interpretations of the Bible, links to other religious websites, and online journals, such as *Biblical Archaeologist.*

Science and Technology
Library

Applied Science and Technology Index. New York: Wilson, 1958–date. A premier source that indexes recent articles in all areas of the applied sciences, engineering, and technology.

Biological Abstracts. Philadelphia: Biological Abstracts, 1926–date. Indexes and gives brief descriptions of books and journal articles, especially for journals such as *American Journal of Anatomy, American Zoologist, BioChemistry,* and *Social Biology.*

Biological and Agricultural Index. New York: Wilson, 1964–date. Indexes about 275 periodicals, including *Field Crop Research, Human Biology, Journal of Bacteriology,* and many more.

Engineering Index. New York: Engineering Information, 1906–date. Covers many subjects, including many topics that relate to engineering.

General Science Index. New York: Wilson, 1978–date. Covers about 100 science periodicals, including *American Naturalist, Biological Bulletin,* and *Human Biology.*

Internet

The Academy of Natural Sciences Related Links <http://www.acnatsci.org/links.html> This site will link you to hundreds of articles and resource materials on various issues and topics in the natural sciences.

Discovery Channel Online <http://www.discovery.com> This site is an online version of television's Discovery Channel, and it features a keyword search engine.

Discover Magazine <http://www.dc.enews.com/magazines/discover> This site is an online version of *Discover Magazine,* including the texts of many articles. Its Archive Library enables you to examine articles from past issues.

National Academy of Sciences <http:// www.nas.edu> This comprehensive site combines the resources of the National Academy of Engineering, the Institute of Medicine, and the National Research Council. It focuses on math and science education, and it has links to scientific societies.

National Weather Service <http:// www.nws.noaa.gov/> Along with providing the satellite imagery and data used for developing weather forecasts, this National Weather Service site offers weather-related data and analysis on such topics as droughts, hurricanes, and global warming.

Network Science <http://www.awod.com/ netsci> The NetSci engine searches out biotechnological literature, with links to other scientific websites. It focuses mainly on chemistry and pharmaceuticals.

Sociology and Social Work

Library

Sociological Abstracts. San Diego: Sociological Abstracts, 1953–date. The key source for skimming sociology articles before going in search of the full article.

Social Sciences Index. New York: Wilson, 1974–date. A vital index to all aspects of topics in sociology, social work, education, political science, geography, and other fields.

Social Work Research and Abstracts. New York: NASW, 1964–date. If your research concerns any area of social work, this reference will prove invaluable.

Internet

Bureau of the Census <http:// www.census.gov> This site from the U.S. Department of Commerce provides census data on geography, housing, and the population. It allows you to examine specific information about your targeted county.

FedStats: One Stop Shopping for Federal Statistics <http://www.fedstats.gov> As the name implies, the site provides access to official U.S. government statistical data. It serves as a gateway to government agencies' web pages where specific data will be found.

Praxis <http://caster.ssu.upenn.edu/~restes/ praxis.html> This site provides a massive collection of articles on socioeconomic

topics, with links to other social science resources.

Social Science Information Gateway (SOSIG) <http://sosig.esrc.bris.ac.uk/Welcome. html#socialsciences> The SOSIG site provides a keyword search that makes available to you many websites in an alphabetical list.

Sociology <http://hakatai.mcli.dist.maricopa. edu/smc/ml/sociology.html> This site gives you access to hundreds of sites that provide articles and resource materials on almost all aspects of sociology issues.

Women's Studies

Library

Larousse Dictionary of Women. Ed. M. Parry. New York: Larousse, 1996. A valuable place to launch your search for basic issues on the women's movement and its key people.

Social Sciences Index. New York: Wilson, 1974–date. Indexes such journals as *Feminist Studies, Ms., Signs, Womanpower, Woman's Journal,* and many others.

Who's Who of American Women. Chicago: Marquis, 1958–date. Identifies and comments on major and minor figures in the history of American women.

Women's Issues. 3 vols. Ed. M. McFadden. Englewood Cliffs, NJ: Salem/Magills, 1997. Provides a comprehensive survey of the major movements and specific issues for a good historical perspective on women.

Women's Studies Index. Boston: Hall, 1989–date. This annual index is considered by many librarians as the best source for immediate information on women's issues.

Women's Studies Abstracts. Rush, NY: Rush, 1972–date. Offers a quick overview of hundreds of articles and books on women's issues.

Women's Studies Encyclopedia. 3 vols. Westport, CT: Greenwood, 1989–91. Although somewhat dated, this multidisciplinary reference touches on all issues relating to women in science, the humanities, and the social sciences.

Internet

The Women's Resource Project <http://sunsite.unc.edu/cheryb/women> This site links you to libraries on the Web that have collections on Women's

Studies. It also has links to women's programs and women's resources on the Web.

Women's Studies Resources
<http:www.inform.umd.edu:8080/EdRes/Topic/WomensStudies> This site features a search engine for a keyword search to women's issues and provides directories to bibliographies, classic texts, references, course syllabi from various universities, and links to other websites.

Women's Studies Librarian <http://www.library.wisc.edu/libraries/WomensStudies>This site at the University of Wisconsin provides information on important contributions by women in science, health, and technology, with links to their activities in literature, government, and business.

Feminist Theory Website <http://www.cddc.vt.edu/feminism/> This site provides "research materials and information for students, activists, and scholars interested in women's conditions and struggles around the world." It consists of three parts: various fields within feminist theory, different national/ethnic feminisms, and individual feminists. Sources of information are listed in each part.

Writing

The Chicago Manual of Style. 4th ed. Chicago: U of Chicago P, 1993. The definitive authority on the footnote style for the humanities. Serves as a style guide for many organizations, associations, and businesses.

MLA Style Manual. 2nd ed. New York: Modern Language Association, 1998. The authoritative source for documentation style in languages and literature.

Publication Manual of the American Psychological Association. 4th ed. Washington, DC: APA, 1994. A new 5th edition is scheduled soon. This is the official guide for most scholarly papers in the social sciences.

Scientific Style and Format: The CBE Manual for Authors, Editors, and Publishers. 6th ed. Cambridge: Cambridge UP, 1994. This work is the definitive guide for papers in the applied and natural sciences. It gives full details on using the number system, as described in Chapter 17.

Strunk, William, Jr., and E. B. White. *The Elements of Style.* Boston: Allyn and Bacon, 1999. Teaches and exhorts writers to avoid needless words, urges writers to use the active voice, and calls for simplicity in style.

Zinsser, William K. *On Writing Well.* New York: HarperCollins, 1998. A well-informed discourse on writing, especially on the best elements of nonfiction prose.

Williams, Joseph M. *Style: Ten Lessons in Clarity and Grace.* New York: Addison, Wesley, Longman, 2000. An excellent discussion of writing style and the means to attain it.

Internet

Internet Resources for English Teachers and Students <http://www.umass.edu/english/resource.html> This site at the University of Massachusetts provides links to articles and instructional materials for the English class.

Research Links for Writers <http://www.siu.edu/departments/cola/english/seraph9k/research.html> This site gives you a method for finding and accessing various articles and discussions about writing, especially research writing.

Writing Research Papers <http://ablongman.com/lester> This is the site that accompanies the text book. You probably noticed cross-reference icons to it throughout the text. It carries you to a wealth of information on research and research writing.

WWW Resources for Rhetoric and Composition <http://www.ind.net/Internet/comp.html> This site provides a number of links to issues on writing and the teaching of writing.

NOTE: See also the websites listed on the tabs in the spiral-bound version of *Writing Research Papers: A Complete Guide.*

Credits

Ch 2 Fig. 2-2 page 22
"Subject Keyword = Diet Therapy" from *Felix G. Cat Online Catalog*. Reprinted by permission of Austin Peay State University, Woodland Library.

Ch 2 Fig 2-3 page 24
From *Microsoft ® Encarta® Online Encyclopedia 2000*, <http://encarta.msn.com>. ©1993-2000 Microsoft Corporation. All rights reserved. "Hughes, Langston" is used with permission from Microsoft Corporation as made available through Encarta® Online.

Ch 3 Fig 3-2 page 37
Entry "Victims of Crime" from *Bibliographic Index*, 2000. ©2000 by The H.W. Wilson Company. Reprinted by permission.

Ch 3 Fig 3-3 page 37
Entry "Heinrich, Richard" from *Subject Guide to Books in Print 1999-2000*, p. 3954. ©1999 by Reed Elsevier, Inc. Reprinted by permission of R.R. Bowker, A Reed Reference Publishing Company.

Ch 3 Fig 3-4 page 39
Sample bibliography from the end of an article in *Encyclopedia of Psychology*, 2nd ed., Vol. 1, p. 287, edited by Raymond J. Corsini. Reprinted by permission of John Wiley & Sons, Inc.

Ch 3 Fig 3-5 page 39
From *Out of the Storm: The End of the Civil War* by Noah Andre Trudeau. Copyright ©1994 by Noah Andre Trudeau. Reprinted by permission of Little, Brown, and Company.

Ch 3 Fig 3-6 page 40
INFOTRAC "Keyword Search—Child Care Education." Copyright ©2000, Gale Group. Reprinted by permission. INFOTRAC is the brand name of the online databases of the Gale Group.

Ch 3 Fig 3-7 page 41
INFOTRAC, Screen shot "Article 14 of 41" is reprinted by permission of the Gale Group. INFOTRAC is the brand name of the online databases of the Gale Group. Barbara Murray's "Create Public Schools at Work: How to Give Working Parents More Time with Their Kids" is reprinted by permission of *U.S. News & World Report*. Copyright, December 29, 1997, U.S. News & World Report. Visit the Web site at www.usnews.com for additional information.

Ch 3 Fig 3-8 page 42
Sample entry "Brain Stimulation Implants" from *Readers' Guide to Periodical Literature*, May 2000, p. 100. ©2000 by The H.W. Wilson Company. Reproduced by permission of the publisher.

Ch 3 Fig 3-9 page 44
From *PsycINFO*. This material is reprinted with permission of the American Psychological Association, publisher of the *PsycINFO Database* (copyright 1887-2001 by APA), and may not be reproduced without prior permission.

Ch 3 Fig 3-10 and Fig 3-11 page 45
From *Dissertation Abstracts International*, Vol. 59, No. 12, June 1999. Published with permission of Bell & Howell Information and Learning Company. Further reproduction is prohibited without permission. Copies of dissertations may be obtained by addressing requests to Bell & Howell Information and Learning Company (formerly UMI), 300 North Zeeb Road, Ann Arbor, MI 48106-1346 USA. (734) 761-7400; E-mail: info@bellhowell.infolearning.com; Web-page: http://www.bellhowell.infolearning.com.

Ch 3 Fig 3-12 page 46
From sample entry "Clinton, Hillary Rodham," *Biography Index*, May 2000, p. 22. ©2000 by The H.W. Wilson Company. Reproduced by permission of the publisher.

Ch 3 Fig 3-13 page 48
"Homepage" from the *Herald Citizen* (online edition),

Ch 3 Fig 3-14 page 49
From *CQ Researcher*, March 3, 2000, p. 181. Reprinted with permission of Congressional Quarterly, Inc.

Ch 3 page 51
From entry "King, Martin Luther, 1929-1968" from *Essay and General Literature Index*, June 1991. Reprinted by permission of The H.W. Wilson Company.

Ch 4 Fig 4-1 page 55
"Library of Congress Homepage," <http://www.loc.gov/homepage/>.
Ch 4 Fig 4-2 page 56
"Thomas Homepage," <http://thomas.loc.gov>.
Ch 4 Fig 4-3 page 58
"H.R.2719" from House Bill Website.
Ch 4 Fig 4-4 and Fig 4-5 page 59 and page 61
Reproduced with permission of Yahoo! Inc. ©2000 by Yahoo! Inc. YAHOO! and the YAHOO! logo are trademarks of Yahoo! Inc.
Ch 4 Fig 4-6 page 64
Web page from About® The Human Internet.™ "The Battle of Gettysburg" by David Schwalbe. ©1997 David Schwalbe <http://americanhistory.about.com>, licensed to About, Inc. Used by permission of About, Inc. which can be found on the Web at <http://www.about.com>. All rights reserved.
Ch 4 Fig 4-7 page 72
Screen shot from a description of the Listserv group *Biochem for Health* found by accessing Tile.net.
Ch 4 Fig 4-8 page 75
"Book Search" results for "Fad Dieting" from Barnes & Noble.com. Reprinted by permission of Barnes & Noble.com (www.bn.com).
Ch 4 Fig 4-9 page 77
Red Earth "homepage" from <http://www.redearth.org/museum.htm>. Copyright ©Red Earth Inc., 2000. Reprinted by permission.
Ch 5 Fig 5-1 page 82
Source: George E. Hall and Courtney M. Slater, eds., 1993 County and City Extra. Reproduced with permission of Slater-Hall Information Products, from Bernan Press, Lanham, MD, 1993 (copyright).
Ch 7 Fig 7-1 page 105
From *Book Review Digest*, August 1997, Vol. 93, No. 5, p. 324. Reprinted by permission of The H.W. Wilson Company.
Ch 7 Fig 7-2 page 107
From *Child Development*, 1997. Copyright ©1997 by The Society for Research in Child Development, Inc. Reprinted by permission.
Ch 7 Fig 7-3 pages 112-114
"Kennedy Led Us to the New Frontier" by Peter Keating is reprinted with permission from *George* Magazine, August 2000. Copyright ©2000 by George Publishing Co., LLC.
Ch 7 pages 114-115
Excerpts from *Oscar Wilde* by Richard Ellman. Vintage Books, 1988. Reprinted by permission of Alfred A. Knopf, a division of Random House, Inc.
Ch 7 Fig 7-4 page 116
Reprinted with permission from Issues in Science and Technology. Screen shot from Issues in Science and Technology Online, David Western, "Conservation in a Human-Dominated World," found at <http://www.nap.edu/issues/16.3/western.htm>. Copyright ©2000 by the University of Texas at Dallas, Richardson, TX.
Ch 7 pages 117-118
"New Rules Proposed by NHTSA to Reduce Dangers of Air bags" from <http://www.nhtsa.dot.gov>.
Ch 8 page 127
From "The New Science of Alzheimer's" by J. Madeline Nash, *Time,* July 17, 2000. ©2000 by Time, Inc. Reprinted by permission.
Ch 9 page 138
From "The Love Song of J. Alfred Prufrock" in *Collected Poems 1909-1962* by T.S. Eliot. Reprinted by permission of the publisher, Faber and Faber Limited.
Ch 11 pages 164-165
From "Parenthood" by Karen S. Peterson, *USA Today*, September 19, 1990. Copyright 1990, USA Today. Reprinted with permission.
Ch 11 page 166
"The Red Wheelbarrow" by William Carlos Williams from *Collected Poems: 1909-1939, Volume I.* Copyright 1938 by New Directions Publishing Corp. Reprinted by permission of New Directions Publishing Corporation.
Ch 11 page 169
Arthur M. Schlesinger, Jr., *A Thousand Days*, Boston: Houghton Mifflin, 1965, p. 820.
Ch 11 page 172
From "The Waste Land" in *Collected Poems 1909-1962* by T.S. Eliot. Reprinted by permission of the publisher, Faber and Faber Limited.
Ch 11 page 173
From "Morning Song" from *Ariel* by Sylvia Plath. Copyright© 1961 by Ted Hughes. Copyright renewed. Reprinted by permission of HarperCollins Publishers, Inc. and by Faber and Faber Limited.
Ch 11 page 174
Sophocles, "Oedipus Rex," *The Oedipus Cycle:An English Version* by Dudley Fitts and Robert Fitzgerald. New York: Harcourt, Brace, 1958, 1949.
Ch 11 page 176
From Elizabeth Barrett Browning, "Cry of the Children," 1844.

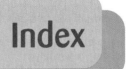

Index

Note: Page numbers followed by the letters *f* and *t* indicate figures and tables, respectively.
Bold page numbers indicate main discussions.